THE ROHINGYA, JUSTICE AND INTERNATIONAL LAW

Written by an international judge, professor and former ambassador with decades of experience in the field, this is an incisive and highly readable book about international law as well as realpolitik in bilateral and multilateral diplomacy in the quest for justice by victims of serious human rights violations amounting to grave crimes of international concern.

Focusing on the plight of the ethnic and religious group of persons called the 'Rohingya', normally residing in Myanmar, as the case study, the book elaborates the complex legal technicalities and impediments in international courts and foreign domestic criminal courts exercising 'universal jurisdiction' in relation to acts amounting to genocide, crimes against humanity and/or war crimes. It builds on and adds value to existing literature on the international law applicable to the protection of human rights as interpreted by the International Court of Justice as well as that on the international criminal justice meted out by domestic criminal courts, ad hoc international criminal tribunals and the permanent International Criminal Court.

The book will be essential reading for students, researchers and academics in public international law, international criminal law, international human rights law as well as government officials and those working for NGOs and international organizations with mandates in these fields.

Kriangsak Kittichaisaree is a Judge of the International Tribunal for the Law of the Sea. He has served as Chairperson of the UN International Law Commission's Working Group on 'The Obligation to Extradite or Prosecute (*aut dedere aut judicare*)'; and Thailand's Ambassador to Iran, Australia and Russia. He has taught international law at renowned law schools in four continents. His publications include *International Criminal Law*, *Public International Law of Cyberspace*, *The Obligation to Extradite or Prosecute* and *International Human Rights Law and Diplomacy*.

THE ROHINGYA, JUSTICE AND INTERNATIONAL LAW

Kriangsak Kittichaisaree

Routledge
Taylor & Francis Group
LONDON AND NEW YORK

First published 2022
by Routledge
2 Park Square, Milton Park, Abingdon, Oxon OX14 4RN

and by Routledge
605 Third Avenue, New York, NY 10158

Routledge is an imprint of the Taylor & Francis Group, an informa business

British Library Cataloguing-in-Publication Data
A catalogue record for this book is available from the British Library

Library of Congress Cataloging-in-Publication Data
Names: Kriangsak Kittichaisaree, 1958- author.
Title: The Rohingya, justice, and international law /
Kriangsak Kittichaisaree.
Description: Abingdon, Oxon [UK] ; New York, NY : Routledge,
2022. | Includes bibliographical references and index.
Identifiers: LCCN 2021022402 | ISBN 9781032123448 (hardback) |
ISBN 9781032123417 (paperback) | ISBN 9781003224211 (ebook)
Subjects: LCSH: Crimes against humanity (International law) |
Crimes against humanity--Law and legislation--Burma. | Genocide
(International law) | Genocide--Law and legislation--Burma. |
Rohingya (Burmese people)--Crimes against--Burma. | International
law and human rights--Burma. | Human rights--Burma.
Classification: LCC KZ7145 .K75 2022 | DDC 345/.0238--dc23
LC record available at https://lccn.loc.gov/2021022402

ISBN: 978-1-032-12344-8 (hbk)
ISBN: 978-1-032-12341-7 (pbk)
ISBN: 978-1-003-22421-1 (ebk)

DOI: 10.4324/9781003224211

Typeset in Bembo
by Deanta Global Publishing Services, Chennai, India

CONTENTS

PREFACE

This book is about the ongoing quest for justice for the group of persons widely known around the world as the 'Rohingya', launched simultaneously in November 2019 in the International Court of Justice, the International Criminal Court and a criminal court in Argentina, which have attracted widespread international interest. This is an area where the international community's human rights concerns face the daunting challenges of complex legal technicalities and practical impediments, including *realpolitik*. The cases will take years before their eventual conclusion, with multifarious possible scenarios and implications for all involved, prior and subsequent thereto.

Rather than determining whether Myanmar and/or Myanmar government officials has or have violated applicable rules of international law, this book will endeavour to objectively and pragmatically explain to readers practical lessons from international responses to situations like the ones faced by the Rohingya, including the applicable international instruments and their supporting mechanisms as well as the overlap or differences between diplomatic responses and legal claims, at multilateral and bilateral levels. The situations concerning the Rohingya covered by the book are all quite current. After the publication of this book, there will be new developments on the various fronts. By presenting the Rohingya's quest for justice as the case study so that lessons can be learned when similar situations arise in the future in various scenarios, whatever the developments in the judicial and diplomatic forums concerning the Rohingya, the analyses in this book will still be useful, and not outdated in five years or so after its publication. Above all, insofar as the Myanmar persons wanted by the International Criminal Court and foreign domestic courts like the one in Argentina are never brought before these forums where they cannot be tried *in absentia*, this book will never be obsolete.

The Rohingya issue is an Asian one, and an authoritative book about their quest for justice should, ideally, be written by an Asian international lawyer with decades of diplomatic experience whose view is not considered inherently Western-centric. I do hope that what I have learnt as Chairperson of the United Nations International Law Commission's Working Group on the topic 'The obligation to extradite or prosecute (*aut dedere aut judicare*)'; as head of delegations to bilateral as well as multilateral negotiations; as an ambassador; as a visiting professor at some renowned law schools in four Continents teaching International Criminal Law, International Human Rights Law, Public International Law, United Nations Law and so forth; as the author of several books and peer-reviewed articles in this field; and as a judge of an international tribunal will be put to good use here.

I have tried to write this book in such a way as to make it a highly readable text and useful not only to those coming to the subject with little prior specialist knowledge, but also those already engaged in international law scholarship.

Sincerest thanks are due to Alison Kirk, Senior Commissioning Editor of Routledge, and her efficient team for bringing this book to life. The painting which has become the cover of this book is by Wadhanee Xivivadh, to whom I am grateful. I also very much appreciate the valuable assistance and support in one way or another from Tsvetelina van Benthem and Gayathree Devi Kalliyat Thazhathuveetil, both of whom are DPhil candidates in public international law at the University of Oxford, and Amanda Wallin, LL.M. (Leiden).

All the webpages referred to in this book are accessible as of 6 August 2021.

ABBREVIATIONS

AA	Arakan Army
ACT	Accountability, Coherence and Transparency
AHA CENTRE	ASEAN Coordinating Centre for Humanitarian Assistance on Disaster Management
AICHR	ASEAN Intergovernmental Commission on Human Rights
AJIL	American Journal of International Law
ANP	Arakan National Party
ARSA	Arakan Rohingya Salvation Army
ASEAN	Association of Southeast Asian Nations
ASG	ASEAN Secretary-General
ASSK	Daw Aung San Suu Kyi
ATS	United States' Alien Tort Statute of 1789
AU	African Union
BNPP	BNP Paribas
CAN	Comprehensive Needs Assessment
CAR	Central African Republic
CEDAW	1979 Convention on the Elimination of All Forms of Discrimination against Women
CESCR	Committee on Economic, Social and Cultural Rights
CILRAP	Centre for International Law Research and Policy
CONVENTION AGAINST TORTURE	1984 UN Convention against Torture and Other Cruel, Inhuman or Degrading Treatment or Punishment
CRC	1989 UN Convention on the Rights of the Child
CRPD	2006 Convention on the Rights of Persons with Disabilities

CRPH	Committee for Representing Pyidaungsu Hluttaw
DR CONGO	Democratic Republic of the Congo
ECOSOC	Economic and Social Council of the United Nations
EJIL	European Journal of International Law
ERAT	ASEAN's Emergency Response and Action Team
ETS	European Treaty Series
EU	European Union
FRY	Federal Republic of Yugoslavia
GID	Syria's General Intelligence Directorate
HRC	United Nations Human Rights Council
ICC	International Criminal Court
ICCPR	1966 International Covenant on Civil and Political Rights
ICESCR	1966 International Covenant on Economic, Social, and Cultural Rights
ICJ	International Court of Justice
ICLQ	International and Comparative Law Quarterly
ICOE	Independent Commission of Enquiry, established by the Government of Myanmar
ICTR	International Criminal Tribunal for Rwanda
ICTY	International Criminal Tribunal for the former Yugoslavia
IDP	internally displaced person
IIFFMM	United Nations Independent International Fact-Finding Mission on Myanmar, set up by the Human Rights Council
IIMM	Independent Investigative Mechanism for Myanmar, set up by the Human Rights Council
ILC	United Nations International Law Commission
ILM	International Legal Materials
ILR	International Law Reports
INT'L	International
J	Journal
JIL	Journal of International Law
JNA	Yugoslav People's Army
LRA	Lord's Resistance Army
MCCAR	*ad hoc* Ministerial Committee on Accountability for Human Rights Violations against the Rohingya, set up by the Organization of Islamic Cooperation
MEC	Myanmar Economic Corporation
MEHL	Myanmar Economic Holdings Limited
MLC	*Mouvement de libération du Congo*
MNHRC	Myanmar National Human Rights Commission
NATO	North Atlantic Treaty Organization
NGO	non-governmental organization
NHRI	national human rights institution
NLD	National League for Democracy

NPFL	National Patriotic Front of Liberia
NPT	1968 Treaty on Non-Proliferation of Nuclear Weapons
NUG	National Unity Government, formed by the CRPH
OAG	Office of the Attorney General of Switzerland
OECD	Organization for Economic Development and Cooperation
OHCRC	Office of the United Nations High Commissioner for Human Rights
OIC	Organization of Islamic Cooperation
OTP	Office of the Prosecutor of the International Criminal Court
PCA	Permanent Court of Arbitration
PNA	Preliminary Needs Assessment
PSC	African Union's Peace and Security Council
REP	Reports
REV	Review
ROME STATUTE	1998 Rome Statute of the International Criminal Court
RSO	Rohingya Solidarity Organization
SAC	State Administrative Council
SAPS	South African Police Service
UEC	Myanmar's Union Election Commission
UKSC	UK Supreme Court
ULIMO	United Liberation Movement of Liberia for Democracy
UN	United Nations
UNDP	United Nations Development Programme
UNHCR	United Nations High Commissioner for Refugees
UNTS	United Nations Treaty Series
USDP	Union Solidarity and Development Party
VRS	Army of Republika Srpska
YBIL	Yearbook of International Law

PART I

Introduction

1

NARRATIVES ABOUT THE 'ROHINGYA' AND THEIR PLIGHT

In November 2019, three parallel legal actions were launched simultaneously against Myanmar and/or its leadership after bilateral and multilateral diplomatic efforts failed to alleviate the Rohingya's alleged plight.

The Gambia has taken Myanmar to the International Court of Justice ('ICJ') for the latter's alleged breaches of the 1948 Convention on the Prevention and Punishment of the Crime of Genocide ('Genocide Convention').[1] To succeed, The Gambia must overcome jurisdictional, evidentiary and other challenges before the ICJ may, if at all, provide redress to the Rohingya through The Gambia.

The Prosecutor of the International Criminal Court ('ICC') has officially started investigating possible crimes against humanity perpetrated against the Rohingya by certain Myanmar individuals. Several legal complexities and practical impediments stand in the way of the ICC Prosecutor.

Criminal proceedings against some high-level Myanmar individuals, including Daw Aung San Suu Kyi ('ASSK'), Myanmar's *de facto* Head of Government from 6 April 2016 to 31 January 2021, have been initiated in Argentina, whose law allows the exercise of universal jurisdiction over crimes committed abroad even though the crimes have no connection with Argentina. However, successes in bringing high-ranking foreign government officials who are still in office to stand trial in foreign domestic courts exercising universal jurisdiction are non-existent as of this writing.

These three tiers of parallel legal actions are unprecedented in terms of their spontaneity, and this is the first time a Nobel Peace Prize laureate – in this instance, ASSK who won the Prize in 1991 for her non-violent struggle for

1 78 UNTS 277, in force 12 Jan 1951.

DOI: 10.4324/9781003224211-1

democracy and human rights in Myanmar – has been accused in court proceedings of having a role in serious crimes of international concern.[2] The court of international public opinion seems to have found Myanmar and the Myanmar individuals implicated in alleged atrocities against the Rohingya guilty as charged. However, the Rohingya's quest for justice in the real world will have to take a long journey through complex legal technicalities in the judicial forums mentioned above.

Throughout this book, those accused of crimes are presumed innocent until proven guilty in a court of competent jurisdiction and according to due process of law.

Who are the people widely called the 'Rohingya'?

The 2014 Population and Housing Census – Myanmar's first national census in 30 years and undertaken by the Ministry of Immigration and Population in cooperation with the United Nations Population Fund – estimated Myanmar's total population as at midnight between 29 and 30 March 2014 at 51,486,253. This figure includes 50,279,900 people enumerated through the field data collection operation, and an additional estimated 1,206,353 people, based on the Census mapping activity, who were not counted. This estimate includes 1,090,000 people in Rakhine state (where the Rohingya mostly live), 69,753 people in Kayin state and 46,600 people in Kachin state.[3] The Census does not record the composition or number of members of ethnic groups living in Myanmar, however. This omission should come as no surprise since ethnic identity and citizenship are tightly interwoven in Myanmar's ethno-political landscape. On the one hand, successive military-backed governments since 1962, which have been dominated by ethnic Bamar-majority leaders, have viewed Burma/Myanmar as an indivisible 'unitary State' bound together by a historic family of 'national race' relatives, and with power concentrated in the central plain and river valleys inhabited by ethnic Bamars. On the other hand, non-Bamar groups and organizations have generally regarded 'ethnic', 'nationality' or 'national race' identities as the basis for claims to autonomy and political rights, and have long sought a devolved 'federal' system of government.[4]

According to *The World Factbook* by the US Central Intelligence Agency as of 24 February 2021, Myanmar is projected to have the total population of 57,069,099 in July 2021, comprising the following ethnic groups: Burman (Bamar) 68%,

2 Although there have been calls for Henry Kissinger, a former US Secretary of State and a joint winner of the Nobel Peace Prize in 1973, to be prosecuted for war crimes, crimes against humanity, torture and so forth, he has never been brought before any court of law. See Christopher Hitchens, *The Trial of Henry Kissinger* (Verso 2001).

3 https://myanmar.unfpa.org/sites/default/files/pub-pdf/MyanmarCensusAtlas_lowres.pdf at 10.

4 Transnational Institute, *Ethnicity without Meaning, Data without Context: The 2014 Census, Identity and Citizenship in Burma/Myanmar*, Myanmar Policy Briefing No 13 (Feb 2014) 3, 6–7, 16.

Shan 9%, Karen 7%, Rakhine 4%, Chinese 3%, Indian 2%, Mon 2% and others 5%. It notes that the Myanmar Government recognizes 135 'indigenous ethnic groups'. Based on the 2014 Census, Buddhists account for 87.9% of the total population, Christians 6.2%, Muslims 4.3%, Animists 0.8%, Hindus 0.5%, others 0.2% and none 0.1%, although as of December 2019 Muslims probably make up less than 3% of Myanmar's total population due to the large outbound migration of the Rohingya population since 2017.[5]

Linking citizenship and rights to ethnic identity in a hugely ethnic diverse nation such as Myanmar has hardened ethnic divides and driven the proliferation of ethnic non-State armed groups, or 'rebels' from the perspective of the Bamar-majority Government. According to the International Crisis Group, there are some twenty 'ethnic armed groups' that have political as well as military wings and hundreds, possibly thousands, of armed militias ranging from small village defence forces to entities with thousands of fighters, more powerful than many of the ethnic armed groups, with nearly all of these militias drawn from a particular ethnic community and are generally formed by, or allied with, the Myanmar military ('Tatmadaw') and are nominally under its command – although the degree of actual Tatmadaw authority over these groups varies.[6] A main flashpoint is Rakhine state where self-identifying 'Rohingya' leaders seek legal recognition for their people as full citizens, whereas no ethnic Bamar or Rakhine political elite, and few among the Buddhist-dominant population in general, appears prepared to consider them as anything except 'Bengalis' – meaning an Indo-Aryan ethnic group native to the Bengal region in South Asia – and 'illegal immigrants'.[7]

In its Order of 23 January 2020 on the indication of provisional measures requested by The Gambia, the ICJ clarifies that references in this Order to the 'Rohingya' should be understood as references to 'the group that self-identifies as the Rohingya group and that claims a longstanding connection to Rakhine state, which forms part of the Union of Myanmar'.[8] This book follows the ICJ in this respect.

Indeed, most countries refer to the Rohingya as a group of people residing within Myanmar although the Myanmar Government and officials do not refer to members of this group as the 'Rohingya'. An attempt to stay neutral regarding

5 www.cia.gov/the-world-factbook/countries/burma/#people-and-society.

6 International Crisis Group, *Identity Crisis: Ethnicity and Conflicts in Myanmar*, Report No 312/ Asia (28 Aug 2020). The location of main ethnic armed groups in Myanmar as of 2016 appears in Appendix B of this Report.

7 Transnational Institute, *Ethnicity without Meaning* 10–1. See also Jane M Ferguson, 'Who's Counting? Ethnicity, Belonging, and the National Census in Burma/Myanmar' (2015) 171 J Humanities & Social Sciences of Southeast Asia 1; Sarah L Clarke, Seng Aung Sein Myint and Zabra Yu Siwa, *Re-Examining Ethnic Identity in Myanmar* (May 2019), https://reliefweb.int/sites/reliefweb.int/files/resources/Ethnic-Identity-in-Myanmar.pdf.

8 *Application of the Convention on the Prevention and Punishment of the Crime of Genocide (The Gambia v Myanmar)* (Provisional Measures), Order of 23 January 2020 para 15.

the identity of this group of people can be found in the work of the Advisory Commission on Rakhine State chaired by former UN Secretary-General Kofi Annan (hereinafter 'the Annan Commission'). In line with ASSK's request, the Annan Commission uses neither the term 'Bengali' nor 'Rohingya', who are referred to instead as 'Muslims' or 'the Muslim community in Rakhine'. This reference does not include the Kaman Muslims, residing primarily in Rakhine state and recognized by the Myanmar Government as among the 135 official ethnic groups, who are simply referred to as 'Kaman'.

This chapter will present the narratives of all sides in the debate, without prejudice to their respective veracity.

Before proceeding to the narratives of those supporting the claims of the Rohingya that they have been subject to serious human rights violations by the Myanmar Government and the narratives of those who deny such claims, the narrative of the Annan Commission is helpful because it represents the narrative of a body officially approved by the Myanmar Government but under the chairmanship of Kofi Annan, a joint Nobel Peace Prize laureate in 2001, whose integrity and reputation would be seriously undermined should the Commission's findings and recommendations were not well-grounded.

In September 2016, following a request from ASSK, then State Counsellor and *de facto* leader of Myanmar,[9] the Kofi Annan Foundation and the Office of the State Counsellor established the Advisory Commission on Rakhine State, six of whose members were Myanmar nationals and the other three members foreigners (namely, Professor Ghassan Salamé from Lebanon, former Dutch Ambassador Laetitia van den Assum and Kofi Annan). Although the Annan Commission included three international commissioners, it was essentially a national mechanism, being established by the Myanmar Government and reporting to the Myanmar national authorities. It was mandated to examine the complex challenges facing Rakhine state and to propose responses to those challenges. The commissioners consulted widely, engaging with political and religious leaders, civil society organizations and communities across Rakhine state, meeting with Myanmar's Commander-in-Chief of the Armed Forces; members of parliament; the Central Committee for the Implementation of Peace, Stability and Development in Rakhin; Union ministers; Rakhine state officials; communities

9 ASSK was barred from becoming the President of Myanmar because of a provision in the 2008 Myanmar Constitution prohibiting anyone with a foreign-born spouse or children from assuming the Presidency. Instead, ASSK became State Counsellor on 6 April 2016 by virtue of the State Counsellor Act, in force on 6 April 2016, after her party won the general election in 2015. It was the second-highest position of authority after the President and was akin to a Prime Minister. The State Counsellor was accountable to the Union Parliament and could not be dismissed by the President. The term of the office for the State Counsellor was equal to the term of the President. ASSK also concurrently held the posts of the President's Office Minister and Foreign Minister from 30 March 2016 until the military took over the government on 1 February 2021.

of faith; NGOs; Myanmar's international and regional partners; and individual experts.

The Annan Commission's 63-page Final Report entitled *Towards a Peaceful, Fair and Prosperous Future for the People of Rakhine*,[10] submitted in August 2017, concludes that Rakhine state faces three crises: development crisis, human rights crisis and security crisis.

According to this Final Report, Rakhine state, separated from the rest of Myanmar by a rugged chain of mountains, has for most of its history been a distinct political entity. The Rakhine kingdom was established in 1430, with its capital in Mrauk U. For the next 350 years, Mrauk U thrived as a prosperous trading hub, until it came under Burmese control in 1784 or 1785. The annexation of Rakhine by Myanmar, then called Burma, was short-lived, as the First Anglo-Burmese War (1824–1826) brought the area under British control and subsequent incorporation into British India. While there had been a Muslim community in Rakhine since *before* the Burmese invasion, its size increased rapidly during colonial times due to British colonial policies to expand rice cultivation in Rakhine that required a significant number of Muslim workers from Bengal, some of whom settled down permanently, thereby altering the ethnic and religious mix of the area. From the 1880s to the 1930s, the size of the Muslim community (as part of Rakhine's total population) seems to have doubled, increasing from about 13 to 25%. Since then, the relative increase of the Muslim population has slowed down significantly, and is now estimated to be around a third of Rakhine's total population.[11] For sustained periods, Rakhines and Muslims lived peacefully together in Rakhine. Yet, since the mid-19th century, periods of Buddhist-Muslim cooperation and cohabitation have repeatedly been interrupted by communal tension and armed upheavals. In 1942–1943, during the Anglo-Japanese War at the height of the Second World War, both communities suffered from violence and widespread displacement. In June and October 2012, Rakhine state was again marked by large-scale inter-communal violence, during which at least 192 people were killed (134 Muslims and 58 Rakhines). Destruction to private property was highly asymmetric, as 7,422 out of 8,614 destroyed houses (about 86%) belonged to Muslims. More than 95% of the approximately 140,000 internally displaced persons ('IDPs') generated by the conflict were Muslims, of whom around 120,000 still remain in squalid IDP camps. In several areas, most Muslims were forced to leave. At different times – and with varying intensity – both Rakhines and

10 www.rakhinecommission.org/app/uploads/2017/08/FinalReport_Eng.pdf.

11 The present author: the Rohingya themselves have claimed to be indigenous to the Arakan region before its conquest by Burma. According to this narrative, from the 14th through the 18th centuries, Muslims played a key role in the history of the Kingdom of Arakan due to the close contacts between Arakan and neighbouring Bengal, which had become Muslim in 1203. Arakan Muslims are Sunnis who call themselves 'Rohinga', 'Rohingya' or 'Roewengya'. See Moshe Yegar, *Between Integration and Secession: The Muslim Communities of the Southern Philippines, Southern Thailand, and Western Burma/Myanmar* (Lexington Books 2002) 23–5.

Muslims have sought to advance their political agendas through armed struggle against the central government. Shortly after Myanmar's independence in 1948, a Muslim 'mujahidin' rebellion erupted in Rakhine, demanding equal rights and an autonomous Muslim area in the north of Rakhine. While the rebellion was eventually defeated, the Rohingya Solidarity Organization ('RSO') revived the armed struggle in the 1980s, but lost its military potency in the late 1990s. When Harakat al-Yakin (later Arakan Rohingya Salvation Army ('ARSA')) attacked government security forces on 9 October 2016, it was one of the largest Muslim attacks on Myanmar government forces in living memory. On the Rakhine side, non-State armed groups of both nationalist and communist stripes have fought the Myanmar Army since independence. At present, the strongest Rakhine insurgency movement is the Arakan Army ('AA'), an ethnic Rakhine and religiously Buddhist armed group founded in Kachin in 2009, which gradually has expanded its presence and operational capabilities in Rakhine. Over the past years, dozens of Myanmar security personnel have reportedly been killed by the AA. To some extent, inter-communal conflict in Rakhine state is 'a clash of narratives', in which both Rakhines and Muslims draw extensively on historical events to legitimize political claims and to demonstrate protracted victimhood and historical injustices. Regretfully, notes the Annan Commission, these narratives are often exclusive and irreconcilable, ignoring the fears and grievances of the other community.

Although Rakhine state is fertile, relatively well-endowed with natural resources, and strategically located, its economy is marked by stagnation, under-investment and under-development. Rakhine state's poverty rate is 78%, almost double the national rate of 37.54%, which makes it one of the poorest parts of Myanmar. All communities in Rakhine state suffer from poverty, poor social services and a scarcity of livelihood opportunities. The bulk of the Rakhine economy is made up of farmers, fishermen and family-run business, and wages in the agricultural sector are low. Landlessness is more common in Rakhine state than other parts of Myanmar – especially in the northern part of the state, where 60% of households are landless. While other parts of Myanmar have seen rapid economic growth over the past years, Rakhine state has fallen further behind. Many obstacles to growth and development are man-made – the waves of inter-communal violence in 2012 significantly reduced trust between the communities, disrupting trade and commerce across Rakhine state as well as cross-border trade with Bangladesh. The Annan Commission, among other things, urges the Myanmar Government to increase the participation of Rakhine state's local communities in decision making affecting the development of the state, and find ways to ensure that local communities benefit from investments – including natural resource extraction – in Rakhine state, as well as to continue to invest heavily in infrastructure, including roads, waterways, jetties, electricity, drinking water and internet provision.

As regards the frustrations of the Muslim population, which feels especially vulnerable because it is deprived of documentation and the freedom of movement, the Annan Commission presents ambitious steps on the central questions of citizenship verification, documentation, rights and equality before the law. In the short-run, it calls for an acceleration of the citizenship verification process in line with Myanmar's 1982 Citizenship Law.[12] The Myanmar Government should develop a clear strategy and timeline for the process, communicated through a broad outreach campaign. Those who have already been verified should immediately be allowed to enjoy all benefits, rights and freedoms associated with citizenship. Complaints regarding the verification process should be addressed swiftly by a government authority independent of the institutions responsible for the process. The rights of those whose citizenship application is not accepted should be clarified. The Commission further notes the need to revisit the law itself and calls on the Myanmar Government to set in motion a process to review the law and align the law with international standards, re-examine the current linkage between citizenship and ethnicity, and consider provisions to allow for the possibility of acquiring citizenship by naturalization, particularly for those who are stateless. The rights of non-citizens who live in Myanmar should be regulated, and residency rights clarified. Pending such a review, the Commission calls on the Myanmar Government to ensure that existing legislation is interpreted and applied in a manner that is non-discriminatory.

The Annan Commission notes that both Rakhines and Muslims face movement restrictions, although Muslims – and in particular IDPs – are particularly affected. The Myanmar Government should ensure freedom of movement for all people irrespective of religion, ethnicity or citizenship status; undertake a mapping exercise to identify all existing restrictions on freedom of movement; and introduce measures to prohibit informal restrictions including unofficial payments and arbitrary roadblocks.

In the Annan Commission's view, urgent steps are needed to promote communal representation and participation for underrepresented groups, including ethnic minority groups, stateless and displaced communities. This affects Muslims disproportionately. Women should be included in political decision-making. Household leaders, Village Administrators and Village Tract Administrators should be directly elected by the residents of each village/village tract.

The Annan Commission also considers it necessary to have a comprehensive strategy towards closing all IDP camps in Rakhine state. The Myanmar Government should cooperate with international partners to ensure that return/relocation is carried out in accordance with international standards, is voluntary, safe and takes place in a dignified manner. In the interim, and without affecting the closure of IDP camps, the Myanmar Government should ensure dignified living conditions in camps, including improved shelter, water and sanitation, education and access to livelihood opportunities.

12 Pyithu Hluttaw Law No 4 of 1982.

The Annan Commission recognizes the threat posed from potential radicalization, but advises against a purely security response in Rakhine state. Commission members have instead called for a calibrated response that combines political, developmental, security and human rights approaches that address the root causes of violence and reduce inter-communal tensions. To strengthen and professionalize policing in Rakhine state, the security infrastructure in Rakhine state should be simplified by creating a unified agency for all policing in the state, with a single chain of command reporting directly to the chief of Myanmar's Police Force. This could be done, for instance, by folding the Border Guard Police into the national police. Improved training – including in human rights, community policing, civilian protection and languages – should be provided to all members of the security forces in order to improve intelligence gathering and relations with local communities. In general, the police force should reflect the population in all components, including women and minorities. This is the reason why the Annan Commission has made several recommendations to enhance inter-communal dialogue and reconciliation to reduce the tension among the communities of Rakhine state, as well as recommendations to strengthen cooperation between local communities and Rakhine state and central government agencies.

The accusation about the plight of the Rohingya

Other narratives may not be as 'neutral' as the one adopted by the Annan Commission.

The 106-page *Countdown to Annihilation: Genocide in Myanmar* by Professor Penny Green, Dr Thomas McManus and Alicia de la Cour Venning of Queen Mary University of London, published by the International State Crime Initiative in 2015, explains the chronology of the Rohingya in Myanmar as follows.

In 1785, the last Rakhine Kingdom was annexed by Burmese King Bodawpaya. After the first Anglo-Burmese War in 1824–1826, Arakan (Rakhine) state was annexed to British India. In 1942–1943 during the Second World War, pro-British Muslims and pro-Japanese Rakhine people clashed, resulting in massacres on both sides and forcing Muslims to flee north and Rakhine people moving south, thereby contributing to segregation between these peoples. In 1948 Burma gained independence from Britain. In 1959, Burma's first President, Sao Shwe Thaike, declared that 'Muslims of Arakan certainly belong to the indigenous races of Burma' and the Rohingya had the right to vote in the elections held in 1960. However, the 1962 military *coup d'état* by General Ne Win led to increasing discrimination of ethnic minorities. In 1974, Rakhine was granted a statehood within Burma as Arakan state. In 1977–1978, the nationwide crackdown on 'illegal immigration' caused 200,000 of the Rohingya to flee to Bangladesh although most of them returned to Burma the following year. In 1982, Burma's Citizenship Law excluded the Rohingya from the country's list of 135 national races and stripped them of citizenship. In 1989 Burma was renamed Myanmar and Arakan state renamed Rakhine state. New citizenship scrutiny cards were issued to Myanmar nationals, excluding most of the Rohingya. In 1990, Rohingya and Kaman parties ran in national elections and several Rohingya representatives were elected. In 1991–1992, the military operation Pyi Thaya in northern Rakhine state caused 250,000 people to flee to Bangladesh. In 1992, the NaSaKa military/border security force was established in northern Rakhine state. In 1993–1995 the Rohingya who had fled during operation Pyi Thaya were repatriated under the watch of the UN High Commission for Refugees ('UNHCR'). In 1993, Myanmar's Border Region Immigration Control restricted marriages of the Rohingya in Maungdaw township, the overwhelmingly large majority of whose population were Muslim Rohingya, and in 1994 Myanmar stopped issuing birth certificates to Rohingya children. In 1997, the Head of the Immigration Office in Sittewe, Rakhine state's capital, restricted the Rohingya from travelling outside their township. In 2001, 28 mosques and Islamic schools were destroyed in and around Maungdaw township. In 2005, the Maungdaw Township Peace and Development Council restricted Rohingya marriages and birth rates. In 2008, the Rohingya were granted temporary registration cards and permitted to vote in the widely discredited Myanmar Constitution referendum. In 2008–2009, the Myanmar Government 'spot-checked' Rohingya homes and restricted the Rohingya's movement. Yet, the Rohingya were allowed to vote in the 2010 Myanmar elections. In 2012, violence erupted in Rakhine state between Buddhists and Muslims. In April 2014, the Rohingya were excluded from Myanmar's nationwide census. In 2015, Myanmar's parliament granted temporary white card holders (mostly Rohingya) the right to vote in a planned constitutional amendment. Days later Myanmar's President reversed the decision and declared the white cards invalid. In June 2015, the UNHCR estimated that more than 150,000 people had fled from the Myanmar/Bangladesh border area since January 2012. In August 2015, the Rohingya representative in northern Rakhine state, U Shwe Maung, was barred from re-election. The authors find Rakhine state to be the second poorest region in Myanmar due to years of economic and development neglect, with the Rakhine community, together with the Rohingya and other ethnic minorities living in the state, having suffered extreme poverty and inadequate access to education, healthcare and livelihood opportunities. As a result, argue the authors, the Rakhine community harbours grievances against both the central Government and its predominantly Bamar rulers, who, in turn, make a scapegoat of the Rohingya, or 'illegal Bengali immigrants' as they are referred to in government and public discourse. Rakhine antagonism also extends to international organizations, which are perceived as disproportionately supportive of the Rohingya. Many of the fears and grievances of members of the Rakhine community related to poverty, economic underdevelopment and State suppression of Rakhine culture 'tended to be expressed most vehemently as a perceived Muslim threat'. The central Myanmar Government and its sponsored actors 'have manipulated and channelled legitimate Rakhine concerns into hostility towards the Rohingya in an effort to deflect anger from government policy', with Myanmar government officials, nationalist Rakhine politicians and civil society leaders and hard-line Buddhist monks being 'all central to the scapegoating process'. To the authors, '[t]he result is a dangerous mix of racism, xenophobia and Islamophobia, and a narrative that dehumanizes and excludes the Rohingya from both Rakhine and Myanmar's "universe of moral obligation"'.

Exiled: The Roots of Myanmar's Persecution of the Rohingya, a 48-minute film by award-winning director and war reporter Shahida Tulaganova, was screened on the Doha/Qatar-based *Al Jazeera* television channel on 25 November 2019.[13] It asserts that despite historical evidence of their long-standing presence in Rakhine state, the Myanmar Government and army refuse to recognize the Rohingya's right to citizenship and classify them as 'illegal migrants' from Bangladesh and India. To the Myanmar Government and army as well as Myanmar nationalists, the Rohingya are 'Bengalis'. When modern Burma was established after gaining independence from Britain in 1948, the Rohingya were first recognized as part of the Burmese nation and were registered as citizens, as an ethnic minority. However, as early as 1966, the Tatmadaw started to see the Rohingya as a problem and the Nasaka border security force was set up by General Khin Nyunt, the former head of Burmese Military Intelligence, who is now alleged to have masterminded the policy of ethnic cleansing leading to the persecution of the Rohingya. According to the General, '[t]hese problems with Muslims have existed since the British rule, because they brought labour from Bangladesh [as migrants whom] we could not accept …'. He adds that his country 'needed to manage the population' by controlling its own border; '[o]therwise, there would be no more Rakhines, just more and more Muslims'. According to one source, the first exodus of Rohingyas from Burma happened in 1978 after a military campaign, which resulted in over 250,000 Rohingya persons escaping to Bangladesh.

Michael McGrath's report entitled 'The forgotten side of the Rohingya crisis' published in *Frontier Myanmar* on 26 August 2019[14] narrates how more than 740,000 Rohingya refugees fled to Bangladesh in 2017 to escape the 'clearance operation' by the Tatmadaw in Rakhine state in response to attacks by ARSA. Survivors reaching Bangladesh told of extrajudicial killings – including of children – as well as the rape of women and girls and the torching of their villages. There are concerns about the safety of the almost 600,000 Rohingyas who remained in Rakhine, the great majority of whom are confined to camps in central Rakhine, or huddled in often partially destroyed villages across the north. They 'continue to eke out a precarious existence, [be] denied citizenship of the country in which they were born, and denied access to livelihoods, education, health care and freedom of movement'. The Rohingya in northern

13 This film is no longer available online.
14 www.frontiermyanmar.net/en/the-forgotten-side-of-the-rohingya-crisis/.

Rakhine are reported to be essentially confined to their villages by curfews and a series of laws and local orders, with some requiring a Village Departure Certificate to move between villages or a 'Form 4' to move between townships. Most desperate of all are perhaps the 128,000 Rohingya – more than half of them children – who have been confined since 2012 in *de facto* detention camps in Sittwe, Pauktaw, Minbya, Mrauk-U and Myebon townships, and in the Aung Mingalar 'ghetto' in downtown Sittwe, the state capital, which are often subject to flooding, cut off by checkpoints and controlled by management committees that regulate every aspect of the lives of the Rohingya, who are dependent on aid handouts. Although children receive a few hours of instruction each day from lightly trained volunteer teachers in basic temporary 'learning spaces', those needing medical care must wait several days to receive permission and then have to pay for an expensive armed escort to travel to Sittwe General Hospital, where Rohingya are confined in a separate ward with barred windows. Interestingly, the reporter asserts that the Rohingya are not alone in being excluded from Myanmar society, since Hindus, Muslims and persons of Chinese or South Asian descent across Myanmar have all suffered discrimination for decades, and the gross human rights abuses endured by the Rohingya have also been felt by many other communities, including the Rakhine, Kachin, Karen and Shan. Therefore, 'the crisis faced by the Rohingya is not unique, but rather emblematic of exclusionary policies that have divided Myanmar for decades'.

In his report 'Rohingya crisis: Villages destroyed for government facilities' for *BBC News* on 10 September 2019,[15] BBC reporter Jonathan Head who was on a Myanmar Government-escorted media tour to Rakhine state saw entire Muslim Rohingya villages in Myanmar had been demolished and replaced by police barracks, government buildings and refugee relocation camps. At four locations, secure facilities had been built on what satellite images show were once Rohingya settlements, being 'clear evidence of the deliberate eradication of Rohingya communities'. According to the Australian Strategic Policy Institute's analysis of satellite images, at least 40% of Rohingya villages damaged by the 2017 violence have since been completely demolished. The media reporters were taken to Hla Poe Kaung transit camp built to accommodate 25,000 returnees, who would stay for two months before moving to permanent housing. The camp, completed nearly a year previously and built on the site of two Rohingya villages – Haw Ri Tu Lar and Thar Zay Kone, demolished after the 2017 violence – was in poor condition. The reporters were also taken to Kyein Chaung, a relocation camp, where houses have been built with Japanese and Indian government funding as long-term accommodation for returning refugees and constructed on where a Rohingya village called Myar Zin had been bulldozed. This relocation camp lies close to a massive new barracks for the Border

15 www.bbc.com/news/world-asia-49596113#:~:text=Entire%20Muslim%20Rohingya%20villages%20in,show%20were%20once%20Rohingya%20settlements.

Guard Police – a unit of the security forces accused by the Rohingya of serious abuses in 2017. In Inn Din, a village notorious for a massacre of ten captured Muslim men in September 2017, and one of the few atrocities the Tatmadaw has admitted to, approximately three-quarters of its population was Muslim, the rest Rakhine Buddhist. As of September 2019, no trace of the Muslim quarter remained, with what had been the Rohingya houses now replaced by barbed-wire fences enclosing an extensive new Border Guard Police barracks. Rakhine Buddhist residents told the reporters they would never accept Muslims living next to them again. On his way back to Yangon, the *BBC News* reporter ran into one of the 130,000 Rohingya displaced in a previous outbreak of violence in 2012 who told him he had been trapped with his family in an IDP camp for seven years, was unable to attend university and was not allowed to travel outside the camp without permission. Jonathan Head concludes from his long-time news coverage on Myanmar that the Myanmar Government has refused Rohingya requests for citizenship and guaranteed freedom of movement, but is willing to give them what are called National Verification Cards, which it says could be a step towards eventual citizenship but which are rejected by most of the Rohingya because they would be required to identify themselves as Bengalis. At the height of the military campaign against the Rohingya in early September 2017, the Commander-in-Chief of the Myanmar Armed Forces Senior General Min Aung Hlaing said they were taking care of 'unfinished business' left from 1942 when Japanese and British forces were fighting in what is now Rakhine state, in which the Rohingya and Rakhine Buddhists backed opposing sides, often killed each other, and caused large-scale movements of displaced civilians. The Senior General added that Muslims had flooded into northern Rakhine from Bangladesh. The two districts of Maungdaw and Buthidaung on the border with Bangladesh, where the great majority of villages destroyed since 2017 were once located, was the only region in Myanmar with a Muslim majority. Since the Rohingya exodus, the remaining Muslims, perhaps only 10% of the original population, may now be in a minority.

There are several 'factual reports' by scholars, private entities and human rights NGOs accusing the Myanmar Government, especially its military, of serious human rights abuses committed against the Rohingya, such as the one by the *pro bono* global law firm Public International Law & Policy Group (which also provides a legal analysis of the alleged facts)[16] and another one by Amnesty International.[17]

16 www.publicinternationallawandpolicygroup.org/rohingya-report.

17 www.amnesty.org/en/latest/news/2018/05/myanmar-new-evidence-reveals-rohingya-armed-group-massacred-scores-in-rakhine-state/. See also Ronan Lee, *Myanmar's Rohingya Genocide: Identity, History and Hate Speech* (I.B. Tauris 2021); Kawser Ahmed and Helal Mohiuddin, *The Rohingya Crisis: Analyses, Responses, and Peacebuilding Avenues* (Lexington Books 2019); Muhammad Abdul Bari, *The Rohingya Crisis: A People Facing Extinction* (Kube Publishing 2018); Sabyasachi Basu Ray Chaudhury and Ranabir Samaddar (eds), *The Rohingya in South Asia:*

In *Application of the Convention on the Prevention and Punishment of the Crime of Genocide (The Gambia v Myanmar)* brought by The Gambia against Myanmar in the ICJ, The Gambia presents the following narrative on 10 and 12 December 2019 during its oral arguments to support its request for the ICJ's indication of provisional measures pending the ICJ's final Judgment in the case.[18]

The Rohingya are a distinct ethnic and religious group in Myanmar's Rakhine state, where they have had historical presence for centuries. The genocidal acts against them have been a long time in the making. They incubated in toxic hate speech – on Facebook and Twitter – by which Myanmar demonized the Rohingya as 'illegal Bengali immigrants', 'terrorists' and 'jihadists'; 'maggots' and 'dogs'; and a 'Muslim invasion' posing an existential threat to Burmese 'racial purity'. The UN Independent International Fact-Finding Mission on Myanmar ('IIFFMM'), set up by the UN Human Rights Council in March 2017, has pointed to the 'systematic oppression and persecution of the Rohingya … from birth to death'; and their 'extreme vulnerability [as] a consequence of State policies and practices implemented over decades'. In 2016, ASSK, State Counsellor and Foreign Minister of Myanmar, is reported to have insisted to the United Nations that it must refrain from even using the word 'Rohingya' because Rohingya are not recognized as among the 135 official ethnic groups.

Beginning in 2016, there was a dramatic escalation of this persecution, in successive waves of what Myanmar described as 'clearance operations', ostensibly against ARSA, but it targeted the Rohingya as such for collective destruction. The IIFFMM has observed that there was not the least effort to make any distinction between ARSA fighters and civilians, or to specifically target a military objective or identify and repel an immediate threat. Everyone was a target and no one was spared: mothers, infants, pregnant women, the old and infirm all fell victim to the ruthless campaign. The targeting of women and girls for rape, gang rape and other forms of sexual violence, as well as the targeting of and impact on children in general, has been shocking.

The IIFFMM has first concluded in its September 2018 report to the Human Rights Council that 'the factors allowing the inference of genocidal intent are

---

People Without a State (Routledge India 2018); Azeem Ibrahim, *The Rohingyas: Inside Myanmar's Hidden Genocide* (Hurst 2018); Norman K Swazo *et al.*, *The Rohingya Crisis: A Moral, Ethnographic, and Policy Assessment* (Routledge India 2020); Nasir Uddin, *The Rohingya: An Ethnography of 'Subhuman' Life* (Oxford University Press 2020); Francis Wade, *Myanmar's Enemy Within: Buddhist Violence and the Making of a Muslim 'Other' (Asian Arguments)* (2nd edn, Zed Books 2019); Anthony Ware and Costas Laoutides, *Myanmar's 'Rohingya' Conflict* (Hurst 2018); Afroza Anwary 'Fractured Lives of the Rohingya Victims of Genocide in Attrition in Myanmar' in Damien Rohgers (ed.), *Human Rights in War* (Springer, forthcoming 2022). Cf. Partha S Gosh, *Migrants, Refugees and the Stateless in South Asia* (SAGE 2016) 160–2 (on 'Rohingyas and Islamic Militancy').

18 *Application of the Convention on the Prevention and Punishment of the Crime of Genocide (The Gambia v. Myanmar)*, Verbatim Record, ICJ Doc CR 2019/18 (10 Dec 2019) and Doc CR 2020 (12 Dec 2019).

present', namely, the intention to destroy the Rohingya in whole or in part, as such. It has specifically noted that: '[d]estruction is understood to mean physical or biological destruction, rather than the disbandment or expulsion of the group'. It has found '[t]he actions of those who orchestrated the attacks on the Rohingya read as a veritable check-list' of what a nation State would have done had it 'wished to destroy the target group in whole or in part'.

In particular, there are detailed accounts of corroborated mass killings of the Rohingya. In hundreds of villages, men, women and children were killed as Tatmadaw soldiers systematically moved from house to house, pulling people out of their homes and executing them, or shooting them inside their houses, or as they left their houses, often in front of family members. The IIFFMM has also verified a pattern of people, including babies and children, being pushed or thrown into burning houses by Tatmadaw soldiers, with the Rohingya children specifically targeted.

In early 2018, a delegation of the Organization of Islamic Cooperation ('OIC') visiting a Rohingya refugee camp in Bangladesh heard from the refugees the stories of mass killings, mass rape, mass torture and of children being burnt alive in their homes and places of worship. Reports from various credible international organizations including the United Nations and the OIC indicate that many thousands of people have already died as a direct result of Myanmar's genocidal actions, and the number of refugees on exodus is of biblical proportions.

In September 2018, the IIFFMM reports on a communication from the Foreign Ministry of Myanmar that include links to four videos about the August 2017 events in Rakhine state. The four videos are each imbued with explicitly anti-Muslim and anti-Rohingya messages. According to the IIFFMM's report, ASSK did not use her *de facto* position as Head of Government, nor her moral authority, to stem or prevent the unfolding events, or seek alternative avenues to meet the Government's responsibility to protect the civilian population or even to reveal and condemn what was happening. On the contrary, the civilian authorities spread false and hateful narratives; denied the Tatmadaw's wrongdoing; blocked independent investigations, including the IIFFMM's; and oversaw the bulldozing of burned Rohingya villages and the destruction of crime sites and evidence.

The IIFFMM in its final report submitted to the Human Rights Council on 16 September 2019 has found a serious risk of genocidal actions recurring, and that Myanmar is failing in its obligation to prevent genocide.

In addition, the IIFFMM has described 'widespread sexual violence' intended 'to contribute to the destruction of the Rohingya as a group and the breakdown of the Rohingya way of life'. In Myanmar, there was a 'notable pattern' of 'mass gang rape, involving multiple perpetrators and multiple victims in the same incident', committed 'in open public spaces, in front of family and neighbours, within forested areas near the village; in large houses within the village; and during detention in military and police compounds'.

The IIFFMM has also concluded that the genocidal intent is evident in the lack of remorse – or even acknowledgment – of any wrongdoing. Instead, the Tatmadaw's actions are glorified in State media.

The IIFFMM has come to such conclusion following an exhaustive two-year investigation by three distinguished jurists. The IIFFMM's Chairperson is Marzuki Darusman, Indonesia's former Attorney General. Another member is Radhika Coomaraswamy, former Chairperson of the Sri Lanka Human Rights Commission, former UN Special Rapporteur on Violence against Women and former UN Special Representative for Children and Armed Conflict. The other member, Christopher Sidoti, is a former Human Rights Commissioner of Australia. The IIFFMM was assisted by experts and advisers from the Office of the UN High Commissioner for Human Rights. Over two years, more than 1,000 victims and witnesses were interviewed and a vast amount of documents, photographs and videos were analyzed. Myanmar refused to cooperate with or give access to the IIFFMM, but that did not prevent what the IIFFMM claims to be 'a thorough and impartial investigation'. The IIFFMM is so convinced of its conclusion that it has taken an extraordinary step of recommending that named senior generals of the Tatmadaw be 'investigated and prosecuted in an international criminal tribunal for genocide'. Those named include Myanmar's Commander-in-Chief, Senior General Min Aung Hlaing. The then UN Special Rapporteur on human rights in Myanmar, Yanghee Lee of Korea, similarly concluded that the Commander-in-Chief and other senior Tatmadaw generals should be held accountable for genocide in Rakhine. The UN Special Adviser on the Prevention of Genocide, Adama Dieng of Senegal, has also concluded Rohingya Muslims have been killed, tortured, raped, burnt alive and humiliated, solely because of who they are, with the perpetrators intending to cleanse northern Rakhine state of their existence, possibly even to destroy the Rohingya as such, which, if proven, would constitute the crime of genocide.

The satellite imagery analysis by the UN Operational Satellite Application Programme, published in October 2018, shows that in northern Rakhine state the Tatmadaw had destroyed, or partially destroyed, 392 villages comprising 37,700 homes and other structures. However, some 600,000 Rohingya have remained in Myanmar and, according to the IIFFMM, they 'remain under serious risk of genocide' due to the steps Myanmar is taking currently, that reflect its continuing intention to destroy the Rohingya as a group. Each of these steps has been reported by the highly credible, independent and eminent investigators acting under the authority of the United Nations, intergovernmental organizations and human rights organizations. The first step is the forceful segregation and confinement of over 20% of the Rohingya in internment camps and ghettos, where they are in situations of extreme precariousness. According to the IIFFMM, Myanmar forcibly transferred over 120,000 Rohingya men, women and children into displacement camps outside Sittwe town in central Rakhine state in June 2012. For over seven years, Myanmar has cordoned them off from the outside world with barbed wire, police checkpoints and military posts; restricted their movements; subjected them to physical and mental abuse; and maintained them in a state of fear for their survival. They remain in Rakhine state, easy targets for the next wave of mass killings, especially as they are guarded by the same Tatmadaw that carried out the 'clearance operations'.

Myanmar claims its confinement of the Rohingya in their displacement camps is for their own good, to ensure the 'protection of the communities' from inter-communal violence between the ethnic Rakhine and the Rohingya. However, as the IIFFMM has pointed out, Myanmar has not shown how any actual risks justify this extreme and indefinite restriction of movement. At times, Myanmar has simply denied there are any restrictions on the interned Rohingya population. The remaining 80% of the Rohingya reside in villages under the Tatmadaw's close watch. As explained in the IIFFMM's September 2018 report, these Rohingya are required to obtain travel permits to leave their villages, and are generally not permitted to travel to ethnic Rakhine areas, including the main towns and markets. The IIFFMM's September 2019 report indicates that the restrictions have increased in severity over the past year. It notes the Myanmar Government's current restriction of the freedom of movement of Rohingya through a combination of local orders, verbal instructions, security checkpoints, soldiers and patrols, which have the cumulative effect of confining them to their villages and camps. This State-mandated segregation thus fosters a 'conducive environment for dehumanization and hate campaigns'. Yet, Myanmar is building more internment camps for those Rohingya who have not yet been interned. The extermination of the Rohingya, who have been rounded up into internment camps and closely-guarded ghettos and villages, can come swiftly, at any time, in the form of a new 'clearance operation' perpetrated by security forces who are stationed there or it can occur in slow motion, through denying them food and other essentials of life. The IIFFMM, in its September 2019 report, has found that while the former method of destruction could be resumed at any time, the latter method is already in progress: 'the Government has severely restricted access to food for Rohingya in Rakhine state' and the resulting 'food insecurity is being caused by government laws and policies'. Myanmar is implementing its policy of denying food to the Rohingya by various means, including its widespread confiscation of agricultural lands on which the Rohingya grew crops essential to their survival. The ongoing land confiscations extend beyond the Rohingya villages destroyed during the 'clearance operations'. The Rohingya are no longer allowed to consume products from their own lands following the confiscation, and the Tatmadaw is also depriving them of food by deliberately killing or confiscating their livestock without permission or payment.

In the past few years, Myanmar has appointed numerous commissions to investigate the genocidal acts reported by the IIFFMM and other international observers. None of Myanmar's commissions has found any violations of internationally protected rights. As the UN High Commissioner for Human Rights concludes in 2019:

> The establishment of commissions of inquiry has become routine after cyclical episodes of violence in Myanmar, with eight such commissions having been established since 2012 … None of the previous commissions has led to the prosecution of any Tatmadaw official; all have indeed exonerated the army.

Likewise, the IIFFMM concludes in September 2019: 'Myanmar is not meeting its obligations under the Genocide Convention to conduct an independent criminal investigation into allegations of genocide'. The IIFFMM draws this conclusion based on the Myanmar Government's pattern of ignoring compelling evidence that genocide took place on its territory and its failure to put in place investigative mechanisms that are independent, prompt, thorough, effective, credible and transparent.

Myanmar's very own Advisory Board for the Committee for Recommendations on Rakhine State[19] was one of a very few investigative mechanisms set up by the Government that included international members. Among them was Ambassador Bill Richardson, a former US Permanent Representative to the United Nations, New York. He resigned after the first round of meetings, denouncing the Board's so-called 'investigation' as a 'whitewash'. Kobsak Chutikul, a former Thai ambassador who served as the Board's Secretary, quit soon thereafter, expressing his concern that the Board's existence was going to divert attention from the issues and give a false impression that things were being done. Instead, he said, Myanmar government officials insisted this was an internal matter, they were handling it, and they had not done anything wrong. Besides, the chairperson of a national-level investigative committee was reported to have said that the widespread and well-documented rape of Rohingya women was 'inconceivable' because they were 'very dirty'; the Bengali/Rohingya women had a very low standard of living and poor hygiene; and they were not attractive to either the local Buddhist men or the soldiers.

The Myanmar Government's defence

The following narrative comes from ASSK and Myanmar's Counsel's oral arguments before the ICJ on 11 and 12 December 2019.[20]

The situation in Rakhine is complex and not easy to fathom. The troubles of Rakhine state and its population, whatever the background, go back into past centuries and have been particularly severe over the past few years. Currently, an internal armed conflict is going on there – between the Arakan Army, an

19 Not to be confused with the Annan Commission.

20 *Application of the Convention on the Prevention and Punishment of the Crime of Genocide (The Gambia v. Myanmar)*, Verbatim Record, ICJ Doc CR 2019/19 (11 Dec 2019) and Doc CR 2019/21 (12 Dec 2019).

organized Buddhist armed group with more than 5,000 fighters, and the regular Myanmar Defence Services. The Arakan Army seeks autonomy or independence for Rakhine – or Arakan as it was called – finding inspiration in the memory of the historic Kingdom of Arakan. This conflict has led to the displacement of thousands of civilians in Rakhine state. Standard security restrictions such as curfew and check-points are in place in the conflict zone and affect the situation of civilians there, regardless of their background.

On 9 October 2016, approximately 400 fighters of the Arakan Rohingya Salvation Army, or ARSA, launched simultaneous attacks on three police posts in Maungdaw and Rathedaung townships in northern Rakhine, near the border with Bangladesh. ARSA claimed responsibility for these attacks, which led to the death of nine police officers, more than 100 dead or missing civilians, and the theft of 68 guns and more than 10,000 rounds of ammunition. This was the start of an internal armed conflict between ARSA and Myanmar's Defence Services which lasted until late 2017. The selective factual propositions contained in The Gambia's Application actually concerns this conflict.

In the months following the 9 October 2016 attacks, ARSA grew in strength in the Maungdaw, Buthidaung and Rathedaung townships in northern Rakhine. It resorted to threats and intimidation against local villagers in order to gain support and allegiance, executing suspected informers. According to the International Crisis Group and other sources, ARSA received weapons and explosives training from Afghan and Pakistani militants.

In the early morning of 25 August 2017, several thousand ARSA fighters launched coordinated attacks on more than 30 police posts and villages and an army base in northern Rakhine. Most of the attacks took place on the narrow Maungdaw plain, which is framed by densely forested hills to the east and the border with Bangladesh to the west. ARSA's objective was apparently to seize Maungdaw township, which has historical significance. When Britain made Burma a colonial entity separate from British India in 1937, the border between Burma and India was drawn along the River Naf, which is today's border between Bangladesh and Myanmar. The historical Kingdom of Arakan had at times extended much further to the north than the River Naf, including most of what is today Chittagong District in Bangladesh. Members of some Rakhine communities therefore felt the border drawn by the British was too far south; for others, it was too far north. Myanmar has never challenged this border since independence in 1948. Britain did not lose control over what is today Maungdaw township during the Second World War. From September 1942, a number of local Muslim families offered fighters to the British irregular V-Force set up to collect intelligence and initially absorb any Japanese advance. Many Muslims gave their lives in combat against the Japanese in Rakhine. The sacrifices made by Muslim fighters motivated a call for the creation of an autonomous Muslim space in northern Rakhine, centred on Maungdaw. Whether or not this was encouraged by British officers, Britain rejected this call as soon as it reoccupied Burma, before Burma's independence in 1948. The Muslim-Buddhist inter-communal violence of 1942 recurred in 1948 and several times thereafter. This cycle of violence has negatively affected life in northern Rakhine, making it the second poorest state in Myanmar.

Many of the ARSA fighters had been recruited from local villages in the weeks and months preceding the attack on 25 August 2017. Myanmar's Defence Services responded to the attacks of ARSA fighters by the use of ground forces. There were armed incidents in more than 60 locations. The main clashes occurred in 12 places: in Min Gyi (Tola Toli) village, Chut Pyin village, Maung Nu village, Gutar Pyin village, Alai Than Kyaw village, Myin Lut village, Inn Din village, Chein Kharli (Koetan Kauk) village, Myo Thugyi ward, Kyauk Pandu village, wards of Maungdaw township and southern Maungdaw.

The term 'clearance operation', *nae myay shin lin yeh* in Myanmar, has been used since as early as the 1950s during military operations against the Burma Communist Party. Since then, the military has used this expression in counter-insurgency and counter-terrorism operations after attacks by insurgents or terrorists. In the Myanmar language, *nae myay shin lin yeh* – literally means 'clearing of locality' – simply means to clear an area of insurgents or terrorists.

It is still not easy to establish clear patterns of events in these 12 locations. Many ARSA fighters died. There may have been several hundred casualties in some locations. There was some inter-communal violence. Buddhist and Hindu minority communities also feared for their security after the original ARSA attacks and many fled from their homes. The use of air power in military operations was avoided as far as possible to minimize the risk of collateral damage. However, in one incident, in order to extract a unit surrounded by hundreds of ARSA fighters, a helicopter was used. There was shooting from the helicopter resulting in fatalities, which may have included non-combatants. *It cannot be ruled out that disproportionate force was used by members of the Defence Services in some cases in disregard of international humanitarian law, or that they did not distinguish clearly enough between ARSA fighters and civilians.* There may also have been failures to prevent civilians from looting or destroying property after fighting or in abandoned villages. However, these are determinations to be made in the due course of the criminal justice process, not by any individual in the Myanmar Government.

This complex situation and the challenge to sovereignty and security in Myanmar must be borne in mind when assessing the intent of those who attempted to deal with the rebellion. Surely, under the circumstances, genocidal intent cannot be the only hypothesis.

Under its 2008 Constitution, Myanmar has a military justice system. Criminal cases against soldiers or officers for possible war crimes committed in Rakhine must be investigated and prosecuted under that system. On 25 November 2019, the Office of the Judge Advocate General announced the start of a court martial for allegations linked to the Gutar Pyin village incident, one of the 12 main incidents referred to earlier. There will be additional court martials if further incriminating evidence is brought up by the Independent Commission of Enquiry ('ICOE'), an independent special-investigation procedure established for Rakhine allegations by the President of Myanmar, chaired by Rosario Manalo, former Deputy Foreign Minister of the Philippines, with three other members – Kenzo Oshima, former UN Under-Secretary-General from Japan, and two Myanmar nationals. On 26 November 2019, the ICOE announced it had taken about 1,500 witness statements from all affected groups in Rakhine and interviewed 29 military personnel deployed to the affected townships in northern Rakhine during the military operations from 25 August 2017 to 5 September 2017, as well as 20 police personnel stationed at the police posts that were attacked on 25 August 2017. There is currently no other fact-finding body in the world that has garnered relevant first-hand information on what occurred in Rakhine in 2017 to the same extent as the ICOE and the Office of the Judge Advocate General in Myanmar. These ongoing criminal justice processes in Myanmar must be allowed to run their course. It is never easy for armed forces to recognize self-interest in accountability for their members, and to implement a will to accountability through actual investigations and prosecutions. This is a common challenge, even in resource-rich countries.

As part of the Myanmar Government's overall efforts to provide justice, a court martial found that ten Muslim men had been summarily executed in Inn Din village, one of the 12 locations of serious incidents referred to earlier. It sentenced four officers and three soldiers each to ten years' imprisonment with hard labour. After serving a part of their sentences, they were given a military pardon although many in Myanmar were unhappy with this pardon.

Other cases are undertaken without controversy. For example, in the Mansi case,[21] a court martial sat close to the location in Kachin state where three internally displaced civilians had been killed. It sentenced six soldiers, each to ten years in prison, in January 2018. Relatives of the victims and local civil society representatives were invited to the proceedings.

Myanmar's Office of the Judge Advocate General is well resourced, with more than 90 staff and a presence in all regional commands throughout Myanmar. The Gutar Pyin court martial is encouraging, and the Office is expected to continue its investigations and prosecutions based on reliable evidence gathered in Rakhine and from persons who witnessed what happened there.

ASSK asks the audience in the ICJ in December 2019, 'Can there be genocidal intent on the part of a State that actively investigates, prosecutes and punishes soldiers and officers who are accused of wrongdoing?' Although the focus here is on members of the military, appropriate action will also be taken against civilian offenders, in line with due process.

Myanmar – like the United Kingdom or the United States – has a military justice system. There are those who wish to *externalize* accountability for 'alleged war crimes' committed in Rakhine, almost automatically, without proper reflection. This not only contradicts Article 20(b) of Myanmar's 2008 Constitution

21 Mansi is a town in Bhamo District, Myanmar's Kachin state, bordering China.

stipulating that the Defence Services have the right to independently administer and adjudicate all affairs of the armed forces, it also undercuts painstaking domestic efforts relevant to the establishing of cooperation between the military and the civilian government in Myanmar, in the context of a Constitution that needs to be amended to complete the process of democratization. The Constitution cannot and should not be ignored, if one is serious about establishing constitutional democracy and rule of law in Myanmar. International criminal tribunals take four to eight years to undertake investigations of core international crimes, sometimes longer. Just over two years passed since the serious internal armed conflict against ARSA, and the second court martial was now underway. The Gambia has not challenged the quality of the military justice in the Inn Din case, only the pardon, which many of Myanmar people regret. The ongoing Gutar Pyin court martial in Buthidaung township should be allowed to run its course. There would be further courts martial after the ICOE's submission of its final report. It is vital for Myanmar's present and future that its civilian and military criminal justice systems function in accordance with its Constitution. Where a country has a military justice system, neutralizing this system by *externalizing justice* in effect surgically removes a critical limb from the body – the limb that helps armed forces to self-correct, to improve and to better perform their functions within the constitutional order.

While no stone should be left unturned to make domestic accountability work, it would not be helpful for the international legal order if the impression takes hold that only resource-rich countries can conduct adequate domestic investigations and prosecutions, and that the domestic justice of countries still striving to cope with the burden of unhappy legacies and present challenges cannot be made good enough.

If 'war crimes' have been committed by members of Myanmar's Defence Services, they will be prosecuted through Myanmar's military justice system, in accordance with Myanmar's Constitution. It is a matter for the competent criminal justice authorities to assess whether, for example, there has been inadequate distinction between civilians and ARSA fighters, disproportionate use of force, violations of human rights, failure to prevent plundering of property, or destruction or acts of forcible displacement of civilians. Such conduct, if proven, could be relevant under international humanitarian law or human rights conventions, but *not* under the 1948 Genocide Convention.

Feeding the flames of an extreme polarization in the context of Rakhine, for example, can harm the values of peace and harmony in Myanmar. Aggravating the wounds of conflict can undermine unity in Rakhine state. Hate narratives are not simply confined to hate speech – language that contributes to extreme polarization also amounts to hate narratives. Cycles of inter-communal violence in Rakhine going back to the 1940s should be countered not just by practical measures aimed at sustainable development and rule of law, but also by nourishing a spiritual mindset of unity. It is a moral responsibility of leaders to guard the aspirations of people for harmony and peace.

Even before the events of 2016–2017, Muslim, Buddhist and other communities in Rakhine faced what the Annan Commission described as complex challenges of low development and poverty rooted in enduring social conflict between the communities. The Myanmar Government is committed to addressing these challenges. Together with its partners, Myanmar is now striving to ensure that all communities enjoy the same fundamental rights. To expedite citizenship verification and application, a mobile team is already in operation. All children born in Rakhine state, regardless of religious background, are issued with birth certificates. Arrangements have been made to enable more Muslim youth to attend classes at universities across Myanmar. With the support of international and local partners, scholarships will also be made available to students from all communities living in Rakhine. The Myanmar Government has started a social cohesion model project in Maungdaw township, to promote social harmony among all communities. Interfaith fora have been encouraged. These are some of the steps taken to improve livelihoods, security, access to education and to health, citizenship and social cohesion for all communities in Rakhine. Three IDP camps have already been closed, and an IDP camp closure strategy has been adopted. Myanmar is also committed to the voluntary, safe and dignified repatriation of displaced persons from Rakhine under the framework agreement reached between Bangladesh and Myanmar.

Rakhine today suffers 'an internal armed conflict' between the Buddhist Arakan Army and Myanmar's Defence Services. Muslims are not a party to this conflict, but may, like other civilians in the conflict area, be affected by security measures that are in place. The ICJ should refrain from taking any action that might aggravate the ongoing armed conflict and peace and security in Rakhine. On 11 December 2019, in northern Rakhine, an army base near Paletwa was under attack by a group of more than 400 Arakan Army fighters, and some 200 insurgents had surrounded a military column near Ann City in Rakhine.

Since Myanmar gained independence in 1948, the greatest challenge for its people is to address the roots of distrust and fear, prejudice and hate that undermine the foundations of Myanmar. One example of what the Myanmar Government is doing on the ground in northern Rakhine to further reconciliation between communities is the launch in January 2019 by the 'In Transformation Initiative' – directed by Roelf Meyer, a transitional justice leader in South Africa – of the 'Rakhine Transformation Project' aiming at preventing the recurrence of historical violence and paving the way for sustainable, voluntary return of peoples displaced by violence.

In her op-ed article in *The Financial Times* published just before the ICJ reading its Order indicating provisional measures on 23 January 2020, ASSK maintains that the case against Myanmar before the ICJ, the statements by the ICC Prosecutor and the private lawsuit brought in Argentina all rely extensively on the IIFFMM, which is 'precariously dependent on statements by refugees in camps in Bangladesh'. The ICOE's final report of 20 January 2020 reveals that some refugees may have provided inaccurate or exaggerated information. In ASSK's view, there is 'a systemic challenge' here since the international justice system 'may not yet be equipped to filter out misleading information before shadows of incrimination are cast over entire nations and governments'. ASSK laments that human rights groups' condemnation of Myanmar based on unproven statements without the due process of criminal investigation has had a negative effect on Myanmar's endeavours to bring stability and progress to Rakhine, undermined painstaking domestic efforts to establish cooperation between the military and the civilian government, hampered Myanmar's ability to lay the foundation for sustainable development in a very diverse country, presented a distorted picture of Myanmar and affected its bilateral relations. In her opinion, an informed assessment of Myanmar's ability to address the issue of violations in Rakhine can only be made if adequate time is given for domestic justice to run its course, and international justice should not itself 'fall victim to the extreme polarization which characterizes discussions on the situation in Rakhine'.[22]

One may wonder whether narratives negative to the Myanmar Government and the Tatmadaw could have been countenanced effectively by narratives of independent mass media operating inside Myanmar free from the dominance and control of Western media which propagate their values for democracy, market economy and human rights. However, press freedom in Myanmar was ranked 138th of the 180 countries listed in Reporters Without Borders' World Press Freedom Index in 2019. Although Myanmar rose 20 places in the Index from 2013 to 2017, the reverse is said to be taking place, with the biggest blow to press freedom being the seven-year prison sentence Reuters journalists Wa Lone and Kyaw Soe Oo received in September 2018 for trying to investigate the allegation of ethnic cleansing of Myanmar's 'Rohingya minority' by Myanmar government security forces. Reporters Without Borders adds that this subject is completely off limits – even the term 'Rohingya' is officially banned, which has forced some media outlets to stop operating in Myanmar. Indeed, according to the Annan Commission's Final Report dated August 2017, since 9 October 2016 media access to the areas of conflict in Rakhine state has been highly restricted, especially for foreign journalists. While recognizing the sensitive nature of the conflict in Rakhine state and the Myanmar Government's reaction to what it perceives to be unfounded rumours and biased narratives, the Annan Commission considers the Myanmar Government's policies based on media restriction, which inhibits the flow of information, to be counterproductive because they undermine trust in the Government and give the impression Myanmar's authorities have something to hide. The Commission believes full transparency is the most effective way to dispel false and inaccurate representations of the situation on the ground. According to the Commission, the Government should provide full and regular access for domestic and international media to all areas affected by recent violence and all other areas of

22 www.ft.com/content/dcc9bee6-3d03-11ea-b84f-a62c46f39bc2.

Rakhine state, as well as increase and improve its public communication related to developments in Rakhine state.

With regard to the Advisory Board for the Committee for Recommendations on Rakhine State lambasted by The Gambia's Counsel in the oral hearings in the ICJ in December 2019, it was to provide external perspectives and advice to Myanmar's national committee entrusted with implementing the Annan Commission's recommendations. Set up on 14 December 2017 by the Office of the State Counsellor ASSK, the Advisory Board comprised four international members[23] and five Myanmar nationals, two of whom had served as members of the Annan Commission. In January 2018, the Advisory Board did recommend, among other things, that the national committee undertake a national initiative to establish an independent fact-finding commission, which could also include international members, to look into the human rights abuses in Rakhine state. What eventually ensued was the ICOE, but, to be fair to the Advisory Board, the ICOE's final report of January 2020 was not the Advisory Board's product. Owing to the huge difference in the domestic and international narratives of the situation in Rakhine state, the Advisory Board also advised the Myanmar Government to grant greater access to the media so as to narrow the gap in perception and understanding of the situation over there. In its final recommendations of August 2018, the Advisory Board added that greater access to Rakhine state was to be granted to not only the media, but also diplomatic corps and international organizations in order to promote transparency and enhance understanding of the situation in Rakhine. The final recommendations encouraged the Myanmar Government to work closely with UN agencies to expedite repatriation of refugees. The Advisory Board considered that peace and prosperity in Rakhine state could be advanced by expediting the implementation of the pilot project for a model township in Rakhine to address the problems confronting the Rakhine 'communities' – including through infrastructure investment, closing IDP camps and promoting freedom of movement, and by convening an inter-communal dialogue as soon as possible to bring all the stakeholders together to work to bring about a lasting peace, bearing in mind that the problem in Rakhine state was an inter-communal conflict and not a religious one. In addition, with a view to implementing the Annan Commission's numerous recommendations on the citizenship issue, the Advisory Board recommended that a comparative study of the citizenship laws and practices of countries facing similar problems be undertaken to understand how these countries had different categories of citizens and steps to achieve full citizenship. The other final recommendations of the Advisory Board were for the Myanmar Government to undertake, from the security perspective, an identity verification process to properly identify the people crossing the border; close the IDP camps in a manner that

23 Surakiart Sathirathai, former Deputy Prime Minister and Foreign Minister of Thailand (chair); Lord Darzi of Denham (UK); Urban Ahlin (Sweden); and Roelof Petrus Meyer (South Africa).

would be a positive incentive for the refugees in Bangladesh to return; and continue to work with the Association of Southeast Asian Nations ('ASEAN'), of which Myanmar is a Member State, and other countries on development projects in Rakhine state. The Advisory Board's critics maintain, nonetheless, that it should have been more assertive in its role and in trying to convince ASSK to take serious steps to ensure accountability of all those implicated in the plight of the Rohingya.

It is interesting to take note of an 'international expert meeting' on 'Colonial Wrongs, Double Standards and Access to International Law' in Yangon, Myanmar, on 16–17 November 2019 as part of a series of events on colonial wrongs and double standards being planned by the Brussels-based Centre for International Law Research and Policy ('CILRAP') together with the Berlin-based European Centre for Constitutional and Human Rights and some other institutes.[24] The meeting was organized by CILRAP in cooperation with the European Centre, China University of Political Science and Law (Beijing), Centre for Diversity and National Harmony (Yangon), Institute for International Peace and Security Law (University of Cologne) and Maharishi Law School (New Delhi). The Yangon meeting was based on CILRAP's 20-page Occasional Paper 'Myanmar, Colonial Aftermath, and Access to International Law' by CILRAP's director Morten Bergsmo published in August 2019,[25] which serves as its concept note. The Paper recounts the narrative of Dr Thant Myint-U – grandson of the late U Thant, the Burmese who became the third UN Secretary-General – which 'soberly describes an important aspect of the current situation in Myanmar, including Rakhine state'. According to this narrative, at the beginning of the 12th century Indians were arriving in Burma at the rate of no less than a quarter million people a year, and the numbers rose steadily until, in the peak year of 1927, there were 480,000 immigrants among the total population of 13 million in Burma, with Burma's then capital city of Rangoon, as Yangon was then called, surpassing New York City as the greatest immigration destination in the world. ASSK herself referred in a 1991 publication to 'a well-justified apprehension' among the Burmese late in the colonial period that 'their very existence as a distinct people would be jeopardized if the course of colonial rule was allowed to run unchecked'. Britain fought three wars in order to occupy the entirety of Burma and establish colonial rule. To fuel its economic interests in rice production and other sectors, Britain allowed the transfer of millions of persons from its colonial India into Burma. The Occasional Paper poses a question whether the transfer of civilians into Burma prior to the Second World War – a process that has contributed significantly to the demographic makeup of, for example, Rakhine state – was a violation of international law. It also contends that by making deportation of Muslims from northern Rakhine state and the question of their return the

24 www.cilrap.org/events/191116-17-yangon/.
25 www.toaep.org/ops-pdf/9-bergsmo.

centrepiece of an investigation by the ICC Prosecutor – 'seemingly recognizing a Rohingya identity' – the ICC Prosecutor is 'inexorably turning the spotlight on the demographic reality and background of Rakhine state'. The Occasional Paper maintains that if the massive transfer of civilians into Burma during the late colonial period is seen as irrelevant to international law and justice, 'international law would be used against Burmese actors for current Rakhine violence, but it would be found to be silent on the past wrongs which make up part of the root causes of the violence'. Interestingly, the Occasional Paper considers it 'particularly important in the Myanmar context to avoid a general externalization of accountability given the relative resourcefulness of its Office of the Judge Advocate General as well as the security and constitutional realities of the country'.

According to CILRAP's website, the Yangon meeting had seven sessions, dealing with both case studies and general issues. The case studies encompassed the Belgian-dominated area in the Great Lakes Region, colonial Burma, Namibia, as well as the Sami and Romani peoples in Norway and Canada's native Americans. The colonial (or similar) wrongs were conduct that could amount to core international crimes as defined by the 1998 Rome Statute of the International Criminal Court.[26] The case studies focused on colonial wrongs that have lingering, negative consequences to the present day and on how measures taken after the end of the colonial period have not fully addressed related grievances in affected populations. The sessions on general issues considered, among other things, relevant patterns identified by the case studies, the extent to which contemporary international law addressed lingering consequences of colonial wrongs, the risks of double standards and related perceptions in affected populations, and whether traditional truth and reconciliation mechanisms were adequate to address lingering grievances linked to colonial wrongs. According to the organizers, the meeting was held in Yangon because the situation in Myanmar was illustrative of problems that could arise if colonial grievances were long ignored by moderate actors and abused by other actors, as well as highlighted why the topic of the meeting was important. The organizers explained, however, that the meeting was 'not about the contemporary armed conflicts in Rakhine'.

This present author should like to make a few comments at this juncture. Blaming colonialism for contemporary problems is not novel. Arguably, arbitrarily drawn colonial boundaries impede the legitimate right to self-determination of numerous ethnic minorities. Nevertheless, there is a cardinal principle of international law called *uti possidetis* to the effect that international law preserves the *status quo* of the frontier at the end of colonization. As the Chamber of the ICJ in *Case Concerning the Frontier Dispute (Burkina Faso/Republic of Mali)* explains in 1986, *uti possidetis* is a general principle with 'its obvious purpose … to prevent

26 2187 UNTS 3, in force 1 July 2002.

the independence and stability of new States being endangered by fratricidal struggles provoked by the challenging of frontiers following the withdrawal of the administering power'.[27] Therefore, every former Western colony has to be content with, and bears relevant international human rights obligations binding on it with regard to, the population of all races, religions, cultures and ethnicities living within its frontiers at the time of and after decolonization.

The Myanmar National Human Rights Commission

A national human rights commission, where it exists in a country, should be a safety net against human rights abuses by the government and/or government officials. The existence and performance of national human rights institutions ('NHRIs') must measure up to the international standards set by the Principles relating to the Status of National Institutions, or the Paris Principles, adopted by UN General Assembly on 20 December 1993.[28] The Paris Principles require NHRIs to *protect* human rights, including by receiving, investigating and resolving complaints, mediating conflicts and monitoring activities relating to human rights. NHRIs are also required to *promote* human rights through education, outreach, the media, publications, training and capacity building, as well as advising and assisting the government in this regard. There are six main criteria for each NHRI to meet. First, its mandate must be as broad as possible, based on universal human rights norms and standards, which shall be clearly set forth in a constitutional or legislative text, specifying its composition and its sphere of competence. Second, it must be autonomous from the government. Third, its independence must be guaranteed by the country's law or constitution. Fourth, its composition must ensure the pluralist representation of the social forces of civilian society involved in the protection and promotion of human rights. Fifth, it must have adequate resources. Sixth, it must have adequate powers of investigation. In particular, a NHRI must draw the attention of the government to situations in any part of the country where human rights are violated and make proposals to the government for initiatives to end such situations and, where necessary, express an opinion on the positions and reactions of the government.

Myanmar's National Human Rights Commission Law of 2014[29] provides a statutory basis for a national human rights body in Myanmar. The Myanmar Government declared to the UN Human Rights Council that the Law was in compliance with the Paris Principles. However, in its self-assessment of 2018 the Myanmar National Human Rights Commission ('MNHRC') recognized the need for law reform and submitted reform proposals to the Myanmar Government.

27 [1986] ICJ Rep 554, 565 [20]. Cf. Mohammad Shahabuddin, 'Post-colonial Boundaries, International Law, and the Making of the Rohingya Crisis in Myanmar' (2019) 9 Asian JIL 334.
28 A/RES/48/134 (4 Mar 1994) Annex.
29 Law No 21/2014 of 28 Mar 2014.

Furthermore, on 12 November 2019 the International Commission of Jurists, a Geneva-based human rights NGO whose membership comprises 60 eminent human rights lawyers from all over the world, issued a briefing note entitled *Four Immediately Implementable Reforms to Enhance Myanmar's National Human Rights Commission*,[30] urging the Myanmar Government to adopt constitutional and legislative guarantees to enable the MNHRC to better protect and promote human rights for all persons in Myanmar. At the same time, MNHRC Commissioners should robustly pursue their mandate, including by advocating for the rights of society's most vulnerable people. According to the International Commission of Jurists, the MNHRC 'generally fails to act on reported human rights violations, from crimes by soldiers in border areas through to regular attacks on the press, rendering it ineffective in providing redress to victims', and 'the MNHRC's routine inaction in critical cases demonstrates its lack of the necessary independence to stand against state actors, particularly the military'. For example, MNHRC Commissioners have been 'notably silent on gross human rights violations against Rohingyas [*sic*], perpetrated by Tatmadaw soldiers in the context of "clearance operations"'. The MNHRC's composition is also said to not reflect Myanmar's ethnic, religious, regional and gender diversity, which further erodes its ability to address the conflict-related violations and abuses particularly prevalent in border areas such as Rakhine, Kachin and Shan states.

The International Commission of Jurists advises Myanmar Government to undertake four immediately implementable reforms as regards the MNHRC. First, the Union President and the Selection Board should appoint MNHRC commissioners through a transparent and fully consultative process that enables its composition to effectively protect human rights and appropriately reflect the full diversity of the population of Myanmar, including ethnic, religious, regional, gender and sexual identities. Second, MNHRC Commissioners should adopt a broad and active interpretation of their mandate, including by taking steps to address the most serious violations, including crimes under international law, and certain human rights cases that have gone before courts. Third, Myanmar's Parliament should amend the 2014 MNHRC Law to include provisions that strengthen the MNHRC's capacity and independence, and improve the appointment process for commissioners. Fourth, in amending the 2008 Constitution, Myanmar's Constitutional Amendment Committee should propose provisions guaranteeing the structural and financial independence of the MNHRC.

On 14 January 2020, the Myanmar Government replaced the entire 11-member MNHRC with 11 new commissioners led by chairman U Hla Myint, a former ambassador and Myanmar's representative to the ASEAN Intergovernmental Commission on Human Rights. The MNHRC's new vice chair, Dr Nanda Hmun, is a retired permanent secretary of the Ministry of Religion and Culture.

30 www.icj.org/wp-content/uploads/2019/11/Myanmar-MNHRC-Advocacy-Briefing-Note-2019-ENG.pdf.

The other MNHRC commissioners are retired civil servants from ministries and government agencies, including a retired official from the Office of the Commander-in-Chief of the Armed Forces, and a professor from the Department of Law at Yangon University. The new composition of the MNHRC seems to fall short of what the International Commission of Jurists has recommended. If the MNHRC is considered by the international community as not measuring up to the international standards set by the Paris Principles, the Myanmar Government itself might have lost a golden opportunity to turn the MNHRC into a credible voice to 'filter out misleading information before shadows of incrimination are cast over entire nations and governments' and to fend off 'the ways in which unsubstantiated narratives are relied upon by the UN and NGOs [which] must be reformed', as demanded by ASSK in her op-ed article in *The Financial Times*.

2

THE ROHINGYA SITUATION AND INTERNATIONAL REACTIONS

There are several possible avenues for international intervention in problems like the Rohingya crisis, bilaterally as well as at regional organizations and global international organizations. Lessons learnt from the Rohingya crisis will hopefully prompt the international community to strive to achieve progress towards designing international processes appropriate to such situations.

ASEAN

The regional intergovernmental organization to which Myanmar belongs is the Association of Southeast Asian Nations, or ASEAN, set up on 8 August 1967 by Indonesia, Malaysia, Philippines, Singapore and Thailand, motivated by their common fear of the spread of communism into Southeast Asia. After the end of the Vietnam War, ASEAN expanded to include Brunei Darussalam on 7 January 1984 – a few days after its independence from Great Britain, Vietnam on 28 July 1995, Lao PDR and Myanmar both on 23 July 1997 and Cambodia on 30 April 1999. The principle of non-interference in international affairs of ASEAN Member States is rooted in the fourth preambular paragraph of the 1967 ASEAN Declaration (or Bangkok Declaration),[1] ASEAN's founding document, stating that ASEAN Member States 'are determined to ensure their stability and security from external interference in any form or manifestation in order to preserve their national identities in accordance with the ideals and aspirations of their peoples'. Article 2(2) of the 2007 ASEAN Charter[2] stipulates, *inter alia*, that ASEAN and its Member States shall act in accordance with the

1 (1967) 6 ILM 1233.
2 2624 UNTS 223, in force 15 Dec 2008.

DOI: 10.4324/9781003224211-2

following Principles: (a) respect for the independence, sovereignty, equality, territorial integrity and national identity of all ASEAN Member States; (b) shared commitment and collective responsibility in enhancing regional peace, security and prosperity; (c) renunciation of aggression and of the threat or use of force or other actions in any manner inconsistent with international law; (d) reliance on peaceful settlement of disputes; (e) *non-interference in the internal affairs* of ASEAN Member States; (f) respect for the right of every Member State to lead its national existence free from external interference, subversion and coercion; (g) enhanced consultations on matters seriously affecting the common interest of ASEAN; (h) adherence to the rule of law, good governance, the principles of democracy and constitutional government; (i) respect for fundamental freedoms, *the promotion and protection of human rights*, and the promotion of social justice; and (j) upholding the UN Charter[3] and international law, including international humanitarian law, subscribed to by ASEAN Member States.

Dispute settlement among ASEAN Member States is based on Chapter IV (Pacific Settlement of Disputes) of the 1976 Treaty of Amity and Cooperation in Southeast Asia,[4] pursuant to which 'friendly negotiations' between the disputing parties are the priority, failing which the High Council comprising a Representative at ministerial level from each of the ASEAN Member States shall recommend to the parties in dispute appropriate means of settlement such as good offices, mediation, inquiry or conciliation. The High Council may offer its good offices, *or upon agreement of the parties in dispute*, constitute itself into a committee of mediation, inquiry or conciliation. When deemed necessary, the High Council shall recommend appropriate measures for the prevention of a deterioration of the dispute or the situation. However, all the parties to the dispute must agree to engage the role of the High Council in this regard. In any case, an ASEAN Member State not party to the dispute may offer all possible assistance to settle the said dispute. Nothing in the 1976 Treaty precludes recourse to the modes of peaceful settlement contained in Article 33(l) of the UN Charter.[5]

As of 2015, the 'ASEAN Community' is founded upon three pillars: Political-Security Community, Economic Community and Socio-Cultural Community. 'Promotion and Protection of human rights' falls under the first of the three pillars, whereby ASEAN Member States undertake to, among other things, establish an ASEAN human rights body by 2009 and encourage cooperation between it and existing human rights mechanisms, as well as with other relevant international organizations.[6] They also undertake to promote and protect the rights of

3 1 UNTS XVI, in force 24 Oct 1945.
4 1022 UNTS 316, in force 15 July 1976.
5 Art 33(1) of the UN Charter reads: 'The parties to any dispute, the continuance of which is likely to endanger the maintenance of international peace and security, shall, first of all, seek a solution by negotiation, enquiry, mediation, conciliation, arbitration, judicial settlement, resort to regional agencies or arrangements, or other peaceful means of their own choice.'
6 ASEAN Secretariat, *ASEAN Political-Security Community Blueprint* (2009) 5.

women and children and migrant workers, human rights and fundamental freedoms of peoples in accordance with the 2007 ASEAN Charter, the UN Charter, the 1948 Universal Declaration of Human Rights[7] and the Vienna Declaration and Programme of Action[8] adopted by the World Conference on Human Rights in Vienna on 25 June 1993.

The ASEAN Intergovernmental Commission on Human Rights ('AICHR') was set up on 23 October 2009, comprising one representative appointed by each ASEAN Member State to serve for a three-year term that is renewable. It works by means of consultation and consensus and it reports to the ASEAN Foreign Ministers. On 19 November 2012, the Heads of State or Governments of the ASEAN Member States approved the ASEAN Human Rights Declaration[9] drafted by the AICHR. The Declaration refers to the civil and political rights; economic, social and cultural rights; the right to development and the right to peace. However, operative paragraph 7 of the Declaration makes it clear the realization of human rights must be considered in the regional and national contexts bearing in mind different political, economic, legal, social, cultural, historical and religious backgrounds. Although operative paragraph 8 of the Declaration stipulates that the human rights and fundamental freedoms of every person may be subject only to such limitations as are determined by law solely for the purpose of securing due recognition for the human rights and fundamental freedoms of others and to meet the just requirements of national security, public order, public health, public safety, public morality, as well as the general welfare of the peoples in a democratic society, there is no supervisory mechanism or enforcement machinery to ensure their observance. Since ASEAN works on the basis of the 'comfort level' of the ASEAN Member States concerned, bearing in mind their different political systems, ASEAN does not adopt punitive measures such as sanctions against an ASEAN Member State. Therefore, ASEAN does not have either a regional human rights court or an international mechanism to hear individual complaints about human rights violations. The ASEAN consensus has, in effect, resulted in not naming and shaming or censuring any ASEAN Member State or Government, but in trying instead to help it find a way out of the problem without anybody losing face.

Whereas the other international institutions can only condemn Myanmar or its officials, ASEAN could be better placed to provide a route to change, in particular on the issue of getting the Myanmar Government to accept the Rohingya as part of the country.

7 A/RES/217(III) (10 Dec 1948).

8 A/CONF.157/23 (12 July 1993).

9 ASEAN Secretariat, *ASEAN Human Rights Declaration and the Phnom Penh Statement on the Adoption of the ASEAN Human Rights Declaration (AHRD)* (2013). For a drafting history of the Declaration and criticisms thereof, see James Gomez and Robin Ramcharan, 'The Protection of Human Rights in Southeast Asia: Improving Effectiveness of Civil Society' (2012) 2 Asia-Pacific J Human Rights & the Law 27.

At the end of 2016 and soon after the start of the 'clearance operations' by the Tatmadaw in 2017, Indonesia's Foreign Minister Retno Marsudi travelled to Myanmar to meet ASSK and Commander-in-Chief Senior General Min Aung Hlaing. In discussions with both, she raised Indonesia's concerns about the crisis and submitted a proposal aimed at restoring stability and preventing further violence. Other senior government officers of Indonesia called on ASEAN Member States to take a more active role in resolving the Rohingya refugee crisis, and for Myanmar to be more open and trust friendly countries in the region to help resolve this problem by choosing who could help. In Indonesia's view, ASEAN's assistance is not a way of interfering in Myanmar's domestic affairs, as ASEAN has no intention of interfering or influencing Myanmar's domestic policies. In late January 2019, Indonesian President Joko Widodo became the first Head of State to visit the Rohingya refugee camps in Bangladesh's Cox's Bazar district, and Indonesia was one of the first countries to dispatch food aid and volunteers to support humanitarian work in the camps. Aceh in Indonesia has been sheltering many Rohingya asylum seekers fleeing Myanmar by boat since late 2015. Although the Indonesian Armed Forces have sought to close the asylum seekers' entry into Indonesian territory, they assist the latter by providing food and water supplies to the boats with Rohingya on board. In June and early September 2020, for example, Indonesia rescued and gave shelters to a total of 395 Rohingya asylum seekers who were stranded in cramped boats at sea off Indonesia.

Among the national leaders of ASEAN Member States, Malaysia's leaders have been the most critical of Myanmar's handling of the Rohingya issue. In December 2016, Malaysia's then Prime Minister Datuk Seri Najib Razak led a rally in Kuala Lumpur to protest the 'ethnic cleansing' of the Rohingya community in Rakhine state, and called on world leaders to take action on the matter despite being warned by Myanmar against it. Thanks to Malaysia's pressure, a meeting of ASEAN Foreign Ministers was convened on 19 December 2016 to discuss Myanmar's ongoing military campaign in Rakhine state. That meeting was followed on 19 January 2017 by an Extraordinary Meeting of the Foreign Ministers of the Organization of Islamic Cooperation ('OIC'), convened in Kula Lumpur under Malaysia's chairmanship, where Najib announced it was the time to end the Rohingya crisis, by Myanmar immediately stopping the killing, the burning of houses, the violation of women and girls, the persecution of men and women and the denial of basic rights to fellow human beings simply on the grounds that they were Muslims. He also demanded that the perpetrators be brought to justice.

Malaysia has sent food aid to the Rohingya refugees in Bangladesh, provided support on the ground and provided a field hospital with 100 beds. Malaysia also disassociated itself from the statement issued by ASEAN on the humanitarian crisis in Rakhine in September 2017 because the statement made no mention of the Rohingya as one of the affected parties. In his meeting with US President Trump, Najib raised the Rohingya issue, resulting in the joint statement following their bilateral discussions. It reads in its pertinent part:

> They discussed the need to end the humanitarian crisis in Myanmar. Both leaders called for an end to the violence targeting civilian populations, and discussed the need for a strong international community response for the hundreds of thousands of individuals who have been victimized and displaced by violence, including those who have arrived in Bangladesh.[10]

Senior US government officers, including Vice-President Mike Pence and Secretary of State Rex Tillerson pursued this matter further in numerous forums, including at the UN Security Council. After his meeting with ASSK and Commander-in-Chief Senior General Min Aung Hlaing on 22 November 2017, Tillerson issued a written statement declaring, '[a]fter a careful and thorough analysis of available facts, it is clear that the situation in northern Rakhine state constitutes ethnic cleansing against the Rohingya', and '[t]hose responsible for these atrocities must be held accountable'. He added that the US would pursue accountability through US law, including possible targeted sanctions.[11] Najib himself continued to raise the issue even in front of ASSK at various forums whenever opportunities arose.

Dr Mahathir Mohamad, Najib's successor, sustained his predecessor's zeal with respect to the Rohingya. In an exclusive interview with *Anadolu Agency*, Turkey's State-run international news agency headquartered in Ankara, on 30 July 2019, Mahathir proposed a separate state for the Rohingya community to resolve the issue 'if Myanmar does not recognize them as its citizens'. In his view,

> Myanmar, of course, at one time was made up of many different states. But the British decided to rule Myanmar as one State, and because of that, many of the tribes were included in the State of Burma. But now, of course, they should either be treated as nationals or they should be given their territory to form their own State.

This proposal has not been well-received even among the Rohingya. At the high-level event on the 'Rohingya Crisis – A Way Forward' held at the UN headquarters on 24 September 2019, Mahathir deplored that the Myanmar Government was clearly unwilling to take any action to resolve the Rohingya crisis, leaving the international community to step in to urgently resolve it. He was unequivocal that '[w]hat happened in Rakhine state [was] genocide' – with 'mass killings, systematic rape and other gross violations of human rights'. In his opinion, the longer the Rohingya refugees stayed in the camps, the more desperate their situation would become, as the refugees had become vulnerable to other forms of exploitation such as human trafficking and sex slavery. He maintained that those

10 www.malaysiakini.com/news/395099.

11 www.voanews.com/east-asia-pacific/tillerson-calls-violence-against-rohingya-myanmar-ethnic-cleansing.

Rohingya remaining in Myanmar had become internally displaced persons languishing in camps in Rakhine, and the Myanmar authorities had denied access to some UN officials and humanitarian aid workers as if they had something to hide. While repatriation should be Myanmar's main priority to demonstrate its seriousness in tackling the crisis, Mahathir pointed out two attempts had been made to repatriate some of the refugees and both had failed since no one would return if they did not feel their safety was guaranteed. Malaysia would continue to insist that repatriation be done in a safe, voluntary and dignified manner, with full citizenship granted to the Rohingya.

In his speech during the General Debate of the 74th session of the UN General Assembly on 27 September 2019, Prime Minister Mahathir stated:

> I must again refer to the fate of the Rohingyas [*sic*] in Myanmar. Many colonies of the West, upon independence, expelled non-natives in their countries. But nowhere have they been as brutal as Myanmar. Even natives massacred, brutally killed and raped in full view of the world backgrounded by the burning houses and villages of the victims. They were forced to migrate and now they dare not return to Myanmar even when offered. They cannot trust the Myanmar military unless some form of non-Myanmar protection is given.
>
> The helplessness of the world in stopping atrocities inflicted on the Rohingyas [*sic*] in Myanmar had reduced the regard for the resolution of the UN.[12]

As of January 2020, Malaysia sheltered more than 100,000 Rohingya refugees who had fled from Rakhine. However, when the COVID-19 pandemic was rampaging everywhere, Malaysian authorities reportedly turned away boats carrying Rohingya for fear of their spreading the pandemic in Malaysia.

Brunei, the other Muslim-majority ASEAN Member State, is more circumspect. In April 2019, Brunei Sultan Haji Hassanal Bolkiah informed the visiting Prime Minister of Bangladesh that emphasis should be placed on 'just and permanent solution' to the Rohingya crisis, with all sorts of efforts exerted for Rohingya to return to Myanmar.

The Philippines has shown compassion to the Rohingya on several occasions. In April 2018, President Rodrigo Duterte said the Philippines wanted to give refuge to the Rohingya fleeing persecution and violence in Myanmar. In February 2019, the President offered citizenship of the Philippines to Rohingya refugees in Bangladesh as a sign of humanitarian assistance. He once remarked that 'genocide' was being committed, but apologized to ASSK a week later, explaining he was not interfering in Myanmar's 'internal affairs' and 'civil war'

12 www.nst.com.my/news/nation/2019/09/525269/dr-ms-full-speech-text-74th-unga.

– his previous remark was a satirical barb at the West for not taking in Rohingya Muslims. He had previously called on Europe to participate in the reception of 'Muslim refugees' from Myanmar.

Apart from the aforesaid individual efforts by some ASEAN Member States, ASEAN as a regional grouping focuses mainly on the process of repatriating the Rohingya back to Myanmar, treating the 'humanitarian situation' in Myanmar's Rakhine state as 'a matter of concern' but without accusing the Myanmar authorities of any wrongs. At the ASEAN Summit in November 2018, ASEAN called on the ASEAN Coordinating Centre for Humanitarian Assistance on Disaster Management ('AHA Centre') to assess Myanmar's readiness to resettle the refugees and how the AHA Centre could help. ASEAN's Emergency Response and Action Team ('ERAT') sent by the AHA Centre to assess Myanmar's readiness to receive returning Rohingya has been accused by human rights NGOs of not seeking inputs from Rohingya refugees and of not even using the term 'Rohingya' in its report on the readiness of reception and transit centres, including potential relocation sites that have been identified by the Myanmar Government. The report has also been criticized for ERAT's failure to address the reality of the lack of trust and confidence between the Rohingya and the Myanmar authorities.

The ASEAN Chairman's Statement of the 34th ASEAN Summit, issued on 23 June 2019, 'reaffirmed' ASEAN's support to Myanmar in providing humanitarian assistance, facilitating the repatriation process with regard to the situation in Rakhine state and promoting sustainable development in cooperation with ASEAN's Dialogue Partners on possible support. The importance of the voluntary return of displaced persons in a safe, secure and dignified manner was emphasized. So was the need to find a comprehensive and durable solution to address the root causes of the conflict in Rakhine and to create a conducive environment so that the affected communities can rebuild their lives. Myanmar was encouraged to continue to implement the remaining recommendations of the Annan Commission's Final Report. ASEAN expected the Independent Commission of Enquiry established by the Government of Myanmar to seek accountability by carrying out an independent and impartial investigation into alleged human rights violations and related issues. The ASEAN Chairman's Statement, issued on 3 November 2019 during the 35th ASEAN Summit, did not add anything substantively different from the previous Statement except for expressing ASEAN's support for the implementation of the agreement among the Foreign Ministers of Myanmar, Bangladesh and China on 23 September 2019 to facilitate the implementation of the bilateral agreements between Myanmar and Bangladesh on repatriation of the Rohingya given shelters in Bangladesh.

Subsequent discussions at ASEAN in 2020 focused on repatriating the Rohingya from Bangladesh to Myanmar. In the second half of 2020, the situation in Rakhine became increasingly complicated due to the worsening of the COVID-19 outbreak over there. Separately, Malaysian Foreign Minister Hishammuddin Hussein voiced his concern that a prolonged crisis in Rakhine would jeopardize the security and the stability in the ASEAN region. He and

Indonesian Foreign Minister Retno urged ASEAN Member States to join forces in addressing transnational crimes, particularly people smuggling and trafficking, as Rohingya asylum seekers were likely to be vulnerable in this regard.

As of the time of writing, there has been no meaningful progress made to repatriate the Rohingya in Bangladesh camps back to Myanmar. The Government of Bangladesh has been facing increasingly serious constraints to accommodate those in the existing camps. In December 2020, in order to ease chronic overcrowding in camps on land, it started relocating Rohingya asylum seekers to Bhasan Char, a remote offshore island of 56 square kilometres in size, even before the UN could determine whether the island was suitable to safely host this vulnerable population and amid human rights NGOs' concerns about the poor living conditions on the island which is also prone to cyclones. Some of the asylum seekers were reportedly willing to be relocated to the island, to be united with their family members and get away from the overcrowded camps on land. The Government is planning to eventually relocate 100,000 Rohingya to the island.

OIC

The Organization of Islamic Cooperation, or OIC, set up in September 1969, is the second largest intergovernmental organization after the United Nations, with a membership of 57 States in four continents. The OIC aims to be the collective voice of the Muslim world. It endeavours to safeguard and protect the interests of the Muslim world in the spirit of promoting international peace and harmony among various peoples of the world.

The OIC has been actively dealing with the plight of the Rohingya since the 4th Extraordinary Islamic Summit Conference on the Rohingya Muslim Community in Myanmar, held in Mecca, Saudi Arabia, in 2012. The OIC Contact Group at the Ministerial Level on the Rohingya in Myanmar made a visit to Myanmar in 2013 to meet with the governmental and religious leaderships and the representatives of civil society and international organizations and institutions, and to the camps in Rakhine state where meetings were held with the displaced. Meetings of the OIC Groups were also held in New York, Brussels and Geneva in December 2016 to discuss the situation of the Rohingya Muslims in Myanmar.

The January 2017 Extraordinary Meeting of the Foreign Ministers of the OIC held in Kuala Lumpur expressed grave concern at the recent outbreak of violence in Myanmar's Rakhine state that resulted in the loss of innocent lives and displaced tens of thousands of Rohingya people, and called upon the Myanmar Government to take decisive steps to restore calm to the affected areas as well as to ensure that Myanmar security forces act in accordance with the rule of law and all perpetrators of acts of violence be held accountable. The Meeting also urged Myanmar to abide by its obligations under international law, international humanitarian law and human rights treaties, and take all necessary measures to stop the violence and discrimination against the Rohingya Muslim minority and continued attempts to deny their culture and identity. The Meeting further urged Myanmar to eliminate the root causes for the Rohingya's grievances, in particular by restoring the citizenship of the Rohingya which was revoked in the Citizenship Act of 1982.[13] The Meeting called on the Myanmar Government to ensure an inclusive and transparent policy towards ethnic and religious communities by including the Rohingya Muslim minority as an integral part of this process and considering them as an ethnic minority, as called for by relevant UN General Assembly and Human Rights Council resolutions. The authorities of Myanmar were also urged to take effective measures to prevent the worsening of the humanitarian crisis in Rakhine state and to take all necessary measures to restore peace and inter-communal harmony through dialogue and a comprehensive national peace and reconciliation process involving all segments of society in Myanmar. In this regard, the importance of moderation was underlined as a core value in countering extremism and terrorism in all their aspects. The Meeting invited OIC Member States to continue to share the substantial costs incurred by those countries that have provided temporary shelter and protection to Rohingya refugees, in accordance with the principles of burden-sharing and shared responsibility, and in the spirit of Islamic solidarity. The Meeting decided to request the OIC Secretary General to coordinate with the Myanmar Government for a high-level delegation from the OIC Contact Group to visit Rakhine state to meet with local officials and the affected Rohingya Muslim minority, as well as to explore joint initiatives with his counterparts in the UN and ASEAN, that could support the Myanmar Government to develop and implement interfaith and inter-communal dialogues in Myanmar and in the wider Southeast Asian region. The OIC Groups in New York, Geneva and Brussels were requested to regularly review the evolving situation and explore sustained engagement strategies with Myanmar, the UN, the European Union and other international organizations. The OIC Independent Permanent Human Rights Commission was encouraged to continue examining the situation of the Rohingya Muslim minority in Myanmar as a priority issue on its agenda.

In early 2018, a delegation of the OIC visited a Rohingya refugee camp in Bangladesh. On 5–6 May 2018, the OIC Council of Foreign Ministers met in Dhaka, Bangladesh, under the theme 'Islamic Values for Sustainable Peace and Development'. The ensuing Dhaka Declaration[14] includes four paragraphs on the Rohingya crisis. It expresses

> deep concern over the recent systematic brutal acts perpetrated by security forces against the Rohingya Muslim community in Myanmar that

13 Pyithu Hluttaw Law No 4 of 1982.

14 https://reliefweb.int/report/world/dhaka-declaration-45th-session-council-foreign-ministers-organization-islamic.

> has reached the level of ethnic cleansing, which constitutes a serious and blatant violation of international law, and which has affected over 370,000 Rohingya who have been forcibly displaced to Bangladesh and other countries across the region, in addition to the burning of their houses and places of worship.

In this regard, it commends the personal leadership of Bangladeshi Prime Minister Sheikh Hasina in addressing the plight of 'the most persecuted people in the world' and seeks strong international support to resolve the crisis and full implementation of the recommendations put forward by the Annan Commission. The Declaration underscores the importance of OIC Members States continuing to remain engaged in the UN system including in the UN General Assembly and the Human Rights Council as well as with other relevant international organizations to address 'the massive human rights violations of the Rohingya Muslims', taking into account the recent developments. It also reaffirms the OIC's full solidarity with Bangladesh in the face of the huge Rohingya influx with its humanitarian and security consequences for Bangladesh and with the Rohingya, 'victims of the state-backed violence in Myanmar' who are 'forcibly displaced … from Myanmar'. It agrees to address the accountability issue for the violations of human rights against the Rohingya in Myanmar through the formation of an *ad hoc* ministerial committee, to be chaired by The Gambia.

A preambular paragraph of the OIC's Resolution No 59/45-POL on the Establishment of an OIC *ad hoc* Ministerial Committee on Accountability for Human Rights Violations against the Rohingyas[15] recognizes that 'ensuring accountability and justice is the most crucial step towards preventing genocide and other mass atrocity crimes'. The Resolution decides to establish a ten-member *ad hoc* Ministerial Committee on Accountability for Human Rights Violations against the Rohingya ('MCCAR') including the OIC Secretariat, to be chaired by The Gambia. The MCCAR will: (a) engage to ensure accountability and justice for gross violations of international human rights and humanitarian laws and principles; (b) assist in information gathering and evidence collection for accountability purposes; (c) mobilize and coordinate international political support for accountability for the human rights violations against the Rohingya in Myanmar; and (d) collaborate with the international bodies, such as the Office of the UN High Commissioner for Human Rights, UN Security Council and other international and regional mechanisms. Malaysia is a member of the MCCAR.

On 1–2 March 2019, the 46th Session of the OIC Council of Foreign Ministers was convened in Abu Dhabi, UAE, under the theme 'Fifty Years of Islamic Cooperation: Roadmap for Prosperity and Development'. It adopted Resolution

15 OIC/CFM-45/2018/POL/RES/FINAL at 164.

No 4/46-MM on the Situation of the Muslim Community in Myanmar,[16] which is 12 pages in length and which, for the first time for the OIC, mentions the term 'genocide' in the context of the Rohingya crisis. It alludes to the opening statement of the Chairperson of the UN Independent International Fact-Finding Mission on Myanmar, or IIFFMM, at the UN Security Council on 24 October 2018, in which he stated that

> [w]ar crimes and crimes against humanity have been committed in Kachin, Shan and Rakhine states [, and that there was] sufficient information to warrant the investigation and prosecution of senior officials in the Tatmadaw on charges of genocide [since] … genocidal intent, meaning the intent to destroy the Rohingya in whole or in part, can be reasonably inferred.

The Resolution welcomes the September 2017 letter addressed by President Haydar Abbadi of Iraq to the heads of Muslim countries and the OIC Secretary General, which addresses the Rohingya crisis and the violations of human rights and genocide against the Rohingya. The letter calls for convening an urgent meeting of the Council of the OIC Foreign Ministers to form an international alliance to counter and stop these violations. Operative paragraph 11 of the Resolution calls upon the Myanmar Government to, among other things, honour its obligations under international law and human rights treaties, and

> to take all measures to immediately halt all vestiges and manifestations of the practice of ethnic cleansing, genocide, violence of all types, vigilantism, acts of dispersion and discriminatory practices against Rohingya Muslims, as well as the continuous attempts to obliterate their Islamic culture and identity immediately, including delisting them from household lists and demolition of places of worship, institutions and houses of Muslim minorities.

Operative paragraph 12 proceeds to call upon OIC Member States to demonstrate solidarity and take up the OIC Charter-bound duty of saving the Rohingya Muslim minority in Myanmar from 'existential threat' and of ensuring justice to heal the wounds, sufferings and grievous losses of lives. In this pursuit, OIC Member States are to 'take concrete steps to bring the perpetrators of atrocities, crimes against humanity and genocide and those responsible for destroying a community, its distinct history and culture to all the international legal and juridical institutions and mechanisms'. Operative paragraph 34 then calls upon Members of the MCCAR 'to carry out the tasks of ensuring accountability and justice for gross violations of international human rights and humanitarian laws

16 OIC/CFM-46/2019/POL/RES/FINAL at 14.

and principles' as well as assisting in information gathering and evidence collection for accountability purposes and mobilizing and coordinating international political support for accountability for the human rights violations against the Rohingya in Myanmar.

Human rights treaty bodies

Individuals in a nation State whose human rights are in peril or violated may have recourse to human rights treaty bodies monitoring the implementation of the respective human rights treaties falling within their competence. For the Rohingya, the most pertinent human rights treaty is the 1966 International Covenant on Civil and Political Rights ('ICCPR'),[17] which aims at protecting the rights to life and freedom from torture, inhuman or degrading treatment or punishment; the freedom of movement; the right to privacy; the freedom of religion, belief and thought; the right to a fair trial; equal protection of the law; the freedom from discrimination; the right to vote and to stand for election; and the freedoms of assembly and association, among others. As of this writing, the ICCPR has 173 parties, but Myanmar is not one of them.

In addition to the 1948 Genocide Convention,[18] which will be dealt with in Chapters 4 and 5, Myanmar is party to four core international human rights treaties – the 1966 International Covenant on Economic, Social and Cultural Rights ('ICESCR')[19] binding upon Myanmar since January 2018, the 1979 Convention on the Elimination of All Forms of Discrimination against Women ('CEDAW')[20] since 1997, the 1989 UN Convention on the Rights of the Child ('CRC')[21] since 1991, and the 2006 Convention on the Rights of Persons with Disabilities ('CRPD')[22] since January 2012.

Article 1 of CEDAW defines 'discrimination against women' as

> any distinction, exclusion or restriction made on the basis of sex which has the effect or purpose of impairing or nullifying the recognition, enjoyment or exercise by women, irrespective of their marital status, on a basis of equality of men and women, of human rights and fundamental freedoms in the political, economic, social, cultural, civil or any other field.

In its General Recommendation 28 on the core obligations of States Parties under Article 2 of CEDAW,[23] the Committee on the Elimination of Discrimination

17 999 UNTS 171, in force 23 Mar 1976.
18 78 UNTS 277, in force 12 Jan 1951.
19 993 UNTS 3, in force 3 Jan 1976.
20 1249 UNTS13, in force 3 Sept 1981.
21 1577 UNTS 3, in force 2 Sept 1990.
22 2515 UNTS 3, in force 3 May 2008.
23 CEDAW/C/GC/28 (16 Dec 2010).

against Women, or the CEDAW Committee entrusted with monitoring the implementation of CEDAW, it is reaffirmed that the objective of CEDAW is 'the elimination of all forms of discrimination against women on the basis of sex' by guaranteeing women the equal recognition, enjoyment and exercise of all human rights and fundamental freedoms as elaborated in Article 1 even where discrimination was not intended. The CEDAW Committee, acting pursuant to Article 18(1)(b) of CEDAW,[24] decided on 17 November 2017 to request the Myanmar Government to submit an exceptional report by May 2018 on the situation of Rohingya women and girls from northern Rakhine state since the onset of the violence on 25 August 2017. In response to the report received belatedly from Myanmar on 1 February 2019, the CEDAW Committee issued its Concluding Observations on 8 March 2019.[25]

The CEDAW Committee notes that in recent decades Rohingya women and girls have been victims of at least four incidences of mass violence with widespread killings, arrests, torture, rape, forced labour and other abuses resulting in waves of mass displacement. In 1977 the Myanmar Government programme Naga Min (Dragon King) resulted in 200,000 Rohingya seeking refuge from violence in Bangladesh; 250,000 Rohingya escaped once again to Bangladesh in 1991; in 2012, almost 200,000 Rohingya found themselves enclosed in internally displaced people's camps in and around Sittwe, the capital of Rakhine state; and in 2016 and 2017 military security 'clearance operations' led to an influx of over 800,000 refugees to Bangladesh. The CEDAW Committee recommends, among other things, that Myanmar: take the measures necessary to amend the provisions of the Constitution that grant government officials, including military and security officers, immunity for human rights abuses and establish civilian jurisdiction over human rights violations; amend the Penal Code of 1861[26] to adopt a definition of violence against women, including rape and other forms of sexual and gender-based violence, in accordance with CEDAW and international standards, and ensure civilian courts have jurisdiction over the military for crimes of violence against women and girls; enact comprehensive legislation

24 Art 18 of CEDAW reads:

> '1. States Parties undertake to submit to the Secretary-General of the United Nations, for consideration by the Committee, a report on the legislative, judicial, administrative or other measures which they have adopted to give effect to the provisions of the present Convention and on the progress made in this respect:
>
> a. Within one year after the entry into force for the State concerned;
> b. Thereafter at least every four years and further whenever the Committee so requests.
>
> 2. Reports may indicate factors and difficulties affecting the degree of fulfilment of obligations under the present Convention.'

25 CEDAW/C/MMR/CO/EP/1.

26 India ACT XLV.1860 (1 May 1861).

that protects women from forced displacement, in particular women belonging to various ethnic minority groups such as the Rohingya; and review promptly its Penal Code to criminalize serious international crimes including genocide, crimes against humanity and war crimes, such as conflict-related sexual violence, and establish civilian jurisdiction over these crimes. The CEDAW Committee urges Myanmar to bring those responsible for such crimes to justice. The Committee also reiterates its previous call for the Myanmar Government to amend the Citizenship Act of 1982 to remove discriminatory provisions based on ethnicity, use objective criteria to determine citizenship, such as descent, and restore citizenship to Rohingya women and girls. Furthermore, Myanmar should take the measures necessary to end conflict-related sexual violence in Rakhine state, and to: (a) establish an effective, accessible and safe mechanism to report incidents of rape and other forms of sexual and gender-based violence to appropriate authorities for investigation; (b) carry out community education programmes aimed at empowering women who want to report violence and in a manner that does not jeopardize their safety; (c) ensure the availability of sexual and reproductive health services as well as preventative and emergency healthcare, under the principles of inclusion and accessibility, to Rohingya women and girls, including psychological health services for victims and survivors of rape and other forms of sexual and gender-based violence; and (d) ensure the participation of Rohingya women and girls in the development and implementation of programmes related to sexual and reproductive health services; set up monitoring mechanisms to ensure access to and quality of those services; and eliminate discriminatory and abusive practices by health care personnel. The other recommendations of the CEDAW Committee focus on the human rights of Rohingya women that are also shared by Rohingya of other genders. Finally, the Committee reminds Myanmar that its sixth periodic report under Article 18 of CEDAW is due in 2020.

In its report to the Human Rights Council on 22 August 2019 entitled 'Sexual and gender-based violence in Myanmar and the gendered impact of its ethnic conflicts',[27] the UN Independent International Fact-Finding Mission on Myanmar, or IIFFMM, concludes that sexual and gender-based violence against ethnic women and girls by Myanmar security forces' operations in northern Myanmar and in Rakhine was committed with the intent to intimidate, terrorize and punish the civilian population and as a tactic of war. The report narrates how men and boys have also been victims of sexual and gender-based violence by the security forces, especially in the context of detention settings. The report emphasizes that Myanmar's obligations under CEDAW do not cease in periods of armed conflict and, therefore, Myanmar must not engage in sexual and gender-based violence, must prevent acts or omissions of sexual and gender-based violence by their own organs and agents, and must investigate, prosecute

27 A/HRC/42/CRP.4 (22 Aug 2019).

and apply appropriate legal or disciplinary sanctions and provide reparations as required. Myanmar must also take all appropriate measures to prevent and investigate, prosecute, punish and provide reparation for acts or omissions by non-State actors that result in sexual and gender-based violence.

With respect to the CRPD, its preambular paragraph (e) recognizes disability as an evolving concept and that disability results from the interaction between persons with impairments and attitudinal and environmental barriers which hinders their full and effective participation in society on an equal basis with others. According to Article 1 of the CRPD, the CRPD's purpose is to promote, protect and ensure the full and equal enjoyment of all human rights and fundamental freedoms by all persons with disabilities, and to promote respect for their inherent dignity. Article 2 defines 'discrimination on the basis of disability' as

> any distinction, exclusion or restriction on the basis of disability which has the purpose or effect of impairing or nullifying the recognition, enjoyment or exercise, on an equal basis with others, of all human rights and fundamental freedoms in the political, economic, social, cultural, civil or any other field; it includes all forms of discrimination, including denial of reasonable accommodation.

The Rohingya situation in Myanmar does not seem to fit in this scenario.

The CRC is applicable to Rohingya children. Article 2 requires its States Parties to respect and ensure the rights set forth in the CRC to each child within their jurisdiction without discrimination of any kind, irrespective of the child's or his or her parent's or legal guardian's race; colour; sex; language; *religion*; political or other opinion; *national, ethnic or social origin*; property; disability; birth *or other status*. States Parties shall take all appropriate measures to ensure the child is protected against all forms of discrimination or punishment on the basis of the *status*, activities, expressed opinions, or *beliefs of the child's parents*, legal guardians or family members. By virtue of Article 3(1), in all actions concerning children, whether undertaken by public or private social welfare institutions, courts of law, administrative authorities or legislative bodies, the best interests of the child shall be a primary consideration. Under Article 6, States Parties recognize every child's inherent right to life and States Parties shall ensure to the maximum extent possible the survival and development of the child. Pursuant to Article 7, the child shall be registered immediately after birth and shall have the right from birth to a name, *the right to acquire a nationality*, and States Parties shall ensure the implementation of these rights in accordance with their national law and their obligations under the relevant international instruments in this field, in particular where the child would otherwise be stateless. Article 8 further requires its States Parties to undertake to respect *the right of the child to preserve his or her identity, including nationality*, name and family relations as recognized by law without unlawful interference. Where a child is illegally deprived of some or all of the elements of his or her identity, States Parties shall provide appropriate assistance and protection, with a view to re-establishing speedily his or her identity. According to Article 30, in those States in which ethnic, religious or linguistic minorities or persons of indigenous origin exist, a child belonging to such a minority or who is indigenous shall not be denied the right, in community with other members of his or her group, to enjoy his or her own culture, to profess and practise his or her own religion or to use his or her own language. Article 37 obligates its States Parties to ensure, among other things, that no child shall be subjected to torture or other cruel, inhuman or degrading treatment or punishment; no child shall be deprived of his or her liberty unlawfully or arbitrarily; every child deprived of liberty shall be treated with humanity and respect for the inherent dignity of the human person, and in a manner which takes into account the needs of persons of his or her age; and every child deprived of his or her liberty shall have the right to prompt access to legal and other appropriate assistance, as well as the right to challenge the legality of the deprivation of his or her liberty before a court or other competent, independent and impartial authority, and to a prompt decision on any such action.

Myanmar is not party to the 2011 Optional Protocol to the CRC on a Communications Procedure[28] that would allow children or their representatives to file with the Committee on the Rights of the Child individual complaints for violation of the rights of children. This Optional Protocol also permits its State Party to recognize the Committee's competence to receive and consider inter-State communications claiming that another State Party is not fulfilling its obligations under the CRC. Therefore, Myanmar is only bound by Article 44 of the CRC to undertake to submit to the Committee, through the UN Secretary-General, reports on the measures it has adopted which give effect to the rights recognized herein and on the progress made on the enjoyment of those rights, within two years of the entry into force of the CRC for Myanmar, and every five years thereafter.

In 2012, the CRC Committee considered Myanmar's third and fourth periodic reports due in 2008 and expressed the following concerns regarding Rohingya children in Myanmar. A large number of children, including Rohingya children, remained unregistered as a result of insufficient awareness-raising on the importance of birth registration; a non-user-friendly system; a lengthy process to obtain birth certificates at the township level; unofficial fees associated with the birth registration system; the existence of the local order restricting marriages for Rohingya people; and the practice aimed at reducing the number of their children. The CRC Committee therefore recommended that Myanmar implement special measures for improving the birth registration system, greater access to registry services and sensitization and training for registry officials, with a view to ensuring that all children, including children born in remote areas, and displaced and stateless children, especially Rohingya children, be duly registered

28 A/RES/66/138 (19 Dec 2011), in force 14 Apr 2014.

at birth and provided with birth certificates and identity cards. In addition, Myanmar should abolish the local order restricting marriages for Rohingya people and cease practices which restrict the number of children of Rohingya people. Moreover, the CRC Committee was deeply concerned about the prohibition on the return of Rohingya people, including children, who fled Myanmar. It thus recommended that Myanmar allow Rohingya people, including children, who fled Myanmar to return to the country and assist them in their reintegration. Finally, the CRC Committee reiterated its concern that children belonging to ethnic, indigenous, religious and other minority groups, in particular Rohingya children, faced multiple restrictions and forms of discrimination and continued to be denied access to basic rights, including the right to food, health care, education, survival and development, as well as the right to enjoy their culture and to be protected from discrimination. The CRC Committee urged Myanmar to gather additional information on all ethnic minorities and other marginalized groups and to elaborate policies and programmes to fully ensure the implementation of their rights without discrimination. In particular, Myanmar should take effective measures to improve access to education and primary health care for children in the northern Rakhine state, taking into account the Committee's General Comment 11[29] which provides States with guidance on how to implement their obligations under the CRC. The CRC Committee invited Myanmar to submit its combined fifth and sixth periodic report by 13 February 2017 and to include in it information on the implementation of the CRC Committee's aforesaid concluding observations.[30] The CRC Committee's consideration of Myanmar's next report on the implementation of the CRC could take years from now and is being effectively overtaken by other developments, especially at the ICJ, the ICC and certain domestic criminal court(s).

Possible rights under the ICESCR in the Rohingya context may include the guarantee that the rights enunciated in the ICESCR will be exercised without discrimination of any kind as to race, colour, sex, language, *religion*, political or other opinion, *national or social origin*, property, birth *or other status* (Article 2(2)); the right of everyone to an adequate standard of living for himself and his family, including adequate food, clothing and housing, and to the continuous improvement of living conditions (Article 11); the right of everyone to the enjoyment of the highest attainable standard of physical and mental health (Article 12); the right to education (Article 13); and the right of everyone to take part in cultural life (Article 15(1)(a)). Nonetheless, Myanmar is not party to the 2009 Optional Protocol to the ICESCR[31] that recognizes the competence of the Committee on Economic, Social and Cultural Rights ('CESCR') – a panel of 18 independent experts that meets twice a year – to receive complaints from persons within their

29 CRC/C/GC/11 (12 Feb 2009).
30 CRC/C/MMR/CO/3–4 (14 Mar 2012).
31 A/RES/63/117 (5 Mar 2009), in force 5 May 2013.

jurisdiction alleging violations of their rights under the ICESCR. Therefore, Myanmar is only bound to submit regular reports as required by Article 17 of the ICESCR. Since Myanmar has become party to the ICESCR only recently, in January 2018, its first report as well as the report's consideration by the CESCR should take years to materialize and is likely to be overtaken by the current developments regarding the Rohingya issue at various forums and levels.

Under the law of treaties, as also codified in Articles 26 and 27 of the 1969 Vienna Convention on the Law of Treaties,[32] to which Myanmar is party as of October 1998, every treaty in force is binding upon the parties to it and must be performed by them in good faith, and a party may not invoke the provisions of its internal law as justification for its failure to perform a treaty. Human rights treaties fall into the category of treaties where reciprocal fulfilment or non-fulfilment of treaty obligations may not serve as a useful mechanism to force another State Party to perform its treaty obligations. Rather than regulating inter-State conduct, human rights treaties regulate States' domestic behaviour, with individuals and domestic communities, as the case may be, as beneficiaries of the treaties. If a State Party fails to perform its human rights treaty obligations, another State Party cannot reciprocate by not performing the same obligations, as this non-performance by the latter State would deprive the individuals the treaty aims to protect of their human rights protection. Instead, the non-complying State will be pressured bilaterally and/or at various human rights forums by other States Parties for the non-complying State to fulfil its human rights treaty obligations.

United Nations

The UN, comprising almost 200 Member States, has six principal organs. The General Assembly comprises all Member States. The Security Council has five permanent members (China, France, Russia, UK and USA) and ten non-permanent members elected by the UN General Assembly for a two-year term. The Economic and Social Council ('ECOSOC') has 54 Member States elected by the UN General Assembly for a three-year term. The ICJ has 15 judges elected simultaneously by the UN General Assembly and the UN Security Council for a nine-year term and may be re-elected. The UN Secretariat is headed by the Secretary-General, the chief administrative UN officer appointed for a five-year term by the UN General Assembly upon the UN Security Council's recommendation. The other principal organ, the Trusteeship Council, has suspended its operations since 1 November 1994, a month after the independence of Palau, the last remaining UN trust territory.

The UN General Assembly, where each UN Member State has one vote, may discuss any questions or any matters within the scope of the UN Charter or

32 1155 UNTS 331, in force 27 Jan 1980.

relating to the powers and functions of any organs provided for in the Charter, and may make recommendations to UN Members States or to the Security Council or to both on any such questions or matters. It may call the attention of the Security Council to situations which are likely to endanger international peace and security. However, when the Security Council is exercising in respect of any dispute or situation the functions assigned to it in the UN Charter, the UN General Assembly shall not make any recommendation with regard to that dispute or situation unless the Security Council so requests.[33]

UN Security Council

It is the UN Security Council that has primary responsibility for the maintenance of international peace and security.[34] Pursuant to Chapter VII of the UN Charter, the Security Council is entrusted with determining the existence of any threat to the peace, breach of the peace or act of aggression and with making recommendations or deciding what measures shall be taken to maintain or restore international peace and security. The UN Secretary-General may bring to the attention of the Security Council any matter which in his opinion may threaten the maintenance of international peace and security. The Security Council may decide what measures not involving the use of armed force are to be employed to give effect to its decisions, and it may call upon UN Member States to apply such measures. These may include complete or partial interruption of economic relations and of rail, sea, air, postal, telegraphic, radio and other means of communication, and the severance of diplomatic relations. Should the Security Council consider that measures just mentioned would be inadequate or have proved to be inadequate, it may take such action by air, sea or land forces as may be necessary to maintain or restore international peace and security, including demonstrations, blockade and other operations by air, sea or land forces of UN Member States. Such decisions shall be carried out by UN Member States directly and through their action in the appropriate international agencies of which they are members.

Decisions of the Security Council on all non-procedural matters must be made by an affirmative vote of at least nine members including the concurring votes of the permanent members,[35] thereby giving each of the five permanent members of the Council the right of veto. All UN Member States agree to accept and carry out the decisions of the Security Council in accordance with the UN Charter.[36]

The UN Security Council has been dealing with the situation in Myanmar since June 2005 after the United States raised concerns about Myanmar at the UN Security Council's closed consultations under the agenda item 'other

33 UN Charter, Chapter IV.
34 Ibid Art 24(1).
35 Ibid Art 27(3).
36 Ibid Art 25.

matters', leading to the Council holding its first-ever briefing on the situation in Myanmar on 16 December 2005. The focus of the Council's attention was on the democratization process in Myanmar that would end decades of military rule. Not until 20 June 2012 was the Security Council briefed, in consultations by the UN Secretary-General's Special Adviser on Myanmar who had visited Myanmar earlier that month, on the recent troubles in Rakhine state, where the communal violence between the ethnic Rakhine Buddhists and Rohingya Muslims had led to a humanitarian crisis.

On 16 April 2013, the Special Adviser updated the Security Council on the situation on the ground in Myanmar in the light of his many visits to Myanmar since his previous briefing. On 17 April 2014, at the UK's request, the Special Adviser on Myanmar briefed Security Council members in informal consultations under the agenda item 'any other business', focusing on the situation in Rakhine, especially the recent rise in inter-communal tensions there, the disruption of humanitarian aid and the controversy surrounding the 2014 census. On 4 February 2015, the UK sent a letter to the Security Council president requesting the retention of the situation in Myanmar on the Security Council's list of active agenda items. On 2 April 2015, at the UK's request, the UN Secretary-General's Special Adviser on Myanmar updated Council members, noting the continuing challenges in Rakhine state, increasing violence in Kachin and northern Shan states and expressing concerns about the human rights situation. This was followed by another briefing by the Special Adviser on 28 August 2015. Earlier, on 28 May 2015, under the agenda item 'any other business', the UN High Commissioner for Human Rights had briefed Security Council members via video teleconference on the human rights situation in Myanmar, in particular on the Rohingya and the related migration crisis in Southeast Asia. On 19 November 2015, the Special Adviser on Myanmar briefed Security Council members in consultations under the agenda item 'any other business', again at the UK's request, about the 8 November 2015 general elections in Myanmar, and he noted as a serious flaw the disenfranchisement of the Rohingya. On 25 February 2016, at the UK's request, the Special Adviser briefed Council members under the agenda item 'any other business', focusing on the political transition, the peace process and the human rights situation. On 17 November 2016, at the request of the United States, the Special Adviser briefed Council members under the agenda item 'any other business', with the ensuing discussion focused on the recent escalation of violence in Rakhine state and the humanitarian and human rights situation. While emphasizing that lack of access made it difficult to assess the situation, the Special Adviser said there were signs of more organized resistance by the Rohingya and a risk of further radicalization of the conflict.

On 17 March 2017, the UN Under-Secretary-General for Political Affairs briefed Security Council members on the situation in Myanmar during informal consultations under the agenda item 'any other business', focusing mainly on the situation in Rakhine, including the humanitarian challenges. At the briefing on 13 September 2017, he informed the Council of the deteriorating situation in

Myanmar's Rakhine state. Following the meeting, press elements were issued in which Council members expressed concern at reports of excessive violence by Myanmar security forces following the 25 August 2017 attacks by Rohingya armed groups on police border posts and called for 'immediate steps to end the violence in Rakhine, de-escalate the situation, re-establish law and order, ensure the protection of civilians, restore normal socio-economic conditions and resolve the refugee problem'. They also called for the Myanmar Government to facilitate humanitarian assistance and to fulfil commitments to provide aid to all displaced people. On 26 September 2017, Council members were briefed again by the Under-Secretary-General under the agenda item 'any other business', followed on the following day by the briefing of the Council by the UN Secretary-General himself and in a public meeting. On 13 October 2017, at the joint initiative of France and the UK, an informal, confidential meeting was held for Security Council members to have a frank and private exchange of views focusing on the situation in Rakhine state, with former UN Secretary-General Kofi Annan giving a briefing in his capacity as chairperson of the Advisory Commission on Rakhine state.

On 6 November 2017, the UN Security Council issued its Presidential Statement[37] condemning the attacks against Myanmar security forces carried out by ARSA on 25 August 2017 in Rakhine state and expressing grave concern over accounts that ARSA had been responsible for human rights abuses. The Statement also strongly condemned the widespread violence that had taken place in Rakhine state since 25 August 2017 leading to the mass displacement of more than 607,000 individuals, the vast majority belonging to the Rohingya community. It further expressed

> grave concern over reports of human rights violations and abuses in Rakhine state, including by the Myanmar security forces, in particular against persons belonging to the Rohingya community, including those involving the systematic use of force and intimidation, killing of men, women, and children, sexual violence, and including the destruction and burning of homes and property.

According to the Statement, the Security Council stressed 'the primary responsibility of the Government of Myanmar to protect its population including through respect for the rule of law and the respect, promotion and protection of human rights', and called upon that Government

> to ensure no further excessive use of military force in Rakhine state, to restore civilian administration and apply the rule of law, and to take immediate steps in accordance with [its] obligations and commitments to respect

37 S/PRST/2017/22 (6 Nov 2017).

> human rights, including the human rights of women, children, and persons belonging to vulnerable groups, without discrimination and regardless of ethnicity, religion, or citizenship status

as well as called on the Government to implement measures in line with Security Council Resolution 2106 (2013)[38] to prevent and respond to incidents of sexual violence, and encouraged the Government to work with the UN Secretary-General's Special Representative on Sexual Violence in Conflict. It expressed grave concern over accounts of inter-communal violence and called upon the Myanmar Government to take all necessary measures to counter incitement to violence or hatred and restore peace and inter-communal harmony through dialogue, a comprehensive reconciliation process and by respecting the rule of law. It likewise expressed alarm at the significantly and rapidly deteriorating humanitarian situation in Rakhine state and grave concern at the increasing number of refugees and internally displaced persons, which has a destabilizing impact in the region. The Council continued expressing its deep concern about the severely limited humanitarian access, with humanitarian needs exceeding the current levels of provision. It asked the Myanmar Government to grant immediate, safe and unhindered access to UN agencies and their partners, as well as other domestic and international NGOs, to provide humanitarian assistance in Rakhine state, as well as to ensure the safety and security of humanitarian personnel. It praised Bangladesh and other countries and organizations providing humanitarian assistance to the Rohingya fleeing from Myanmar. It then called upon the Myanmar Government

> to address the root causes of the crisis in Rakhine state by respecting, promoting and protecting human rights, without discrimination and regardless of ethnicity or religion, including by allowing freedom of movement, equal access to basic services, and equal access to full citizenship for all individuals.

It stressed 'the importance of undertaking transparent investigations into allegations of human rights abuses and violations, including sexual violence and abuse and violence against children, and of holding to account all those responsible for such acts to provide justice for victims'. The Government was called upon 'to urgently grant domestic and international media organizations full and unhindered access to Rakhine state and throughout the country and to ensure the safety and security of media personnel'. The Statement ended by affirming the Security Council would remain determined to continue to closely follow the situation in Myanmar, and requested the UN Secretary-General to brief the

38 S/RES/2106 (2013) (24 June 2013).

Security Council on developments on the situation in Rakhine after 30 days from the adoption of this Statement.

On 12 December 2017, the Security Council was briefed by the Under-Secretary-General for Political Affairs and the Secretary-General's Special Representative on Sexual Violence in Conflict on developments in Myanmar. Representatives of relevant UN agencies as well as the representatives from Bangladesh and Myanmar also participated in the meeting. According to the Under-Secretary-General, although the violence had subsided, the flow of refugees to Bangladesh was continuing and Myanmar leaders needed to adopt measures to defuse tensions and create an environment for safe and dignified repatriation of refugees and internally displaced persons. The Special Representative reported on her visit to Rohingya refugee camps and informed the Council of the stories she had heard of sexual atrocities against girls and women in Rakhine state, which indicated a pattern of grave violations of international humanitarian and human rights law.

On 13 February 2018, the Security Council was briefed by the UN High Commissioner for Refugees via video teleconference and by the Assistant UN Secretary-General for Political Affairs. The meeting was held at the request of eight members of the Council: Equatorial Guinea, France, Kazakhstan, Netherlands, Poland, Sweden, UK and USA. Several Council members emphasized the need for humanitarian access and the safe return of refugees. In addition, there were calls for the implementation of the Annan Commission's recommendations.

On 14 May 2018, the Security Council was briefed by the Ambassadors of Kuwait, Peru and the UK, the three co-leaders on the Council's visiting mission to Bangladesh and Myanmar from 28 April to 1 May 2018. Following the briefing, Council members met in consultations, during which the UN High Commissioner for Refugees briefed them by video teleconference.

On 28 August 2018, the Security Council was briefed by the UN Secretary-General António Guterres, UNHCR Goodwill Ambassador Cate Blanchett and UN Development Programme Associate Administrator Tegegnework Gettu on the situation in Myanmar and the Rohingya refugee crisis. The Council discussed developments one year after 'the violent reaction by Myanmar military forces' to the 25 August 2017 attacks by ARSA on security posts had led to an exodus of refugees from Myanmar to Bangladesh. The UN Secretary-General asked the Council to urge Myanmar's leaders to ensure immediate, unimpeded and effective access for UN agencies and partners and to release journalists arrested for reporting on the human tragedy. He also called for accountability as an essential prerequisite for regional security and stability, and for the Security Council to give serious consideration to the report released on 27 August 2018 by the IIFFMM.[39] The Chairperson of the IIFFMM himself briefed the Security Council on 24 October 2018

39 A/HRC/39/64 (27 Aug 2018).

In December 2018, the UK circulated a draft resolution aiming at establishing a timeframe for Myanmar to allow the repatriation of more than 700,000 Rohingya Muslim refugees from Bangladesh as well addressing accountability of those involved in the plight of the Rohingya. However, China and Russia reportedly boycotted discussions on the British-drafted resolution.

The Security Council was briefed on 28 February 2019 by the UN Secretary-General's Special Envoy for Myanmar Christine Schraner Burgener, who had visited Myanmar at the end of January 2019. On 2 July 2019, the Special Envoy once again briefed Council members, under the agenda item 'any other business', about UN activities in Myanmar, likely tensions in the run-up to the general election in Myanmar in 2020, the Rohingya situation, and the continuing clashes between the Arakan Army and the Myanmar government forces. On 21 August 2019, at the joint request of Belgium, France, Germany, UK and the United States following the Myanmar Government's announcement that it had cleared 3,450 people for repatriation on 22 August 2019 from a list of 22,000 provided by Bangladesh, Security Council members discussed the return of Rohingya refugees to Myanmar under the agenda item 'any other business'. Members were briefed by the UN High Commissioner for Refugees and the Assistant UN Secretary-General and UNDP Director of the Bureau of Policy and Programme Support. On 23 August 2019, there was an informal meeting organized by Germany, Peru and Kuwait on 'Mass Atrocity Crimes in Myanmar: Where do we stand on accountability?'

The Special Representative of the Secretary-General on Sexual Violence in Conflict briefed Security Council members under the agenda item 'any other business' on 20 March 2019 about her visit to Yangon and Nay Pyi Taw, Myanmar's capital city, from 5 to 8 February 2019, including the outcome of her meetings with Myanmar government officials and the follow-up to the joint communiqué signed on 7 December 2018 between the UN and the Myanmar Government to prevent and respond to conflict-related sexual violence.[40]

It should be noted that Security Council's official meetings on the Rohingya situation were usually held under the agenda item 'any other business', meaning that certain Council members would prefer not to give it a prominent status as a discrete agenda item on the Council's agenda. On the whole, due to geopolitical divides among Council members, the Council has not made any substantive progress in addressing the Rohingya issue except for the issuance of its Presidential Statement on 6 November 2017. Security Council Presidential statements are routinely resorted to when a permanent member has threatened to veto a draft Security Council resolution. Paragraph 105 of the IIFFMM's aforesaid report

40 www.un.org/sexualviolenceinconflict/wp-content/uploads/joint-communique/joint-communique-of-myanmar-un-on-prevention-response-to-crsv/Joint_Communique_of_Myanmar_UN_Prevention_Response_to_CRSV_2018.pdf.

in 2018 has called upon the UN Security Council to 'ensure accountability for crimes under international law committed in Myanmar, preferably by referring the situation to the International Criminal Court or, alternatively, by creating an *ad hoc* international criminal tribunal' as well as 'adopt targeted individual sanctions, including travel bans and asset freezes, against those who appear most responsible for serious crimes under international law' and to also impose an arms embargo on Myanmar.[41] However, the Council has not taken up that recommendation as of this writing.

China, with its veto power in the UN Security Council, is Myanmar's immediate neighbour to the north, and China does have strong geopolitical and economic interests in Myanmar. As a matter of principle, China and Russia, another veto-wielding permanent member of the Security Council, consistently oppose resolutions in multilateral forums that condemn specific countries on human rights grounds since they consider such country-specific human rights resolutions to be inherently 'politicized', bearing in mind also that these two permanent members have been accused of several human rights violations in their respective territories. The rare occasions when the UN Security Council has been able to adopt enforcement measures under Chapter VII of the UN Charter were when the targeted countries had become failed States and China and/or Russia did not have vested interest in these countries – as in, for example, by allowing the Security Council to set up the International Criminal Tribunal for the former Yugoslavia ('ICTY') to punish perpetrators of atrocities committed since 1 January 1991 during the disintegration of the former Yugoslavia[42] and the International Criminal Tribunal for Rwanda ('ICTR') to punish perpetrators of genocide, crimes against humanity and war crimes committed in 1994 in Rwanda, and, in the case of war crimes, by Rwandan citizens in Rwanda's neighbouring States.[43]

As of this writing, China has facilitated and hosted three foreign minister meetings between China, Myanmar and Bangladesh to work for an early repatriation of the Rohingya from Bangladesh. China has also helped arrange facilities as well as offered incentives for the repatriation.

On 17 and 18 January 2020, just over a month after the oral hearings in the ICJ, Chinese President Xi Jinping paid a State visit to Myanmar, being the first visit to Myanmar by China's President since 2001. As of the end of 2020, China was Myanmar's second-biggest investor behind Singapore with US$21.5 billion in approved foreign capital, or a quarter of foreign direct investment in Myanmar. The Chinese telecommunications giant Huawei has been building Myanmar's 5G telecommunications networks. China also accounts for approximately

41 Reiterated in para 1700 of the full report by the IIFFMM issued on 17 Sept 2018 (A/HRC/39/CRP.2).
42 S/RES/827 (25 May 1993).
43 S/RES/955 (8 Nov 1994).

one-third of all Myanmar's trade, making it Myanmar's most important trading partner, with their bilateral trade accounting for approximately US$11 billion in 2018. China is interested in pursuing with Myanmar its Belt and Road Initiative,[44] China-Myanmar Economic Corridor, including the Kyaukphyu Special Economic Zone to serve as China's strategic route to the Indian Ocean, and Chinese investment projects such as the 6,000 megawatt Myitsone Dam project. Myanmar is strategically situated to give China's landlocked western provinces potential port access to the Indian Ocean and the Bay of Bengal and onto the Middle East and Africa. This access will also help China bypass the need to navigate through the Straits of Malacca and Singapore. China is also reported to have set up a maritime reconnaissance and electronic intelligence station on Myanmar's Great Coco Island in the Bay of Bengal, approximately 300 kilometres south of Myanmar's mainland, and another one on Little Coco Island in the Alexandra Channel between the Indian Ocean and the Andaman Islands. During President Xi's visit, China and Myanmar signed 33 agreements to expedite infrastructure projects in Myanmar that are part of China's Belt and Road Initiative, including the development of the China-Myanmar Economic Corridor, worth billions of US dollars, with agreements on railways linking southwestern China to the Indian Ocean; a US$1.3 billion deep sea-port in Kyaukpyu in Rakhine state; a special economic zone on the border between the two countries; and a letter of intent for new urban development in Yangon, Myanmar's biggest city. However, the two sides did not publicly mention the controversial US$3.6-billion Myitsone dam project desired by China, the work on which has been suspended since 2011 by the then Myanmar President Thien Sein, who informed Myanmar's Parliament that other hydropower projects which posed no threat to Myanmar would be implemented through thorough survey for availability of electricity needed for the nation. The Myitsone dam project is controversial owing to its threat to the environment. In particular, the dam would submerge local people, historical temples, churches, and cultural heritage sites important to Kachin identity and history and the natural heritage of the Kachin people located in the area. ASSK was reported by a State-run Chinese media to have said to the visiting Chinese President that some countries intended to interfere in internal affairs of other countries with such excuses as human rights, ethnicities and religions, but Myanmar would never accept such interference and hoped China would continue to maintain justice for small countries, including Myanmar.

Interestingly, in November 2019 and mid-2020 the Commander-in-Chief of Myanmar's Armed Forces and Myanmar military spokesperson stated that a 'foreign country' was behind the Arakan Army ('AA') active in the Rakhine

44 A global infrastructure development strategy adopted by the Chinese Government in October 2013 to connect China with more than 70 countries across Asia, Europe and Africa via a 'New Silk Road' of railways, highways and ports.

state in western Myanmar bordering China, citing China-made weapons used by the AA to attack the Myanmar military in 2019 that prompted suspicions about China's role as part of an effort to keep Myanmar unstable with the AA as a bargaining chip for smooth implementation of China's Belt and Road Initiative projects. China has denied it supplies weapons to armed rebel groups in Myanmar, and Chinese President Xi pointed out to the Myanmar Command-in-Chief when they met in January 2020 that there were other ways for the rebels to acquire Chinese weapons. Yet, suspicions of Chinese involvement seem to linger in Myanmar which shares a 2,227-kilometre-long land border with China and there have been only two joint inspections – in 1984–1986 and 1992–1995 – of the demarcated land boundary although the 1961 boundary protocol between the two countries requires these joint inspections to be conducted every five years. A dispute over the border between Myanmar's northern Shan state and China has simmered on and off since 2008.

Russia, another veto-wielding permanent member of the UN Security Council, is also unlikely to support any UN Security Council's sanction against Myanmar. In June 2020, Myanmar's Senior General Min Aung Hlaing paid a one-week visit to Russia as official guest of the Russian Government despite his being named by the IIFFMM as one of those who are to be 'investigated and prosecuted in an international criminal tribunal for genocide'. Besides, Russia has long been Myanmar's main partner in military cooperation, and Myanmar is one of the biggest customers of Russian-manufactured weaponry.[45]

Indeed, after the establishment of the ICTY in 1993 and the ICTR in 1994 there are only two occasions when the UN Security Council has succeeded in taking action against serious human rights violations amounting to international crimes. The first is the Security Council's exercise of its mandate under Chapter VII of the UN Charter to adopt Resolution 1593 of 2005[46] to refer the situation in Darfur, Sudan, to the ICC. The Resolution was adopted with 11 votes in favour and four abstentions (Algeria, Brazil, China and the United States). Explaining its position regarding the Resolution, China, one of the four abstaining States, would have preferred the perpetrators to stand trial in Sudanese courts and China did not favour the referral to the ICC without the consent of the Sudanese Government. Besides, China, a non-State Party to the 1998 Rome Statute of the International Criminal Court,[47] had major reservations regarding some of the provisions under that Statute. The United States abstained because, as a non-State Party to the Rome Statute, it opposed the ICC's exercise of jurisdiction over nationals of non-States Parties. For Algeria, the African Union was the best organization to bring peace and justice to Sudan.

45 See, e.g., Pieter D Wezeman *et al.*, 'Trend in International Arms Transfer, 2019', Stockholm International Peace Research Institute (SIPRI) *Fact Sheet* (Mar 2020) 6.

46 S/RES/1595 (31 Mar 2005).

47 2187 UNTS 3, in force 1 July 2002.

Brazil abstained because it was against the operative paragraph inserted at the United States' instigation to exempt from the ICC's jurisdiction UN peacekeeping force members who are nationals of countries that are not parties to the Rome Statute. The other Security Council Members, including the UK and France, cited accountability and the lack of impunity of those responsible for the atrocities in Darfur as their respective reasons for supporting the Resolution.

The only other UN Security Council resolution referring a situation in a nation State to the ICC is Resolution 1970 (2011),[48] unanimously adopted by the Security Council on 26 February 2011 to refer the situation in Libya since 15 February 2011 to the ICC Prosecutor. Libya was by then a failed State. The United States, which had abstained from voting to adopt Security Council Resolution 1593 of 2005, made no mention of the fact that Libya, like the United States, was not party to the Rome Statute. China, another Security Council member which had abstained from voting to adopt Resolution 1533, said the special circumstances in Libya made it necessary to urgently cease the violence, to end the bloodshed and civilian casualties, to resolve the crisis through peaceful means, such as dialogue, as well as to assure the safety and interest of the foreign nationals in Libya.

The ongoing efforts to reform the UN Security Council include proposals to prevent any of its five permanent members from using veto power in the face of the threats or occurrence of gross atrocities of international concern such as genocide. The Accountability, Coherence and Transparency ('ACT') Group, comprising 27 UN Member States working to improve the working methods of the UN Security Council, proposed, in July 2015, a one-page 'Code of Conduct regarding UN Security Council action against genocide, crimes against humanity and war crimes'.[49] The Code is not only for the permanent members of the Council, but also for its non-permanent members as well as for any UN Member State that may, at some point in time, become UN Security Council members. The Code comprises a general and positive pledge to support the Security Council's action to prevent or end the crimes covered by the Code that the UN Secretary-General has brought to the Security Council's attention. This general and positive pledge is complemented by a more specific pledge to be made by all the 15 members of the UN Security Council not to vote against any credible draft resolution aiming at preventing or halting these crimes. Also in 2015, France and Mexico presented a one-page 'Political Statement on the suppression of the veto in case of mass atrocities',[50] open to signature by UN Member States to propose a collective and voluntary agreement among the UN Security Council permanent members to refrain from using the veto in case of mass

48 S/RES/1970 (26 Feb 2011).
49 A/70/621–S/2015/978 (14 Dec 2015) Annex I.
50 https://s156658.gridserver.com/media/files/2015-07-31-veto-political-declaration-final-eng.pdf.

atrocities, with the veto being considered not as a privilege but 'an international responsibility'. Of the five permanent members, the UK supports the Code of Conduct, while France supports both the Code of Conduct and the Political Statement.[51] Silence by the other three permanent members – China, Russia and the United States – does not bode well for the future realization of either the Code or the Political Statement.[52]

Human Rights Council and UN General Assembly

When the UN Security Council does not effectively perform the role expected of it in protecting human rights, the UN General Assembly often steps in. Human rights matters come before the Human Rights Council ('HRC')[53] and the UN General Assembly's Third Committee (Social, Humanitarian and Cultural Affairs), which is open to all UN Member States. The Third Committee scrutinizes human rights issues within the UN system, including reports from the HRC, before draft resolutions on human rights are submitted to the UN General Assembly for further action.

The HRC was set up on 15 March 2006 as a subsidiary organ of the UN General Assembly to promote universal respect for the protection of all human rights and fundamental freedoms for all individuals, without distinction of any kind and in a fair and equal manner. It addresses situations of violations of human rights, including gross and systematic violations, and makes recommendations thereon as well as promotes the effective coordination and the mainstreaming of human rights within the UN system. The HRC works under the principles of universality, impartiality, objectivity and non-selectivity, constructive international dialogue and cooperation. The HRC consists of 47 UN Member States, elected directly and individually by secret ballot by the majority of the Members of the UN General Assembly based on equitable geographical distribution for a period of three years. A HRC Member is not eligible for immediate re-election after serving two consecutive terms.

The mandate of the Special Rapporteur on the situation of human rights in Myanmar was first established in 1992 by Resolution 58 of the HRC's predecessor, the Commission on Human Rights,[54] and has been extended annually. The HRC's Resolution 25/26[55] adopted on 15 April 2014 broadened the mandate to

51 Source: International Coalition for the Responsibility to Protect. According to the Global Centre for the Responsibility to Protect, as of 1 January 2019 the Code had been signed by 117 UN Member States and two observers.

52 See also PM Butchard, *The Responsibility to Protect and the Failures of the United Nations Security Council* (Hart 2020).

53 Cf. Universal Rights Group, *Building a coherent Human Rights Council-Security Council relationship: The prevention of human rights crises, violent conflict and atrocity crimes* (Mar 2021) 8–17, 40–4.

54 E/CN.4/RES/1992/58 (3 Mar 1992) adopted without a vote.

55 A/HRC/RES/25/26 (15 Apr 2014) adopted without a vote.

include reporting on the progress in the electoral process and reform in the run-up to the 2015 election in Myanmar. The HRC's Resolution 31/24[56] adopted on 24 March 2016 further broadened the mandate to include identifying benchmarks for progress and priority areas for technical assistance and capacity-building. The Special Rapporteur is instrumental in bringing the Rohingya issue before the HRC with her regular reports. For example, in 2018, the Special Rapporteur presented her concept for an accountability mechanism for Myanmar, including a proposal for victim support and the referral of the situation in Myanmar to the International Criminal Court by the UN Security Council, or a State Party or group of States Parties to the Rome Statute of the ICC. In her oral statement to the HRC on 11 March 2019 she expressed her deep concern at the Myanmar Government's serious downplaying of the ongoing humanitarian crisis and suppression of human rights in Rakhine where the conflict between the Arakan Army and the Tatmadaw was continuing, forcing up to 10,000 civilians to flee their homes as a result of the violence, and there was little humanitarian assistance as a result of the Government's imposed restrictions. She had received a report from Buthidaung in Rakhine that 24 Rohingya houses in Kun Taing Nar Yar Gone village were burned down on 2 March 2019, and on 4 March 2019, 100 houses were burned down in Nga Yan Chaung village. This occurred in circumstances in which the Government of Bangladesh had said that it would not receive any new Rohingya refugees after up to 16,000 of them had crossed over to Bangladesh in 2018. On 23 October 2019, the Special Rapporteur appeared before the UN General Assembly to call for targeted sanctions against Myanmar military-run companies and commanders responsible for serious human rights violations against the Rohingya as well as for the international community to work with civil society to develop transformative processes in accordance with the pillars of justice, truth, reparations and guarantees of non-recurrence.

In March 2017, the HRC set up the IIFFMM, which finished its task in September 2019 after submitting its final report to the HRC.

On 27 September 2018, the HRC adopted Resolution 39/2 on the situation of human rights of Rohingya Muslims and other minorities in Myanmar[57] by the vote of thirty-five in favour, three against, seven abstentions, with two either not voting or being absent. The resolution was an outcome of joint efforts by all Member States of the European Union and those of the OIC. The Resolution expresses grave concern at the IIFFMM's findings that there is sufficient information to warrant the investigation and prosecution of senior officials in Myanmar's military chain of command so that a competent court may determine their liability for genocide in relation to the situation regarding the Rohingya Muslims in Rakhine state. The IIFFMM also finds crimes against humanity and war crimes have been committed in Kachin, Rakhine and Shan states. The resolu-

56 A/HRC/RES/31/24 (20 Apr 2016).
57 A/HRC/RES/39/2 (3 Oct 2018).

tion, therefore, strongly condemns all the violations and abuses of human rights in Myanmar as reported by the IIFFMM. It takes an unprecedented step for the HRC by setting up the Independent Investigative Mechanism for Myanmar ('IIMM') as an ongoing independent mechanism to collect, consolidate, preserve and analyse evidence of the most serious crimes and violations of international law committed in Myanmar since 2011, in order to facilitate and expedite fair and independent criminal proceedings, in accordance with international law standards, in national, regional or international courts or tribunals that have or may in the future have jurisdiction over these crimes, in accordance with international law. It also requests the IIMM to cooperate closely with any of the ICC Prosecutor's future investigations pertaining to human rights violations in Myanmar. In December 2018, the UN General Assembly's Administrative and Budgetary Committee approved without a vote approximately US$28 million for the IIMM to perform its task. In December 2019, the UN General Assembly decided, for the first time, that in 2020 the budgets for the Myanmar investigations would be transferred to the UN regular budget to be financed by annual budget contributions from the 193 UN Member States. The IIFFMM handed over its evidence of serious crimes under international law to the IIMM at the time when the former finished its mandate.

China, Philippines and Burundi voted against the HRC's Resolution 39/2. For China, the Rakhine state issue was a complex one, involving history and ethnicity and could not be solved overnight, and the immediate priority was to address repatriation and practical measures that had to be taken. In China's view, the HRC had to play a constructive role, but the Resolution would only deteriorate the situation and would not address the issue comprehensively. The Philippines 'did not see the value in implementing resolutions that polarized'. In its opinion, the IIFFMM's report recognized the social and political situation as well as the presence of terrorist groups within Myanmar, and there was a will of the Myanmar leadership to cooperate in good-will towards an end to the human rights violations, which needed to be supported by the HRC. Burundi, which did not explain why it voted against the Resolution, has ceased to be a State Party to the Rome Statute since 27 October 2017, in response to a preliminary investigation launched in April 2016 by the ICC Prosecutor into possible crimes against humanity in Burundi.

Of the abstaining HRC members – Angola, Ethiopia, Japan, Kenya, Mongolia, Nepal and South Africa – only Japan explained why it abstained, emphasizing it was vital for Myanmar itself to undertake a transparent and credible investigation into the situation in Rakhine although Japan would continue to participate in discussions with the international community to improve the human rights situation in Myanmar.

Japan is Myanmar's sixth-largest foreign direct investor, third-largest importer of Myanmar products and seventh-largest exporter to Myanmar. Japanese businesses continue to expand their businesses in Myanmar. For example, in December 2020 Mitsubishi Corp. signed two contracts worth US$663 million to deliver railroad cars to Myanmar Railways, owned by the Myanmar Government. Japan has been providing more than US$7 billion in foreign aid to Myanmar since 2016. Japan considers the Rohingya crisis a complicated and serious issue that Japan will work bilaterally with Myanmar and support the Myanmar Government's efforts to resolve it. In order to stay 'neutral', the Japanese Government refers to the Rohingya as 'the Muslims in Rakhine', 'Rohingya (Bangladeshi Muslims)' or simply 'Muslims'. Japan has been providing humanitarian aid to Rakhine state, giving US$3 million to Myanmar in January 2018 to assist displaced Rohingya Muslims returning from Bangladesh. The Independent Commission of Enquiry on Rakhine, or ICOE, set up by the Myanmar Government to investigate alleged human rights violations concerning the Rohingya, has two foreign members, one of whom is a former Japanese career diplomat who subsequently served as UN Under-Secretary-General for Humanitarian Affairs and Emergency Relief Coordination. Japan has also been urging Bangladesh, another State receiving huge foreign aid from Japan, to cooperate with Myanmar in repatriating the Rohingya living in overcrowded camps in Bangladesh since August 2017. In October 2019, Commander-in-Chief of the Myanmar Armed Forces Senior General Min Aung Hlaing was invited by Japan's Ministry of Defence to officially visit Japan, where he also called upon the Prime Minister of Japan who, in turn, expressed his appreciation to the Senior General for his tolerance in dealing with the Rakhine situation. On 26 December 2019, Japan's Ambassador to Myanmar informed the media he did not think the Tatmadaw had committed genocide or had the intent of genocide, or the intention to kill all the Muslim residents in Rakhine. In his view, the actions by the Tatmadaw came in response to a series of attacks by ARSA on police outposts in 2016 and 2017, although Japan would not rule out the possibility that human rights violations occurred in Rakhine state during clashes between the military and ARSA and urged the Myanmar Government and military to take action against those responsible. His statement to the media followed a visit to Myanmar by Natsuo Yamaguchi, a member of Japan's Upper House from the Komeito Party, a member of Japan's coalition government, to explain the Japanese Government's stance on the genocide allegation against Myanmar. During his stay in Myanmar from 21 to 25 December 2019, Yamaguchi met ASSK and Senior General Min Aung Hlaing. He promised Japan would continue to help Myanmar solve the problems in Rakhine state, but urged the Myanmar military to take serious action against those who committed crimes in Rakhine in accordance with the ICOE's final report scheduled for 20 January 2020.

Those absent or not voting were Cuba and Venezuela. On the same day as the adoption of the HRC's Resolution 39/2, the ICC Prosecutor received a referral from a group of States Parties to the Rome Statute – Argentina, Chile, Colombia, Paraguay, Peru and Canada – requesting her to initiate an investigation into crimes against humanity allegedly committed in Venezuela since 12 February 2014, with the view to determining whether one or more persons should be charged with the commission of such crimes. The ICC Prosecutor herself has already initiated a preliminary examination of the situation in Venezuela concerning crimes allegedly committed in Venezuela since at least April 2017, in the context of mass demonstrations and related political unrest. As for Cuba, it usually opposes human rights resolutions in international organizations, placing blame on specific countries, since Cuba itself has been frequently targeted by such resolutions introduced by Cuba's unfriendly countries.

On 22 December 2018, the UN General Assembly adopted Resolution 73/264[58] by the vote of 136 in favour (including Bangladesh, Brunei, Indonesia and Malaysia), 8 against (Belarus, Cambodia, China, Lao PDR, Myanmar, Philippines, Russia and Vietnam), 22 abstentions (including Japan, India, Singapore, Thailand and Venezuela) and 27 non-voting (including, surprisingly, The Gambia). The Resolution, among other things, strongly condemns all violations and abuses of human rights in Myanmar, as set out in the IIFFMM's 2018 report, including the widespread, systematic and gross human rights violations and abuses committed in Rakhine state, including the presence of elements of extermination and deportation and the systematic oppression and discrimination that the IIFFMM has concluded may amount to persecution and to the crime of apartheid. The Resolution calls upon the Myanmar authorities to ensure that those responsible for violations of international law, including human rights violations and abuses, are held accountable and removed from positions of power. The three Muslim-majority Member States of ASEAN voted in favour of the Resolution, whereas five other ASEAN Member States voted against it and the other two ASEAN Member States abstained from voting.

Almost a year later, on 14 Nov 2019, the Third Committee of the UN General Assembly approved the draft resolution on the human rights situation in Myanmar, introduced by Saudi Arabia, by a recorded vote of 140 in favour to 9 against (Belarus, Cambodia, China, Lao PDR, Myanmar, Philippines, Russia, Vietnam and Zimbabwe), with 32 abstentions. The draft resolution expressed grave concern at continuing reports of serious human rights violations – as well as violations of international humanitarian law – in Myanmar, against Rohingya Muslims and other minorities, including those involving arbitrary arrests, deaths in detention, torture and other cruel, inhuman or degrading treatment or punishment. It called upon Myanmar, in particular its security and armed forces, to immediately end all violence and ensure the protection of the human rights of all persons in Myanmar, including Rohingya Muslims and persons belonging to other minorities. Myanmar's delegate criticized the draft resolution for having 'grossly mischaracterized' the situation in Rakhine state because the issue was not one of religious persecution, but rather a complex political and economic situation involving a variety of factors, including poverty and cross-border migration. Certain delegations deplored that the draft resolution did not go far enough. For example, in Liechtenstein's opinion the draft resolution failed to allude to the

58 A/RES/73/264 (22 Dec 2018).

UN Security Council's authority given under Article 13(b) of the 1998 Rome Statute of the International Criminal Court to refer the situation in Myanmar to the International Criminal Court.[59]

Some of those voting against the draft resolution in the Third Committee explained their respective positions. Russia said the dramatic situation of Rohingya and other minorities in Myanmar required attention in order to provide real assistance to tackle the causes of this issue, and Russia lauded the serious commitment by Myanmar in this area. Russia advocated a non-confrontational approach, welcoming steps by Myanmar to work with the UN Development Programme and the UN Secretary-General, as well as welcomed ASEAN's efforts to help normalize the humanitarian situation in Rakhine state, stressing that country-specific resolutions are not effective. For the Philippines, the universal periodic review by the HRC in which all UN Member States take turns having their respective human rights records scrutinized at regular intervals would be the appropriate mechanism to assess the human rights situations of States. The Philippines supported Myanmar's ICOE and was confident of its ability to bring accountability. The Philippines also supported the continued dialogue between Bangladesh and Myanmar for the return of displaced persons to Myanmar. China, for its part, considered divergences should be addressed through dialogue and cooperation and China opposed the politicization of human rights issues, including through country-specific human rights resolutions. Lao DPR said it understood the complex situation in Myanmar, as it closely followed developments in Rakhine state. Lao DPR stressed the importance of engaging with Myanmar, noting that country-specific resolutions would not help human rights in any country. For Zimbabwe, it expressed concern over country-specific reports or resolutions, calling for constructive dialogue as a more productive approach to tackle human rights issues. Vietnam regretted the draft did not fully reflect its views and took issue with an unconstructive approach that only exacerbated the challenges Myanmar was trying to overcome in its democratic transition. In Vietnam's opinion, the most important factor in addressing the situation was mutual trust, which could only be achieved through dialogue, whereas country-specific resolutions only undermined such efforts.

On 27 December 2019, the UN General Assembly adopted Resolution 74/246 on the Situation of human rights of Rohingya Muslims and other minorities in Myanmar,[60] forwarded to it by the Third Committee, by the vote of 134 in favour to 9 against (Belarus, Cambodia, China, Lao PDR, Myanmar, Philippines, Russia, Vietnam and Zimbabwe) and 28 abstentions. The Resolution, among other things, expresses alarm at the continuing influx of Rohingya to Bangladesh over the past four decades – then numbering 1.1 million, including 744,000 who had arrived since August 2017 – 'in the aftermath

59 This possibility will be analysed in Chapter 5.
60 A/RES/74/246 (27 Dec 2019).

of atrocities committed by the security and armed forces of Myanmar'. It alludes to the findings of the IIFFMM 'of gross human rights violations and abuses suffered by Rohingya Muslims and other minorities' by Myanmar's security forces, which the IIFFMM describes as 'the gravest crimes under international law'. It strongly condemns all violations and abuses of human rights in Myanmar, and calls upon Myanmar, in particular its security and armed forces, to end immediately all violence and all violations of international law in Myanmar, to ensure the protection of the human rights of all persons in Myanmar, including of Rohingya Muslims and persons belonging to other minorities, and to take all measures necessary to provide justice to victims, to ensure full accountability and to end impunity for all violations and abuses of human rights law and violations of international humanitarian law, starting with a full, transparent and independent investigation into reports of all these violations. The Resolution emphasizes the importance of 'holding accountable all those responsible for brutal acts and crimes against all persons, including the Rohingya Muslims, in order to deliver justice to victims using all legal instruments and domestic, regional and international judicial mechanisms'. The Resolution also urges the Myanmar Government to expedite efforts to eliminate statelessness and the systematic and institutionalized discrimination' against the Rohingya and other minorities, to dismantle camps for Rohingyas and others displaced in Rakhine, and to create the conditions necessary for the safe, voluntary, dignified and sustainable return of all refugees, including Rohingya Muslim refugees. It notes that the Rohingya twice refused to return to Myanmar from Bangladesh because of the absence of these conditions. Moreover, the Resolution urges the IIMM to expedite its work and requests the UN Secretary-General to extend the appointment of his Special Envoy on Myanmar. In response, Myanmar's Permanent Representative to the UN, New York, condemned the Resolution as 'another classic example of double-standards [and] selective and discriminatory application of human rights norms' designed 'to exert unwanted political pressure on Myanmar'. In his view, the Resolution did not attempt to find a solution to the complex situation in Rakhine state and refused to recognize government efforts to address the challenges, including by preparing to put suitable conditions in place for the safe and voluntary return of verified displaced people from Bangladesh. The Resolution, in his view, would sow seeds of distrust and create further polarization of different communities in the region.

Although UN General Assembly resolutions are not legally binding by themselves, they reflect the view or position of the international community of States, which often have international political impact and have sometimes led to formulation of legally binding norms of international law, as in the case of the UN General Assembly's Resolution 217 of 10 December 1948 on the Universal Declaration of Human Rights[61] that has given rise to the conclu-

61 A/RES/217(III) (10 Dec 1948).

sion of the 1966 International Covenant on Civil and Political Rights and the 1966 International Covenant on Economic, Social and Cultural Rights. The Universal Declaration of Human Rights itself has been referred to as the yardstick and main source of inspiration for several regional human rights instruments. As another example, the UN General Assembly's Resolution 1761 of 6 November 1962[62] formally condemning South Africa's apartheid regime and imploring UN Member States to halt all diplomatic, military and economic relations with South Africa has eventually resulted in the end of apartheid in South Africa.

On the whole, up to November 2019 both bilateral and multilateral diplomatic forums had failed to meaningfully alleviate the Rohingya's sufferings. To the accusers, there was no realistic prospect for justice in Myanmar, especially when the country would hold the national general election in 2020, and nationalistic rhetoric was used by politicians in Myanmar, like anywhere else, to garner support from their electorate. China and Russia, two of the veto-wielding permanent members of the Security Council, consistently opposed every Rohingya-related resolution within the UN system that specifically blamed the Myanmar Government and/or its officials. Reform of existing regional and global organizations so that they can better protect human rights and punish perpetrators of serious human rights violations is not feasible in the near future, if ever.

Resorting to the International Court of Justice, the International Criminal Court and certain sympathetic domestic criminal courts has thus become the only viable option left to those accusing Myanmar and its government officers of grave violations of the Rohingya's human rights that are also tantamount to crimes punishable under international law and domestic criminal law. Parts II, III and IV of this book will analyse daunting challenges faced by the accusers in their efforts to protect and seek redress for the Rohingya.

Part II (The International Court of Justice: State responsibility) comprises two chapters. Chapter 3 (The Gambia's case before the ICJ) introduces readers to the ICJ including its jurisdiction and applicable law, the meaning of State responsibility as opposed to individual criminal responsibility, The Gambia's Application to the ICJ against Myanmar and the hurdles confronting The Gambia as regards its legal standing to institute the Application against Myanmar and proving the existence of a dispute between them under the Genocide Convention. Chapter 4 (Proving violations of the 1948 Genocide Convention) explains the provisions of the Genocide Convention, the burden and standard of proof in order to find Myanmar responsible for violating this Convention and explores possible outcomes if Myanmar is held by the ICJ to have breached the Convention. The provisional measures indicated by the ICJ on 23 January 2020 and their potential ramifications are also analysed.

Part III (The International Criminal Court: Individual criminal responsibility) also has two chapters. Chapter 5 (Introduction to the International Criminal

62 A/RES/1761 (XVII) (6 Nov 1962).

Court) introduces readers to the ICC, including crimes under the ICC's jurisdiction and essential preconditions to its exercise of jurisdiction. Direct responsibility and command/superior responsibility will be explained. The Chapter will indicate necessary steps to be taken by the ICC *vis-à-vis* Myanmar accused and explores how high-ranking civilians have been prosecuted before international criminal tribunals, including the ICC. Chapter 6 (Practical difficulties faced by the ICC) then narrates how and why the ICC Prosecutor has succeeded in having some, but not other, accused brought to stand trial before the ICC. In this respect, the implication of the existence or non-existence of the personal immunity (immunity *ratione personae*) of incumbent high-ranking government officials will be discussed in length. So will the prospect of the Office of the ICC Prosecutor discharging its mandate in relation to the Situation in Bangladesh/ Myanmar as regards the Rohingya.

In Part IV (Justice in foreign domestic courts), Chapter 7 (Exercise of universal criminal jurisdiction by Argentina and other nation States) explains why and how the law of several States permit the exercise of jurisdiction over offences and persons with no connection with the forum States and the likely consequences for the Myanmar individuals concerned in the context of the Rohingya's quest for justice. This is followed by Chapter 8 (Sanctions and redress under domestic law for victims of serious human rights violations abroad) which studies unilateral sanctions actually imposed by certain States against Myanmar and/or Myanmar nationals and the legality of such sanctions as well as of Myanmar's possible countermeasures against the sanctioning States. The chapter then explores damages and other forms of reparation under the domestic law that may be available to the Rohingya in some foreign States.

In the final Part V (Stock taking), Chapter 9 (Lessons learnt and future possibilities) sums up what is discussed in Chapters 1–8, assesses the likely future scenarios and their legal implications, especially after the 1 February 2021 *coup d'état* in Myanmar.

PART II

The International Court of Justice

State responsibility

3

THE GAMBIA'S CASE BEFORE THE ICJ

Introduction to the ICJ

The International Court of Justice, or ICJ, based in The Hague, Netherlands, is the principal judicial organ of the United Nations.[1] It is composed of 15 judges, no two of whom may be nationals of the same nation State. The judges are elected with an absolute majority of votes in both the UN General Assembly and the UN Security Council, proceeding independently of one another, from among persons of high moral character, who possess the qualifications required in their respective countries for appointment to the highest judicial offices, or are experts of recognized competence in international law. At every election, the electors shall bear in mind not only the persons' requisite personal qualifications, but also the need for the ICJ as a whole to have the representation of the main forms of civilization and of the principal legal systems of the world. ICJ judges are elected for a term of nine years, and may be re-elected. A judge who is elected to replace a judge whose term of office has not expired shall hold office for the remainder of his/her predecessor's term. If the ICJ includes upon its Bench a judge of the nationality of one of the parties to a case pending before the ICJ, the other party may choose a person to sit as judge *ad hoc* in that case. If the ICJ includes upon the Bench no judge of the nationality of the parties, each of these parties may proceed to choose a judge *ad hoc* in that case.[2]

The ICJ has two types of jurisdiction: advisory and contentious.

The ICJ may give advisory opinions on any legal question at the request of the UN General Assembly or the Security Council. The ICJ may also give advisory

1 Art 92 UN Charter (1 UNTS XVI, in force 24 Oct 1945).

2 Chapter I, Statute of the International Court of Justice (1945) 39 AJIL Supp 215, in force 24 Oct 1945.

DOI: 10.4324/9781003224211-3

opinions to other UN organs and specialized agencies, which may at any time be authorized by the UN General Assembly to request advisory opinions of the ICJ on legal questions arising within the scope of their activities.[3]

The ICJ exercised its contentious jurisdiction to settle disputes between nation States. Article 36(1) of the ICJ Statute provides that the ICJ has jurisdiction over all cases which the parties refer to it and all matters specially provided for in the UN Charter or in treaties or conventions in force between the disputing parties. In addition, Article 36(2) of the Statute stipulates that UN Member States may at any time deposit with the UN Secretary-General declarations recognizing as compulsory and without special agreement, in relation to any other State accepting the same obligation, the ICJ's jurisdiction on the interpretation of a treaty; any question of international law; the existence of any fact which, if established, would constitute a breach of an international obligation; or the nature or extent of the reparation to be made for the breach of an international obligation. Article 36(3) of the Statute adds that the acceptance of the ICJ's jurisdiction under Article 36(1) and (2) may be unconditional or on condition of reciprocity on the part of several or certain States, or for a certain time.

The ICJ settles the dispute by applying international agreements (also called 'conventions' or 'treaties'), whether general or particular, establishing rules expressly recognized by the contesting States; international custom, as evidence of a general practice accepted as law binding on States; the general principles of law recognized by civilized nations; and – subject to the fact that the decision of the ICJ has no binding force except between the parties and only in respect of that particular case – judicial decisions and the teachings of the most highly qualified publicists of the various nations, as subsidiary means for the determination of rules of law.[4]

The ICJ, therefore, applies international law which regulates relations between and among nation States. Violation of international law entails international responsibility of the State, and not responsibility of individuals within that State. However, State responsibility arises because of international wrongs resulting from conduct of individuals within the State. The UN International Law Commission ('ILC'), comprising 34 independent international law experts elected by the UN General Assembly for a five-year term to codify and progressively develop international law, has compiled the Articles on the Responsibility of States for Internationally Wrongful Acts,[5] submitted to the UN General Assembly in 2001. Several of the Articles have been relied on extensively by the ICJ to interpret international law in this matter, including in its Judgments in *Case Concerning the Application of the Convention on the Prevention and Punishment of the Crime of Genocide (Bosnia and Herzegovina v Serbia and Montenegro)*,[6] or

3 Art 96 UN Charter.

4 Art 38(1) ICJ Statute.

5 A/RES/56/83 (12 Dec 2001) Annex and A/56/49(Vol. I)/Corr.4.

6 [2007] ICJ Rep 43.

the Bosnian genocide case, in 2007, and *Case Concerning the Application of the Convention on the Prevention and Punishment of the Crime of Genocide (Croatia v Serbia)*,[7] or the Croatian genocide case, in 2015.

Chapter II of the ILC's Articles, entitled 'Attribution of conduct to a State', explains the rules which are relevant to the Rohingya context as follows. Every internationally wrongful act of a State entails that State's international responsibility. The State is treated as a unity, consistent with its recognition as a single legal person in international law. Therefore, the conduct of any State organ is considered an act of that State under international law, whether the organ exercises legislative, executive, judicial or any other functions, whatever position it holds in the organization of the State, and whatever its character as an organ of the central government or of a territorial unit of the State. In this connection, a State organ includes any person or entity which has that status in accordance with the internal law of the State. The conduct of a person or entity which is *not* an organ of the State but which is empowered by the law of that State to exercise elements of the governmental authority is considered an act attributed to the State under international law if the person or entity is acting in that capacity in the particular instance. The conduct of such an organ of a State or a person or entity is considered an act attributed to the State under international law if the organ, person or entity acts in that capacity, even if it exceeds its authority (*ultra vires*) or contravenes instructions.

The ICJ has ruled in the Bosnian genocide case that the conduct of a person or group of persons which are *not* formally recognized as official organs of the State under its internal law is considered an act attributed to that State under international law if the person or group of persons is in a relationship of *complete dependence* on the State. Apart from such a situation, a State's responsibility can be incurred for acts committed by persons or groups of persons – neither State organs nor to be equated with such organs – only if, assuming those acts to be internationally wrongful, they are attributable to it because an organ of the State gave the *instructions in respect of each operation* in which the alleged violations occurred or provided the *direction* pursuant to which the perpetrators of the wrongful act acted or where it exercised *effective control* over the action during which the wrong was committed.[8]

As a general rule, the conduct of an insurrectional movement cannot be attributed to the State. However, the conduct of an insurrectional movement which becomes the new government of a State shall be considered an act of that State under international law. The conduct of a movement, insurrectional or other, which succeeds in establishing a new State in part of the territory of a pre-existing State or in a territory under its administration shall be considered an act of the new State under international law. This is without prejudice to the

7 [2015] ICJ Rep 3.
8 [2007] ICJ Rep 43, 208 [400] and 210 [406].

State responsibility of the pre-existing State in exceptional cases where it was in a position to adopt measures of vigilance, prevention or punishment in respect of the movement's conduct but improperly failed to do so and this has resulted in an injury or damage to another State.[9]

Where a State acknowledges and adopts the conduct as its own, that conduct is considered an act of that State under international law to the extent acknowledged and adopted as such by the State.[10]

Finally, State A is internationally responsible for *aiding or assisting* State B in the commission of an international wrongful act by State B if State A does so with knowledge of the circumstances of the internationally wrongful act and if the act would be internationally wrongful if committed by State A itself. This requires a close connection between the act of aiding or assisting and the eventual wrongful act of State B. The support must have a substantial effect in the sense of making it materially easier to commit the wrongful act which State A is obligated not to commit itself.[11]

General international law also imposes on every State the obligation 'not to allow knowingly its territory to be used for acts contrary to the rights of other States'.[12]

Pursuant to Article 94 of the UN Charter, each UN Member State must comply with the decision of the ICJ in any case to which it is a party; otherwise the other party may ask the UN Security Council to enforce the decision against the non-complying party. However, under Article 27(3) of the UN Charter, each of the five permanent members of the Security Council – China, France, Russia, UK and the United States – has a right of veto against any non-procedural decision by the Security Council.

The Gambia's Application

On 11 November 2019, The Gambia instituted proceedings against Myanmar and asked the ICJ to also indicate provisional measures pending its final Judgment.

According to The Gambia, Myanmar has violated the 1948 Convention on the Prevention and Punishment of the Crime of Genocide,[13] to which both The Gambia and Myanmar are party, through 'acts adopted, taken and condoned by the Government of Myanmar against members of the Rohingya group'. Specifically, argues The Gambia, from around October 2016 the Myanmar military, or Tatmadaw, and other Myanmar security forces began widespread and systematic 'clearance operations' – the term used by Myanmar itself – against the Rohingya group. The genocidal acts committed during these operations were intended to destroy the Rohingya as a group, in whole or in part, by the

9 Art 10, Articles on State Responsibility and the ILC's Commentary thereto.
10 Ibid Art 11.
11 Ibid Art 16 and the ILC's Commentary thereto.
12 *Corfu Channel (UK v Albania)* [1949] ICJ Rep 4, 22.
13 78 UNTS 277, in force 12 Jan 1951.

use of mass murder, rape and other forms of sexual violence,[14] as well as the systematic destruction by fire of their villages, often with inhabitants locked inside burning houses. From August 2017 onward, such genocidal acts continued with Myanmar's resumption of 'clearance operations' on a more massive and wider geographical scale. The Gambia contends that these acts constitute violations of the Genocide Convention. The Gambia has made this claim known to Myanmar since September 2018, but Myanmar has continued to deny any wrongdoing.

The Gambia seeks to found the ICJ's jurisdiction to entertain this dispute on Article 36(1) of the ICJ Statute, stating the ICJ's jurisdiction 'comprises … all matters specially provided for … in treaties and conventions in force', and on Article IX of the Genocide Convention. The latter reads:

> Disputes between the Contracting Parties relating to the interpretation, application or fulfilment of the present Convention, including those relating to the responsibility of a State for genocide or for any of the other acts enumerated in Article III [i.e., conspiracy to commit genocide, direct and public incitement to commit genocide, attempt to commit genocide and complicity in genocide], shall be submitted to the International Court of Justice at the request of any of the parties to the dispute.

Myanmar, then called Burma, ratified the Genocide Convention in March 1956, with two reservations – one as regards Article VI and the other with respect to Article VIII.

Pursuant to Article VI of the Genocide Convention, persons charged with genocide or any of the other acts enumerated in Article III

> shall be tried by a competent tribunal of the State in the territory of which the act was committed, or by such international penal tribunal as may have jurisdiction with respect to those Contracting Parties which shall have accepted its jurisdiction.

Burma's reservation is to the effect that nothing contained in Article VI shall be construed as depriving the courts and tribunals of Burma of jurisdiction or as

14 The present author: in its report entitled 'Sexual and gender-based violence in Myanmar and the gendered impact of its ethnic conflicts ' submitted to the Human Rights Council, the IIFFMM concludes 'on reasonable grounds that the sexual violence perpetrated against Rohingya women and girls in Rakhine state on and after 25 August 2017 was an indicator of the Tatmadaw's genocidal intent to destroy the Rohingya people in whole or in part'. The IIFFMM also concludes the Myanmar Government has failed, and continues to fail, in its obligation to hold perpetrators for sexual violence accountable, so the Myanmar Government bears continuing State responsibility under the Genocide Convention for its failure to investigate and punish acts of genocide (A/HRC/42/CRP.4 (22 Aug 2018) para. 255).

giving foreign courts and tribunals jurisdiction over any cases of genocide or any of the other acts enumerated in Article III committed within Burma's territory.

By virtue of Article VIII of the Genocide Convention,

> [a]ny Contracting Party may call upon the competent organs of the United Nations to take such action under the Charter of the United Nations as they consider appropriate for the prevention and suppression of acts of genocide or any of the other acts enumerated in Article III.

Burma's reservation is to the effect that Article VIII shall not apply to Burma.

Bangladesh, Myanmar's immediate neighbour to the west which bears the biggest burden of sheltering the Rohingya fleeing from Myanmar, is party to the Genocide Convention since January 1999. Bangladesh's reservation as regards the application of Article IX of the Genocide Convention reads: 'For the submission of any dispute in terms of this Article to the jurisdiction of the International Court of Justice, the consent of all parties to the dispute will be required in each case'. Hence, Bangladesh cannot take Myanmar to the ICJ without the latter's prior consent, and this consent will never be given. Bangladesh has not withdrawn this reservation presumably because Bangladesh also wants to shield itself from being unilaterally brought before the ICJ without its prior consent by another State Party.[15]

The Gambia became party to the Genocide Convention in 1979 without any reservation.

In its Application to the ICJ, The Gambia requests the ICJ to adjudge and declare that Myanmar:

- Has breached and continues to breach its obligations under the Genocide Convention, in particular the obligations provided under Articles I,[16] III, IV,[17] V[18] and VI

15 Bangladesh has been accused of maltreatment of the ethnic Bihari Muslim minority in Bangladesh, labelled as 'stranded Pakistanis' and pro-Pakistan collaborators for their role in support of Pakistan during Bangladesh's war of independence from Pakistan in 1971. See, e.g., Rock Ronald Rozario and Stephan Uttom, 'Violence highlights plight of Bangladesh's Bihari Muslims', *Union of Catholic Asian News* (10 Oct 2019), www.ucanews.com/news/violence-highlights-plight-of-bangladeshs-bihari-muslims/86284#. According to Sarmila Bose ('The question of genocide and the quest for justice in the 1971 war' (2011) 13 J Genocide Research 393, 410) the killing by the pro-liberation forces in 1971 of non-Bengali minorities – West Pakistani and Bihari – on the grounds of their ethnicity, as part of a bid to establish what is now Bangladesh, would constitute genocide under the Genocide Convention.

16 The Contracting Parties confirm that genocide, whether committed in time of peace or in time of war, is a crime under international law which they undertake to prevent and to punish.

17 Persons committing genocide or any of the other acts enumerated in Article III shall be punished, whether they are constitutionally responsible rulers, public officials or private individuals.

18 The Contracting Parties undertake to enact, in accordance with their respective Constitutions, the necessary legislation to give effect to the provisions of the Genocide Convention and, in

- Must cease forthwith any such ongoing internationally wrongful act and fully respect its obligations under this Convention, in particular the obligations provided under Articles I, III, IV, V and VI
- Must ensure that persons committing genocide are punished by a competent tribunal, including before an international penal tribunal, as required by Articles I and VI
- Must perform the obligations of reparation in the interest of the victims of genocidal acts who are members of the Rohingya group, including but not limited to allowing the safe and dignified return of forcibly displaced Rohingya and respect for their full citizenship and human rights and protection against discrimination, persecution and other related acts, consistent with the obligation to prevent genocide under Article I
- Must offer assurances and guarantees of non-repetition of violations of the Genocide Convention, in particular the obligations provided under Articles I, III, IV, V and VI

The provisions of the Genocide Convention invoked by The Gambia will be explained in Chapter 4.

Myanmar, for its part, requests the ICJ: (1) to remove the case from its List; (2) in the alternative, to reject the request for the indication of provisional measures submitted by The Gambia.

As neither The Gambia nor Myanmar has its national as a judge of the ICJ, each of them appoints a judge *ad hoc* for the case. The Gambia's judge *ad hoc* is Navanethem Pillay, a South African who has served as a judge of the International Criminal Tribunal for Rwanda and the International Criminal Court before becoming UN High Commissioner for Human Rights from 2008 to 2014. Myanmar's judge *ad hoc* is Professor Claus Kress, a German who is director of the Institute of International Peace and Security Law at the University of Cologne, Germany.

The Gambia's legal standing to institute the Application against Myanmar

The first hurdle for The Gambia to overcome is the requirement that a State suing another State before the ICJ must have legal standing (*locus standi*) to bring the case.

The Gambia argues this is very much a dispute between The Gambia and Myanmar, as The Gambia is seeking to protect not only the rights of the Rohingya, but The Gambia's own rights. Since each State Party to the Genocide Convention has a common interest in compliance with the relevant obligations

particular, to provide effective penalties for persons guilty of genocide or any of the other acts enumerated in Article III.

under the Convention, each State Party is entitled to make a claim concerning the cessation of an alleged breach by another State party – in this case for Myanmar to abide by its obligations under the Convention not to commit genocide, not to incite genocide and to prevent and punish genocide.

Myanmar contends, however, that these proceedings are in fact brought by The Gambia on behalf of and funded by the OIC, with The Gambia acting in its capacity as an OIC Member State and chair of an OIC organ, its *ad hoc* committee. It is unprecedented for a State to invoke the ICJ's contentious jurisdiction as the proxy for an international organization, and not in its capacity as a Contracting Party to the Genocide Convention. The Gambia blurs the crucial difference between the right to invoke another State's responsibility and the question whether a State has legal standing before the ICJ. In Myanmar's view, it is not possible to circumvent the principle that it is the right of an injured State to decide if, and eventually how, to invoke the responsibility of another State, and that the right of non-injured States to invoke such responsibility is subsidiary. A State that is specially affected by the events, the subject-matter of these proceedings, is obviously Bangladesh, but Bangladesh could not have instituted these proceedings without Myanmar's consent because of a reservation made by Bangladesh to Article IX of the Genocide Convention. None of Myanmar's neighbours, with the exception of Laos, could have done so, since each of the others is either not a party to the Genocide Convention or has made a reservation that Article IX applies either not at all or only with the consent of all parties to the dispute. If a State such as The Gambia that is not specially affected by an alleged breach of a treaty could bring a case, in circumstances where a State that is specially affected cannot, this would represent a major inroad into fundamental principles concerning the consensual nature of the ICJ's contentious jurisdiction.

According to Myanmar, because of its reservation to Article VIII, 'not any Contracting Party' may submit to the ICJ a dispute it might have with Myanmar – only those Contracting Parties which are specifically affected by the alleged violations of the Genocide Convention may do so, if the ICJ has jurisdiction under Article IX.

At this juncture, this present author should like to make some observations.

First, the fact that a nation State has brought a case in an international court or tribunal with external financial support has never given rise to the case being dismissed for this reason. For example, Ghana National Petroleum Corporation is reported to have funded the cost of the litigation on Ghana's maritime boundary dispute with Cote d'Ivoire before the International Tribunal for the Law of the Sea,[19] and this has not led the Tribunal to dismiss the case on the grounds of lack of jurisdiction or inadmissibility.

19 *Delimitation of the Maritime Boundary in the Atlantic Ocean (Ghana/Côte d'Ivoire)* ITLOS Reports 2017, 4.

Second, apart from the possibility of a directly injured State Party to a human rights treaty to sue the injuring State Party in a competent international court or tribunal, the right of any State to take legal action in vindication of a public interest (*actio popularis*) at the international level is quite limited. In *South West Africa (Ethiopia v South Africa; Liberia v South Africa) (Second Phase)*, decided in 1966, neither Liberia nor Ethiopia has legal standing to challenge the apartheid policy implemented by South Africa in South West Africa (Namibia) in disregard of the League of Nations' Mandate entrusted to South Africa to promote the material and moral well-being and the social progress of the inhabitants of South West Africa. The ICJ rejects the principle of 'sacred trust of civilization' invoked by Liberia and Ethiopia as a basis of their legal standing, treating it as a mere moral political ideal. The ICJ affirms that international law as it stood in 1966 did not know 'an *action popularis*, or right resident in any member of the international community in vindication of a public interest'.[20]

Third, The Gambia's legal standing to bring the present case against Myanmar depends on how the ICJ will interpret its own Judgment of 2012 in *Questions relating to the Obligation to Prosecute or Extradite (Belgium v Senegal)*.[21] The case was brought by Belgium against Senegal in respect of a dispute concerning Senegal's compliance with its obligation to prosecute Hissène Habré, former President of Chad who had been living in exile in Senegal, for acts including crimes of torture and crimes against humanity committed in Chad, or, alternatively, to extradite him to Belgium for the purposes of criminal proceedings. Belgium based its claims on the 1984 UN Convention against Torture and Other Cruel, Inhuman or Degrading Treatment or Punishment[22] as well as on customary international law. Pursuant to Article 30(1) of the Convention against Torture, any dispute between two or more States Parties concerning the interpretation or application of the Convention which cannot be settled through negotiation shall, at the request of one of them, be submitted to arbitration. If within six months from the date of the request for arbitration the Parties are unable to agree on the organization of the arbitration, any one of those Parties may refer the dispute to the ICJ by request in conformity with the ICJ Statute.

Paragraphs 67–70 of the ICJ's Judgment in the *Belgium v Senegal* case deal with the question whether being a party to the Convention against Torture is sufficient for a State to be entitled to bring a claim to the ICJ concerning the cessation of alleged violations by another State Party of its obligations under that Convention. As stated in its Preamble, the object and purpose of the Convention against Torture is 'to make more effective the struggle against torture … throughout the world'. Therefore, reasons the ICJ, States Parties to

20 *South West Africa Cases (Ethiopia v South Africa; Liberia v South Africa)* (Second Phase) [1966] ICJ Rep 6, 34–5 [52]–[54], 47 [88].

21 [2012] ICJ Rep 422.

22 1465 UNTS 85, in force 26 June 1987.

the Convention against Torture have a common interest to ensure, in view of their shared values, that acts of torture are prevented and that, if they occur, their authors do not enjoy impunity. The obligations of a State Party to conduct a preliminary inquiry into the facts and to submit the case to its competent authorities for prosecution are triggered by the presence of the alleged offender in its territory, regardless of the nationality of the offender or the victims, or of the place where the alleged offences occurred. All the other States Parties have a common interest in compliance with these obligations by the State in whose territory the alleged offender is present. Such common interest implies that the obligations in question are owed by any State Party to all the other States Parties to the Convention against Torture. All the States Parties 'have a legal interest' in the protection of the rights involved. These obligations may be defined as 'obligations *erga omnes partes*' – each State Party has an interest in compliance with these conventional obligations in any given case. In this respect, the ICJ considers the relevant provisions of the Convention against Torture to be 'similar to' those of the Genocide Convention, with regard to which the ICJ observed:

> In such a convention the contracting States do not have any interests of their own; they merely have, one and all, a common interest, namely, the accomplishment of those high purposes which are the *raison d'être* of the Convention. (*Reservations to the Convention on the Prevention and Punishment of the Crime of Genocide, Advisory Opinion, ICJ Reports 1951*, p 23).[23]

The ICJ deems the common interest in compliance with the relevant obligations under the Convention against Torture to imply the entitlement of each State Party to the Convention against Torture to make a claim concerning the cessation of an alleged breach by another State Party. If a special interest were required for that purpose, in many cases no State would be in the position to make such a claim. Thus, any State Party to the Convention against Torture may invoke the responsibility of another State Party with a view to ascertaining the alleged failure to comply with its obligations *erga omnes partes*, and to bring that failure to an end. For these reasons, concludes the ICJ, Belgium, as a State Party to the Convention against Torture, has legal standing to invoke the responsibility of Senegal for the alleged breaches of its obligations under the relevant provisions of that Convention. Consequently, the ICJ finds no need to pronounce on whether Belgium also has a special interest with respect to Senegal's compliance with the relevant provisions of the Convention against Torture in the case of Mr Habré.[24]

Since the ICJ in the *Belgium v Senegal* case specifically alludes to the Genocide Convention as being similar to the Convention against Torture, its reasoning should also apply to the legal standing of The Gambia to institute the proceedings

23 [2012] ICJ Rep 422, 449 [68].
24 Ibid 450 [69] [70].

against Myanmar regarding their dispute relating to the interpretation, application or fulfilment of the obligations under the Genocide Convention.

The next jurisdictional hurdle for The Gambia is to prove the existence of such dispute between The Gambia and Myanmar.

Existence of a dispute between The Gambia and Myanmar

The ICJ has explained its case law on the requirement of the existence of a dispute between the parties, as follows.[25] A dispute is 'a disagreement on a point of law or fact, a conflict of legal views or of interests' between parties. In principle, the date for determining the existence of a dispute is the date on which the Application is submitted to the ICJ, when the evidence must show the parties hold clearly opposite views with respect to the issue brought before the ICJ. Whether there is a dispute in a given case is a matter for 'objective determination' by the ICJ. It must be shown that the claim of one party is positively opposed by the other. For a dispute to exist, it must be demonstrated, on the basis of the evidence, that the party against whom the Application is instituted 'was aware, or could not have been unaware', that its views were positively opposed by the applicant. The ICJ's determination must turn on an examination of the facts, taking into account in particular any statements or documents exchanged between the parties with special attention to the author of the statement or document, their intended or actual addressee and their content. The matter is one of substance, not of form. The conduct of the parties may also be relevant, especially when there have been no diplomatic exchanges. Therefore, the existence of a dispute may be inferred from the failure of a State to respond to a claim in circumstances where a response is called for. While the existence of a dispute and the undertaking of negotiations are distinct as a matter of principle, the negotiations may help demonstrate the existence of the dispute and delineate its subject-matter. Prior negotiations are not required where the ICJ has jurisdiction on the basis of declarations made pursuant to Article 36(2) of its Statute, unless one of the relevant declarations requires that there be prior negotiations before a dispute may be submitted to the ICJ. Moreover, although a formal diplomatic protest may be an important step to bring a claim of one party to the attention of the other, such a formal protest is not a necessary condition for the existence of a dispute. Similarly, notice of an intention to file a case is not required as a condition for the ICJ's jurisdiction over the dispute. Conduct subsequent to the Application (or the Application itself) may be relevant for various purposes, in

25 *Application of the International Convention on the Elimination of All Forms of Racial Discrimination (Georgia v Russian Federation), Preliminary Objection*, Judgment [2011] ICJ Rep 70, 84–5 [30]; *Obligations concerning Negotiations relating to Cessation of the Nuclear Arms Race and to Nuclear Disarmament (Marshall Islands v United Kingdom), Preliminary Objections*, Judgment [2016] ICJ Rep 833, 849–51 [37]–[43].

particular to confirm the existence of a dispute or to determine whether the dispute has disappeared as of the time when the ICJ makes its decision.

The Gambia must discharge its burden of proving the dispute between it and Myanmar regarding the 1948 Genocide Convention did exist when The Gambia instituted the proceedings against Myanmar in the ICJ on 11 November 2019. This burden is not to be taken lightly, as evidenced from the example of the Marshall Islands' failure to prove before the ICJ the existence of its disputes with the UK, India and Pakistan on the latter three States' respective obligations to negotiate cessation of the nuclear arms race and to nuclear disarmament. The Marshall Islands relied heavily on the positions taken by it and the aforesaid States on these issues in multilateral fora. In the Rohingya case brought by The Gambia against Myanmar, The Gambia's contestation of claim against Myanmar was mostly notified through multilateral fora.

On 24 April 2014, the Marshall Islands filed an Application instituting proceedings in the ICJ against the UK, in which the Marshall Islands claims the UK has breached treaty and customary international law obligations concerning negotiations relating to cessation of the nuclear arms race and to nuclear disarmament. The Marshall Islands contends more specifically that the UK violates Article VI of the 1968 Treaty on Non-Proliferation of Nuclear Weapons ('NPT'),[26] to which they are both party. According to that Article, each party

> undertakes to pursue negotiations in good faith on effective measures relating to cessation of the nuclear arms race at an early date and to nuclear disarmament, and on a treaty on general and complete disarmament under strict and effective international control.

The Marshall Islands further accuses the UK of, among other things, opposing UN General Assembly resolutions calling for such negotiations to begin; engaging in 'negative and obstructive' conduct with regard to the cessation of the nuclear arms race at an early date; and repeatedly declaring its intention to rely on its nuclear arsenal for decades to come. The UK raises preliminary objections to the ICJ's jurisdiction and the admissibility of the Marshall Islands' Application. In its Judgment on 5 October 2016,[27] the ICJ rules it cannot proceed with the case since that the Marshall Islands has failed to show there was, at the time of the filing of the Application, a legal dispute between the parties for the following reasons.

First, the Marshall Islands refers to a number of statements made in multilateral fora before the date of the filing of its Application to establish the existence of a dispute. It relies on the statement made at the High-level Meeting of the UN

26 729 UNTS 161, in force 5 Mar 1970.

27 *Obligations concerning Negotiations relating to Cessation of the Nuclear Arms Race and to Nuclear Disarmament (Marshall Islands v United Kingdom), Preliminary Objections*, Judgment [2016] ICJ Rep 833.

General Assembly on Nuclear Disarmament, held on 26 September 2013, by its Minister for Foreign Affairs, 'urg[ing] all nuclear weapons States to intensify efforts to address their responsibilities in moving towards an effective and secure disarmament'. However, the ICJ considers this statement to be hortatory and cannot be understood as an allegation that the UK (or any other nuclear power) was in breach of any of its legal obligations. It does not mention the obligation to negotiate, nor does it say the nuclear-weapon States are failing to meet their obligations in this regard. It suggests that they are making 'efforts' to address their responsibilities, and calls for an intensification of those efforts, rather than deploring a failure to act. A statement can give rise to a dispute only if it refers to the subject-matter of a claim with sufficient clarity to enable the State against which that claim is made to identify that there is, or may be, a dispute with regard to that subject-matter. The 2013 statement relied upon by the Marshall Islands does not meet these requirements. Although the Marshall Islands' statement at the Nayarit Conference on 13 February 2014 goes further than the 2013 statement, with a sentence asserting that 'States possessing nuclear arsenals are failing to fulfil their legal obligations' under Article VI of the NPT and customary international law, the UK was not present at the Nayarit Conference. Furthermore, the subject of the Conference was not specifically the question of negotiations with a view to nuclear disarmament, but the broader question of the humanitarian impact of nuclear weapons, and while this statement contains a general criticism of the conduct of all nuclear-weapon States, it does not specify the UK's conduct that gave rise to the alleged breach. Such a specification would have been particularly necessary if, as the Marshall Islands contends, the Nayarit statement was aimed at invoking the UK's international responsibility on the grounds of a course of conduct which had remained unchanged for many years. Given its very general content and the context in which it was made, that statement did not call for a specific reaction by the UK. Accordingly, no opposition of views can be inferred from the absence of any such reaction. The Nayarit statement is insufficient to bring into existence, between the Marshall Islands and the UK, a specific dispute as to the scope of Article VI of the NPT and the asserted corresponding customary international law obligation, or as to the UK's compliance with such obligations. In addition, none of the other more general statements relied on by the Marshall Islands in that case supports the existence of a dispute, since none articulates an alleged breach by the UK of the obligation enshrined in Article VI of the NPT or the corresponding customary international law obligation invoked by the Marshall Islands. Therefore, in all the circumstances, on the basis of those statements – whether taken individually or together – it cannot be said that the UK was aware, or could not have been unaware, that the Marshall Islands was alleging that the UK was in breach of its obligations.

Secondly, the ICJ rejects the Marshall Islands' argument that the very filing of the Application and statements made in the course of the proceedings before the ICJ by both parties suffice to establish the existence of a dispute.

Thirdly, the Marshall Islands refers to the parties' voting records in multilateral fora on nuclear disarmament to demonstrate the existence of a dispute. In the ICJ's view, considerable care is required before inferring from votes cast on resolutions before political organs such as the UN General Assembly any conclusion as to the existence or not of a legal dispute on some issue covered by a resolution. The wording of a resolution, and votes or patterns of voting on resolutions of the same subject-matter, may constitute relevant evidence of the existence of a legal dispute in some circumstances, particularly where statements were made by way of explanation of vote. However, some resolutions contain a large number of different propositions; a State's vote on such resolutions cannot by itself be taken as indicative of the position of that State on each and every proposition within that resolution, let alone of the existence of a legal dispute between that State and another State regarding one of those propositions.

Fourthly, the ICJ assesses the Marshall Islands' argument that the UK's conduct in declining to cooperate with certain diplomatic initiatives, in failing to initiate any disarmament negotiations, and in replacing and modernizing its nuclear weapons, together with the UK's statements that its conduct is consistent with its treaty obligations, shows the existence of a dispute between the parties. However, the ICJ finds none of the statements made in a multilateral context by the Marshall Islands offer any particulars regarding the UK's conduct. On the basis of such statements by the Marshall Islands, it cannot be said the UK 'was aware, or could not have been unaware', that the Marshall Islands was alleging the UK was in breach of its obligations. In this context, the UK's conduct does not provide a basis for finding a dispute between the two States before the ICJ.

Therefore, the ICJ, by eight votes to eight, by the President's casting vote, upholds the UK's preliminary objection to jurisdiction based on the absence of a dispute between the parties. All the judges from States in possession of nuclear weapons (United States, France, UK, Russia, China and India) join the ICJ judges from Japan and Italy in voting in favour of this decision, which is decided by the casting vote of ICJ President Abraham of France. The other eight judges voting against this decision are from Somalia, Slovakia, Morocco, Brazil, Uganda, Jamaica, Australia and Algeria (who was the judge *ad hoc* appointed by the Marshall Islands).

One may wonder whether the existence of a dispute can always be objectively determined. According to dissenting Judge Yusuf of Somalia, Judge Sebutinde of Uganda and Judge *ad hoc* Bedjaoui from Algeria, the ICJ's introduction of the 'awareness' criterion in that case conflicts with the ICJ's previous case law requiring the existence of a dispute to be objectively determined and the existence of a dispute to stand objectively by itself. In their opinions, this new legal criterion of 'awareness' introduces a degree of subjectivity into an equation that ought to remain objective, since it requires both an applicant and the ICJ to delve into the mind of a respondent State. Dissenting Judge Robinson of Jamaica adds that the requirement of 'awareness' is a departure from the empirical and pragmatic enquiry the ICJ must undertake. Dissenting Judge Crawford of Australia disagrees with the 'objective awareness' test for the existence of a dispute adopted by the majority since no such legal requirement was to be found in the ICJ's previous case law and an objective awareness test is difficult to distinguish from a formal notice requirement, which the ICJ had rejected. By contrast, Judge Owada of Japan and Judge Donoghue of the United States defend the majority's reasoning, contending that the ICJ actually applies the objective standard in that case, and that in reality the element of awareness is the common denominator running through the ICJ's case law because the awareness of the respondent State demonstrates the transformation of a mere disagreement into a true legal dispute and is thus an essential minimum common to all cases. However, dissenting Judge *ad hoc* Bedjaoui rebuts that if the awareness test were to apply, the UK must have been 'aware' of the Marshall Islands' anti-nuclear views in opposition to its own nuclear conduct, given, among other things, the history of the Marshall Islands and its 2013 and 2014 statements made at international events which were open to all, and were aimed at all States possessing nuclear weapons, without distinction, including the UK.

Also on 24 April 2014, the Marshall Islands filed an Application against India and another one against Pakistan, accusing the latter two of not fulfilling their obligations relating to the cessation of the nuclear arms race at an early date and to nuclear disarmament. Although neither India nor Pakistan is party to the NPT, the Marshall Islands – which has ratified the NPT – argues that certain obligations laid down in the NPT apply to all States as a matter of customary international law, particularly Article VI of the NPT, whereby the parties '[undertake] to pursue negotiations in good faith on effective measures relating to cessation of the nuclear arms race at an early date and to nuclear disarmament, and on a treaty on general and complete disarmament under strict and effective international control'. The ICJ delivered its Judgments on the preliminary objections raised by India and Pakistan to the ICJ's jurisdiction and the admissibility of the Applications on 5 October 2016, upholding, by nine votes to seven, India and Pakistan's objection to jurisdiction based on the absence of a dispute between the parties. It further concludes that, lacking jurisdiction under Article 36(2) of its Statute, it cannot proceed to the merits of the case.[28] Judge Yusuf from Somalia who is in the minority in the case brought by the Marshall Islands against the UK votes with the majority in these two cases. He finds no evidence in the record showing positively opposed views held by India and Pakistan, on the one side, and the Marshall Islands, on the other, prior to the submission of the Application to the ICJ by the Marshall Islands. Instead, the record shows all these States have been advocating in various multilateral forums, including at the

28 *Obligations concerning Negotiations relating to Cessation of the Nuclear Arms Race and to Nuclear Disarmament (Marshall Islands v India), Jurisdiction and Admissibility*, Judgment [2016] ICJ Rep 255; *Obligations concerning Negotiations relating to Cessation of the Nuclear Arms Race and to Nuclear Disarmament (Marshall Islands v Pakistan), Jurisdiction and Admissibility*, Judgment [2016] ICJ Rep 552.

Nayarit Conference, but most of all at the UN General Assembly, the necessity for all States, including nuclear-weapon States, to pursue in good faith and to conclude negotiations on nuclear disarmament. Rather than positive opposition or conflict of legal views on the subject-matter of the alleged dispute, Judge Yusuf finds the evidence pointing towards a convergence of views between the parties on the negotiation and conclusion of a comprehensive convention on nuclear disarmament.

Did the dispute between The Gambia and Myanmar regarding the Genocide Convention exist at the time when The Gambia instituted the Application against Myanmar in the ICJ on 11 November 2019?

According to The Gambia, it has been accusing Myanmar of failure to fulfil Myanmar's obligations under the Genocide Convention, and of carrying out genocide against the Rohingya, since early 2018, and The Gambia has done so regularly in its public and official statements ever since. Myanmar has long been well aware of The Gambia's views, and has opposed them, by denying all responsibility for the acts of genocide, and by denying Myanmar has violated the Genocide Convention. There being an unresolved dispute between the parties, The Gambia has come to the ICJ to protect its rights under the Genocide Convention. Myanmar was put on notice of this dispute under the Genocide Convention on several occasions, and it acknowledged receipt of that notice prior to The Gambia's filing of this case. The followings are details of The Gambia's actions in this regard.

From 5 to 6 May 2018, the OIC, including The Gambia, met at a ministerial level in Dhaka, Bangladesh, where, among other actions, they promulgated the Dhaka Declaration,[29] expressing concern over the 'systematic brutal acts perpetrated by security forces against the Rohingya ... which constitute a serious and blatant violation of international law', and sought to address 'the accountability issue for the violations ... against the Rohingya in Myanmar through [the] formation of an *ad hoc* ministerial committee, to be chaired by [The] Gambia'. In response, Myanmar's Ministry of Foreign Affairs issued a press statement three days later to 'categorically reject[]' the Declaration's description of 'events in Rakhine state' as 'State-backed violence'. Myanmar was thus put on notice as early as May of 2018 of the newly formed OIC *ad hoc* Committee on Accountability for Crimes against the Rohingya, chaired by The Gambia, and its allegations of State-sponsored violence against the Rohingya.

In September 2018, the IIFFMM released its first series of reports in which it found evidence of genocidal acts and genocidal intent attributable to Myanmar in the context of its crimes against the Rohingya.[30] Myanmar dismissed those findings as biased. The Gambia, on the contrary, made clear in its remarks at the

29 https://reliefweb.int/report/world/dhaka-declaration-45th-session-council-foreign-ministers -organization-islamic.

30 A/HRC/39/64 (12 Sept 2018).

UN General Assembly later that month that 'The Gambia has undertaken … to champion an accountability mechanism that would ensure that perpetrators of the terrible crimes against the Rohingya Muslims are brought to book'. On 2 March 2019, the OIC held another ministerial-level meeting, at which they, including The Gambia, adopted a resolution on Myanmar's crimes against the Rohingya, which emphasized that accountability was necessary for 'preventing genocide' and endorsed the recommendation of the *ad hoc* Committee chaired by The Gambia to hold Myanmar accountable under the Genocide Convention. In response, Myanmar again denied responsibility and criticized the resolution as an interference with its sovereignty. On 16 September 2019, the IIFFMM submitted its final report.[31] Myanmar rejected wholesale that report, which welcomed 'the efforts of States, in particular The Gambia … to encourage and pursue a case against Myanmar before the International Court of Justice (ICJ) under the Genocide Convention'. The Gambia, in remarks before the UN General Assembly on 26 September 2019, at which Myanmar was present, confirmed The Gambia's readiness to lead the concerted efforts to take the Rohingya issue to the ICJ on behalf of the OIC, and The Gambia would call on all stakeholders to support the process in which, '[a]s a global community with a conscience, we cannot continue to ignore the plight of the Rohingya'.

On 11 October 2019, further to its support of the IIFFMM's conclusions, The Gambia's Permanent Mission to the UN sent a Note Verbale to Myanmar's Permanent Mission, expressing The Gambia's concerns 'regarding the ongoing genocide against the Rohingya people … in violation of Myanmar's obligations under the … Genocide Convention'. Noting Myanmar's rejection of the IIFFMM's final report, The Gambia 'emphatically rejects Myanmar's denial of its responsibility for the ongoing genocide against Myanmar's Rohingya population, and its refusal to fulfill its obligations under the Genocide Convention and customary international law'. The Gambia concluded its Note Verbale by declaring:

> With somber reflection on the goals of the Genocide Convention and its obligations on all States, The Gambia understands Myanmar to be in ongoing breach of those obligations under the Convention and under customary international law. The Gambia insists that Myanmar take all necessary actions to comply with these obligations, including but not limited to its obligations to make reparations to the victims and to provide guarantees and assurances of non-repetition.

Myanmar received The Gambia's Note Verbale on the date it was sent and confirmed this by means of its own Note Verbale to The Gambia's Mission to the UN, sent from the same email address to which The Gambia had sent its Note

31 A/HRC/42/50 (16 Sept 2019).

Verbale. Although the ICJ previously held that a 'formal diplomatic protest' is not required, here there is one, in addition to direct statements and actions in multilateral settings and additional indicia of Myanmar's awareness of this dispute with The Gambia under the Genocide Convention.

For its part, Myanmar rebuts The Gambia's aforesaid contention as follows.

While the OIC decided to bring this case as early as March 2019, the earliest official reference to the Genocide Convention as the basis of the claim was in August 2019. Moreover, The Gambia's lawyers were instructed to initiate proceedings a week before The Gambia even sent its 11 October 2019 Note Verbale to Myanmar.

In May 2018, the OIC passed a resolution establishing an *ad hoc* Ministerial Committee on Accountability for Human Rights Violations against the Rohingya, to be chaired by The Gambia, whose functions were, among other things, to '[e]ngage to ensure accountability and justice for gross violations of international human rights and humanitarian laws and principles', and to '[m]obilize and coordinate international political support'. According to a preambular paragraph, 'ensuring accountability and justice is the most crucial step towards preventing genocide and other mass atrocity crimes'.

In Myanmar's opinion, the *erga omnes partes* character of obligations under the Genocide Convention does not mean The Gambia can bring these proceedings in the absence of a dispute specifically between the two Parties now before the ICJ. In the *Belgium v Senegal* case, while the ICJ accepts that the *erga omnes partes* character of a treaty obligation may be of some relevance to legal standing to bring a case before the ICJ, the ICJ's consideration ofjurisdiction proceeds on the obvious premise that there has to be a dispute between Belgium and Senegal for there to be jurisdiction under the Convention against Torture. In Myanmar's submission, there is no dispute between it and The Gambia for the following reasons.

First, The Gambia relies on various OIC documents. These clearly do not give rise to a relevant dispute between The Gambia and Myanmar. They contain no positive statement that Myanmar is in breach of its obligations under the Genocide Convention. Indeed, the preamble to the two OIC resolutions implies the opposite. In any event, the ICJ has affirmed that a State's vote on a resolution of an international organization is not of itself indicative of that State's position on each proposition within the resolution, let alone of the existence of a legal dispute with another State regarding one of those propositions. Furthermore, Myanmar is not an OIC member and there is nothing to indicate that Myanmar was put on notice of all of the OIC's resolutions.

Secondly, The Gambia relies on the IIFFMM's reports. However, statements in those reports do not constitute claims by The Gambia or the OIC or OIC Member States. Statements by the IIFFMM do not put Myanmar on notice of what particular claims those States and the OIC might be intending to make in proceedings in the ICJ.

Thirdly, the general statement by the Vice-President of The Gambia before the UN General Assembly on 26 September 2019 that The Gambia is 'ready to lead concerted efforts' to bring this case does not even mention the Genocide Convention. Similarly, the statement in reply by Myanmar's Union Minister for the Office of the State Counsellor does not mention the Genocide Convention.

As regards the 11 October 2019 Note Verbale, The Gambia's case is that because Myanmar failed to respond to it within a month, by 11 November 2019, a dispute between the parties concerning the matters set out in that document had suddenly arisen. However, submits Myanmar, the existence of a dispute can be inferred from a failure to respond to a claim only in circumstances where a response is called for, and where an acceptable time for any response has expired. This Note Verbale did not call for a response. It contained only a sweepingly general claim that Myanmar had 'responsibility for the ongoing genocide against Myanmar's Rohingya population', without specifying which particular facts are relied on in support of the assertion of that responsibility and without specifying which provisions of the Genocide Convention are claimed to have been violated by which facts. It provided no particulars of the facts alleged to constitute 'Myanmar's refusal to acknowledge and remedy its responsibility'. It referred only in the most general way to the IIFFMM's reports and findings and to OIC resolutions (but specifies only one of each), and generically to obligations under the Genocide Convention, customary international law and human rights covenants. It did not make any particular legal or factual claim that could be positively opposed by Myanmar. It merely stated a legal conclusion – that there was an ongoing genocide for which Myanmar was responsible – without stating any claim to justify that conclusion.

The Gambia sent another Note Verbale, on 24 November 2019, after this case had already been brought before the ICJ on 11 November 2019. In Myanmar's submission, this cannot *ex post facto* bring about a relevant dispute. In any event, it does nothing further to identify a legal claim.

Furthermore, argues Myanmar, the OIC, on whose behalf the proceedings are brought, has never directly accused Myanmar of violations of the Genocide Convention. Rather, the OIC has expressed support more generally for 'using all international legal instruments to hold accountable the perpetrators of crimes'. These proceedings are the initiative of an OIC sub-committee whose task is generally to '[e]ngage to ensure accountability and justice for gross violations of international human rights and humanitarian laws and principles'. The OIC apparently wanted to bring 'a' case before the ICJ, but was not particularly concerned with the legal basis of the claim – Article IX of the Genocide Convention was simply identified at some point by someone as a vehicle for invoking the ICJ's jurisdiction, and the OIC would have been equally prepared to use any other treaty it could identify for that purpose.

Myanmar concludes by asking: if The Gambia had a genuine dispute with Myanmar concerning the interpretation, application or fulfilment of the Genocide Convention, why did it not give notice of this claim to Myanmar in March 2019, when a decision to bring these proceedings was made – or in August 2019 when 'the 2019 IIFFMM's report noted its intended to bring a claim based on the Genocide Convention'? Why did The Gambia not give notice of this claim to Myanmar *before* instructing lawyers on 4 October 2019 to institute proceedings? The inference is that the Note Verbale of 24 November 2019 was sent as a legal formality, considered necessary to enable proceedings to be issued, once all preparations for the proceedings were already in place.

How the ICJ will apply the majority's reasoning in its Judgments in the three cases brought by the Marshall Islands against the UK, India and Pakistan, respectively, to the facts presented by The Gambia and Myanmar regarding the existence or non-existence of a dispute between them will be decisive for The Gambia's Application.

In February 2020, the Maldives announced its intention to join The Gambia in the latter's on-going lawsuit against Myanmar in the ICJ concerning the Rohingya. Subsequently, on 2 September 2020, Canada and the Netherlands indicated their intention to intervene by joining The Gambia in the case against Myanmar. Third-State intervention in ICJ proceedings involves complex procedural law which is beyond the remit of this book, however.

4

PROVING VIOLATIONS OF THE 1948 GENOCIDE CONVENTION

Should The Gambia succeed in overcoming the jurisdictional and admissibility hurdles in its case against Myanmar in the ICJ, The Gambia will still have to discharge the burden of proving Myanmar has breached the relevant provisions of the 1948 Genocide Convention.[1] In particular, The Gambia must prove certain individuals have committed acts proscribed in Articles II and III of the Genocide Convention against the Rohingya. Once that is proven, The Gambia will need to prove such acts are attributable to Myanmar under the international law of State responsibility and, finally, that Myanmar has failed to prevent and/or punish the genocidal acts.

Genocide Convention

Under Article I of the 1948 Genocide Convention, its Contracting Parties confirm that genocide, whether committed in time of peace or in time of war, is a crime under international law which they undertake to *prevent* and to *punish*.

Article II of this Convention defines genocide as any of the following acts committed with intent to destroy, in whole or in part, a national, ethnical, racial or religious group, as such: (a) killing; (b) causing serious bodily or mental harm; (c) deliberately inflicting on the group conditions of life calculated to bring about its physical destruction in whole or in part; (d) imposing measures intended to prevent births within the group; (e) forcibly transferring children of the group to another group.

1 78 UNTS 277, in force 12 Jan 1951.

DOI: 10.4324/9781003224211-4

Killing as a proscribed act is self-evident – it is homicide, a destruction of a human life, committed with the intent to cause death.[2]

The International Criminal Tribunal for Rwanda ('ICTR') and the International Criminal Tribunal for the former Yugoslavia ('ICTY') have explained the meaning of 'causing serious bodily or mental harm' in the context of genocide. The bodily or mental harm inflicted on members of a group must be of such a serious nature as to threaten its destruction in whole or in part. Serious mental harm includes 'more than a minor or temporary impairment of mental faculties such as the infliction of strong fear or terror, intimidation or threat'. Nearly all convictions for the causing of serious bodily or mental harm as an act of genocide involve rapes or killings. Rape is a 'quintessential' example of serious bodily harm.[3] The systemic rape of and sexual violence against Tutsi women by Hutu men in Rwanda in 1994 have been held by the ICTR to be steps to achieve the destruction of the Tutsi group. These acts were committed by Hutu men solely against Tutsi women, many of whom were subjected to the worst public humiliation, mutilated and raped several times, often in public and by more than one assailant. They resulted in physical and psychological destruction of Tutsi women, their families and their communities as an integral part of the process of systematic destruction of the Tutsi group as a whole. As part of the propaganda campaign geared to mobilizing the Hutu against the Tutsi, Tutsi women were presented as sexual objects, a step in the process of destruction of the Tutsi group – destruction of the spirit, of the will to live and of life itself. [4]

The ICTY Appeals Chamber has held that, generally speaking, some acts such as rapes in themselves cause the suffering of those upon whom they were inflicted, and such suffering occurs even without a medical certificate.[5] In addition, sexual violence necessarily gives rise to severe pain or suffering, whether physical or mental, and in this way justifies its characterization as an act of torture.[6]

Threats of death and knowledge of impending death have been accepted as amounting to serious mental harm as an act of genocide. During the 1990s Balkan wars, the suffering of the Bosnian Muslim women, children and elderly forcibly transferred from the town where they lived resulted in serious mental

2 *Prosecutor v Jean-Paul Akayesu*, Case ICTR-96-4, ICTR Trial Chamber I, 2 Sept 1998 para 501; *Prosecutor v Rutaganda*, Case ICTR-96-3, ICTR Trial Chamber I, 6 Dec 1999 para 55; *Prosecutor v Alfred Musema*, Case ICTR-96-13-T, ICTR Trial Chamber I, 27 Jan 2000 para 155.

3 *Prosecutor v Callixte Nzabonimana*, Case ICTR-98-44D, ICTR Trial Chamber III, 31 May 2012 para 1703, citing, among others, the Judgment of the ICTR Appeals Chamber in *Prosecutor v Seromba* (Case ICTR-2001-66-A, 12 Mar 2008 para 46) and that of the ICTY Appeals Chamber in *Prosecutor v Kunarac et al.* (Case IT-96-23&IT-96-23/1-A, 12 June 2002 para 150).

4 *Akayesu* paras 731–2, followed by the ICJ in *Application of the Convention on the Prevention and Punishment of the Crime of Genocide (Bosnia and Herzegovina v Serbia and Montenegro)* [2007] ICJ Rep 43, 167 [300].

5 *Kunarac et al.* para 150.

6 Ibid. One could also imagine how the victims might suffer severe psychological traumas to the extent that they would abhor sexual intercourse altogether and thereby stopping to procreate.

harm within the meaning of genocide when assessed in a holistic manner, taking into consideration the painful separation process from their male family members, the fear and uncertainty as to their fate and that of their detained male relatives, and the appalling conditions of the journey to Muslim-held territory by bus and on foot, coupled with the continuation of their profound trauma, as well as the financial and emotional difficulties they faced in their drastically changed lives following the forced transfer. While the forcible transfer is not in itself an act of genocide, all the relevant acts perpetrated against the Bosnian Muslim women, children and elderly arising from the forcible transfer operation and the separation from and killings of their male relatives could determine whether their suffering amounted to serious mental harm. Each of those factors are not to be viewed in isolation, but holistically.[7]

An oft-cited example of the proscribed genocidal act of deliberately inflicting on the group conditions of life calculated to bring about its physical destruction in whole or in part is the Ottoman Empire's systematic transportation of Armenians from their homeland to the desert of Northern Syria in 1915 without food and water and subjecting them to periodic robbery, rape and massacre.[8]

According to the ICJ in the Bosnian genocide case, 'ethnic cleansing' can only be a form of genocide, within the meaning of the Genocide Convention, if it corresponds to or falls within one of the categories of acts prohibited by Article II of the Convention. Neither the intent, as a matter of policy, to render an area 'ethnically homogeneous', nor the operations that may be carried out to implement such policy, can as such be designated as genocide. However, this does not mean acts described as 'ethnic cleansing' may never constitute genocide, if they are such as to be characterized as, for example, 'deliberately inflicting on the group conditions of life calculated to bring about its physical destruction in whole or in part', contrary to Article II(c) of the Genocide Convention, provided that such action is carried out with the necessary specific intent to destroy the group, as distinct from its removal from the region.[9]

Imposing measures intended to prevent births within the group as a proscribed act of genocide when accompanied by the requisite genocidal intent is self-evident. According to the ICJ in the Croatian genocide case, rape and other acts of sexual violence, which may also fall within Article II(b) and (c) of the

7 *Prosecutor v Zdravko Tolimir*, Case IT-05-88/2-A, ICTY Appeals Chamber, 8 Apr 2015 paras 206, 210–1.

8 In 2019, the US House of Representatives and the US Senate each adopted a resolution recognizing this as a genocide (H.Res.296 of 29 Oct 2019 and S.Res.150 of 12 Dec 2019). On 24 April 2021, Joe Biden became the first US President to formally recognize what happened to the Armenians as a genocide. Turkey always denies there was genocide against the Armenians, see: www.mfa.gov.tr/the-armenian-allegation-of-genocide-the-issue-and-the-facts.en.mfa.

9 *Application of the Convention on the Prevention and Punishment of the Crime of Genocide (Bosnia and Herzegovina v Serbia and Montenegro)* [2007] ICJ Rep 43, 123 [190]. Cf. Martin Steinfeld, 'When Ethnic Cleansing is not Genocide: A Critical Appraisal of the ICJ's Ruling in *Croatia v Serbia* in relation to Deportation and Population Transfer' (2015) 28 Leiden JIL 937.

Genocide Convention, are capable of constituting proscribed acts of genocide within the meaning of Article II(d), if they are of a kind which prevent births within the group and the circumstances of the commission of those acts as well as their consequences are such that the capacity of members of the group to procreate is affected, taking into account also the systematic nature of such acts.[10]

By proscribing forcibly transferring children of the group to another group as an act of genocide, the Genocide Convention makes it clear there can be no defence that such transfer is for a eugenic or welfare reason if this will result in the destruction of the group in whole or in part. The proscription not only sanctions a direct act of forcible physical transfer, but also sanctions acts of threats or trauma which would lead to the forcible transfer of children from one group to another.[11] It could thus be argued that forced removal of children of the group to another group causes serious mental harm to these children as well as to their parents and close relatives, and that the perpetrators of such forced removal could also be punished under the rubric of the genocidal crime of 'causing serious bodily or mental harm to members of the group' as well.

To be an act of genocide, any of the conducts enumerated in Article II of the Genocide Convention must be 'committed with intent to destroy, in whole or in part, a national, ethnical, racial or religious group, as such'.

In its *Akayesu* Judgment of 2 September 1998, the ICTR Trial Chamber I defines the groups protected from genocidal acts as follows. A national group is a collection of people who are perceived to share a legal bond based on common citizenship, coupled with reciprocity of rights and duties.[12] An ethnic group is a group whose members share a common language and culture.[13] A racial group is distinguished from other racial groups by hereditary physical traits frequently identified with geographical areas, irrespective of linguistic, cultural, national or religious factors.[14] A religious group is a group whose members share the same religion, denomination or mode of worship or common beliefs.[15] Subsequently, the ICTR Trial Chamber II's Judgment of 21 May 1999 in *Kayishema and Ruzindana*, while endorsing the above definitions of the protected groups, additionally defines an ethnic group as 'one whose members share a common language and culture; or, a group which distinguishes itself, as such (self identification); or, a group identified as such by others, including perpetrators of the crimes (identification of others)'.[16] The ICTR Trial Chamber I's Judgment of 4 December 1999 in

10 *Application of the Convention on the Prevention and Punishment of the Crime of Genocide (Croatia v Serbia)* [2015] ICJ Rep 3, 72 [166]. Cf. Giulia Pecorella, 'Rape and Sexual Violence in the ICJ's Judgment in *Croatia v Serbia*' (2015) 28 Leiden JIL 945.

11 *Akayesu* para 509, followed in, e.g., *Rutaganda* para 53 and *Musema* para 159.

12 *Akayesu* para 512.

13 Ibid para 513.

14 Ibid para 514.

15 Ibid para 515.

16 *Prosecutor v Kayishema and Ruzindana*, Case ICTR-95-1-T, ICTR Trial Chamber II, 21 May 1999 para 98.

Rutaganda considers the membership of a protected group as a subjective rather than an objective one – the victim is perceived by the perpetrator of genocide as belonging to a group slated for destruction, and, in some instances, the victim may perceive himself/herself as belonging to the said group.[17] This was followed by the ICTR Trial Chamber II's Judgment of 1 December 2003 in *Kajelijeli*.[18] For its part, the ICTY Trial Chamber I's Judgment of 14 December 1999 in *Jelisic* propounds that although the objective determination of a religious group still remains possible, to attempt to define a national, ethnical or racial group today using objective and scientifically irreproachable criteria would be a perilous exercise whose result would not necessarily correspond to the perception of the persons concerned by such categorization. Therefore, the ICTY Trial Chamber finds it more appropriate to use a subjective criterion to evaluate the status of a national, ethnical or racial group from the point of view of those persons who wish to single that group out from the rest of the community – it is the stigmatization of a group as a distinct national, ethnical or racial unit by the community which allows it to be determined whether a targeted population constitutes a national, ethnical or racial group in the eyes of the alleged perpetrators. A group may be stigmatized in this manner by way of positive or negative criteria – positively by the perpetrators of the crime distinguishing a group by the characteristics which they deem to be particular to a national, ethnical, racial or religious group; negatively by identifying individuals as not being part of the group to which the perpetrators of the crime consider they themselves belong and which to them displays specific national, ethnical, racial or religious characteristics.[19] Subsequent judgments of the ICTR and the ICTY apply either a subjective criterion and/or an objective one to determine whether the victim is a member of a protected group.[20]

Of special relevance to the Rohingya case before the International Court of Justice is the ruling by the ICJ in the Bosnian genocide case that since the essence of the genocidal intent is to destroy the protected group, in whole or in part, as such, it is 'a group which must have particular positive characteristics – national, ethnical, racial or religious – and not the lack of them'. The requisite genocidal intent 'requires an intent to destroy a collection of people who have a particular group identity' – it is a matter of who those people are, not who they are not and the etymology of the word – killing a group – also indicates a positive definition and not a negative one.[21]

17 *Rutaganda* para 56.

18 *Prosecutor v Kajelijeli*, Case ICTR-98-44-A-T, Trial Chamber II, 1 Dec 2003 para 811.

19 *Prosecutor v Goran Jelisic*, Case IT-95-10-T, Trial Chamber I, 14 Dec 1999 paras 70–71.

20 Carola Lingass, *Defining the Protected Groups of Genocide Through the Case Law of International Courts* (International Crime Database Brief 18, Dec 2015) and *The Concept of Race in International Criminal Law* (Routledge 2020) Chapter 3.

21 [2007] ICJ Rep 43, 124–6 [193]–[196]. The ICJ thus endorses the view of the ICTY Appeals Chamber in *Stakic* (Case IT-97-24-A, 22 Mar 2006 paras 20–28) that the group must be defined positively.

According the IIFMM's report of 17 September 2018, both the negative and positive criteria to identify the Rohingya as a group protected under the Genocide Convention are satisfied – the Rohingya can be seen as an ethnic, racial or religious group or a combination thereof and the Rohingya also consider themselves as a distinct group, as do the Myanmar authorities and security forces.[22]

A most difficult hurdle is discharging the burden of proving that the accused committed any of the enumerated acts with 'the specific intent to destroy, in whole or in part', any one of the aforesaid groups, 'as such'. According to the well-established case law of the ICTR and the ICTY, although there is no numeric threshold, the perpetrator must act with the intent to destroy at least a substantial part of the group. The perpetrator need not be solely motivated by a criminal intent to commit genocide, nor does the existence of personal motive preclude him from having the specific intent to commit genocide. In the absence of direct evidence, a perpetrator's intent to commit genocide may be inferred from relevant facts and circumstances that lead *beyond any reasonable doubt* to the existence of the intent. Factors that may establish the specific intent include the general context, the perpetration of other culpable acts systematically directed against the same group, the scale of atrocities committed, the systematic targeting of victims on account of their membership in a protected group or the repetition of destructive and discriminatory acts. In other words, genocidal intent may be proven by circumstantial evidence, inferred from a number of facts and circumstances, including overt statements by the accused, the general context, the perpetration of other culpable acts systematically directed against the same group, the scale of the atrocities committed, the systematic targeting of victims on account of their membership of a particular group or the repetition of destructive and discriminatory acts. The specific intent need not be formed prior to the commission of the acts, but must be possessed at the moment of commission. However, when based on circumstantial evidence, any finding that the accused had genocidal intent must be *the only reasonable inference* from the totality of the evidence.[23]

The ICJ has closely followed the case law of the ICTR and the ICTY in this regard. In its Judgment in the Croatian genocide case, the ICJ rules that the destruction of the group 'in part' within the meaning of Article II of the Genocide Convention must be assessed by reference to several criteria. First, 'the intent must be to destroy at least a substantial part of the particular group', and this is a 'critical' criterion. Furthermore, 'it is widely accepted that genocide may be found to have been committed where the intent is to destroy the group within

22 A/HRC/39/CRP.2 (17 Sept 2018) paras 85, 477, 481–8, 491, 606, 664, 702, 708, 1182, 1328, 1331–2, 1425.

23 *Prosecutor v Ephrem Setako*, Case ICTR-04-81-T, ICTR Trial Chamber I, 25 Feb 2010 paras 466–7 and the ICTR and ICTY's Judgments cited therein.

a geographically limited area' and, accordingly, '[t]he area of the perpetrator's activity and control are to be considered'. Account must also be taken of the prominence of the allegedly targeted part within the group as a whole. In particular, the ICJ must consider whether 'a specific part of the group is emblematic of the overall group, or is essential to its survival'. In the absence of a State plan expressing the intent to commit genocide, such an intent may be inferred from the individual conduct of perpetrators of the acts contemplated in Article II of the Genocide Convention. The ICJ goes on to explain that, in order to infer the existence of the specific intent to destroy (*dolus specialis*) from a pattern of conduct, it is necessary that this is *the only inference that could reasonably be drawn* from the acts in question.[24]

Prosecutor v Radislav Krstić, decided by the ICTY Trial Chamber in August 2001 and upheld by the ICTY Appeals Chamber in April 2004, is illustrative of what is meant by destruction 'in part'. The case concerns the mass extermination in Srebrenica, situated in Eastern Bosnia, of Bosnian Muslims by Bosnian Serb paramilitary men. The armed attack of the Serbian forces on the Srebrenica enclave followed several years of confrontation. In July 1995, seven to eight thousand Bosnian Muslim men were captured by the Serbian forces known as the Army of Republica Srpska ('VRS'), most of whom were executed between 13 and 19 July 1995 with only very few survivors.

The ICTY Appeals Chamber in *Krstić* emphasizes that the determination of when the targeted part is substantial enough to meet this requirement may involve many considerations. The numeric size of the targeted part of the group is the necessary and important starting point, though not in all cases the ending point of the inquiry. The number of individuals targeted should be evaluated not only in absolute terms, but also in relation to the overall size of the entire group. In addition to the numeric size of the targeted portion, its prominence within the group can be a useful consideration. If a specific part of the group is emblematic of the overall group, or is essential to its survival, that may support a finding that the part qualifies as substantial for the purpose of genocide.[25]

Having identified the protected group as the national group of Bosnian Muslims, the ICTY Appeals Chamber rules in *Krstić* that the part the Serbian forces targeted was the Bosnian Muslims of Srebrenica, or the Bosnian Muslims of Eastern Bosnia. The size of the Bosnian Muslim population in Srebrenica prior to its capture by the VRS forces in 1995 amounted to approximately forty thousand people. Although this population constituted only a small percentage of the overall Muslim population of Bosnia and Herzegovina at the time, the

24 [2015] ICJ Rep 3, 64–7 [140]–[148].

25 *Prosecutor v Radislav Krstić*, Case IT-98-33-A, ICTY Appeals Chamber, 19 Apr 2004 para 12. Quoted with approval in *Prosecutor v. Radovan Karadžić*, Case IT-95-5/18-AR98bis.1, ICTY Appeals Chamber, 11 July 2013 para 66. See also *Prosecutor v Ratko Mladić*, Case MICT-13-56-A, International Residual Mechanism for Criminal Tribunals, Appeals Chamber, 8 June 2021 paras 569, 572, 576–583.

importance of the Muslim community of Srebrenica was not captured solely by its size. Srebrenica and the surrounding Central Podrinje region were of immense strategic importance to the Bosnian Serb leadership. Without Srebrenica, the ethnically Serb state of Republica Srpska they sought to create would remain divided into two disconnected parts, and its access to Serbia proper would be disrupted. The capture and ethnic purification of Srebrenica would therefore severely undermine the military efforts of the Bosnian Muslim State to ensure its viability, a consequence the Bosnian Muslim leadership fully realized and tried to prevent. Control over the Srebrenica region was consequently essential not only to the goal of some Bosnian Serb leaders of forming a viable political entity in Bosnia, but also to the continued survival of the Bosnian Muslim people. Because most of the Muslim inhabitants of the region had, by 1995, sought refuge within the Srebrenica enclave, the elimination of that enclave would have accomplished the goal of purifying the entire region of its Muslim population. In addition, Srebrenica was important due to its prominence in the eyes of both the Bosnian Muslims and the international community. The town of Srebrenica was the most visible of the 'safe areas' established by the UN Security Council in Bosnia 'free from armed attack or any other hostile act'. This guarantee of protection was re-affirmed by the commander of the UN Protection Force in Bosnia and reinforced with the deployment of UN troops. The elimination of the Muslim population of Srebrenica, despite the assurances given by the international community, would have served as a potent example to all Bosnian Muslims of their vulnerability and defencelessness in the face of Serb military forces. The fate of the Bosnian Muslims of Srebrenica would be 'emblematic' of that of all Bosnian Muslims. In executing the captured Bosnian Muslim men, the VRS did not differentiate between men of military status and civilians, the healthy and those severely handicapped. The group killed by the VRS included boys and elderly men. The ICTY was entitled to consider the long-term impact that the elimination of seven to eight thousand men from Srebrenica would have on the survival of that community. The scale of the killing, combined with the VRS Main Staff's awareness of the detrimental consequences it would have for the Bosnian Muslim community of Srebrenica and with the other actions the VRS Main Staff took to ensure that community's physical demise, was a sufficient factual basis for the finding of specific genocidal intent. The ICTY finds the killing was engineered and supervised by some members of the Main Staff of the VRS. The fact that genocidal intent was not attributed to a particular official within the Main Staff did not undermine the conclusion that Bosnian Serb forces carried out genocide against the Bosnian Muslims. They targeted for extinction the forty thousand Bosnian Muslims living in Srebrenica, a group emblematic of the Bosnian Muslims in general. They stripped all the male Muslim prisoners, military and civilian, elderly and young, of their personal belongings and identification, and deliberately and methodically killed them solely on the basis of their identity. The Bosnian Serb forces were aware, when they embarked on this genocidal venture, that the harm they caused would continue to plague the

Bosnian Muslims. The ICTY, therefore, concludes genocide has been committed in the extermination of the Bosnian Muslim men of Srebrenica.

Evidence of limited and selective assistance towards a few individuals who are members of a group targeted for genocide does not generally preclude a reasonable finding of the requisite intent to commit genocide, although it may be a factor in mitigation of the sentence to be imposed on the person convicted of genocide.[26]

Article III of the Genocide Convention lists the following acts as punishable under the Convention: (a) genocide; (b) conspiracy to commit genocide; (c) direct and public incitement to commit genocide; (d) attempt to commit genocide; and (e) complicity in genocide. Article IV adds that persons committing genocide or any of the other acts enumerated in Article III shall be punished, whether they are constitutionally responsible rulers, public officials or private individuals. Article V obligates the Contracting Parties to the Genocide Convention to undertake to enact, in accordance with their respective Constitutions, the necessary legislation to give effect to the provisions of the Genocide Convention, and, in particular, to provide effective penalties for persons guilty of genocide or any of the other acts enumerated in Article III.

By virtue of Article VI of the Genocide Convention, persons charged with genocide or any of the other acts enumerated in Article III shall be tried by a competent tribunal of the State in the territory of which the act was committed, or by such international penal tribunal as may have jurisdiction with respect to those Contracting Parties which shall have accepted its jurisdiction. Therefore, if genocide against the Rohingya is committed in Myanmar, the perpetrator must be tried by a competent tribunal of Myanmar or by an international criminal court or tribunal having jurisdiction over the crime. Since Myanmar is not party to the 1998 Rome Statute of the International Criminal Court,[27] the ICC may have jurisdiction over genocide committed in Myanmar only if the UN Security Council, exercising its authority under Chapter VII of the UN Charter[28] in response to threats to the peace, breaches of the peace and acts of aggression, refers the situation in Myanmar to the ICC Prosecutor pursuant to Article 13(b) of the Rome Statute, with retroactive effect.[29] Alternatively, Myanmar can, either voluntarily or as ordered by the ICJ, lodge a declaration with the ICC Registrar in accordance with Article 12(3) of the Rome Statute accepting the

26 *Prosecutor v Georges Ruggiu*, Case ICTR-97-32-I, ICTR Trial Chamber I, 1 June 2000 paras 73–4. See also *Prosecutor v Pauline Nyiramasuhuko et al.*, Case ICTR-98-42-T, ICTR Trial Chamber II, 24 June 2011 para 5723 and the cases cited in the accompanying footnote 14665.

27 2187 UNTS 3, in force 1 July 2002.

28 1 UNTS XVI, in force 24 Oct 1945.

29 As the UN Security Council, acting under Chapter VII of the UN Charter, did on 31 March 2005 by adopting a resolution (S/RES/1595 (2005) to ask the ICC Prosecutor to investigate alleged genocide, war crimes and crimes against humanity committed in in Darfur, Sudan, since 1 July 2002 (when the Rome Statute entered into force).

ICC's exercise of jurisdiction with respect to the crime of genocide in Myanmar, with retroactive effect.[30]

Article VII of the Genocide Convention adds that genocide and the other acts enumerated in Article III shall *not* be considered as political offences – which constitute an exception to extradition in general,[31] and the Contracting Parties pledge themselves in such cases to grant extradition in accordance with their laws and treaties in force.

Burden and standard of proof

How will the ICJ actually proceed to determine whether genocide or the other acts enumerated in Article III of the Genocide Convention have been committed in Myanmar and whether Myanmar has failed to prevent and/or punish such acts?

Guidance may be sought from the ICJ's Judgment in the Bosnian genocide case and the Croatian genocide case.

In the Bosnian genocide case, the ICJ must answer the question whether it may make a finding of genocide by a State in the absence of a prior conviction of an individual for genocide by a competent court. The ICJ reasons that the different procedures followed by, and powers available to, the ICJ and to the courts and tribunals trying persons for criminal offences do not themselves indicate there is a legal bar to the ICJ itself finding that genocide or the other acts enumerated in Article III of the Genocide Convention have been committed. Under the ICJ's Statute,[32] the ICJ has the capacity to undertake that task, while *applying the standard of proof appropriate to charges of exceptional gravity.* Turning to the terms of the Genocide Convention itself, the ICJ has jurisdiction under Article IX to find a State responsible if genocide or other acts enumerated in Article III are committed by its organs or persons or groups whose acts are attributable to it. Any other interpretation could mean there would be no legal recourse available under the Convention in some readily conceivable circumstances: genocide has allegedly been committed within a State by its leaders but they have not been

30 As in the case of Côte d'Ivoire, which accepted the ICC's jurisdiction on 18 April 2003, 14 December 2010 and 3 May 2011, before it ratified the Rome Statute on 15 February 2013. On 3 October 2011 and 22 February 2012, the ICC Pre-Trial Chamber III authorized the ICC Prosecutor to open an investigation in the situation in Côte d'Ivoire with respect to alleged crimes within the ICC's jurisdiction committed between 19 September 2002 and 28 November 2010 as well as with regard to crimes that may be committed in the future in the context of that situation.

31 The political offence exception to extradition is based on a two-fold rationale of maintaining a neutral position in internal political conflicts in another State and preventing the surrender of an offender to a jurisdiction where there is a risk that his trial or punishment might be unfairly influenced by political considerations (*per* Lord Diplock in the UK House of Lords' Judgment in *Cheng v Governor of Pentonville Prison* [1973] AC 931, 945).

32 (1945) 39 AJIL Supp 215, in force 24 Oct 1945.

brought to trial because, for instance, they are still very much in control of the powers of the State including the police, prosecution services and the courts and there is no international penal tribunal able to exercise jurisdiction over the alleged crimes; or the responsible State may have acknowledged the breach. The ICJ accordingly concludes that State responsibility can arise under the Genocide Convention for genocide and complicity without an individual being convicted by a competent court of the crime of genocide or an associated crime.[33]

The Applicant must discharge the *burden of proof* of establishing its case and a party asserting a fact must establish it.[34] As for the *standard of proof*, the ICJ has long recognized that claims against a State involving charges of exceptional gravity must be proved by evidence that is fully conclusive. The ICJ must be fully convinced that allegations made in the proceedings, that the crime of genocide or the other acts enumerated in Article III have been committed, have been clearly established. The same standard applies to the proof of attribution for such acts.[35] In respect of the Applicant's claim that the Respondent has breached its undertakings to prevent genocide and to punish and extradite persons charged with genocide, the ICJ requires proof at a high level of certainty appropriate to the seriousness of the allegation.[36] With regard to *methods of proof*, the parties in the Bosnian genocide case submitted a vast array of material, from different sources, including reports, resolutions and findings by various UN organs; documents from other intergovernmental organizations; documents, evidence and decisions from the ICTY; publications from governments; documents from NGOs; as well as media reports, articles and books. They also called witnesses, experts and witness-experts. The ICJ must itself make its own determination of the facts which are relevant to the law which the Applicant claims the Respondent has breached.[37]

Importantly, the ICJ acknowledges that the Bosnian genocide case does have *an unusual feature since many of the allegations before it have already been the subject of the processes and decisions of the ICTY*. Evidence obtained by examination of persons directly involved, and who were subsequently cross-examined by judges skilled in examination and experienced in assessing large amounts of factual information, some of it of a technical nature, merits special attention. The ICJ stresses this was the case with *the fact-finding process of the ICTY*, which gives rise to evidence obtained by persons directly involved, tested by cross-examination, the credibility of which has not been challenged subsequently.[38] Having set out the arguments of the parties on the weight to be given to the ICTY's material evidence and having reviewed the various ICTY processes, the ICJ concludes

33 [2007] ICJ Rep 43, 119–20 [181]–[182].
34 Ibid 128 [204].
35 Ibid 129 [209].
36 Ibid 130 [210].
37 Ibid 130 [211]–[212].
38 Ibid 130–1 [212]–[214], 134 [223].

it should in principle accept as highly persuasive relevant findings of fact made by the ICTY at trial, unless they have been overturned on appeal. For the same reasons, any evaluation by the ICTY based on the facts, for instance about the existence of the requisite intent for genocide, is also entitled to due weight. The ICJ also comments on the report entitled 'The Fall of Srebrenica', submitted by the UN Secretary-General to the UN General Assembly in November 1999. In the light of the care taken in preparing the aforesaid report, its comprehensive sources and the independence of those responsible for its preparation, the ICJ accords considerable authority to that report.[39]

According to the ICJ, the specific intent to destroy the group in whole or in part, has to be convincingly shown by reference to particular circumstances, *unless a general plan to that end can be convincingly demonstrated to exist*; and for a pattern of conduct to be accepted as evidence of its existence, it would have to be such that *it could only point to the existence of such intent*.[40]

In the genocide case brought by Bosnia and Herzegovina (the Applicant) against Serbia and Montenegro (the Respondent), the ICJ finds the Applicant has failed to establish the existence of that intent on the part of the Respondent, either on the basis of a concerted plan, or on the basis that the events reveal a consistent pattern of conduct which could only point to the existence of such intent. However, having concluded in the specific case of the massacres at Srebrenica in July 1995 that acts of genocide were committed, the ICJ turns to the question whether those acts at Srebrenica are attributable to the Respondent.[41]

To ascertain whether the Respondent's international responsibility can have been incurred, on whatever basis, in connection with the massacres committed in the Srebrenica area during the period in question, the ICJ must consider three interrelated questions in turn. *First*, it is to be determined whether the acts of genocide could be attributed to the Respondent because those acts were committed by its organs or persons whose acts are attributable to it under customary rules of State responsibility. *Second*, the ICJ is to ascertain whether acts of the kind referred to in Article III(b) to (e) of the Genocide Convention, other than genocide itself, were committed by persons or organs whose conduct is attributable to the Respondent under those same rules of State responsibility: that is to say, the acts referred to in Article III(b) to (e), one of these being complicity in genocide. *Finally*, it will be for the ICJ to rule on the issue as to whether the Respondent complied with its twofold obligation deriving from Article I of the Genocide Convention to *prevent and punish genocide*.[42]

On the *first* question, under the law of State responsibility, the conduct of any State organ is to be considered an act of the State under international law, and

39 Ibid 135–7 [228]–[230].
40 Ibid 196–7 [373].
41 Ibid 198 [376].
42 Ibid 199–200 [379].

therefore gives rise to the responsibility of the State, if it constitutes a breach of an international obligation of the State. When applied to the Bosnian genocide case, this rule first calls for a determination whether the acts of genocide committed in Srebrenica were perpetrated by 'persons or entities' having the status of organs of the Federal Republic of Yugoslavia, or FRY (as the Respondent was known at the time), under its internal law then in force. The ICJ finds nothing which could justify an affirmative response to this question. It has not been shown that the FRY army took part in the massacres, nor that the political leaders of the FRY had a hand in preparing, planning or in any way carrying out the massacres. Furthermore, neither the Republika Srpska nor the VRS was a *de jure* organ of the FRY, since none of them had the status of organ of that State under its internal law. According to the ICJ's case law, persons, groups of persons or entities may, for purposes of international responsibility, be equated with State organs even if that status does not follow from internal law, provided that in fact the persons, groups or entities act in 'complete dependence' on the State, of which they are ultimately merely the instrument. Nonetheless, the ICJ cannot find the persons or entities that committed the acts of genocide at Srebrenica had such ties with the FRY so that they could be deemed to have been completely dependent on it. The ICJ therefore finds the acts of genocide at Srebrenica cannot be attributed to the Respondent as having been committed by its organs or by persons or entities wholly dependent upon it, and thus do not on this basis entail the Respondent's international responsibility. The ICJ then determines whether the massacres at Srebrenica were committed by persons who, though not having the status of organs of the Respondent, nevertheless acted on its instructions or under its direction or control. For this purpose, it must be shown that '*effective control*' was exercised, or that the State's *instructions* were given, in respect of *each* operation in which the alleged violations occurred, *not generally in respect of the overall actions* taken by the persons or groups of persons having committed the violations. The ICJ finds, in the light of the information available to it, that it has not been so established.[43]

On the *second* question whether the Respondent is responsible for 'complicity in genocide', the ICJ must examine whether those organs or persons furnished 'aid or assistance' in the commission of the genocide at Srebrenica, in a sense not significantly different from that of those concepts in the general law of international responsibility. The ICJ also has to consider whether the organ or person furnishing *aid or assistance* to a perpetrator of the crime of genocide acted *knowingly*, that is to say, in particular, the organ or person was aware or should have been aware of the principal perpetrator's specific intent to destroy the Bosnian Muslim group, as such. The ICJ is not convinced by the evidence furnished by the Applicant that these conditions were met. In particular, it has not been established *beyond any doubt* whether the authorities of the FRY supplied — and

43 Ibid 202–15 [385]–[415].

continued to supply — the VRS leaders who decided upon and carried out those acts of genocide with their aid and assistance, at a time when those authorities were clearly aware that genocide was about to take place or was under way. What is clearly decisive in this connection is that it was not conclusively shown that the decision to eliminate physically the adult male population of the Muslim community from Srebrenica was brought to the attention of the authorities in Belgrade, the FRY's capital city, when it was taken.[44]

On the *third* and final question regarding the Respondent's alleged breach of the obligation to prevent and punish genocide, the duty to prevent genocide and the duty to punish its perpetrators are two distinct yet connected obligations under the Genocide Convention.[45]

The *obligation to prevent genocide* is one of *conduct and not one of result* – a State cannot be under an obligation to succeed, whatever the circumstances, in preventing the commission of genocide. The obligation of States Parties is rather to employ all means reasonably available to them, so as to prevent genocide so far as possible. A State does not incur responsibility simply because the desired result is not achieved; responsibility is however incurred if the State *manifestly failed* to take all measures to prevent genocide which were within its power, and which might have contributed to preventing the genocide.[46] In any event, a State can be held responsible for breaching the obligation to prevent genocide *only if* genocide was actually committed, and it is at the time when commission of the prohibited act (genocide or any of the other acts listed in Article III of the Convention) begins that the breach of the obligation of prevention occurs.[47]

In this regard, the ICJ underlines the significant differences between the requirements to be met before a State can be held to have violated the obligation to prevent genocide — within the meaning of Article I of the Genocide Convention — and those to be satisfied in order for a State to be held responsible for 'complicity in genocide' — within the meaning of Article III(e). Complicity always requires that some positive action has been taken to furnish aid or assistance to the perpetrators of the genocide, while a violation of the obligation to prevent results from mere failure to adopt and implement suitable measures to prevent genocide from being committed. In other words, while complicity results from commission, violation of the obligation to prevent results from omission; this is merely the reflection of the notion that the ban on genocide and the other acts listed in Article III, including complicity, places States under a negative obligation, the obligation not to commit the prohibited acts, while the duty to prevent places States under positive obligations, to do their best to ensure that such acts do not occur. There cannot be a finding of complicity against a

44 Ibid 215–9 [416]–[424].
45 Ibid 219–20 [427].
46 Ibid 221 [430].
47 Ibid 221–2 [431].

State unless at the least its organs were aware that genocide was about to be committed or was under way, and if the aid and assistance supplied, from the moment they became so aware onward, to the perpetrators of the criminal acts or to those who were on the point of committing them, enabled or facilitated the commission of the acts. Put differently, an accomplice must have given support in perpetrating the genocide with full knowledge of the facts. By contrast, a State may be found to have violated its obligation to prevent even though it had no certainty, at the time when it should have acted but failed to do so, that genocide was about to be committed or was under way; for it to incur responsibility on this basis it is enough that the State was aware, or should normally have been aware, of the serious danger that acts of genocide would be committed.[48]

Considering the FRY's conduct *vis-à-vis* the Srebrenica massacres, the ICJ notes that, during the period under consideration, the FRY was in *a position of influence* over the Bosnian Serbs who devised and implemented the genocide in Srebrenica, unlike that of any of the other States Parties to the Genocide Convention, owing to the strength of the political, military and financial links between the FRY, on the one hand, and the Republika Srpska and the VRS, on the other, which, though somewhat weaker than in the preceding period, nonetheless remained very close. The ICJ further notes that, on the relevant date, the FRY was bound by very specific obligations by virtue of the two Orders of the ICJ indicating provisional measures delivered in 1993. In particular, in its Order of 8 April 1993,[49] the ICJ ordered the FRY to, among other things, ensure

> that any military, paramilitary or irregular armed units which may be directed or supported by it, as well as any organizations and persons which may be subject to its control, direction or influence, do not commit any acts of genocide, of conspiracy to commit genocide, of direct and public incitement to commit genocide, or of complicity in genocide.

The ICJ's use of the term 'influence' is particularly revealing of the fact that the Order concerned not only the persons or entities whose conduct was attributable to the FRY, but also all those with whom the Respondent maintained close links and on which it could exert a certain influence.[50]

Finally, although it has not found that the information available to the Belgrade authorities indicated, as a matter of certainty, *that genocide was imminent* (which is why complicity in genocide was not upheld by the ICJ), they could *hardly have been unaware of the serious risk* of it once the VRS forces had decided to militarily occupy the Srebrenica enclave. Therefore, in view of their undeniable

48 Ibid 222–3 [432].

49 *Application of the Convention on the Prevention and Punishment of the Crime of Genocide*, Provisional Measures, Order of 8 Apr 1993 [1993] ICJ Rep 3, 24 [52 A (2)].

50 [2007] ICJ Rep 43, 223–4 [434]–[435].

influence and of the information, voicing serious concern, in their possession, the FRY authorities should have made the best efforts within their power to try and prevent the tragic events then taking shape, whose scale, though it could not have been foreseen with certainty, might at least have been surmised. The FRY leadership, and its President Milošević above all, were fully aware of the climate of deep-seated hatred between the Bosnian Serbs and the Muslims in the Srebrenica region. Yet the Respondent has not shown it took any initiative to prevent what happened, or any action on its part to avert the atrocities which were committed. In the ICJ's opinion, the organs of the Respondent did nothing to prevent the Srebrenica massacres, claiming they were powerless to do so, which hardly tallies with their known influence over the VRS. *For a State to be held responsible for breaching its obligation of prevention, there is no need to prove that the State concerned definitely had the power to prevent the genocide; it is sufficient that it had the means to do so and manifestly refrained from using them.* The Respondent was held by the ICJ to have violated its obligation to prevent the Srebrenica genocide in such a manner as to engage its international responsibility.[51]

On the Respondent's *obligation to punish the genocide* in Srebrenica, the genocide was not carried out in the Respondent's territory. Hence, the Respondent cannot be charged with not having tried before its own courts those accused of having participated in the Srebrenica genocide, either as principal perpetrators or as accomplices, or of having committed one of the other acts mentioned in Article III of the Genocide Convention in connection with the Srebrenica genocide. The ICJ then proceeds to consider whether the Respondent fulfilled its obligation to cooperate with the 'international penal tribunal' referred to in Article VI of the Genocide Convention. The ICJ deems the ICTY to constitute an 'international penal tribunal' within the meaning of Article VI and the Respondent must be regarded as having 'accepted the jurisdiction' of the ICTY within the meaning of the provision from, at the latest, 14 December 1995, the date of the signing and entry into force of the General Framework Agreement for Peace in Bosnia and Herzegovina between Bosnia and Herzegovina, Croatia and the FRY.[52] Annex 1A of that Agreement, made binding on the parties by virtue of its Article II, obligates them to fully cooperate, notably with the ICTY.[53]

In its Judgment of 2015 in the Croatian genocide case, the ICJ reiterates that the value of reports from official or independent bodies depends, among other things, on (1) the source of the item of evidence, (2) the process by which it has been generated and (3) the quality or character of the item.[54] In its general conclusion on the specific genocidal intent, the ICJ finds Croatia has not established that the only reasonable inference that can be drawn from the pattern of conduct

51 Ibid 224–6 [436]–[438].
52 (1996) 35 ILM 89, 172.
53 [2007] ICJ Rep 43, 226–9 [442]–[449].
54 [2015] ICJ Rep 3, 76 [190].

it relied upon was the intent to destroy, in whole or in part, the Croat group. The acts constituting genocide within the meaning of Article II(a) and (b) of the Genocide Convention were not committed with the specific intent required for them to be characterized as acts of genocide. Besides, the ICTY Prosecutor has never charged any individual on account of genocide against the Croat population in the context of the armed conflict which took place in the territory of Croatia in the period 1991–1995.[55] Accordingly, held the ICJ, no issue of State responsibility under the Genocide Convention for the commission of genocide can arise in that particular case. Nor can there be any question of responsibility for a failure to prevent genocide, a failure to punish genocide or complicity in genocide. Because *dolus specialis* has not been established by Croatia, its claims of conspiracy to commit genocide, direct and public incitement to commit genocide and attempt to commit genocide also necessarily fail.[56]

The ICJ's high threshold of proving the specific genocidal intent *without* prior trial by an international criminal court or tribunal such as the ICTY or the ICTR has been referred to by Myanmar in the oral hearings in the ICJ in December 2019.

Myanmar points out that in both the Bosnian and Croatian genocide cases the ICJ was assisted immensely by the work of the two *ad hoc* tribunals. Although more limited, there is some activity at the International Criminal Court that may be of help to the ICJ. It manifests the drawing of an alternative inference, *other than genocidal intent*, for the alleged conduct of Myanmar. In April 2018, the ICC Prosecutor applied to a Pre-Trial Chamber for a form of advisory opinion as to whether she might be able to exercise jurisdiction over the crime against humanity of deportation given the huge cross-border flows from Myanmar into Bangladesh in 2017. Her application, as well as all of the subsequent proceedings in this matter before the ICC, relied very heavily on the same materials that The Gambia invokes in this case before the ICJ, principally the reports by the UN Fact-Finding Mission, or IIFFMM. In this connection, Myanmar reminds the ICJ that its previous Judgments in the two genocide cases have taken into account the activities of the Prosecutors of international criminal tribunals.

In her application, the ICC Prosecutor said 'the Rohingya people were specifically and intentionally deported into Bangladesh'. She referred to the initiation on 25 August 2017 of a 'clearance operation' aimed at deporting all remaining Rohingya across the border to Bangladesh. She expressly distinguished the situation 'from a mass exodus of civilians from one State caused for instance by an ongoing armed conflict, without evidence of deportation *per se*'. In other words, in her view, the intent of the so-called 'clearance operation' was deportation from Myanmar, not physical destruction. Myanmar alludes to the ICJ's reasoning in its Judgment in the Bosnian genocide case that the forced displacement

55 Ibid 128 [440].
56 Ibid 128–9 [441].

of a population, even if proved, would not in itself constitute the prohibited act of genocide, and that neither the intent, as a matter of policy, to render an area 'ethnically homogeneous', nor the operations that may be carried out to implement such policy, can *as such* be designated as genocide, since the deportation or displacement of the members of a group, even if effected by force, is not necessarily equivalent to destruction of that group.

Myanmar stresses that the most substantial discussion of genocidal intent and the one on which the Application largely relies is that of the IIFFMM in its 2018 report. In Myanmar's view, while the IIFFMM concludes without equivocation that crimes against humanity and war crimes were committed, the IIFFMM is somewhat more circumspect regarding genocide, saying there is 'sufficient information to warrant the investigation and prosecution of senior officials in the Tatmadaw chain of command, so that a competent court can determine their liability for genocide in relation to the situation in Rakhine state'. The IIFFMM also adds the following *caveat*: 'This standard of proof is lower than that required in criminal proceedings.' The IIFFMM devotes 113 words in a 440-page supplement to considering whether the intent may have been 'to displace the Rohingya population, but not to seek its ultimate destruction', doing a little bit of textual sleight of hand by referring to the 'physical destruction of Rohingya life as it once was', a formulation that, submits Myanmar, ever so slightly blurs an important distinction between physical and cultural genocide. Elsewhere, the IIFFMM states: 'The crimes in Rakhine state, and the manner in which they were perpetrated, are similar in nature, gravity and scope to those that have allowed genocidal intent to be established in other contexts', but without providing any reference or examples to what those other contexts are. The IIFFMM is thus 'campaigning for a case' rather than assessing a situation in an objective and impartial manner, and the IIFFMM is indifferent as to factors that tend to prove the contrary. Moreover, continues Myanmar, the IIFFMM is not entirely consistent on the subject of intent. For example, when it discusses what it calls a policy of 'food starvation', the IIFFMM says such 'targeted actions to deny access to food appear to constitute a policy of forcing Rohingya to flee through food deprivation', which is not the same thing and does not necessarily point to physical destruction. Other statements in the IIFFMM's report also point to an intent other than one to destroy. It speaks in the report of the so-called 'Four Cuts' counter-insurgency policy, which has allegedly been practised since the 1960s and implemented through 'clearance operations', essentially scorched earth campaigns in which large numbers of civilians are killed and entire villages destroyed, leading to mass displacement. However, argues Myanmar, nobody is seriously alleging there has been a policy driven by genocidal intent underway since the 1960s.

With respect to the IIFFMM's September 2019 report alleging that genocidal intent has 'strengthened', Myanmar submits that there is no explanation why the IIFFMM has reached such a conclusion especially when there is no real evidence of any aggravation of the situation described in the report of the previous year.

If anything, the absence of allegations of significant numbers of killings in the 2019 report ought to suggest the contrary to what the IIFFMM concludes.

The IIFFMM's mandate from the UN Human Rights Council was 'to establish the facts and circumstances', not to make legal findings. Most importantly, maintains Myanmar, the validity of the IIFFMM's opinion about genocidal intent is undermined by its failure to consider, in any substantive manner, the issue of alternative explanations. In Myanmar's view, although the IIFFMM's reports may contain valuable factual information, its legal determination should simply be disregarded by the ICJ because of its flawed approach.

Myanmar also points out that nowhere does The Gambia's Application specify the number of deaths or the total number of deaths, and compare this with the size of the population that was allegedly attacked and that crossed the border into Bangladesh. Information on this point can be found in the lengthy annex to the IIFFMM's 2018 report, estimating 10,000 deaths, 725,000 refugees who fled to Bangladesh and 600,000 who remained in Myanmar. The application by the ICC Prosecutor also alleges 'the killing of up to 10,000 Rohingya' and 'the deportation of over 700,000 Rohingya into Bangladesh'. Myanmar thus questions whether The Gambia has neglected to provide the ICJ with allegations and evidence of the estimated total number of deaths because The Gambia sees this as weakening The Gambia's claim that the intent was physical destruction of the Rohingya. In any event, Myanmar will produce evidence challenging the figure of 10,000 as an exaggeration. Any estimate of the number of killings ought also to provide some indication of the number of combatant deaths, and those attributable to the Arakan Rohingya Salvation Army, or ARSA. In the Croatian genocide case, the ICJ also considers it relevant to compare the size of the targeted part of the protected group with the number of Croat victims, in order to determine whether the Yugoslav People's Army ('JNA') and Serb forces used opportunities to destroy that part of the group. In this connection, Croatia put forward a figure of 12,500 Croat deaths, which was contested by Serbia. The ICJ notes that, even assuming this figure is correct – an issue on which it will make no ruling – the number of victims alleged by Croatia is small in relation to the size of the targeted part of the group. The ICJ thus concludes Croatia has not established that the only reasonable inference that can be drawn from the pattern of conduct it relied upon was the intent to destroy, in whole or in part, the Croat group.

Myanmar refers to the IIFFMM's estimate of 600,000 Rohingya who stayed on in Myanmar as signifying this is a claim of human rights violations, of persecution, but not of destruction of the Rohingya. Had there been a genocidal plan afoot, argues Myanmar, one would expect a more sinister fate for the Rohingya. The similarities with the situation in Myanmar, as alleged in The Gambia's Application, and the ICJ's findings in the Croatian genocide case are striking in other respects. In the Croatian genocide case, the ICJ has found that, as emerges in particular from the ICTY's findings, forced displacement was the instrument of a policy aimed at establishing an ethnically homogeneous Serb State. In that context, the expulsion of the Croats was brought about by the creation of a coercive atmosphere, generated by the commission of acts including some that constitute the act of genocide within the meaning of Article II(a) and (b) of the Genocide Convention. Those acts had an objective, namely the forced displacement of the Croats, which did not entail their physical destruction. The ICJ finds the acts committed by the JNA and Serb forces essentially had the effect of making the Croat population flee the territories concerned; it was not a question of systematically destroying that population, but of forcing it to leave the areas controlled by these armed forces.

The Gambia rebuts Myanmar's above arguments as follows. Myanmar has not denied that the IIFFMM has concluded 'there is no reasonable conclusion to draw, other than the inference of genocidal intent, from the State's pattern of conduct'. Nor has Myanmar denied the IIFFMM's aforesaid conclusion is based on seven specific indicators, which it finds to be 'indicators of genocidal intent in international case law'. First, the Tatmadaw's extreme brutality during its attacks on the Rohingya. Second, the organized nature of the Tatmadaw's destruction. Third, the enormity and nature of the sexual violence perpetrated against women and girls during the 'clearance operations'. Fourth, the insulting, derogatory, racist and exclusionary utterances of Myanmar officials and others prior, during and after the 'clearance operations'. Fifth, the existence of discriminatory plans and policies, such as the Citizenship Law and the national verification card process, as well as the Myanmar Government's efforts to clear, raze, confiscate and build on land in a manner that sought to change the demographic and ethnic composition of Rakhine state. Sixth, the Myanmar Government's tolerance for public rhetoric of hatred and contempt for the Rohingya. Seventh, Myanmar's failure to investigate and prosecute gross violations of international human rights law and serious violations of international humanitarian law.

According to The Gambia, there is very little evidence that the Tatmadaw's 'clearance operations' were primarily directed at insurgents or terrorists, and not at the Rohingya population. The Gambia does not say there were no insurgents, or Myanmar does not have the right to take military action against them – but armed conflict can never be an excuse for genocide. The IIFFMM's conclusions, in its 2019 report, do summarize the evidence of Myanmar's genocidal intentions having 'strengthened' over the past year, including the Myanmar Government's hostile policies toward the Rohingya such as its continued denial of citizenship and ethnic identity, the living conditions to which it subjects them, its failure to reform laws that subjugate the Rohingya people, the continuation of hate speech directed at the Rohingya, its prior commission of genocide and its disregard for accountability in relation to the 'clearance operations' of 2016 and 2017. Much of the IIFFMM's report consists of extensive details supporting all of these findings. Incidentally, the Associated Press has located at least five mass graves of Rohingya inside Myanmar.

In its ruling in the Croatian genocide case, the ICJ states that for a pattern of conduct to be accepted as evidence of genocidal intent, it would have to be such that it could only point to the existence of such intent, that is to say, that it can only reasonably be understood as reflecting that intent. The Gambia's Application is based squarely on that standard. So are the conclusions of the IIFFMM and of the Special Rapporteur and the US Holocaust Memorial Museum, which is a US federal institution with a Board of Trustees which includes four members of the US Senate and five members of the US House of Representatives. The latter has found 'compelling evidence that the Burmese military committed ethnic cleansing, crimes against humanity, and genocide against the Rohingya'.

On Myanmar's argument that it cannot possibly be a genocide if the ICC has not said it is a genocide, The Gambia explains that as Myanmar is not a party to the Rome Statute, but Bangladesh is, the ICC's jurisdiction only extends to acts occurring on the territory of Bangladesh and no element of the crime of genocide has been committed on Bangladesh's territory. However, the crime of deportation which is a crime against humanity might have been committed on Bangladesh's territory, as it is a transboundary crime. This is in no way inconsistent with the existence of a genocidal intent in respect of other acts. Indeed, the ICTY's genocide cases relating to Srebrenica also include the crime against humanity of deportation.[57] As the ICJ has made clear in its Judgment in the Bosnian genocide case, acts of 'ethnic cleansing' may occur in parallel to acts prohibited by Article II of the Genocide Convention, and may be significant as indicative of the presence of a specific intent inspiring those acts. In 2015, the ICJ has reaffirmed in its Judgment in the Croatian genocide case that acts of 'ethnic cleansing' can indeed be elements in the implementation of a genocidal plan.

Myanmar, availing itself of the right to counter-rebut The Gambia's rebuttal, argues that the seven specific indicators mentioned by The Gambia consist of long recitals of human rights violations which indeed may be present, and in fact are inevitably present, if the genocide takes place. But, contends Myanmar, these are also present in so many other environments and in so many other contexts where genocide has not taken place, is not taking place and is highly, highly unlikely to take place. First, one can well imagine how many countries will generate evidence of 'extreme brutality'. Second, the organized nature of the activities or of the acts is present in many situations. Third, sexual violence regrettably occurs in many parts of the world. Fourth, hate speech is a phenomenon not reserved to Myanmar and some countries even insist it may even fall within the protected domain of freedom of expression. The IIFFMM refers to only one fact of hate speech, a reference by the Tatmadaw Commander-in-Chief to 'clearance operations', and cites this famous Facebook post that 'The Bengali problem is a long-standing one which

57 The Gambia cites *Prosecutor v Vujadin Popovic* (Judgment), Case IT-05-88-T, ICTY Trial Chamber II, 10 June 2010; *Prosecutor v. Momir Nikolic* (Sentencing Judgment), Case IT-02-60/1-S, ICTY Trial Chamber I(A), 2 Dec 2003.

has become an unfinished job despite the efforts of the previous government to solve it. The government in office is taking great care in solving the problem'. This is the damning evidence of genocidal intent, allegedly. However, argues Myanmar, there is no reference here to 'clearance operations', despite what is said later in the report and the suggestion that this reference in the Facebook post is to 'clearance operations'. Myanmar concludes the IIFFMM is not very careful in its reference to the Facebook post although this allegation seems to it to be crucial to its claim of genocidal intent. Be that as it may, continues Myanmar, the statement on the Facebook post is one to which many different meanings can be attached – it certainly could not be described as hate speech of the sort one hears about circulating on Facebook and other social media in many parts of the world. The fifth of the list of indicators of genocide is discriminatory policies about citizenship and residency, but the existence of discriminatory plans and policies dealing with citizenship and mobility and entry to the country is hardly the monopoly of Myanmar in our modern world. The sixth indicator is the tolerance of public rhetoric of hate speech, but examples in other countries abound. Finally, the failure to prosecute is a problem in many parts of the world.

Myanmar points out The Gambia's Application is the first Application submitted to the ICJ based on the Genocide Convention where an estimate of the total number of victims is not provided by the Applicant. Recently, the ICTY Prosecutor attempted, as he had done on other occasions, to invoke the Srebrenica precedent in order to charge the crime of genocide with respect to much lower levels of killing than that in Srebrenica, levels of killings similar to the ones mentioned by The Gambia in the ICJ, drawn from the IIFFMM's report, and the ICTY judges have consistently refused to follow him.

At this juncture, the present author should like to make the following observations.

When an international court or tribunal, including the ICJ, is asked to rely on third-party findings of facts, it gives weight to findings through a court-like process that are tested in an adversarial setting, such as the ICTY. As the ICJ explains in one case, it will treat with caution evidentiary materials specially prepared for a case before it and also materials emanating from a single source. It prefers contemporaneous evidence from persons with direct knowledge. It gives particular attention to reliable evidence acknowledging facts or conduct unfavourable to the State represented by the person making them. The ICJ also gives weight to evidence that has not, even before the litigation before it, been challenged by impartial persons for the correctness of what it contains. The ICJ, moreover, notes that evidence obtained by examination of persons directly involved, and who were subsequently cross-examined by judges skilled in examination and experienced in assessing large amounts of factual information, some of it of a technical nature, merits special attention. In that particular case, the ICJ gives appropriate consideration to the report of a commission of judicial inquiry set up by the Respondent which gathered evidence in this manner, whose credibility has not been challenged since its publication and which has been accepted by both parties in that particular case before the ICJ.[58] In the Bosnian genocide case, the ICJ gives considerable authority to the report entitled 'The Fall of Srebrenica', which the UN Secretary-General submitted to UN the General Assembly in November 1999, due to the care taken in its preparation, its comprehensive sources and the independence of those responsible for its preparation. In the Croatian genocide case, the ICJ gives evidential weight to the report on the situation of human rights in the territory of the former Yugoslavia of 7 November 1995, presented to the UN General Assembly and the UN Security Council by Mrs Elisabeth Rehn, Special Rapporteur of the Commission on Human Rights, because of the independent status of its author and because it was prepared at the request of organs of the UN for purposes of the exercise of their functions. Croatia has not disputed the objective nature of that report, even though it does not agree with certain of its factual findings.[59]

The ICJ has been careful to treat press reports with great caution. The ICJ concedes, however, that although press information is not to be treated in itself as evidence for judicial purposes, public knowledge of a fact may nevertheless be established by means of these sources of information and the ICJ can attach a certain amount of weight to such public knowledge. Widespread reports of a fact may prove on closer examination to derive from a single source, and such reports, however numerous, will in such cases have no greater value as evidence than the original source. It is with this important reservation that newspaper reports should be examined in order to assess the facts of the case, and in particular to ascertain whether such facts were matters of public knowledge. In one case, on the basis of information, including press and broadcast material, which was 'wholly consistent and concordant as to the main facts and circumstances of the case', the ICJ was able to declare it was satisfied that the allegations of fact were well-founded.[60]

Witnesses may be called by the ICJ who may be cross-examined. For example, in the Croatian genocide case the ICJ gives evidential weight to the statements by the eight individuals called by Serbia to testify before it. The fact that Croatia declined to cross-examine those witnesses in no sense implies an obligation on the ICJ to accept all of their testimony as accurate. Moreover, Croatia clearly stated that its decision not to cross-examine the witnesses did not mean it accepted their testimonies as accurate; on the contrary, it expressed significant reservations in relation to some of them. The other documents and testimony were duly considered by the ICJ, without, however, being regarded as conclusive proof of the facts alleged.

58 *Armed Activities on the Territory of the Congo (Democratic Republic of the Congo v Uganda)* [2005] ICJ Rep 168, 201 [61].

59 [2015] ICJ Rep 3, 133 [459].

60 *Military and Paramilitary Activities in and against Nicaragua (Nicaragua v United States of America)* [1986] ICJ Rep 14, 40–1 [63].

In addition, Article 50 of the ICJ Statute allows the ICJ, at any time, to entrust any individual, body, bureau, commission or other organization that it may select with the task of carrying out an enquiry or giving an expert opinion. Article 66 of the ICJ's Rules allows the ICJ at any time, either at its own initiative or at the request of a party, to exercise its functions with regard to the obtaining of evidence at a place or locality to which the case relates. Pursuant to Article 67 of the Rules, if the ICJ considers it necessary to arrange for an enquiry or an expert opinion, it shall, after hearing the parties, issue an order to that effect, defining the subject of the enquiry or expert opinion, stating the number and mode of the persons to hold the enquiry or of the experts, and laying down the procedure to be followed. The ICJ has used experts appointed by it to verify facts on the ground as well as to assess the actual amount of damages in the *Corfu Channel* case between Albania and the UK.[61]

The UN Human Rights Council has set up the Independent Investigative Mechanism for Myanmar, or IIMM, as an ongoing independent mechanism to collect, consolidate, preserve and analyse evidence of the most serious crimes and violations of international law committed in Myanmar since 2011, in order to facilitate and expedite fair and independent criminal proceedings, in accordance with international law standards, in national, regional or international courts or tribunals that have or may in the future have jurisdiction over these crimes, in accordance with international law. In addition, the Jurisdiction, Complementarity and Cooperation Division of the Office of the ICC Prosecutor has been collecting evidence for a case involving crimes against humanity against the Rohingya, including through interviews with Rohingya refugees and witnesses. The Division is working in cooperation with the ICJ in this respect. One has to wait and see whether the outcome of the work of these two bodies will be held by the ICJ to be as authoritative as the factual and evidentiary findings of an international criminal court such as the ICTY.

There seems to be some confusion as regards the *standard of proving* genocide or other acts enumerated in Article II of the Genocide Convention. In the two previous genocide cases before the ICJ, the ICJ rules it must be 'fully convinced' that the Applicant's allegations about genocide have been 'clearly established'. The ICJ goes on to state that 'the same standard applies to the proof of attribution for such acts'. As regards the Applicant's claim that the Respondent has breached its undertakings to prevent genocide and to punish and extradite persons charged with genocide, the ICJ requires 'proof at a high level of certainty appropriate to the seriousness of the allegation'. With due respect, the ICJ should have made it clear that, as a general principle of criminal law, criminal courts, including the ICTY, ICTR and ICC, use the standard of proof of 'beyond reasonable doubt'

61 *Corfu Channel*, Order of 17 Dec 1948 [1948] ICJ Rep 124; *Corfu Channel*, Judgment [1949] ICJ Rep 4, 20–2; *Corfu Channel (Assessment of compensation due from Albania to the UK)*, Judgment [1949] ICJ Rep 244.

to establish individual criminal responsibility, as opposed to State responsibility, and convict the accused.[62] As the Appeals Chamber of the ICTR has held in *Sylvestre Gacumbitsi*, in order to find a person guilty of genocide the Prosecution must discharge 'its burden to prove each element of its case, including genocidal intent, beyond reasonable doubt'.[63] The ICTR has also consistently ruled that in the absence of direct evidence, a perpetrator's intent to commit genocide may be inferred from relevant facts and circumstances that lead 'beyond any reasonable doubt' to the existence of the intent.[64]

Guidance may also be sought from the oft-cited Articles on Responsibility of States for Internationally Wrongful Acts,[65] submitted by the UN International Law Commission, or ILC, to the UN General Assembly in 2001. These Articles do not deal with issues of evidence or the burden of proof to establish State responsibility.[66] Nevertheless, Article 2 (Elements of an internationally wrongful act of a State) of the Articles reads: 'There is an internationally wrongful act of a State when conduct consisting of an action or omission: (a) is attributable to the State under international law; and (b) constitutes a breach of an international obligation of the State'. According to paragraph 3 of the ILC's Commentary to Article 2, there are *other standards* outside of the context of Article 2 just mentioned and '[*s*]*uch standards vary from one context to another* for reasons which essentially relate to the object and purpose of the treaty provision or other rule giving rise to the primary obligation' – '[*e*]*stablishing these is a matter for the interpretation and application of the primary rules engaged in the given case*'.[67]

The primary rules governing commission of genocide are to the effect that the elements of the crime of genocide comprise the commission of any of the acts enumerated in Article II and Article III of the Genocide Convention with intent to destroy, in whole or in part, a national, ethnical, racial or religious group, as such. In order to be punished, it must be proven beyond reasonable doubt in accordance with the general principle of criminal law that the accused individual has committed any of such acts.

Therefore, in order to find Myanmar 'individuals' guilty of the crime of genocide pursuant to Article II or of any acts enumerated in Article III of the Genocide Convention, the ICJ must, first of all, find them so guilty beyond reasonable doubt. Moreover, as the ICTY Appeals Chamber has affirmed, the principle that the accused must be given the benefit of the doubt (*in dubio pro reo*),

62 *Prosecutor v Goran Jelisić*, Case IT-95-10-A, ICTY Appeals Chamber, 5 July 2001 paras 35–7, followed in *Prosecutor v Laurent Gbagbo and Charles Blé Goudé*, Case 02/11-01/15 A, ICC Appeals Chamber, Judgment, 31 Mar 2021 paras 305–17.

63 *Sylvestre Gacumbitsi v Prosecutor*, Case ICTR-2001-64-A, ICTR Appeals Chamber, 7 July 2006 para 41.

64 *Ephrem Setako* para 467 and the cases cited therein.

65 A/RES/56/83 (12 Dec 2001) Annex and A/56/49(Vol. I)/Corr.4.

66 As explained in para 8 of the ILC's Commentary to Chapter V (Circumstances precluding wrongfulness) of the Articles on Responsibility of States for Internationally Wrongful Acts.

67 Emphasis added, footnote omitted.

as a corollary to the presumption of innocence and the burden of proof beyond a reasonable doubt, applies to findings required for conviction, such as those which make up the elements of the crime charged.[68]

Only after the guilt of an individual has been proved beyond reasonable doubt may the ICJ proceed to determine whether the conduct of the individual is attributable to Myanmar, as a nation State, and, if so determined, whether Myanmar has breached its obligations under the Genocide Convention – the standard of proof here for the purpose of State responsibility under international law has been referred to by the ICJ in numerous Judgments. For example, the ICJ in *Oil Platform (Islamic Republic of Iran v USA)* uses the terms 'direct evidence', which is not merely 'suggestive', and 'conclusive' evidence by the State making the assertion.[69] In other cases, the ICJ refers to the need for 'conclusive evidence',[70] 'a degree of certainty',[71] 'inferences of fact ...[which] leave *no room* for reasonable doubt',[72] 'degree of certainty ... supported by convincing evidence',[73] 'clear evidence',[74] '[relevant facts] convincingly established by the evidence',[75] 'evidence [that is] weighty and convincing'[76] and 'evidence that is fully conclusive'.[77]

Provisional measures indicated by the ICJ

The Gambia's Application also requests the ICJ to indicate provisional measures, seeking to protect the rights of the Rohingya group and those of The Gambia under the Genocide Convention, and to prevent the aggravation or extension of the dispute pending the ICJ's final Judgment in this case.

Specifically, The Gambia's requested provisional measures duplicate the provisional measures indicated by the ICJ on 8 April 1993 in the Bosnian genocide case.[78] In that Order, the ICJ indicates three provisional measures. First, the Government of the Federal Republic of Yugoslavia (Serbia and Montenegro) should immediately, in pursuance of its undertaking in the 1948 Genocide Convention, take all measures within its power to prevent commission of the crime of genocide. Second, the aforesaid Government should in particular ensure

68 *Prosecutor v Limaj et al.*, Case IT-03-66-A, ICTY Appeals Chamber, 29 Sept 2007 para 21 and the cases cited therein.
69 [2003] ICJ Rep 161, 190 [59] and 195 [71].
70 *Corfu Channel* [1949] CJ Rep 4, 17.
71 Ibid.
72 Ibid 18 (emphasis original).
73 *Military and Paramilitary in and against Nicaragua* [1986] ICJ Rep 14, 24 [29].
74 Ibid 62 [109].
75 *DR Congo v Uganda* [2005] ICJ Rep 168, 205 [72]. The ICJ in that case also uses the term 'convincing evidence' (ibid 209 [91]).
76 Ibid 220 [136].
77 Bosnian genocide case [2007] ICJ Rep 43, 129 [209].
78 *Application of the Convention on the Prevention and Punishment of the Crime of Genocide*, Provisional Measures, Order of 8 Apr 1993 [1993] ICJ Rep 3.

that any military, paramilitary or irregular armed units which may be directed or supported by it, as well as any organizations and persons which may be subject to its control, direction or influence, do not commit any acts of genocide, of conspiracy to commit genocide, of direct and public incitement to commit genocide or of complicity in genocide, whether directed against the Muslim population of Bosnia and Herzegovina or against any other national, ethnical, racial or religious group. Third, the aforesaid Government and the Government of Bosnia and Herzegovina should not take any action and should ensure that no action is taken which may aggravate or extend the existing dispute over the prevention or punishment of the crime of genocide, or render it more difficult of solution. In addition, The Gambia elaborates the specific acts to be covered by the ICJ's Order as

> extrajudicial killings or physical abuse; rape or other forms of sexual violence; burning of homes or villages; destruction of lands and livestock, deprivation of food and other necessities of life, or any other deliberate infliction of conditions of life calculated to bring about the physical destruction of the Rohingya group in whole or in part.

The Gambia also adds to the aforesaid requested provisional measures the following three requested provisional measures. First, Myanmar shall not destroy or render inaccessible any evidence related to the events described in the Application, including without limitation by destroying or rendering inaccessible the remains of any member of the Rohingya group who is a victim of alleged genocidal acts, or altering the physical locations where such acts are alleged to have occurred in such a manner as to render the evidence of such acts, if any, inaccessible. Second, Myanmar and The Gambia shall each provide a report to the ICJ on all measures taken to give effect to this Order for provisional measures, no later than four months from its issuance. Third, Myanmar shall grant access to, and cooperate with, all UN fact-finding bodies that are engaged in investigating alleged genocidal acts against the Rohingya, including the conditions to which the Rohingya are subjected.

Requests for provisional measures of interim protection are urgent proceedings, with priority over other non-urgent proceedings.[79] The ICJ's decision on a request for provisional is a preliminary one that is without prejudice to the merits of the case. The requisite threshold for the ICJ to indicate provisional measures is that the ICJ considers that it has *prima facie* jurisdiction over the issues covered by the Application.[80] This merely requires the ICJ to satisfy itself that the rights the requesting party claims on the merits and seeks to protect are 'at least plausible',

79 Art 74 Rules of the ICJ.

80 See also Shabtai Rosenne, *Provisional Measures in International Law: The International Court of Justice and the International Tribunal for the Law of the Sea* (Oxford University Press 2004).

taking into account the legal arguments made by the parties and evidence available before it, and there is a link between the rights claimed by the requesting party and the provisional measures it seeks.[81]

On 23 January 2020, the ICJ renders its *unanimous* decision on The Gambia's request for indication of provisional measures, indicating all but two of the provisional measures requested by The Gambia.[82]

At the outset, the ICJ proceeds to consider whether it has *prima facie* jurisdiction over the case. The Gambia seeks to found its jurisdiction on Article IX of the Genocide Convention, making the ICJ's jurisdiction conditional on the existence of a dispute between the parties relating to the interpretation, application or fulfilment of the Convention. The ICJ rejects the Myanmar's contention that there was no dispute between the Parties since The Gambia acted as a 'proxy' for the OIC. The ICJ finds that The Gambia instituted proceedings in its own name, and that The Gambia maintains it has a dispute with Myanmar regarding its own rights under the Genocide Convention. The fact that The Gambia may have sought and obtained the support of other States or international organizations in its endeavour to request the ICJ to take up the case does not preclude the existence between the parties of a dispute relating to the Genocide Convention.

Turning to the question whether, at the time of the filing of the Application, there appeared to exist a dispute between the parties, the ICJ considers the statements made by the parties in September 2019 before the UN General Assembly suggest the existence of a divergence of views concerning the events which allegedly took place in Rakhine state in relation to the Rohingya. In addition, the ICJ takes into account The Gambia's Note Verbale of 11 October 2019, in which The Gambia specifically referred to the IIFFMM's reports and indicated The Gambia's opposition to Myanmar's views, in particular as regards Myanmar's denial of its responsibility under the Genocide Convention. In the light of the gravity of the allegations made therein, the ICJ considers the lack of response may be another indication of the existence of a dispute between the parties.

On the question whether the acts complained of by The Gambia are capable of falling within the provisions of the Genocide Convention, the ICJ recalls that The Gambia contends that Myanmar's military and security forces and persons or entities acting on its instructions or under its direction and control have been responsible, among other things, for killings, rape and other forms of sexual violence, torture, beatings, cruel treatment and for the destruction or denial of access to food, shelter and other essentials of life, all with the intent to destroy the Rohingya group, in whole or in part. Myanmar, for its part, denied it has committed any of the violations of the Genocide Convention alleged by The

81 *Questions relating to the Obligation to Prosecute or Extradite (Belgium v Senegal)*, Provisional Measures, Order of 28 May 2009 [2009] ICJ Rep 139, 151 [57] and 152 [60].

82 *Application of the Convention on the Prevention and Punishment of the Crime of Genocide (The Gambia v Myanmar), Provisional Measures*, Order of 23 Jan 2020 [2020] ICJ Rep 3.

Gambia, arguing in particular the absence of any genocidal intent. In the ICJ's view, at least some of the acts alleged by The Gambia are capable of falling within the provisions of the Convention. The ICJ therefore finds the above-mentioned elements sufficient at this stage to establish *prima facie* the existence of a dispute between the parties relating to the interpretation, application or fulfilment of the Genocide Convention.

The ICJ rejects Myanmar's argument that its reservation to Article VIII of the Genocide Convention prevented The Gambia from requesting the ICJ to take up the case pursuant to Article IX of the Convention. Pursuant to Article VIII of the Convention, any Contracting Party may call upon the competent organs of the UN to take such action under the UN Charter as they consider appropriate for the prevention and suppression of acts of genocide or any of the other acts enumerated in Article III. The ICJ considers that, although the terms 'competent organs of the United Nations' under Article VIII are broad and may be interpreted as encompassing the ICJ within their scope of application, other terms used in Article VIII suggest a different interpretation. In particular, notes the ICJ, Article VIII only addresses in general terms the possibility for any Contracting Party to 'call upon' the competent UN organs to take 'action' which is 'appropriate' for the prevention and suppression of acts of genocide. It does not refer to the submission of disputes between Contracting Parties to the Genocide Convention to the ICJ for adjudication. This is a matter specifically addressed in Article IX of the Convention, to which Myanmar has not entered any reservation. Article VIII and Article IX of the Convention can therefore be said to have distinct areas of application. It is only Article IX of the Convention which is relevant in the context of the ICJ's taking up the present case.

In the light of the foregoing, the ICJ concludes that, *prima facie*, it has jurisdiction pursuant to Article IX of the Genocide Convention to deal with the case.

The ICJ then examines Myanmar's contention that The Gambia did not have *prima facie* standing to bring a case before it in relation to Myanmar's alleged breaches of the Genocide Convention because The Gambia was not specially affected by such alleged violations. The ICJ recalls its observation in its Advisory Opinion on *Reservations to the Convention on the Prevention and Punishment of the Crime of Genocide*[83] in 1951 that in such convention as the Genocide Convention, the Contracting States do not have any interests of their own; they merely have, one and all, a common interest, namely, the accomplishment of those high purposes which are the *raison d'être* of the convention. That common interest implies the obligations in question are owed by any State Party to all the other States parties to the Genocide Convention. In *Questions relating to the Obligation to Prosecute or Extradite (Belgium v Senegal)*, the ICJ observed that the relevant provisions in the 1984 Convention against Torture and Other Cruel, Inhuman or

83 [1951] ICJ Rep 15, 23.

Degrading Treatment and Punishment[84] were 'similar' to those in the Genocide Convention. The ICJ held that these provisions generated 'obligations [which] may be defined as "obligations *erga omnes partes*" in the sense that each State Party has an interest in compliance with them in any given case'.[85] Consequently, any State Party to the Genocide Convention, and not only a specially affected State, may invoke the responsibility of another State Party with a view to ascertaining the alleged failure to comply with its obligations *erga omnes partes*, and to bring that failure to an end. The ICJ thus concludes The Gambia has *prima facie* standing to submit to it the dispute with Myanmar on the basis of alleged violations of obligations under the Genocide Convention.

Addressing the question whether the rights claimed by The Gambia on the merits, and for which it is seeking protection, are plausible, the ICJ observes that the provisions of the Genocide Convention are intended to protect the members of a national, ethnical, racial or religious group from acts of genocide or any other punishable acts enumerated in Article III. In the ICJ's view, the Rohingya in Myanmar appear to constitute a protected group within the meaning of Article II the Genocide Convention.

The ICJ then recalls that, at the hearings, Myanmar admitted violations of international humanitarian law may have occurred during what it characterizes as 'clearance operations' carried out in Rakhine State in 2017. The ICJ further refers to Resolution 73/264 adopted on 22 December 2018 by the UN General Assembly,[86] condemning the widespread and systematic crimes committed by Myanmar forces against the Rohingya in Rakhine state, as well as to the IIFFMM's reports affirming there are reasonable grounds to conclude that serious crimes under international law were committed that warranted criminal investigation and prosecution, including the crime of genocide, against the Rohingya in Myanmar. The ICJ also recalls that following the events which occurred in Rakhine state in 2016 and 2017, hundreds of thousands of Rohingya have fled to Bangladesh. *In view of the function of provisional measures, which is to protect the respective rights of either party pending its final decision, the ICJ does not consider that the exceptional gravity of the allegations is a decisive factor warranting, as argued by Myanmar, the determination, at the present stage of the proceedings, of the existence of a genocidal intent.* In the ICJ's view, these facts and circumstances are sufficient to find that the rights claimed by The Gambia and for which it is seeking protection – namely the right of the Rohingya group in Myanmar and of its members to be protected from acts of genocide and related prohibited acts mentioned in Article III, and the right of The Gambia to seek compliance by Myanmar with its obligations not to commit and to prevent and punish genocide in accordance with the Convention – are *plausible*.

84 1465 UNTS 85, in force 26 June 1987.
85 [2012] ICJ Rep 422, 449–50 [68]–[69].
86 A/RES/73/264 (22 Dec 2018).

The ICJ subsequently turns to the issue of the link between the rights claimed and the provisional measures requested. The ICJ finds such a link in those provisional measures sought by The Gambia aiming at preserving the rights it asserts on the basis of the Genocide Convention in the present case, namely the right of the Rohingya group in Myanmar and of its members to be protected from acts of genocide and other acts mentioned in Article III, and the right of The Gambia to have Myanmar comply with its obligations under the Genocide Convention to prevent and punish acts identified and prohibited under Articles II and III of the Convention, including by ensuring the preservation of evidence. However, there is *no* such link with regard to the provisional measures requested by The Gambia directed at preventing any action which may aggravate or extend the existing dispute or render it more difficult to resolve, and at providing information on the compliance by the parties with any specific provisional measure indicated by the ICJ. As to the provisional measure requested by The Gambia for Myanmar to grant access to, and cooperate with, all UN fact-finding bodies engaged in investigating alleged genocidal acts against the Rohingya, including the conditions to which the Rohingya are subjected, the ICJ does not consider its indication for provisional measures is necessary in the circumstances of the case. In sum, the ICJ finds some of the provisional measures sought by The Gambia are aimed at preserving the rights claimed in the present case, and therefore the requisite link has been established.

The ICJ recalls it has the power to indicate provisional measures when irreparable prejudice could be caused to rights which are the subject of judicial proceedings or when the alleged disregard of such rights may entail irreparable consequences. Yet, the ICJ's power to indicate provisional measures will be exercised only if there is *urgency*, in the sense that there is a real and imminent risk that *irreparable prejudice* will be caused before the ICJ gives its final decision. The condition of urgency is met when the acts susceptible of causing irreparable prejudice can 'occur at any moment' before the ICJ makes a final decision on the case. *In view of the fundamental values sought to be protected by the Genocide Convention, the ICJ considers the rights in question in these proceedings, in particular the right of the Rohingya group in Myanmar and of its members to be protected from killings and other acts threatening their existence as a group, are of such a nature that prejudice to them could cause irreparable harm.* The ICJ notes the IIFFMM's reports have indicated that, since October 2016, the Rohingya in Myanmar have been subjected to acts capable of affecting their right of existence as a protected group under the Genocide Convention, such as mass killings, widespread rape and other forms of sexual violence, as well as beatings, the destruction of villages and homes, denial of access to food, shelter and other essentials of life. In the ICJ's opinion, the Rohingya in Myanmar remain extremely vulnerable, observing in particular the IIFFMM's conclusion in September 2019 that the Rohingya people remained at serious risk of genocide. The ICJ takes note of the statement of Myanmar during the oral proceedings that it is currently engaged in repatriation initiatives to facilitate the return of Rohingya refugees present in Bangladesh and that it intends to promote ethnic reconciliation, peace and stability in Rakhine state, and to make its military accountable for violations of international humanitarian and human rights law. However, the ICJ finds these steps insufficient in themselves to remove the possibility that acts causing irreparable prejudice to the rights invoked by The Gambia for the protection of the Rohingya in Myanmar could occur. In particular, notes the ICJ, '*Myanmar has not presented to the [ICJ] concrete measures aimed specifically at recognizing and ensuring the right of the Rohingya to exist as a protected group under the Genocide Convention*'. Moreover, the UN General Assembly has, as recently as on 27 December 2019, expresses its regret that 'the situation has not improved in Rakhine state to create the conditions necessary for refugees and other forcibly displaced persons to return to their places of origin voluntarily, safely and with dignity', while, at the same time, the General Assembly reiterates

> its deep distress at reports that unarmed individuals in Rakhine state have been and continue to be subjected to the excessive use of force and violations of human rights and international humanitarian law by the military and security and armed forces, including extrajudicial, summary or arbitrary killings, systematic rape and other forms of sexual and gender-based violence, arbitrary detention, enforced disappearance and government seizure of Rohingya lands from which Rohingya Muslims were evicted and their homes destroyed.

Finally, observes the ICJ, irrespective of the situation the Myanmar Government is facing in Rakhine state, including the fact that there may be an ongoing internal conflict between armed groups and the Myanmar military and that security measures are in place, Myanmar remains under the obligations incumbent upon it as a State Party to the Genocide Convention. Pursuant to Article I of the Convention, States Parties expressly confirmed their willingness to consider genocide as a crime under international law which they must prevent and punish independently of the context 'of peace' or 'of war' in which it takes place. The context invoked by Myanmar does not stand in the way of the ICJ's assessment of the existence of a real and imminent risk of irreparable prejudice to the rights protected under the Convention.

In the light of these considerations, the ICJ finds a real and imminent risk of irreparable prejudice to the rights invoked by The Gambia.

From all of the above considerations, the ICJ concludes the conditions required by its Statute for it to indicate provisional measures are met. It is therefore necessary, pending its final decision, for the ICJ to indicate the following measures in order to protect the rights claimed by The Gambia, as identified above.

First, Myanmar shall, in accordance with its obligations under the Genocide Convention, in relation to the members of the Rohingya group in its territory, take all measures within its power to prevent the commission of all acts within the scope of Article II of this Convention, in particular: (a) killing members of the group; (b) causing serious bodily or mental harm to the members of the group; (c) deliberately inflicting on the group conditions of life calculated to bring about its physical destruction in whole or in part; and (d) imposing measures intended to prevent births within the group.

Second, Myanmar shall, in relation to the members of the Rohingya group in its territory, ensure that its military, as well as any irregular armed units which may be directed or supported by it and any organizations and persons which may be subject to its control, direction or influence, do not commit any acts described in the first point above, or of conspiracy to commit genocide, of direct and public incitement to commit genocide, of attempt to commit genocide or of complicity in genocide.

Third, Myanmar shall take effective measures to prevent the destruction and ensure the preservation of evidence related to allegations of acts within the scope of Article II of the Genocide Convention.

Fourth, Myanmar shall submit a report to the ICJ on all measures taken to give effect to this Order within four months, as from the date of this Order, and thereafter every six months, until a final decision on the case is rendered by the ICJ.

At this juncture, the present author wishes to make some observations regarding the ICJ's Order of 23 January 2020.

As explained in paragraph 66 of the Order, the ICJ is not called upon, for the purposes of its decision on the Request for the indication of provisional measures, to establish the existence of breaches of the Genocide Convention, but to determine whether the circumstances require the indication of provisional measures for the protection of rights under this instrument, and it cannot at this stage make definitive findings of fact, and the right of each Party to submit arguments in respect of the merits remains unaffected by the ICJ's decision on the Request for the indication of provisional measures. The ICJ reaffirms in paragraph 85 of the Order that the decision given in the present proceedings in no way prejudges the question of the ICJ's jurisdiction to deal with the merits of the case or any questions relating to the admissibility of the Application or to the merits themselves. Nonetheless, it can reasonably be expected that, from the ICJ's reasoning in that Order, when the time has come for the ICJ to determine whether it has jurisdiction on the merits in this case, the ICJ will most likely rule that The Gambia has legal standing to institute the proceedings against Myanmar and there was 'dispute' between the parties regarding the Genocide Convention at the time when The Gambia instituted its Application on 11 November 2019.

By contrast, despite the ICJ's frequent references to and reliance on the IIFFMM's reports as well as statements in and some resolutions of the UN General Assembly, these reports, statements and resolutions will have to be assessed by the ICJ during the merits stage of the proceedings, according to the standards of proof mentioned above, to determine whether acts proscribed under Articles II and III of the Genocide Convention have been committed, and whether Myanmar has violated its obligations under the Convention thereby entailing

Myanmar's State responsibility *vis-à-vis* The Gambia. Notably in this connection is ICJ's Vice President Xue Hanqing's Separate Opinion attached to the Order expressing her view that '[t]he evidence and documents submitted to the [ICJ] in the present case, while displaying an appalling situation of human rights violations, present a case of a protracted problem of ill-treatment of ethnic minorities in Myanmar rather than of genocide'.[87] In a similar vein, the Declaration of Judge *ad hoc* Kress, appointed by Myanmar, attached to the Order states that

> even on the basis of the low standard [of plausibility of rights for the indication of provisional measures of protection under the Genocide Convention] applied by the [ICJ] in this case, it is not entirely without hesitation that [he has] come to the conclusion that the materials provided by The Gambia so far are sufficient to enable the [ICJ] to conclude that the plausibility test was met with respect to the question of genocidal intent.[88]

By virtue of Article 41(2) of the ICJ Statute, pending the final decision, notice of the measures suggested shall forthwith be given to the parties and to the UN Security Council. Article 94 of the UN Charter obligates each Member of the UN to undertake to comply with the ICJ's decision in any case to which it is a party, and if any party to a case fails to perform the obligations incumbent upon it under a Judgment rendered by the ICJ, the other party may have recourse to the Security Council, which may, if it deems necessary, make recommendations or decide upon measures to be taken to give effect to the Judgment. However, on 4 February 2020, owing to China and Vietnam's objection, the Council failed to agree on a statement urging Myanmar to abide by the ICJ's Order indicating provisional measures. This shows that in the event of Myanmar's failure to comply with the Order, it may not be realistic to expect the Council to take measures to give effect to the ICJ's Order.

Before the Rohingya case, the ICJ indicated provisional measures regarding allegations of genocide in only one case: the Bosnian genocide case. These provisional measures were not observed in the ongoing war in the former Yugoslavia.

The ICJ's provisional measures, even when they are not observed, may generate non-legal impacts such as giving further publicity to the situation the provisional measures are intended to alleviate. Besides, the provisional measures in the Bosnian genocide case were granted in the context of a large-scale armed conflict with both internal and international dimensions, which is different from the Rohingya situation in Myanmar. Even prior to the ICJ's Order of 8 April 1993, on 22 February 1993 the UN Security Council had adopted a resolution[89] to set up the ICTY for the prosecution of persons responsible for serious

87 [2020] ICJ Rep 3, 32 [3].
88 Ibid 66 [5].
89 S/RES/808 (22 Feb 1993).

violations of international humanitarian law committed in the territory of the former Yugoslavia since 1991. The fact that the Respondent in the Bosnian genocide case did not comply with the ICJ's ordered provisional measures eventually led the ICJ to rule in its Judgment on the Merits of 26 February 2007 that the Respondent violated its obligation to prevent the Srebrenica genocide in such a manner as to engage its international responsibility.[90] It may be recalled that the ICJ's Order of 8 April 1993 used the wording similar to the one issued against Myanmar on 23 January 2020, stating, *inter alia*, that the Respondent was required to ensure

> any military, paramilitary or irregular armed units which may be directed or supported by it, as well as any organizations and persons which may be subject to its control, direction or influence, do not commit any acts of genocide, of conspiracy to commit genocide, of direct and public incitement to commit genocide, or of complicity in genocide.

Additionally, the case brought by The Gambia before the ICJ also differs from the genocide case brought by Bosnia and Herzegovina and the one by Croatia against Serbia in that The Gambia's case is about what has happened and is happening to the Rohingya, whereas the ICJ was requested to rule *retrospectively* on Serbia's State responsibility in the other two genocide cases. Indeed, the ICJ ruled in 2007 in the Bosnian genocide case that Serbia had breached its duty to prevent genocide in Srebrenica in 1995. The ICJ's Order of 23 January 2020 is thus of current and practical relevance to what has been going on with regard to the Rohingya.

ASSK's presence in the ICJ also makes it difficult for Myanmar to totally ignore the ICJ's Order of 23 January 2020 and Judgment on the merits if Myanmar is the losing party. The Ministry of Foreign Affairs of Myanmar's Press Release issued immediately after the ICJ's Order 'takes note' of the Order but reiterates that, as concluded by the Independent Commission of Enquiry ('ICOE'), established by the Myanmar Government, in its report of 20 January 2020, 'there has been no genocide in Myanmar' although war crimes occurred and 'those are now being investigated and prosecuted by Myanmar's national criminal justice system'. The Press Release asserts it is important for Myanmar that the ICJ 'reaches a factually correct decision on the merits of the case' since the 'unsubstantiated condemnation of Myanmar by some human rights actors has presented a distorted picture of the situation in Rakhine and affected Myanmar's bilateral relations with several countries', thereby hampering Myanmar's ability to lay the foundation for sustainable development in Rakhine. The historical functions of provisional measures, continues the Press Release, has been to protect the ICJ against possible accusations of failure

90 [2007] ICJ Rep 43, 223–6 [435]–[438].

to take preventive action at the start of a case and, as the ICJ states, its decision given in the present proceedings in no way prejudges the question of the ICJ's jurisdiction to deal with the merits of the case or any questions relating to the admissibility of the application or to the merits themselves. On 24 January 2020, in a telephone interview with Reuters, a spokesperson of the National League for Democracy, Myanmar's then ruling political party, insisted Myanmar had already put in place most of the measures indicated in the ICJ's Order and the only thing the Myanmar Government would do was to submit reports to the ICJ. Myanmar's stance may be perceived by the international community as stubbornness and defiance to the view and sentiment of the majority of UN Members States as expressed on various occasions, and this is a bad public relations strategy for Myanmar to sustain in the years leading to the ICJ's final Judgment, which might eventually turn out to be in Myanmar's favour. Myanmar could have reacted to the ICJ's Order in a more constructive way, for example, by stating something which is not prejudicial to its case as follows:

> Myanmar will seriously study the ICJ's Order and comply with it in good faith insofar as practicable in the prevailing circumstances. In particular, the Myanmar Government will take concrete steps to investigate 'allegations' of genocide in the IIFFMM's reports. As Myanmar will rightly prove by substantiating evidence during the merits phase of the proceedings before the ICJ, Myanmar has never harboured any genocidal intent or committed any act to destroy any racial, ethnic, national or religious group in Myanmar, as such. Meanwhile Myanmar will also heighten its efforts to take measures to protect the personal safety of members of such group as well as accelerate economic and social developments in Rakhine. Myanmar looks forward to cooperation from the international community towards this end.

One may hope the ICJ's Order of 23 January 2020 should at least ensure that the situation of the 600,000 Rohingya still inside Myanmar will not worsen, and those Rohingya who are voluntarily repatriated to Rakhine will be under even more watchful eye of the international community of nations. However, on 25 January 2020, amidst escalating violence, two women were killed and seven others injured when a Rohingya village in Rakhine state was under artillery fire, although the Tatmadaw has denied accusations that it was responsible.

On 3 February 2020, the Myanmar Government reimposed a mobile internet blackout in several townships in Rakhine. The information blockade meant lack of information on the ground to verify Myanmar's compliance with the ICJ's Order. In March 2020, hundreds of websites, including media outlets covering the ongoing armed conflict in Rakhine, were blocked. The Government explained these measures were to prevent the Arakan Army from using the internet to coordinate attacks against soldiers and even to detonate landmines.

On 8 April 2020, the Myanmar Government issued three presidential directives. The Directive on Compliance with the Convention on the Prevention and Punishment of the Crime of Genocide instructed 'all Ministries and all Regions and States Governments' to 'ensure that its personnel, officers, staff…and local people do not commit the acts mentioned in Articles II and III of the Genocide Convention'. The Directive on the Preservation of Evidence and Property in Areas in Northern Rakhine state prohibited 'all Ministries and the Rakhine state government' from destroying, removing or permitting the destruction or removal of evidence referred to in the ICOE's final report and anything that could be evidence of the underlying acts described in Article II of the Genocide Convention, and violations of the Directive are criminalized. The third directive instructed officials to take all possible measures to denounce and prevent all forms of hate speech. These measures have been criticized as meaningless and impractical to address the problems faced by the Rohingya, since they provide no clear guidelines for implementation and monitoring, and leave untouched the key issues of structural discrimination and persecution under, among others, the 1982 Citizenship Law,[91] the four laws passed in 2015 and known collectively as 'Race and Religion Protection Laws'[92] and the 2014 Myanmar National Human Rights Commission Law.[93] On 22 May and 30 November 2020, Myanmar submitted to the ICJ its first and second reports, respectively, on its compliance with the ICJ's Order of 23 January 2020. The reports have been shared with The Gambia but have not been made public. The Gambia could include its reactions thereto in its Memorial to be submitted to the ICJ.[94]

As of this writing, Myanmar has not submitted any subsequent report due every 6 months, until a final decision on the case is rendered by the ICJ.

On 3 September 2020, the Office of the UN High Commissioner for Human Rights released its report on the situation of human rights of Rohingya Muslims and other minorities in Myanmar.[95] This 15-page report concludes, among other things, there has been no tangible progress towards accountability for serious human rights violations, with both the Government and the Tatmadaw using 'closed and arcane processes whereby the military leadership claims to hold itself accountable through its own chain of command' – it 'embodies a view of a military which is above the law, both national and international, and which is

91 Pyithu Hluttaw Law No 4 of 1982.

92 They are monogamy law, religious conversion law, interfaith marriage law and population control law.

93 Pyithu Hluttaw Law No 21 of 2014.

94 By its Order of 23 January 2020, the ICJ fixed 23 July 2020 and 25 January 2021, respectively, as the time-limits for the filing of a Memorial by The Gambia and of a Counter-Memorial by Myanmar. At The Gambia's request for at least a three-month extension for the filing of the Memorial due to the COVID-19 pandemic, the ICJ extended to 23 October 2020 the time-limit for the filing of the Memorial of The Gambia and 23 July 2021 the time-limit for the filing of the Counter-Memorial of Myanmar.

95 A/HRC/45/5 (3 Sept 2020).

accountable to no one but itself'. Independent, transparent, civilian-run mechanisms that guarantee impartiality and, consequently, build credibility and public trust are required to ensure accountability. Accountability must also be supported by transitional justice processes, which include ensuring the right to truth, reparations and guarantees of non-recurrence, all of which are currently lacking. While the Myanmar authorities emphasize 'the rule of law', this must go beyond a 'law and order' approach that justifies oppressive policies and discriminatory attitudes which remain deeply entrenched, to one that promotes inclusiveness and respect for rights and democratic principles. Journalists, activists and civil society must be allowed to operate freely and unhindered, and be permitted to express themselves without fear of retribution for exercising such rights as independent voices and institutions, including those with a specific human rights mandate. The report reiterates the recommendations contained in previous reports by the High Commissioner and human rights mechanisms, including the Special Rapporteur on the situation of human rights in Myanmar and the fact-finding mission. In addition, the report recommends that the Myanmar Government: (i) immediately extend the ceasefire throughout the whole country and end violations of international humanitarian law and international human rights law, including all restrictions on humanitarian access; (ii) conduct prompt, independent, impartial and thorough investigations into all allegations of violations of international humanitarian law, including into conduct that may constitute war crimes and crimes against humanity in Rakhine and Chin states, and all allegations of human rights violations, and ensure that perpetrators are brought to justice through transparent and credible processes; (iii) acknowledge that sexual crimes have occurred in Rakhine state and other parts of the country, take concrete measures to identify perpetrators and hold them accountable, and ensure health-care and psycho-social services for survivors; (iv) strengthen institution-building and structural reforms to uphold the rule of law, human rights and democratic principles, through a participatory and inclusive approach – including efforts to ensure the independence of the judiciary, and reforming the security sector to enhance civilian control; (v) facilitate access by the Office of the UN High Commissioner for Human Rights to the country and engage with the Office on technical cooperation; (vi) amend the Citizenship Law of 1982, removing links between ethnicity and citizenship, and restore the citizenship of the Rohingya; (vii) ensure sustainable solutions for displaced persons and implement the national strategy for the closure of camps for internally displaced persons, in compliance with international standards; (viii) ensure that the Myanmar National Human Rights Commission fully comply with the Paris Principles, that commissioners be appointed through a transparent process, and that the Commission include representatives from civil society and ethnic minority groups; (ix) issue a moratorium on land expropriation carried out under the Farmland Law of 2012,[96] the Vacant, Fallow and Virgin Lands

96 Pyidaungsu Hluttaw Law No II of 2012.

Management Act of 2012,[97] and the Land Acquisition Act of 1894 as amended by the Land Acquisition, Resettlement and Rehabilitation Law of 2019,[98] until a land governance framework, compliant with the Land Use Policy adopted in 2016, is established; (x) create an enabling environment for the independent media and civil society, including by publicly acknowledging their value in a democratic society and by ceasing to criminalize their exercise of rights and freedoms; and (xi) cooperate and engage meaningfully with Thomas Andrews, the then newly appointed Special Rapporteur on the situation of human rights in Myanmar, and with relevant international justice and accountability mechanisms.

For its part, the Myanmar state media reported on 15 September 2020 that the Office of the Judge Advocate General was investigating possible wider patterns of violations in the region of northern Rakhine in 2016–2017, with allegations regarding villages in the Maungdaw area on the border with Bangladesh being included. However, according to *Al Jazeera* citing United Nations sources, since early September 2020 the Myanmar Government has erased from official maps the name of the Rohingya village of Kan Kya, situated approximately five kilometres from the Naf River which marks the border between Myanmar's Rakhine state and Bangladesh, with dozens of government and military buildings now occupying where Kan Kya once stood.[99]

On 21 December 2020, as part of the ongoing review of its procedures and working methods, the ICJ adopted a new Article 11 of the Resolution concerning the ICJ's Internal Judicial Practice. The article provides for the establishment of an *ad hoc* committee, composed of three judges to assist the ICJ in monitoring the implementation of the provisional measures that it indicates. The committee will examine the information supplied by the parties in this regard, report periodically to the ICJ and recommend potential options for it. Any decision, if required, will be taken by the ICJ. Myanmar's implementation of the provisional measures ordered by the ICJ in January 2020 will certainly be under scrutiny by the committee. Closely related to this is Article 76(1) of the Rules of the ICJ, as amended on 21 October 2019, providing that, at the request of a party or on its own initiative, the ICJ may, at any time before the final judgment in the case, revoke or modify any decision concerning provisional measures if, in its opinion, some change in the situation justifies such revocation or modification. Any application by a party proposing such a revocation or modification shall specify the change in the situation considered to be relevant. Before taking any decision in this regard, the ICJ shall afford the parties an opportunity of presenting their observations on the subject.

97 Pyidaungsu Hluttaw Law No 10/2012.

98 Pyidaungsu Hluttaw Law No 24/2019.

99 'Myanmar army probes "wider patterns" of abuse against Rohingya', *Al Jazeera* (16 Sept 2020), https://www.aljazeera.com/news/2020/9/16/myanmar-army-probes-wider-patterns-of-abuse-against-rohingya.

Possible outcomes if Myanmar is held to have breached the Genocide Convention

In its Application of 11 November 2019, The Gambia requests the ICJ to adjudge and declare that Myanmar:

- Has breached and continues to breach its obligations under the Genocide Convention, in particular the obligations provided under Articles I, III, IV, V and VI
- Must cease forthwith any such ongoing, internationally wrongful act and fully respect its obligations under the Genocide Convention, in particular the obligations provided under Articles I, III, IV, V and VI
- Must ensure that persons committing genocide are punished by a competent tribunal, including before an international penal tribunal, as required by Articles I and VI
- Must perform the obligations of reparation in the interest of the victims of genocidal acts who are members of the Rohingya group, including but not limited to allowing the safe and dignified return of forcibly displaced Rohingya and respect for their full citizenship and human rights and protection against discrimination, persecution and other related acts, consistent with the obligation to prevent genocide under Article I
- Must offer assurances and guarantees of non-repetition of violations of the Genocide Convention, in particular the obligations provided under Articles I, III, IV, V and VI.

If the ICJ does eventually rule Myanmar has indeed violated and continues to breach Myanmar's obligations under the relevant provisions of the Genocide Convention, the declaration will in and of itself be significant in giving some form of satisfaction to The Gambia and, of course, to the Rohingya. Those interested in taking measures to sanction Myanmar and the individuals concerned will have legitimate reasons to do so. Certain States whose national law permits the exercise of criminal jurisdiction over foreign nationals for their acts of genocide committed outside the territory of the forum States exercising such jurisdiction may take steps to prosecute Myanmar individuals so implicated by the ICJ.

If the ICJ does find the genocide is continuing in Myanmar against the Rohingya, the ICJ is expected to order Myanmar to cease forthwith any such ongoing internationally wrongful act and fully respect its obligations under the Genocide Convention. Ordering Myanmar to ensure that persons committing genocide are punished by a competent tribunal, including before an international penal tribunal, is practically difficult for the Myanmar Government. Can members of the Tatmadaw be brought to justice at all, especially after the *coup d'état* on 1 February 2021? What if the ICJ finds that ASSK is also implicated? The possibility of the International Criminal Court prosecuting Myanmar individuals will be analysed in detail in Chapters 5 and 6. At this juncture, what can be said is that the UN Security Council *should* exercise its authority under

Chapter VII of the UN Charter to refer the alleged genocide in Myanmar to the ICC Prosecutor to take necessary steps to prosecute the individuals involved. One can imagine that at least one permanent member of the Council which is Myanmar's close ally will veto any draft resolution to make such referral to the ICC Prosecutor. Alternatively, the ICJ may order Myanmar to accept the ICC's jurisdiction on an *ad hoc* basis pursuant to Article 12(3) of the Rome Statute, with retroactive effect, in which case questions arises as to how Myanmar can be realistically compelled to do so.

Myanmar may be ordered by the ICJ to provide reparation in the interest of the victims of genocidal acts who are members of the Rohingya group, including but not limited to allowing the safe and dignified return of forcibly displaced Rohingya and respect for their full citizenship and human rights and protection against discrimination, persecution and other related acts, consistent with the obligation to prevent genocide under Article I of the Genocide Convention. The extent to which the ICJ orders the losing party to provide reparation varies from case to case, depending on the facts and circumstances of each case. In the Bosnian genocide case, the Applicant recognized it was inappropriate to ask the ICJ to find that the Respondent was under an obligation of restitution to the original position before the wrongs. Insofar as restitution is not possible, an injured State is entitled to obtain compensation from the State which has committed an internationally wrongful act for the damage caused by it. In order to rule on the claim for reparation, the ICJ must ascertain whether, and to what extent, the injury asserted by the Applicant is the consequence of wrongful conduct by the Respondent with the consequence that the Respondent should be required to make reparation for it. In this context, the question in the Bosnian genocide case as to whether the genocide at Srebrenica would have taken place even if the Respondent had attempted to prevent it by employing all means in its possession becomes directly relevant. However, the ICJ clearly cannot conclude from that particular case as a whole and with a sufficient degree of certainty that the genocide at Srebrenica would in fact have been averted if the Respondent had acted in compliance with its legal obligations. Since the ICJ cannot regard as proven a causal nexus between the Respondent's violation of its obligation of prevention and the genocide at Srebrenica, financial compensation is not the appropriate form of reparation for the breach of the obligation to prevent genocide. Yet the Applicant is clearly entitled to reparation in the form of 'satisfaction', and this may take the most appropriate form, as the Applicant itself suggested, of a declaration in the Judgment that the Respondent has failed to comply with the obligation imposed by the Convention to prevent genocide. Turning to the question of the appropriate reparation for the breach by the Respondent of its obligation under the Convention to punish acts of genocide, the ICJ is satisfied that the Respondent has outstanding obligations as regards the transfer to the ICTY of persons accused of genocide, in order to comply with its obligations under Articles I and VI of the Convention. In any event, the ICJ does not find it appropriate to give effect to the Applicant's request for an order for symbolic compensation in respect of the non-compliance of the Respondent with the ICJ's Order of 8 April 1993 on provisional measures.[100]

With regard to the ICJ's ordering Myanmar to offer assurances and guarantees of non-repetition of violations of the Genocide Convention, in particular the obligations provided under Articles I, III, IV, V and VI, it all depends on whether Myanmar is willing to fulfil these obligations at all.

Should Myanmar refuse to abide by the ICJ's Judgment, Article 94 of the UN Charter allows The Gambia to have recourse to the UN Security Council, which may, if it deems necessary, make recommendations or decide upon measures to be taken to give effect to the ICJ's Judgment. Once again, at least one of the five permanent member of the Security Council may cast a veto against any decision to enforce the ICJ's Judgment against Myanmar.

When Myanmar appeared before the ICJ in December 2019, Myanmar was scheduled to hold the next general elections in November 2020. It was not unusual for politicians of all stripes to drum up nationalistic or patriotic sentiment to gain popular support. Against this background, ASSK was seen as opting to be a national heroine who wanted to stay in power to govern Myanmar rather than an icon of human rights. In his open letter posted on social media on 7 September 2017, Archbishop Desmond Tutu of South Africa, Nobel Peace Prize laureate in 1984, appeals to ASSK to intervene in the escalating violence being perpetrated against members of the Rohingya, which some have called 'ethnic cleansing' and others 'a slow genocide'. The Archbishop adds:

> My dear sister: If the political price of your ascension to the highest office in Myanmar is your silence, the price is surely too steep. A country that is not at peace with itself, that fails to acknowledge and protect the dignity and worth of all its people, is not a free country. It is incongruous for a symbol of righteousness to lead such a country.[101]

It could be that if The Gambia wins in the ICJ, there may be a new wave of violence against the Rohingya. If the ICJ dismisses The Gambia's case for lack of jurisdiction or because The Gambia's Application is not admissible or the ICJ substantially finds in favour of Myanmar on merits, this may provoke even more discontent among the Rohingya, especially the Arakan Rohingya Salvation Army that has been fighting the Myanmar military.

Since it will take some years before the ICJ renders its final Judgment in the case brought by The Gambia, the Myanmar leadership has plenty of opportunities to refute and disprove allegations that it does harbour a specific intent to destroy the Rohingya, a group protected by the Genocide Convention, as

100 [2007] ICJ Rep 43, 232–7.

101 https://www.iol.co.za/news/opinion/an-open-letter-from-desmond-tutu-to-aung-san-su-kyi-11123972.

such. Instead of deflecting The Gambia's accusation of genocide by asserting that war crimes and some human rights violations, and not genocide, might have been committed against the Rohingya and that these wrongs are not subject to the ICJ's jurisdiction, the Myanmar leadership could take constructive steps to assimilate the Rohingya, including those voluntarily repatriated from Bangladesh and elsewhere, into the mainstream of the Myanmar society and duly protect their human rights under the relevant human rights treaties binding on Myanmar. In this sense, The Gambia's Application may not be a waste of time and efforts after all.

What is more urgent and worrying for the Myanmar individuals implicated in the IIFFMM's report as well as any other Myanmar individuals who may be so implicated as a result of the investigation by the Independent Investigative Mechanism for Myanmar, or IIMM, is the possibility that even before the ICJ's final Judgment in the case brought by The Gambia, the ICC may issue international arrest warrants for them to be surrendered to stand trial before the ICC. This possibility and its ramifications are discussed in the next two chapters.

PART III

The International Criminal Court

Individual criminal responsibility

5

INTRODUCTION TO THE INTERNATIONAL CRIMINAL COURT

The ICC

The International Criminal Court ('ICC') is the world's first-ever permanent international criminal court. It was set up by the 1998 Rome Statute of the International Criminal Court,[1] which came into force on 1 July 2002. As of this writing, there are 123 parties to the Rome Statute. Thirty-three of them are from Africa;[2] 19 from Asia-Pacific;[3] another 18 from Eastern Europe;[4] 28 from Latin American and the Caribbean;[5] and the other 25 from Western Europe and other States.[6] Myanmar is not party to the Rome Statute, but both The Gambia and Bangladesh are.

1 2187 UNTS 3.

2 Benin, Botswana, Burkina Faso, Cabo Verde, Central African Republic, Chad, Comoros, Congo, Côte d'Ivoire, DR Congo, Djibouti, Gambon, *Gambia*, Ghana, Guinea, Kenya, Lesotho, Liberia, Madagascar, Malawi, Mali, Mauritius, Namibia, Niger, Nigeria, Senegal, Seychelles, Sierra Leone, South Africa, Tunisia, Uganda, Tanzania and Zambia.

3 Afghanistan, *Bangladesh*, Cambodia, Cook Islands, Cyprus, Fiji, Japan, Jordan, Kiribati, Maldives, Marshall Islands, Mongolia, Nauru, Republic of Korea, Samoa, State of Palestine, Tajikistan, Timor-Leste and Vanuatu.

4 Albania, Bosnia and Herzegovina, Bulgaria, Croatia, Czech Republic, Estonia, Georgia, Hungary, Latvia, Lithuania, Montenegro, North Macedonia, Poland, Moldova, Romania, Serbia, Slovakia and Slovenia.

5 Antigua and Barbuda, Argentina, Barbados, Belize, Bolivia, Brazil, Chile, Colombia, Costa Rica, Dominica, Dominican Republic, Ecuador, El Salvador, Grenada, Guatemala, Guyana, Honduras, Mexico, Panama, Paraguay, Peru, Saint Kitts and Nevis, Saint Lucia, Saint Vincent and the Grenadines, Suriname, Trinidad and Tobago, Uruguay and Venezuela.

6 Andorra, Australia, Austria, Belgium, Canada, Denmark, Finland, France, Germany, Greece, Iceland, Ireland, Italy, Liechtenstein, Luxembourg, Malta, Netherlands, New Zealand, Norway, Portugal, San Marino, Spain, Sweden, Switzerland and the United Kingdom.

DOI: 10.4324/9781003224211-5

Ideally, having a permanent ICC would do away with the need to set up *ad hoc* international criminal tribunals such as the International Military Tribunal at Nuremberg and the International Military Tribunal for the Far East, set up by the victorious Allied Powers after the Second World War to try major Nazi war criminals and Japanese war crime suspects, respectively, both of which are sometimes criticized for dispensing 'victors' justice' and violation of the principle that no one shall be held guilty of any penal offence on account of any act or omission which did not constitute a penal offence, under national or international law, at the time when it was committed.[7] The setting up by the UN Security Council of the ICTY and the ICTR is unique and has not been emulated owing to geopolitics coupled with the veto power of the Council's permanent members as well as the huge financial implications of such *ad hoc* tribunals on the UN's budget. It is also not always practical to establish special or 'hybrid' courts with foreign judges and chief prosecutors working side by side with national judges and prosecutors to render criminal justice in particular States, as in the case of, for example, the Special Court for Sierra Leone, the Extraordinary Chambers in the Courts of Cambodia (or the Khmer Rouge Tribunal), the Serious Crimes Panels in the District Court of Dili (East Timor), and, since 22 October 2018, the Special Criminal Court of the Central African Republic which is cooperating closely with the ICC to bring to justice perpetrators of serious violations of international human rights law and international humanitarian law committed in the Central African Republic since 1 January 2003.[8]

7 See, e.g., UN Secretary-General, *Historical Survey of the Question of International Criminal Jurisdiction* (United Nations 1949) 25–30; Y Onuma, 'The Tokyo Trial: Between Law and Politics' in C Hosoya, N Ando, Y Onuma and R Minear (eds.), *The Tokyo War Crime Trial: An International Symposium* (Kodansha 1986) 45 ff; Kirsten Sellars, 'Imperfect Justice at Nuremberg and Tokyo' (2010) 21 EJIL 1085; Yuki Tanaka, Tim McCormack and Gerry Simpson (eds.), *Beyond Victor's Justice?: The Tokyo War Crimes Trial Revisited* (Martinus Nijhoff 2010); William A Schabas, 'Victor's Justice: Selecting Situations at the International Criminal Court' (2010) 43 John Marshall L Rev 535; David M Crowe, 'The Tokyo and Nuremberg International Military Tribunal Trials: A Comparative Study' in Viviane E Dittrich, Kerstin von Lingen, Philipp Osten and Jolana Makraiová (eds.), *The Tokyo Tribunal: Perspectives on Law, History and Memory* (Torkel Opsahl Academic EPublisher 2020) 31; Kerstin von Lingen, 'The Tokyo Tribunal: A Transcultural Endeavour' ibid 61.

8 See also Phani Dascalopoulo-Livada, *Contemporary Issues in International Law* (Eleven International Publishing 2019) 35–48; Luc Reydams and Jan Wouters, 'The Politics of Establishing International Criminal Tribunals' in Luc Reydams, Jan Wouters and Cedric Ryngaert (eds.), *International Prosecutors* (Oxford University Press 2012) Chapter 2; Cesare P R Romano, André Nollkaemper and Jann K Kleffner (eds.), *Internationalized Criminal Courts: Sierra Leone, East Timor, Kosovo, and Cambodia* (Oxford University Press 2004); Phillip Rapoza, 'Hybrid Criminal Tribunals and the Concept of Ownership: Who Owns the Process?' (2005) 21 American University Int'l L Rev 525; Errol P Mendes, *Peace and Justice at the International Criminal Court: A Court of Last Resort* (2nd edn, Edward Elgar Publishing 2020) Chapter 1; Julian Elderfield, 'The Rise and Rise of the Special Criminal Court', *Opinio Juris* (7 Apr 2021).

The ICC, based in The Hague, has more than 900 staff members from approximately 100 nation States. It has six field offices in Africa[9] and one in Tbilisi, Georgia. Its budget for the financial year 2020 was €149,205,600.

The ICC's 18 judges are elected from two lists of candidates who are nationals of States Parties to the Rome Statute and who have excellent knowledge of and are fluent in English or French. List A comprises those with established competence in criminal law and procedure, and the necessary relevant experience, whether as judge, prosecutor, advocate or in other similar capacity, in criminal proceedings. List B comprises those with established competence in relevant areas of international law such as international humanitarian law and the law of human rights, and extensive experience in a professional legal capacity which is of relevance to the ICC's judicial work. The judges are elected by secret ballot at a meeting of the Assembly of States Parties to the Rome Statute convened for that purpose. Those elected must obtain the highest number of votes to fill the vacancies and a two-thirds majority of the States Parties present and voting. The States Parties shall, in the election of judges, take into account the need, within the ICC's membership, for the representation of the principal legal systems of the world; equitable geographical representation; and a fair representation of female and male judges. No two judges may be nationals of the same nation State. ICC judges are elected for one nine-year term and are not eligible for re-election.[10]

The ICC is composed of the following organs: (a) the Presidency; (b) an Appeals Division, a Trial Division and a Pre-Trial Division; (c) the Office of the Prosecutor; and (d) the Registry.[11] The Appeals Division is composed of the ICC President and four other judges, the Trial Division of not fewer than six judges and the Pre-Trial Division of not fewer than six judges. The assignment of judges to divisions shall be based on the nature of the functions to be performed by each division and the qualifications and experience of the judges elected to the ICC, in such a way that each division shall contain an appropriate combination of expertise in criminal law and procedure and in international law. The Trial and Pre-Trial Divisions shall be composed predominantly of judges with criminal trial experience. The functions of the Trial Chamber is carried out by three judges of the Trial Division, whereas the functions of the Pre-Trial Chamber shall be carried out either by three judges of the Pre-Trial Division or by a single judge of that Division in accordance with the Rome Statute and the ICC's Rules of Procedure and Evidence.[12]

The Office of the ICC Prosecutor ('OTP') is an independent, separate organ of the ICC. It is responsible for receiving referrals and any substantiated information on crimes within the ICC's jurisdiction, for examining them and for

9 Kinshasa and Bunia (DR Congo); Kampala (Uganda); Bangui (Central African Republic); Abidjan (Côte d'Ivoire); and Bamako (Mali).

10 Rome Statute Art 36.

11 Ibid Art 34.

12 Ibid Art 39.

conducting investigations and prosecutions before the ICC. The OTP is headed by the ICC Prosecutor, who is assisted by one or more Deputy Prosecutors. The Prosecutor and the Deputy Prosecutors shall be of different nationalities, serve on a full-time basis, be persons of high moral character, be highly competent and have extensive practical experience in the prosecution or trial of criminal cases, and shall have an excellent knowledge of and be fluent in English or French. The ICC Prosecutor is elected by secret ballot by an absolute majority of the members of the Assembly of States Parties. The Deputy Prosecutors are elected in the same way from a list of candidates provided by the ICC Prosecutor who shall nominate three candidates for each position of Deputy Prosecutor to be filled. Unless a shorter term is decided upon at the time of their election, the ICC Prosecutor and the Deputy Prosecutors hold office for a term of nine years and are not eligible for re-election.[13]

As regards the applicable law, Article 21(1) of the Rome Statute requires the ICC to apply: (a) in the first place, this Statute, Elements of Crimes and its Rules of Procedure and Evidence; (b) in the second place, where appropriate, applicable treaties and the principles and rules of international law, including the established principles of the international law of armed conflict;[14] (c) failing that, general principles of law derived by the ICC from national laws of legal systems of the world including, as appropriate, the national laws of States that would normally exercise jurisdiction over the crime, provided that those principles are not inconsistent with this Statute and with international law and internationally recognized norms and standards. By virtue of Article 21(2), the ICC may apply principles and rules of law as interpreted in its previous decisions. However, paragraph 3 of Article 21 adds that the application and interpretation of law pursuant to Article 21 must be consistent with internationally recognized human rights, and be without any adverse distinction founded on grounds such as gender, age, race, colour, language, religion or belief, political or other opinion, national, ethnic or social origin, wealth, birth or other status. Case law of international criminal tribunals such as the ICTY and the ICTR is not legally binding on the ICC.[15] Yet, unless and until the ICC itself has rendered judgments or decisions to the contrary, well-established jurisprudence of other international criminal tribunals serves as 'the principles and rules of international law' referred to in Article 21(1)(b) of the Rome Statute.

13 Ibid Art 42.

14 According to the International Committee of the Red Cross, the law of armed conflict is synonymous with international humanitarian law or the law of war (ICRC Advisory Service on International Humanitarian Law, *What is International Humanitarian Law?* (July 2004) 1).

15 *Prosecutor v Thomas Lubanga Dyilo*, Case ICC-01/04-01/06 A 5, ICC Appeals Chamber, Judgment, 1 Dec 2014 para 472.

Crimes under the ICC's jurisdiction

By virtue of Article 5 of the Rome Statute, the ICC has jurisdiction in accordance with the Statute with respect to the following crimes: the crime of genocide, crimes against humanity, war crimes and – as of 17 July 2018 and only for those States Parties accepting the ICC's jurisdiction over this crime or unless the UN Security Council acting under Chapter VII of the UN Charter[16] refers it to the ICC Prosecutor – the crime of aggression.

The crime of aggression is not relevant in the Rohingya context. Aggression is the planning, preparation, initiation or execution, by a person in a position effectively to exercise control over or to direct the political or military action of a nation State, of the use of armed force against the sovereignty, territorial integrity or political independence of another nation State, or in any other manner inconsistent with the UN Charter which, by its character, gravity and scale, constitutes a manifest violation of the UN Charter.[17]

The crime of genocide is already explained in Chapter 4.

War crimes

War crimes are crimes committed in violation of a body of rules known collectively as 'international humanitarian law' during an armed conflict. An armed conflict is deemed to exist whenever there is a resort to armed forces between nation States or protracted armed violence between governmental authorities and organized armed groups or between such groups fighting with a certain level of intensity within a nation State.[18] An armed conflict is international if it takes place between two or more nation States, and in case of an internal armed conflict breaking out on the territory of one nation State, it may become international or, depending on the circumstances, international in character alongside an internal armed conflict if another nation State intervenes in that conflict through its troops, or if some of the participants in the internal armed conflict act on behalf of that other nation State.[19] An armed conflict is not limited to the specific geographical municipalities where acts of violence and actual fighting

16 1 UNTS XVI, in force 24 Oct 1945.

17 Rome Statute Art 8 *bis* (1).

18 *Prosecutor v Dusko Tadic*, Case IT-94-1-AR72, ICTY Appeals Chamber, Decision of 2 Oct 1995 on the Defence Motion for Interlocutory Appeal on Jurisdiction paras 70, 562.

19 *Prosecutor v Dusko Tadic*, Case IT-94-1-A, ICTY Appeals Chamber Judgment of 15 July 1999 paras 84, 120–1, 145. See also *Prosecutor v Thomas Lubanga Dyilo*, Case ICC-01/04-01/06, Trial Chamber, Judgment Pursuant to Article 74 of the Statute, 14 Mar 2012 paras 503, 541, 551; *Prosecutor v Germain Katanga*, Case ICC-01/04-01/07, ICC Trial Chamber II, Judgment pursuant to Article 74 of the Statute, 7 Mar 2014 paras 1177–87; *Prosecutor v. Ntaganda*, Case ICC-01/04-02/06, ICC Trial Chamber VI, Judgment, 8 July 2019 paras 700–28; *Prosecutor v Dominic Ongwen*, Case ICC-02/04-01/15, ICC Trial Chamber IX, Judgment, 4 Feb 2021 paras 700–3, 726–7. Cf. Rogier Bartels, 'The Classification of Armed Conflicts by International Criminal Courts and Tribunals' (2020) 20 Int'l Criminal L Rev 595.

occur, or to the specific periods of actual combat – whether a specific situation constitutes an 'armed conflict' requires a holistic evaluation of the parameters of the alleged conflict.[20]

The perpetrator need not have made a legal evaluation whether an international or non-international armed conflict existed, or have realized that the situation qualified as either of the two, but he or she must have been aware of the factual circumstances that established the existence of the armed conflict.[21]

There is no international armed conflict in the Rohingya context although Myanmar has conceded certain war crimes in an internal armed conflict, also known as an armed conflict not of an international character, might have been committed by its security forces.

If the ICC somehow has jurisdiction over war crimes in Myanmar, the following provisions of the Rome Statute will be applicable. By virtue of Article 8(1), the ICC shall have jurisdiction in respect of war crimes in particular when committed as part of a plan or policy or as part of a large-scale commission of such crimes. Article 8(2)(c) enumerates as war crimes in an armed conflict not of an international character 'serious violations of Article 3 common to the four Geneva Conventions of 12 August 1949',[22] namely, any of the following acts committed against persons taking no active part in the hostilities, including members of armed forces who have laid down their arms and those placed *hors de combat* by sickness, wounds, detention or any other cause: (i) violence to life and person, in particular murder of all kinds, mutilation, cruel treatment and torture; (ii) committing outrages upon personal dignity, in particular humiliating and degrading treatment; (iii) taking of hostages; (iv) the passing of sentences and the carrying out of executions without previous judgment pronounced by a regularly constituted court, affording all judicial guarantees which are generally recognized as indispensable. Article 8(2)(d) clarifies that Article 8(2)(c) applies to armed conflicts not of an international character and thus does not apply to situations of internal disturbances and tensions, such as riots, isolated and sporadic acts of violence or other acts of a similar nature.

Article 8(2)(e) additionally lists the following acts as war crimes in an internal armed conflict: (i) intentionally directing attacks against the civilian population as such or against individual civilians not taking direct part in hostilities;[23] (ii) intentionally directing attacks against buildings, material, medical units and

20 *Prosecutor v Jadranko Prlić et al.*, Case IT-04-74-A, ICTY Appeals Chamber, 29 Nov 2017 para 230.

21 *Ongwen*, ICC Trial Chamber IX, Judgment, 4 Feb 2021 para 1172.

22 Convention for the Amelioration of the Condition of the Wounded and Sick in Armed Forces in the Field (75 UNTS 31); Convention for the Amelioration of the Condition of the Wounded, Sick, and Shipwrecked Members of Armed Forces at Sea (75 UNTS 85); Convention Relative to the Treatment of Prisoners of War (75 UNTS 135); and Convention Relative to the Protection of Civilian Persons in Time of War (75 UNTS 287). They came into force on 21 Oct 1950.

23 See *Katanga*, ICC Trial Chamber II, Judgment pursuant to Article 74 of the Statute, 7 Mar 2014 paras 795–808; *Ntaganda*, ICC Trial Chamber VI, Judgment, 8 July 2019 para 904.

transport, and personnel using in conformity with international law the distinctive emblems of the four Geneva Conventions of 1949 on the humanitarian treatment and protection of victims during armed conflicts; (iii) intentionally directing attacks against personnel, installations, material, units or vehicles involved in a humanitarian assistance or peacekeeping mission in accordance with the UN Charter, as long as they are entitled to the protection given to civilians or civilian objects under the international law of armed conflict; (iv) intentionally directing attacks against buildings dedicated to religion, education, art, science or charitable purposes, historic monuments, hospitals and places where the sick and wounded are collected, provided they are not military objectives;[24] (v) pillaging a town or place, even when taken by assault;[25] (vi) committing rape, sexual slavery, enforced prostitution, forced pregnancy;[26] (f) enforced sterilization, and any other form of sexual violence of a gravity comparable to that of a serious violation of Article 3 common to the four Geneva Conventions of 1949; (vii) conscripting or enlisting children under the age of 15 years into armed forces or groups or using them to participate actively in hostilities;[27] (viii) ordering the displacement of the civilian population for reasons related to the conflict, unless the security of the civilians involved or imperative military reasons so demand;[28] (ix) killing or wounding treacherously a combatant adversary; (x) declaring that no quarter will be given; (xi) subjecting persons who are in the power of another party to the conflict to physical mutilation or to medical or scientific experiments of any kind which are neither justified by the medical, dental or hospital treatment of the person concerned nor carried out in his or her interest, and which cause death to or seriously endanger the health of such person or persons; (xii) destroying or seizing the property of an adversary unless such destruction or seizure be imperatively demanded by the necessities of the conflict.[29] Article 8(2)(f) clarifies that Article 8(2)(e) applies to armed conflicts not of an international character and thus does not apply to situations of internal disturbances

24 See *Prosecutor v Ahmad Al Faqi Al Mahdi*, Case ICC-01/12-01/15, ICC Trial Chamber VIII, Judgment and Sentence, 27 Sept 2016; *Ongwen*, ICC Trial Chamber IX, Judgment, 4 Feb 2021 para 1136.

25 See *Prosecutor v Thomas Lubanga Dyilo*, Case ICC-01/04-01/06, ICC Trial Chamber I, Judgment pursuant to Article 74 of the Statute, 14 Mar 2012; *Katanga*, ICC Trial Chamber II, Judgment pursuant to Article 74 of the Statute, 7 Mar 2014 paras 902–14.

26 On rape and sexual slavery, see *Katanga*, ICC Trial Chamber II, Judgment pursuant to Article 74 of the Statute, 7 Mar 2014 paras 961–84; *Ntaganda*, ICC Trial Chamber VI, Judgment, 8 July 2019 paras 930, 932–5; 951–2.

27 See *Katanga*, ICC Trial Chamber II, Judgment pursuant to Article 74 of the Statute, 7 Mar 2014 paras 1038–50; *Ntaganda*, ICC Trial Chamber VI, Judgment, 8 July 2019 paras 1102–9; *Ongwen*, ICC Trial Chamber IX, Judgment, 4 Feb 2021 paras 1104–9.

28 See *Prosecutor v Bosco Ntaganda*, Case ICC-01/04-02/06 A A2, ICC Appeals Chamber, Judgment, 30 Mar 2021 paras 530–68.

29 See *Katanga*, ICC Trial Chamber II, Judgment pursuant to Article 74 of the Statute, 7 Mar 2014 paras 887–901; *Ntaganda*, ICC Trial Chamber VI, Judgment, 8 July 2019 paras 1151–2, 1158, 1164–6; *Ongwen*, ICC Trial Chamber IX, Judgment, 4 Feb 2021 paras 1151–2, 1158–67.

and tensions, such as riots, isolated and sporadic acts of violence or other acts of a similar nature. Furthermore, Article 8(2)(e) applies to armed conflicts that take place in the territory of a State when there is protracted armed conflict between governmental authorities and organized armed groups or between such groups. Article 8(3) stipulates that nothing in paragraph 2(c) and (e) of Article 8 shall affect the responsibility of a Government to maintain or re-establish law and order in the State or to defend the unity and territorial integrity of the State, by all 'legitimate means'.[30]

Crimes against humanity

Under international criminal law, crimes against humanity are distinguished from ordinary crimes in their respective contexts.[31] Crimes against humanity are serious crimes committed in the context of widespread *or* systematic attacks, and not just random acts of violence, against civilian population.[32]

Article 7(1) of the Rome Statute defines 'crime against humanity' as any of the following acts when committed as part of a widespread *or* systematic attack directed against any civilian population, with knowledge of the attack: (a) murder;[33] (b) extermination; (c) enslavement; (d) *deportation or forcible transfer of population*; (e) imprisonment or other severe deprivation of physical liberty in violation of fundamental rules of international law; (f) torture; (g) rape, sexual slavery, enforced prostitution, forced pregnancy, enforced sterilization, or any other form of sexual violence of comparable gravity;[34] (h) persecution against any identifiable group or collectivity on political, racial, national, ethnic, cultural, religious, gender or other grounds that are universally recognized as impermissible under international law, in connection with any act referred to in this paragraph or any crime within the ICC's jurisdiction; (i) enforced disappearance of persons; (j) the crime of apartheid; (k) other inhumane acts of a similar character intentionally causing great suffering, or serious injury to body or to mental or physical health.

30 See further Knut Dörmann, *Elements of War Crimes under the Rome Statute of the International Criminal Court: Sources and Commentary* (Cambridge University Press 2003) Chapters 7 and 8; Eve La Haye, *War Crimes in International Armed Conflicts* (Cambridge University Press 2008).

31 See, generally, Egon Schwelb, 'Crimes against Humanity' (1946) 23 British YBIL 178; Mark Lattimer and Philippe Sands, *Justice for Crimes Against Humanity* (Hart 2003); Larry May, *Crimes against Humanity: A Normative Account* (Cambridge University Press 2004); M Cherif Bassiouni, *Crimes against Humanity: Historical Evolution and Contemporary Application* (Cambridge University Press 2011); Guénaël Mettraux, *International Crimes: Law and Practice*, vol II (Crimes against Humanity) (Oxford University Press 2020).

32 *Tadic*, Case IT-94-1-A, ICTY Appeals Chamber Judgment, 15 July 1999 para 271.

33 See *Katanga*, ICC Trial Chamber II, Judgment pursuant to Article 74 of the Statute, 7 Mar 2014 paras 765–782.

34 See ibid paras 967, 970–1, 974–9, 981–3; *Ntaganda*, ICC Trial Chamber VI, Judgment, 8 July 2019 paras 930–1, 933–5, 952.

Article 7(2)(a) of the Rome Statute adds that, for the purpose of paragraph 1 of Article 7: 'attack directed against any civilian population' means a course of conduct involving the multiple commission of acts referred to in paragraph 1 against any civilian population, pursuant to or in furtherance of a State or organizational policy to commit such attack.

The first session of the Assembly of States Parties to the Rome Statute, held in September 2002, has adopted the Elements of Crimes[35] to guide the ICC in interpreting the relevant provisions of the Statute. The Elements of Crimes reiterate that a conduct criminalized as a crime against humanity must be committed as part of a widespread or systematic attack directed against a civilian population, and clarify that the perpetrator 'knew the conduct was part of or intended the conduct to be part of a widespread or systematic attack directed against a civilian population'. However, the requisite element of knowledge by the perpetrator should not be interpreted as requiring proof that the perpetrator had knowledge of all characteristics of the attack or the precise details of the plan or policy of the State or organization. In the case of an emerging widespread or systematic attack against a civilian population, the intent requirement is satisfied if the perpetrator intended to further such an attack.[36] 'Attack directed against a civilian population' is defined as a course of conduct involving the multiple commission of acts referred to in Article 7 of the Rome Statute against any civilian population, pursuant to or in furtherance of a State or organizational *policy* to commit such attack. The acts need not constitute a military attack. 'Policy to commit such attack' requires that the State or organization actively promote or encourage such an attack against a civilian population. A policy which has a civilian population as the object of the attack would be implemented by State or organizational action. Such a policy may, in exceptional circumstances, be implemented by a deliberate failure to take action, which is consciously aimed at encouraging such attack. The existence of such a policy cannot be inferred solely from the absence of governmental or organizational action.

35 Elements of Crimes (as amended), 2 Nov 2000 (ICC-ASP/1/3 (Pt II-B), UN Doc PCNICC/2000/1/Add.2).

36 However, according to the ICC Trial Chamber II in *Katanga*, the requirement that the perpetrator of the act knowingly participated in the attack directed against a civilian population should not be interpreted to require proof that the perpetrator had knowledge of all of the characteristics of the attack or the precise details of the plan or policy of the State or organization. Nor is it required that the perpetrator of the act subscribed to the State or the organization's criminal design, any more than it must be shown that the perpetrator deliberately intended his or her act to form part of the attack against the civilian population, even though the Elements of Crimes mention this scenario. The perpetrator's motive is hence irrelevant to such proof, and for his or her act to be characterized as a crime against humanity it suffices to establish, in view of the context, knowledge of the particular fact that his or her act formed part of the attack (*Katanga*, ICC Trial Chamber II, Judgment pursuant to Article 74 of the Statute, 7 Mar 2014 para 1125). See also *Ongwen*, Trial Chamber IX, Judgment, 4 Feb 2021 para 1170.

The ICC has held that 'attack directed against any civilian population' denotes a 'campaign, an operation or a series of actions directed against the civilian population, *viz.* a course of conduct and not a single isolated act'. The proof required to establish the existence of an attack cannot be confused with the proof required to demonstrate the widespread nature of the attack, lest the alternative possibilities foreseen, *viz.* that the attack may be widespread or systematic, be rendered meaningless. This first step consists of proving only that the course of conduct involved the multiple commission of acts referred to in Article 7(1). In this connection, where established that it involved such multiple commission of acts, a single event may well constitute an attack directed against any civilian population, provided that the other elements of Article 7 are met.[37] Whereas a civilian population under Article 7(1) cannot constitute a limited and randomly selected group of individuals, the use of 'any' indicates that the provision should not be understood as being limited to populations defined by a common nationality, ethnicity or other similar distinguishing features.[38] Also, Article 7 of the Statute requires a finding that the attack was 'directed against any civilian population' and does not require a separate finding that the civilian population was the *primary*, as opposed to incidental, object of the attack – an attack directed against a civilian population may also serve other objectives or motives.[39]

According to the ICC, the 'policy' element refers essentially to the fact that a State or organization intends to carry out an attack against a civilian population, whether through action or deliberate failure to take action. 'Policy' does not preclude a design adopted by a State or organization with regard to a certain population in a given geopolitical situation. However, the Rome Statute does not require the existence of a formal design. In any event, the policy must always target a particular civilian population or a part thereof. It is relatively rare, although cannot be wholly excluded, for a State or organization seeking to encourage an attack against a civilian population to adopt and disseminate a pre-established design or plan to that effect. In most cases, the existence of such a State or organizational policy can be inferred by discernment of, *inter alia*, (i) the fact that the attack was planned or directed; (ii) the existence of a recurrent pattern of violence, for example, repeated actions occurring according to a same sequence; (iii) the use of public or private resources to further the policy; (iv) the involvement of the State or organizational forces in the commission of crimes; (v) statements, instructions or documentation attributable to the State or the organization condoning or encouraging the commission of crimes; (vi) an underlying motivation; and (vii) the existence of preparations or collective mobilization orchestrated and coordinated by that State or organization.

37 *Katanga*, ICC Trial Chamber II, Judgment pursuant to Article 74 of the Statute, 7 Mar 2014 para 1101. See also *Ongwen*, ICC Trial Chamber IX, Judgment, 4 Feb 2021 paras 660–3

38 *Ntaganda*, ICC Trial Chamber VI, Judgment, 8 July 2019 para 667; *Ongwen*, ICC Trial Chamber IX, Judgment, 4 Feb 2021 para 667.

39 *Ntaganda*, ICC Appeals Chamber, Judgment, 30 Mar 2021 paras 417–8, 424.

Furthermore, some aspects of the policy pursued against a civilian population will only crystallize and develop as actions are set in train and undertaken by the perpetrators. The State or organizational policy may therefore become clear to the perpetrators, as regards its modalities, only in the course of its implementation, such that definition of the overall policy is possible only *in retrospect*, once the acts have been committed and in the light of the overall operation or course of conduct pursued. Otherwise stated, the State or organizational policy may be part of an ongoing process whose every aspect is not always predetermined before the operation or course of conduct pursued against the targeted civilian population has commenced or even once it has started.[40]

Neither the Rome Statute nor the Elements of Crime define(s) 'widespread or systematic attack'. In the case law of international criminal tribunals, a widespread attack is an attack directed against a multiplicity of victims, whereas a systematic attack is an attack carried out pursuant to a preconceived policy or plan. Phrased differently, 'widespread' means massive, frequent, large-scale action occurring in different locations, carried out collectively with considerable seriousness and directed against a multiplicity of victims, whereas 'systematic' means thoroughly organized and following a regular or consistent, and not random or accidental, pattern on the basis of a preconceived policy or plan, although this policy or plan may not be adopted formally as the policy or plan of a State.[41] The ICC has clarified that the systematic nature of the attack is understood to refer to the organized nature of the acts of violence. Any attack directed against a civilian population that may be considered 'systematic' will in principle presuppose the existence of a State or organizational policy, but that does not mean that the terms 'policy' and 'systematic' are to be considered synonymous. The adjective 'systematic' allows the nature of the attack, understood in a broad sense, to be characterized and to bring to the fore the existence of a pattern of repeated conduct or the recurring or continuous perpetration of interlinked, non-random acts of violence that establish the existence of a crime against humanity. To establish a 'policy', it need be demonstrated only that the State or organization meant to commit an attack against a civilian population. An analysis of the systematic nature of the attack therefore goes beyond the existence of any policy

40 *Katanga*, ICC Trial Chamber II, Judgment pursuant to Article 74 of the Statute, 7 Mar 2014 paras 1108–13. See also *Ntaganda*, ICC Trial Chamber VI, Judgment, 8 July 2019 paras 673–4; *Ongwen*, ICC Trial Chamber IX, Judgment, 4 Feb 2021 paras 673–4; *Ntaganda*, ICC Appeals Chamber, Judgment, 30 Mar 2021 paras 375–6.

41 *Prosecutor v Kayishema and Ruzindana*, Case ICTR-95-1-T, ICTR Trial Chamber II, 21 May 1999 para 123; *Prosecutor v Jean-Paul Akayesu*, Case ICTR-96-4, ICTR Trial Chamber I, 2 Sept 1998 para 580; *Prosecutor v Rutaganda*, Case ICTR-96-3, ICTR Trial Chamber I, 6 Dec 1999 para 67; *Prosecutor v Alfred Musema*, Case ICTR-96-13-T, ICTR Trial Chamber I, 27 Jan 2000 para 204; *Prosecutor v Dusko Tadic*, Case IT-94-1-T, ICTY Trial Chamber II, 7 May 1997 para 648; *Prosecutor v Tihomir Blaskic*, Case IT-95-14-T, ICTY Trial Chamber, 3 Mar 2000 paras 206–7. Followed in *Katanga*, ICC Trial Chamber II, Judgment pursuant to Article 74 of the Statute, 7 Mar 2014 para 1123; *Ongwen*, ICC Trial Chamber IX, Judgment, 4 Feb 2021 paras 691–2.

seeking to eliminate, persecute or undermine a community. Such analysis also entails inquiry as to whether a series of repeated actions seeking to produce always the same effects on a civilian population was undertaken with consideration – identical acts or similarities in criminal practices, continual repetition of a same *modus operandi*, similar treatment meted out to victims or consistency in such treatment across a wide geographic area.[42] The organization promoting or encouraging such attack need not be structured so as to assume the characteristics of a State or a quasi-State. Of prime importance are the capacities for action, mutual agreement and coordination, which are essential features to defining an organization that, by very reason of the means and resources it possesses and its membership, allow an attack to be executed.[43]

Article 7(2)(d) defines 'deportation or forcible transfer of population', which clearly has a transboundary effect, as 'forced displacement of the persons concerned by expulsion or other coercive acts from the area in which they are lawfully present, without grounds permitted under international law'. This is further elaborated by the Elements of Crimes to mean the perpetrator must have deported or forcibly transferred, without grounds permitted under international law, one or more persons to another State or location, by expulsion or other coercive acts. The term 'forcibly' is not restricted to physical force, but may include threat of force or coercion, such as that caused by fear of violence, duress, detention, psychological oppression or abuse of power against such person or persons or another person, or by taking advantage of a coercive environment. 'Deported or forcibly transferred' is interchangeable with 'forcibly displaced'. Such person or persons must have been lawfully present in the area from which they were so deported or transferred, and the perpetrator was aware of the factual circumstances that established the lawfulness of such presence.

As part of its response to the ICC Prosecutor's request for a ruling on a question whether the ICC may exercise jurisdiction over the alleged deportation of the Rohingya people from Myanmar to Bangladesh, the ICC Pre-Trial Chamber I rules that Article 7(1)(d) of the Rome Statute sets forth two separate crimes, namely deportation *and* forcible transfer. The Elements of Crimes pertaining to Article 7(1)(d) of the Statute support this interpretation by linking the conduct and the destinations. In more specific terms, 'deported' is linked to the destination of 'another State', while 'forcibly transferred' is linked to the destination of 'another [...] location' (which specifically entails another location within the same State). This means that, if all other requirements are met, the displacement of persons lawfully residing in an area to another State amounts to deportation, whereas such displacement to a location within the borders of a State must be

42 *Katanga*, ICC Trial Chamber II, Judgment pursuant to Article 74 of the Statute, 7 Mar 2014 paras 1111–3; *Ntaganda*, ICC Trial Chamber VI, Judgment, 8 July 2019 paras 691–3.

43 *Katanga*, ICC Trial Chamber II, Judgment pursuant to Article 74 of the Statute, 7 Mar 2014 paras 1120–2.

characterized as forcible transfer. In this connection, the Pre-Trial Chamber disagrees with the formulation in the Elements of Crimes that 'deported or forcibly transferred' is interchangeable with 'forcibly displaced' since such formulation is not consistent with Article 7(2)(d) of the Rome Statute. The prohibition against deportation as a crime against humanity is strongly embedded in international law, having been included in a number of international instruments, including Statutes of international tribunals. Moreover, individuals have been held accountable for this crime by different international courts and tribunals, including the International Military Tribunal at Nuremberg after the Second World War. On the other hand, the prohibition against forcible transfer as a crime against humanity was first expressed following the recognition of deportation as a crime against humanity. The legal interest commonly protected by the crimes of deportation and forcible transfer is the right of individuals to live in their area of residence. However, the legal interest protected by the crime of deportation further extends to the right of individuals to live in the State in which they are lawfully present. According to the ICC's jurisprudence, the destination requirement distinguishes between deportation and forcible transfer. The Pre-Trial Chamber adds that deportation or forcible transfer of population is an open-conduct crime, meaning a perpetrator may commit several different conducts which can amount to 'expulsion or other coercive acts'. This means, in the Rohingya context, various types of conduct may, if established to the relevant threshold, qualify as 'expulsion or other coercive acts' for the purposes of the crime against humanity of deportation, including deprivation of fundamental rights, killing, sexual violence, torture, enforced disappearance, destruction and looting.[44]

According to the ICTY, an essential element for the crime against humanity of deportation or forcible transfer of population is the involuntary nature of the displacement. It is the absence of 'genuine choice' that makes a given act of displacement unlawful. In this context, genuine choice cannot be inferred from the fact that consent was expressed where the circumstances deprive the consent of any value. In addition, a lack of genuine choice may be inferred from threatening and intimidating acts calculated to deprive the civilian population of exercising its free will, such as the shelling of civilian objects, the burning of civilian property, and the commission of or the threat to commit other crimes calculated to terrify the population and make them flee the area with no hope of return. There are two general grounds under international law according to which displacement of persons is legitimate: it may be carried out either for the security of a civilian population or for imperative military reasons. In either case, the chief distinction between an illegitimate forcible displacement and a permissible evacuation is that, in the case of the latter, persons thus evacuated are transferred back to their homes as soon as the hostilities in the area in question have ceased. It is

44 *Decision on the 'Prosecution's Request for a Ruling on Jurisdiction under Article 19(3) of the Statute'*, Case ICC-RoC46(3)-01/18, 6 Sept 2018 paras 52–61.

therefore unlawful to use evacuation measures as a pretext to forcibly dislocate a population and seize control over a territory. The offences of deportation and forcible transfer do not require intent that the victims be displaced permanently, only that they be intentionally displaced. As with the knowledge requirement for all crimes against humanity and the specific intent requirement for persecution, the intent to displace the victims may be that of either the physical perpetrator or the planner, orderer or instigator of the physical perpetrator's conduct.[45]

The ICTY has also ruled that the underlying offence of forcible transfer constitutes the statutory crime of 'other inhumane acts'. For a physical perpetrator's act or omission to constitute an inhumane act as a crime against humanity, four specific requirements must have been identified: (a) the conduct must cause serious mental or physical suffering to the victim or constitute a serious attack upon human dignity; (b) the conduct must be of equal gravity to the conduct enumerated as crimes against humanity; and (c) the physical perpetrator must have performed the act or omission deliberately (d) with the intent to inflict serious physical or mental harm upon the victim or commit a serious attack upon human dignity or with the knowledge that his act or omission would probably cause serious physical or mental harm to the victim or constitute a serious attack upon human dignity. Applying the above analysis, in order to prove that forcible transfer as the crime against humanity of 'other inhumane acts' was committed, the Prosecution must prove: (a) the act and intent of forcible displacement, (b) the general requirement of crimes against humanity and (c) the four specific requirements for other inhumane acts, set out above.[46]

With respect to the Rome Statute, the Elements of Crimes explain that in the case of the crime against humanity of other inhumane acts proscribed by Article 7(1)(K) of the Statute the perpetrator must have inflicted great suffering, or serious injury to body or to mental or physical health, by means of an inhumane act of the nature and gravity similar to any other act referred to in Article 7(1) of the Statute, being aware of the factual circumstances that established the nature and gravity of the act. The conduct must have been committed as part of a widespread or systematic attack directed against a civilian population and the perpetrator knew that the conduct was part of or intended the conduct to be part of a widespread or systematic attack directed against a civilian population.

The crime against humanity of persecution under Article 7(1)(h) of the Rome Statute is defined in Article 7(2)(g) to mean 'the intentional and severe deprivation of fundamental rights contrary to international law by reason of the

45 *Prosecutor v Milan Milutinović et al.*, Case IT-05-87-T, ICTY Trial Chamber, 26 Feb 2009 paras 165–7. The ICTY Trial Chamber also held that the intent to displace the victims may be that of a member of the 'joint criminal enterprise' carried out by groups or individuals acting in pursuance of a common criminal design. As will be explained below, the ICC has not adopted the notion of joint criminal enterprise, first propounded by the ICTY Appeals Chamber in *Tadic*, Judgment of 15 July 1999 para 185 ff.

46 *Prosecutor v Milutinović et al.*, Case IT-05-87-T, ICTY Trial Chamber, 26 Feb 2009 paras 170–1.

identity of the group or collectivity'. The Elements of Crimes further elaborate the elements of the crime of persecution as follows. First, the perpetrator severely deprived, contrary to international law, one or more persons of fundamental rights. Second, the perpetrator targeted such person or persons by reason of the identity of a group or collectivity or targeted the group or collectivity as such. Third, such targeting was based on political, racial, national, ethnic, cultural, religious, gender or other grounds that are universally recognized as impermissible under international law. Fourth, the conduct was committed in connection with any act referred to in Article 7(1) of the Rome Statute or any crime within the ICC's jurisdiction. Fifth, the conduct was committed as part of a widespread or systematic attack directed against a civilian population, and the perpetrator knew that the conduct was part of or intended the conduct to be part of a widespread or systematic attack directed against a civilian population.

In *Ongwen*, the ICC further explains the elements of persecution as a crime against humanity as follows. For the purpose of identifying those rights whose severe infringement may constitute persecution, more defined parameters for the definition of human dignity can be found in international standards on human rights such as those laid down in the 1948 Universal Declaration of Human Rights,[47] the 1966 International Covenant on Civil and Political Rights[48] and the 1966 International Covenant on Economic Social and Cultural Rights,[49] and other international instruments on international human rights, as well as the rights reflected in international humanitarian law. Drawing upon the various provisions of these texts, it is possible to identify a set of fundamental rights pertaining to any human being, the gross infringement of which may amount to, depending on the surrounding circumstances, a crime against humanity. Examples of such rights include the right to life, liberty and the security of person, the right not to be subjected to cruel, inhuman or degrading treatment or punishment, and the right not to be subjected to arbitrary arrest, detention or exile. Persecution consists of a severe attack on those rights. The determination as to which acts will result in the severe deprivation of one or more individuals' fundamental rights must be made on a case-by-case basis. For the purpose of this assessment, the ICC will examine the acts 'in their context and with consideration of their cumulative effect' to ascertain whether taken alone or in conjunction with other acts, they resulted in the 'gross or blatant denial' of fundamental rights. With respect to the mention in the first legal element that the deprivation of a fundamental right must be contrary to international law, this means no justification must exist under international law for the impediment of the concerned right. Furthermore, while human rights law lays down obligations for States to be respected *vis-à-vis* individuals on its territory (or under its overall control), for

47 A/RES/217(III) (10 Dec 1948).
48 993 UNTS 171, in force 23 Mar 1976.
49 993 UNTS 3, in force 3 Jan 1976.

the purpose of its assessment as to whether a deprivation of fundamental rights is 'contrary to international law' as *per* the first element, what matters is that the right cannot be enjoyed by the person entitled to it. Indeed, Article 7(1)(h) would become meaningless if non-State armed groups cannot be held accountable for serious human rights violations. In this connection, the contextual elements of crimes against humanity need to be met for the conduct to qualify as a crime pursuant to Article 7(1)(h). This ensures that not any infringement of a person's right(s) by individuals other than State agents amount to persecution, but only those committed by a sufficiently organized entity, pursuant to a policy to attack a civilian population in a widespread or systematic manner. Against this background, the commission of any act considered to be a crime against humanity will, in principle, result in a deprivation of fundamental rights of one or more individuals, as envisaged in Article 7(2)(h), and meet, in and of itself, the minimum level of severity required. Acts of murder and the causing of serious injury as well as rape and sexual slavery, may, for example, constitute underlying acts of persecution.[50]

Trigger mechanisms and preconditions for the ICC's exercise of jurisdiction

A State which becomes a party to the Rome Statute thereby accepts the ICC's jurisdiction with respect to the crimes referred to in Article 5.[51]

By virtue of Article 13 of the Statute, the ICC's jurisdiction is triggered by: (a) referrals by its States Parties; (b) the UN Security Council acting under Chapter VII of the UN Charter to refer a situation in which one or more of the crimes enumerated in Article 5 appears to have been committed; or (c) the ICC Prosecutor initiating investigations on his or her own initiative on the basis of information on crimes within the ICC's jurisdiction.

In the case of Article 13(a) or (c), Article 12(2) of the Statute stipulates that the ICC may exercise its jurisdiction *only if* one or more of the following States are parties to the Rome Statute *or* have accepted the ICC's jurisdiction in accordance with paragraph 3 of Article 12 on an *ad hoc* basis: (a) the State on the territory of which the conduct in question occurred or, if the crime was committed on board a vessel or aircraft, the State of registration of that vessel or aircraft; (b) the State of which the person accused of the crime is a national. Pursuant to Article 12(3), if the acceptance of a State which is not a party to this Statute is required, that State may, by declaration lodged with the ICC Registrar, accept the exercise of jurisdiction by the ICC with respect to the crime in question, in which case the accepting State shall cooperate with the ICC without any delay or exception. On 18 April 2003, Côte d'Ivoire, which was then not party to the

50 *Ongwen*, ICC Trial Chamber IX, Judgment, 4 Feb 2021 paras 991–4.
51 Rome Statute Art 12(1).

Rome Statute, invoked Article 12(3) to declare its acceptance of the ICC's jurisdiction over the situation in that country, and this declaration was reconfirmed on 14 December 2010 and 3 May 2011 before Côte d'Ivoire became party to the Statute in 2013. Ukraine, another State not yet party to the Rome Statute, has lodged two declarations under Article 12(3) in April 2014 and September 2015, respectively. Ukraine's first declaration accepts the ICC's jurisdiction over alleged crimes committed in Ukraine's territory from 21 November 2013 to 22 February 2014, whereas its second declaration accepts such jurisdiction since 20 February 2014.

The following situations currently under investigation by the ICC Prosecutor have been referred by States Parties to the Rome Statute: Uganda (in January 2004), DR Congo (in April 2004), Central African Republic (in December 2004 and, again, in the context of renewed violence starting in 2012, in May 2014) and Mali (in July 2012).

The UN Security Council has referred to the ICC Prosecutor the situation in Darfur, Sudan, which is not party to the Rome Statute. The Council's Resolution 1593 (2005)[52] determines that 'the situation in Sudan continues to constitute a threat to international peace and security', taking note of the report of the International Commission of Inquiry on violations of international humanitarian law and human rights law in Darfur, set up by the UN Secretary-General 'to investigate reports of violations of international humanitarian law and human rights law in Darfur by all parties, to determine also whether or not acts of genocide have occurred, and to identify the perpetrators of such violations with a view to ensuring that those responsible are held accountable'. The Resolution authorizes the ICC to exercise its jurisdiction over crimes listed in the Rome Statute committed on the territory of Darfur, Sudan, or by its nationals from 1 July 2002, when the Rome Statute entered into force, onward.

In Resolution 1970 (2011),[53] the UN Security Council refers the situation in Libya, another non-State Party to the Rome Statute, to the ICC Prosecutor after condemning the violence and use of force against civilians, deploring the gross and systematic violation of human rights, including the repression of peaceful demonstrators, expressing deep concern at the deaths of civilians, and rejecting unequivocally the incitement to hostility and violence against the civilian population made from the highest level of the Libyan Government, then under President Muammar Gaddafi. The referral notes that the widespread and systematic attacks against the civilian population may amount to crimes against humanity, and expresses concern at the plight of refugees forced to flee the violence and at the reports of shortages of medical supplies to treat the wounded. It underlines 'the need to respect the freedoms of peaceful assembly and of

52 S/RES/1593 (31 Mar 2005).
53 S/RES/1970 (26 Feb 2011).

expression, including freedom of the media' and stresses 'the need to hold to account those responsible for attacks, including by forces under their control, on civilians'.

The ICC Prosecutor has initiated investigations on his or her own initiative with regard to the situations in, for example, Kenya (in March 2010), Georgia (in February 2016), Burundi (in October 2017), *Bangladesh/Myanmar* (in July 2019) and Nigeria (in December 2020). In the case of Nigeria, the ICC Prosecutor's Office found a reasonable basis to believe, after reviewing the conflict between Nigerian government forces and Boko Haram and its various splinter groups in western and northern Nigeria since 2010, that Boko Haram and its splinter groups had committed war crimes and crimes against humanity in Nigeria, through murder, rape, sexual slavery and torture, and that members of the Nigerian security forces had also committed crimes including murder, rape, torture and cruel treatment, as well as enforced disappearance and forcible transfer of the population and attacks directed at civilians.

As regards the situation in Bangladesh/Myanmar, the ICC Pre-Trial Chamber I has clarified a question of law regarding the ICC's jurisdiction over allegations that members of the Rohingya people from Myanmar (a State which is not party to the Rome Statute and which has not accepted the ICC's jurisdiction pursuant to Article 12(3) of the Statute) were deported to Bangladesh (a State Party to the Statute). The Pre-Trial Chamber rules the preconditions for the exercise of the ICC's jurisdiction pursuant to Article 12(2)(a) of the Statute are, as a minimum, fulfilled if *at least one legal element of a crime within the ICC's jurisdiction or part of such a crime is committed on the territory of a State Party.* An element of the crime of deportation as a crime against humanity under the Statute is forced displacement across international borders, which means the conduct related to this crime necessarily takes place on the territories of at least two States. What is more, the drafters of the Statute did not limit the crime of deportation from one State Party to another State Party. Article 7(2)(d) only speaks of displacement from 'the area in which they were lawfully present' and the elements of crimes generally refer to deportation to 'another State'. Therefore, the inclusion of the inherently transboundary crime of deportation in the Statute without limitation as to the requirement regarding the destination reflects the intentions of the drafters to, among other things, allow for the exercise of the ICC's jurisdiction when one element of this crime or part of it is committed on the territory of a State Party. Phrased differently, acts of deportation initiated in a State not party to the Statute (through expulsion or other coercive acts) and completed in a State Party to the Statute (by virtue of victims crossing the border to a State) fall within the parameters of Article 12(2)(a). Consequently, in the circumstances identified in the ICC Prosecutor's request, the ICC has jurisdiction over the alleged deportation of members of the Rohingya people from Myanmar to Bangladesh, provided that such allegations are established to the required threshold. This conclusion is without prejudice to subsequent findings on jurisdiction at a later stage of the proceedings.[54]

The ICC Pre-Trial Chamber emphasizes that the rationale of its determination as to the ICC's jurisdiction over the crime of deportation may apply to other crimes within the ICC's jurisdiction as well if at least an element of another crime within the ICC's jurisdiction or part of such a crime is committed on the territory of a State Party. In this regard, the Pre-Trial Chamber refers to two examples of such crimes – persecution and other inhumane acts as crimes against humanity. Denying the Rohingya finding refuge outside Myanmar the right to return to Rakhine state in Myanmar could be tantamount to persecution. In addition, Article 7(1)(k) stipulates that '[o]ther inhumane acts of a similar character intentionally causing great suffering, or serious injury to body or to mental or physical health', amount to a crime against humanity within the ICC's jurisdiction. The Pre-Trial Chamber notes that, following their deportation, members of the Rohingya people allegedly live in appalling conditions in Bangladesh and the Myanmar authorities supposedly impede their return to Myanmar. If these allegations are to be established to the required threshold, the ICC is able to exercise jurisdiction over these two trans-boundary crimes in Bangladesh, a State Party to the Rome Statute.[55]

After the above ruling on the question of jurisdiction, on 4 July 2019 the ICC Prosecutor submitted a request to the ICC for authorization to investigate the situation in Bangladesh/Myanmar in the period since 9 October 2016, specifically as regards crimes within the ICC's jurisdiction in which at least one element occurred on Bangladesh's territory and which occurred within the context of two waves of violence, in 2016 and 2017, in Rakhine state on Myanmar's territory, as well as *any other crimes* sufficiently linked to these events. In its Decision of 14 November 2019, the ICC Pre-Trial Chamber III accepts there is a reasonable basis to believe that: since at least 9 October 2016, widespread and/or systematic acts of violence may have been committed against the Rohingya population, including murder, imprisonment, torture, rape, sexual violence as well as other coercive acts, resulting in their large-scale deportation; these coercive acts could qualify as the *crimes against humanity of deportation and persecution* on grounds of ethnicity and/or religion against the Rohingya population; and there may have been a State policy to attack the Rohingya population, given that there are many sources indicating the heavy involvement of several Myanmar government forces and other government agents, and that members of the Tatmadaw, jointly with other Myanmar security forces and with some participation of local civilians, may have committed these crimes against humanity.[56] On the important issue

54 *Decision on the 'Prosecution's Request for a Ruling on Jurisdiction under Article 19(3) of the Statute'* paras 64, 69–73.

55 Ibid paras 74–9.

56 *Decision Pursuant to Article 15 of the Rome Statute on the Authorisation of an Investigation into the Situation in the People's Republic of Bangladesh/Republic of the Union of Myanmar*, No ICC-0-1/19, 14 Nov 2019 paras 104–10.

of territorial jurisdiction, the ICC Pre-Trial Chamber III has agreed with the 6 September 2018 ruling by the ICC Pre-Trial Chamber I that the ICC may exercise jurisdiction over crimes when part of the criminal conduct takes place on the territory of a State Party to the Rome Statute. The Pre-Trial Chamber III has also concluded the alleged deportation of civilians across the Myanmar-Bangladesh border, which involved victims crossing that border, clearly establishes a territorial link on the basis of the proscribed conduct of this crime (i.e., the crossing into Bangladesh by the victims).[57]

Besides, the Pre-Trial Chamber III has authorized an investigation with broad parameters. Specifically, it has authorized an investigation in relation to *any crimes* within the ICC's jurisdiction, including any future crimes, committed at least in part on Bangladesh's territory, or on the territory of any other State Party or State which would accept the ICC's jurisdiction in accordance with Article 12(3) of the Statute, insofar as such crimes are sufficiently linked to the Rohingya situation. Similarly, the Prosecutor is also not restricted to the persons or groups of persons identified in the Request. This is because the information available to the Prosecutor at the preliminary examination stage is necessarily limited.[58] As for the time period, the Pre-Trial Chamber has authorized the investigation of crimes allegedly committed on or after 1 June 2010, the date of entry into force of the Rome Statute for Bangladesh, and, in relation to crimes allegedly committed, at least in part, on the territory of *other* State Parties – after the date of entry in force of the Rome Statute for those States Parties. Regarding alleged crimes that have a continuous nature, the Prosecutor may extend her investigation even when such crimes commenced before 1 June 2010 (or the date of entry into force of the Statute for any other relevant State Party) insofar as the crimes continued after this date.[59] Also, taking into account the gravity of the crime and the interests of victims, there is *no* substantial reason to believe an investigation into the Rohingya situation would not be in the interests of justice.[60]

57 Ibid paras 43–62.

58 At the preliminary examination stage, the OTP does not enjoy investigative powers other than for the purpose of receiving testimony at the seat of the ICC in The Hague and receiving information on alleged crimes. It may seek additional information from States, UN organs, intergovernmental and non-governmental organizations and other reliable sources appropriate for the purpose of analysing the seriousness of the information received. The OTP may also undertake field missions to the territory concerned to consult with the competent national authorities, the affected communities and other relevant stakeholders, such as civil society organizations (Office of the Prosecutor, *Policy Paper on Preliminary Examinations* (International Criminal Court 2013) para 85).

59 *Decision Pursuant to Article 15 of the Rome Statute on the Authorisation of an Investigation into the Situation in the People's Republic of Bangladesh/Republic of the Union of Myanmar* paras 126–33.

60 Ibid paras 118–9. Under Article 53(1)(c) and (2)(c) of the Rome Statute, the ICC Prosecutor shall, having evaluated the information made available to him/her, initiate an investigation unless he/she determines there is no reasonable basis to proceed under this Statute. In deciding whether to initiate an investigation, the Prosecutor shall consider whether, taking into account the gravity of the crime and the interests of victims, there are nonetheless substantial reasons

The ICC Prosecutor explains that the OTP is not restricted to investigating only the events, persons or groups identified in her request, or their provisional legal characterization, since the ICC Pre-Trial Chamber III has emphasized that the OTP may, on the basis of the evidence gathered during the investigation, extend its investigation to other crimes against humanity or other crimes under Article 5 of the Statute, as long as these crimes remain within the parameters of the authorized investigation. The OTP, aware that a number of acts of violence have also allegedly been committed in Myanmar by the Arakan Rohingya Salvation Army will keep these allegations under review as well as the question of whether these acts amount to a crime or crimes under the Statute and were committed in part on the territory of a State Party to the Statute.[61]

Complementarity

The ICC operates on the principle of 'complementarity', deferring to national criminal jurisdictions.[62]

By virtue of Article 17(1) of the Rome Statute, the ICC shall determine that a case is inadmissible where: (a) the case is being investigated or prosecuted by a State which has jurisdiction over it, unless the State is unwilling or unable genuinely to carry out the investigation or prosecution; (b) the case has been investigated by a State which has jurisdiction over it and the State has decided not to prosecute the person concerned, unless the decision resulted from the unwillingness or inability of the State genuinely to prosecute; (c) the person concerned has already been tried for conduct which is the subject of the complaint, and a trial by the ICC is not permitted under Article 20(3);[63] (d) the case is not of sufficient gravity to justify further action by the ICC.

Pursuant to Article 17(2) of the Statute, in order to determine unwillingness in a particular case, the ICC must consider, having regard to the principles of due process recognized by international law, whether one or more of the following

---

to believe an investigation would not serve the interests of justice. For a critical analysis of this provision, see Talita de Souza Dias, '"Interests of justice": Defining the scope of prosecutorial discretion in Article 53(1)(c) and (2)(c) of the Rome Statute of the International Criminal Court' (2017) 30 Leiden JIL 731. See also Anni Pues, *Prosecutorial Discretion at the International Criminal Court* (Hart 2020).

61 www.icc-cpi.int/Pages/item.aspx?name=20191122-otp-statement-bangladesh-myanmar.

62 Para 10 of the preamble to the Rome Statute. See also Muyiwa Adigun, 'The Principle of Complementarity: A Reflection on Its Meaning, Origin and Types in International Criminal Law' (2021) 29 African J Int'l & Comparative Law 82.

63 Art 20(3) Rome Statute reads: 'No person who has been tried by another court for conduct also proscribed under Article 6, 7 or 8 shall be tried by the [ICC] with respect to the same conduct unless the proceedings in the other court: (a) [w]ere for the purpose of shielding the person concerned from criminal responsibility for crimes within the jurisdiction of the [ICC]; or (b) [o]therwise were not conducted independently or impartially in accordance with the norms of due process recognized by international law and were conducted in a manner which, in the circumstances, was inconsistent with an intent to bring the person concerned to justice.'

exist, as applicable: (a) the proceedings were or are being undertaken or the national decision was made for the purpose of shielding the person concerned from criminal responsibility for crimes within the ICC's jurisdiction; (b) there has been an unjustified delay in the proceedings which in the circumstances is inconsistent with an intent to bring the person concerned to justice; (c) the proceedings were not or are not being conducted independently or impartially, and they were or are being conducted in a manner which, in the circumstances, is inconsistent with an intent to bring the person concerned to justice. Article 17(3) adds that in order to determine inability in a particular case, the ICC is to consider whether, due to a total or substantial collapse or unavailability of its national judicial system, the State is unable to obtain the accused or the necessary evidence and testimony or otherwise unable to carry out its proceedings. For example, on 11 October 2013 the ICC declared inadmissible the ICC Prosecutor's case against Colonel Abdullah Al Senussi, former head of Libya's Military Intelligence accused of two counts of crimes against humanity allegedly committed in 2011 in Libya. This was due to the then on-going national proceedings in Libya against him regarding the same crimes, culminating in his conviction and sentence to death by a Libyan trial court in July 2015. He has appealed against his conviction and sentence, and the ICC has continued to monitor the progress of the Libyan legal proceedings against him.[64]

The Gambia contended at the oral hearings before the ICJ in December 2019 that the Myanmar Government was unable and unwilling to bring justice to the Rohingya. According to both the IIFFMM's reports submitted to the Human Rights Council in September 2018 and September 2019, the Tatmadaw acts with complete impunity and has never been held accountable. The Myanmar Government's standard response is to deny, dismiss and obstruct. It publicly lauds the discipline of Myanmar troops and operations conducted 'in full accordance with the law'. It promotes perpetrators. Occasional superficial investigations have only been undertaken when the Tatmadaw has been faced with public exposure of undeniable evidence. It consistently fails to attribute responsibility, thereby reinforcing its message to troops that they will face no consequences. This pattern is a result of the political and legal construct of Myanmar, whereby the Tatmadaw is removed from all civilian oversight and is given the constitutional right to adjudicate its own affairs. Impunity is also structural; it is built into the legal framework and the system of governance, including Myanmar's Constitution of 2008,[65] Article 343(b) of which stipulates that decisions of the Commander-in-Chief of the Defence Services concerning military justice matters are 'final and

64 *Decision on the admissibility of the case against Abdullah Al-Senussi*, Case ICC-01/11-01/11-466-Red, Pre-Trial Chamber I, 11 Oct 2013. See also *Decision following the declaration of inadmissibility of the case against Abdullah Al-Senussi before the Court*, Case ICC-01/11-01/11, Pre-Trial Chamber I, 7 Aug 2014.

65 www.wipo.int/edocs/lexdocs/laws/en/mm/mm009en.pdf.

conclusive', with no right of appeal.[66] The documented history of crimes committed by the Tatmadaw demonstrates an absence of responsible command and of measures to prevent or repress crimes. Justice has remained elusive for victims in Myanmar for decades, with the Myanmar authorities systematically failing to condemn, investigate and prosecute perpetrators. In the face of the Rakhine crisis, the Myanmar authorities have created *ad hoc* inquiry commissions and boards. The IIFFMM has examined eight such efforts since 2012, finding none meet the standard of an impartial, independent, effective and thorough human rights investigation, and none having led to any prosecution for gross human rights violations and redress for victims. The rare cases, brought mostly before military courts without transparency, are wholly insufficient to counter the overall trend of impunity. Furthermore, Myanmar's military courts are inadequate forums to deal with large-scale human rights violations perpetrated by the military. Nor are Myanmar civilian courts the answer since Myanmar's domestic justice system is not independent and lacks the capacity to respect fair trial standards or to deal with the breadth and gravity of the violations perpetrated by high-level officials, especially crimes under international law. Those who file complaints often face intimidation and reprisals. In short, concludes the IIFFMM, accountability at the domestic level in Myanmar is currently unattainable.

The ICC Prosecutor, in her request for authorization of an investigation pursuant to Article 15 of the Statute, has concluded much the same – the Myanmar Government is simply unwilling to end impunity for these violations, especially those committed by security forces. The Myanmar Government's outright rejection of the IIFFMM's findings in 2018 is also indicative of its unwillingness to pursue accountability at the domestic level. Instead, of the six individuals publicly named by the IIFFMM, two highest-ranking military officials remain in their command positions. According to media reports quoting Commander-in-Chief Senior General Min Aung Hlaing, Major General Maung Soe, Commander of Western Regional Military Command, was removed not for human rights violations but for 'shortcomings in timely response to the early warnings of the use of force and lawless acts'. The Tatmadaw also announced Lieutenant-General Aung Kyaw Zaw had resigned in mid-2018 due to poor health and 'weakness in serving duty'. The Myanmar Government's unwillingness to pursue accountability was demonstrated graphically by the release of seven Tatmadaw soldiers in November 2018. The seven had been convicted and sentenced to ten years' imprisonment for killing ten Rohingya civilians in Inn Din village, Maungdaw township, on 2 September 2017. They were pardoned by the Senior General and released after less than a year in detention. By contrast, two *Reuters* journalists

66 See also Melissa Crouch, *The Constitution of Myanmar: A Contextual Analysis* (Hart 2019).

whose investigation of the incident had led to the soldiers' convictions were themselves imprisoned for 18 months.[67]

On 30 July 2018, shortly before the IIFFMM released its first report, the Myanmar Government established the Independent Commission of Enquiry ('ICOE') to examine the events of 2017 in Rakhine state. The ICOE comprised two national and two international 'personalities', none of whom appeared to have a background in complex human rights or criminal investigations. Several public statements from the Myanmar authorities and the selected commissioners suggested prejudice, compromising its impartiality from the outset. Under its mandate, the ICOE's recommendations could only be directed to enhancing peace and stability and ensuring law enforcement and the rule of law. The ICOE's chairperson emphasized it was not an accountability mechanism for human rights violations and abuses and violations of international humanitarian law. She considered accountability to be unhelpful and to amount to 'quarrelling'. One of the national commissioners was the chief coordinator of the Myanmar Government's 'Union Enterprise for Humanitarian Assistance, Resettlement and Development in Rakhine', mandated to implement development projects in Rakhine state, who was extensively quoted in the media denying that any ethnic cleansing or genocide took place. The IIFFMM has therefore concluded 'on reasonable grounds' that the ICOE would not and could not provide a real avenue for accountability, even with some international involvement.[68]

At the December 2019 oral hearings in the ICJ, Myanmar defends its domestic criminal justice system, as detailed in Chapter 1. The followings are the essence of its defence. Under its 2008 Constitution, Myanmar has a military justice system to investigate and prosecute soldiers or officers for 'possible war crimes' committed in Rakhine. On 25 November 2019, the Office of the Judge Advocate General announced the start of a court martial for allegations linked to the Gutar Pyin village incident, one of the 12 main incidents concerning the Rohingya. The Office has also announced there will be additional court martials if further incriminating evidence is brought up by the ICOE. These ongoing criminal justice processes in Myanmar must be allowed to run their course. It is never easy for armed forces to recognize self-interest in accountability for their members, and to implement a will to accountability through actual investigations and prosecutions. As part of the Myanmar Government's overall efforts to provide justice, a court martial found that ten Muslim men had been summarily executed in Inn Din village, one of the 12 locations of serious incidents concerning the Rohingya. It sentenced four officers and three soldiers each to ten years' imprisonment with hard labour. After serving a part of their sentences, they were given a military pardon *although many in Myanmar were unhappy with this pardon.* Other cases are

67 *Situation in the People's Republic of Bangladesh/Republic of the Union of Myanmar: Request for authorization of an investigation pursuant to article 15*, ICC-01/19, 4 July 2019 para 234 ff.
68 A/HRC/39/CRP.2 (17 Sept 2018) para 1619.

undertaken without controversy. The Office of the Judge Advocate General in Myanmar is well resourced. The Gutar Pyin court martial is encouraging, and the Office is expected to continue its investigations and prosecutions based on reliable evidence gathered in Rakhine and from persons who witnessed what happened there. The military justice system under the Constitution cannot and should not be ignored, if one is serious about establishing constitutional democracy and rule of law in Myanmar. International criminal tribunals take four to eight years to undertake investigations of core international crimes, sometimes longer. Just over two years have passed since the serious internal armed conflict against ARSA, and the second court martial is now underway. The ongoing Gutar Pyin court martial in Buthidaung township should be allowed to run its course. There will be further courts martial after the ICOE's submission of its final report.

On 20 January 2020, the ICOE presented its 461-page final report to Myanmar's President and ASSK. The ICOE's evidence-collection teams interviewed approximately 1,500 witnesses from various communities in northern Rakhine, including Muslims and ethnic Rakhine, Mro and Daingnet people, as well as military and police personnel. No mention is made of speaking to the Rohingya in the refugee camps in Bangladesh, though. The ICOE finds 'insufficient evidence to argue, much less conclude, that the crimes committed [against the Rohingya or any other community in northern Rakhine] were undertaken with the intent to destroy, in whole or in part, a national, ethnical, racial or religious group, or with any other requisite mental state for the international crime of genocide'. Yet, it finds war crimes, serious human rights violations and violations of domestic law did take place during security operations between 25 August and 5 September 2017. Although these serious crimes and human rights violations were committed by multiple actors, there are reasonable grounds to believe that members of Myanmar's security forces were involved during their security operations in response to ARSA's attacks. The ICOE concludes the killing of innocent villagers and destruction of their homes were committed by some members of the Myanmar security forces through disproportionate use of force during the internal armed conflict, and makes 22 recommendations, essentially urging the Myanmar Government and Defence Services to continue their respective investigations, taking into account the findings of the ICOE's evidence-collection teams.[69]

The ICOE's conclusion is more or less similar to the explanation given by ASSK to the ICJ in December 2019. Accepting the ICOE's conclusion as justifiable would mean the ICC has no jurisdiction over what has happened to the Rohingya. The war crimes in internal armed conflict identified by the ICOE were committed in Myanmar by Myanmar nationals and Myanmar is not party to the Rome Statute and has not accepted the ICC's jurisdiction on an *ad hoc* basis pursuant to Article 12(3) of the Statute.

69 https://reliefweb.int/sites/reliefweb.int/files/resources/BM.pdf. Access to the full text of the final report has been blocked as of this writing.

In an important related development, from 10–20 March 2020, Myanmar's Parliament voted on 135 proposed amendments to the Constitution drafted by the then military regime. Myanmar's ruling National League for Democracy ('NLD') led by ASSK and ethnic parties submitted 114 of these proposed amendments to limit or revoke the special powers and privileges granted under the Constitution to military and its chief in the legislative, administrative and judicial branches of government by, for example, gradually reducing the military's share of seats in Parliament – from 25 per cent to 15 per cent after the November 2020 election, 10 per cent after the 2025 election, and 5 per cent after the 2030 election – and ending both the Commander-in-Chief's role as the supreme commander of the armed forces and his right to take power during an emergency, including the right to control the legislature, executive and judiciary. None of these proposed amendments received the necessary three-fourths majority of Members of Parliament for them to be adopted. This was due to the fact that in the 664-seat bicameral Parliament, the NLD had approximately merely 59 per cent of seats and ethnic parties 11 per cent, compared to the military-backed Union Solidarity and Development Party's 5 per cent and the military's constitutionally-allocated 25 per cent of seats. Only four minor amendments have been adopted – to change Burmese-language references to 'disabled military officers' in three provisions, and to remove language deemed unnecessary from a provision under the Constitution on the appointment of state and regional ministers. Most importantly, only 408 MPs (or 62.3 per cent) approved and 218 MPs opposed the NLD's proposed amendment to remove Article 445 in the 'Transitory Provisions' chapter of the Constitution stipulating that no proceeding shall be instituted against the former junta (i.e., the State Law and Order Restoration Council and the State Peace and Development Council) or any member thereof or *any member of the Government, in respect of any act done in the execution of their respective duties.*

Myanmar's above rebuttal in the ICJ, the ICOE's final report and the failed attempt to amend the Constitution to end immunity of Myanmar's military must be objectively assessed by the ICC according to the criteria of inability or unwillingness under the domestic criminal justice system as enumerated in Article 17(2) and (3) of the Rome Statute. After the *coup d'état* staged by the Tatmadaw on 1 February 2021, the Tatmadaw is most unlikely to allow its leaders and key military personnel to be prosecuted for what has happened to the Rohingya.

Direct responsibility or command/superior responsibility

There are two types of individual criminal responsibility under the Rome Statute: direct and indirect.[70]

70 See also Elies van Sliedregt, *Individual Criminal Responsibility in International Law* (Oxford University Press 2012) Chapters 1–6.

Article 25 of the Statute covers *direct individual criminal responsibility.* It provides that the ICC shall have jurisdiction over 'natural persons';[71] hence, governments, corporations and entities that are not 'natural persons' are not subject to the ICC's jurisdiction although the nation State may bear State responsibility under international law under certain circumstances,[72] as explained in Part II of this book. By virtue of Article 25(3), a natural person who commits a crime within the ICC's jurisdiction shall be individually responsible and liable for punishment in accordance with this Statute if that person:

> (a) Commits such a crime, whether as an individual, jointly with another or through another person, regardless of whether that other person is criminally responsible;
> (b) Orders, solicits or induces the commission of such a crime which in fact occurs or is attempted;
> (c) For the purpose of facilitating the commission of such a crime, aids, abets or otherwise assists in its commission or its attempted commission, including providing the means for its commission;
> (d) In any other way contributes to the commission or attempted commission of such a crime by a group of persons acting with a common purpose. Such contribution shall be intentional and shall either:
>   (i) Be made with the aim of furthering the criminal activity or criminal purpose of the group, where such activity or purpose involves the commission of a crime within the jurisdiction of the [ICC]; or
>   (ii) Be made in the knowledge of the intention of the group to commit the crime;
> (e) In respect of the crime of genocide, directly and publicly incites others to commit genocide;
> (f) Attempts to commit such a crime by taking action that commences its execution by means of a substantial step, but the crime does not occur because of circumstances independent of the person's intentions. However, a person who abandons the effort to commit the crime or otherwise prevents the completion of the crime shall not be liable for punishment under this Statute for the attempt to commit that crime if that person completely and voluntarily gave up the criminal purpose.

Article 25(3)(b) and (f) are self-evident and the modes referred thereto are criminalized in domestic criminal law.[73] Article 25(3)(e) is not relevant to the pre-

71 Rome Statute Art 25(1)(2).
72 Ibid Art 25(4).
73 In the ICC's case law, attempted commission of a crime is characterized by the incompleteness of its objective elements; accordingly, there are no distinctions between the mental elements required for, e.g., murder in its consummated form and those required for its attempted form (*Ntaganda*, Case ICC-01/04-02/06, ICC Trial Chamber VI, Judgment, 8 July 2019 para 861).

sent discussion about the Rohingya since the ICC in the Bangladesh/Myanmar Situation does not have jurisdiction over genocide, except for the most unlikely event when the UN Security Council refers the situation in Myanmar to the ICC Prosecutor under Article 13(b) of the Statute.

As regards co-perpetration under Article 25(3)(a), the ICC Appeals Chamber explains in *Lubanga* that this does not require co-perpetrators to carry out the crime personally and directly. In order to establish that an accused person committed a crime under the ICC's jurisdiction 'jointly with another [...] person', two or more individuals must have worked together in the commission of the crime. This requires an agreement between these perpetrators – express or implied, previously arranged or materializing extemporaneously. This agreement may take the form of a 'common plan' between individuals, although it may not be specifically directed at the commission of a crime. It is sufficient for the common plan to involve a critical element of criminality by reference to Article 30 of the Statute, stipulating in its pertinent part that the material elements of a crime within the ICC's jurisdiction must be committed with intent and knowledge, and that a person has intent where: (a) in relation to conduct, that person means to engage in the conduct; (b) in relation to a consequence, that person means to cause that consequence or is aware that it will occur in the ordinary course of events. Article 30 defines 'knowledge' as 'awareness that a circumstance exists or a consequence will occur in the ordinary course of events'. The Appeals Chamber considers that the words '[a consequence] will occur' refer to future events, and that the standard for the foreseeability of events is *virtual* certainty. In circumstances where a plurality of individuals are involved in the commission of a crime, the question of whether an accused 'committed' a crime – and therefore not only contributed to the crime committed by someone else – cannot only be answered by reference to how close the accused was to the actual crime and whether he or she directly carried out the incriminated conduct. Rather, what is required is a normative assessment of the role of the accused person in the specific circumstances of the case. The most appropriate tool for conducting such an assessment is an evaluation of whether the accused had *control over the crime*, by virtue of his or her *essential contribution* to it *and the resulting power to frustrate its commission*, even if that essential contribution was not made at the execution stage of the crime. This 'control over the crime' theory distinguishes those who are considered to have 'committed' the crimes from those who have contributed to crimes of others. A co-perpetrator is one who makes, within the framework of a common plan, an essential contribution with the resulting power to frustrate the commission of the crime. The essential contribution can be made not only at the execution stage of the crime, but also, depending on the circumstances, at its planning or preparation stage, including when the common plan is conceived. At the core of this approach is the assumption that a co-perpetrator may compensate for his or her lack of contribution at the execution stage of the crime if, by virtue of his or her essential contribution, the person nevertheless had control over the crime. This approach applies objective criteria to determine whether a person is a perpetrator rather than an accessory and does not rely primarily on subjective criteria.[74]

The ICC Appeals Chamber also notes that the Rome Statute differentiates between principal (Article 25(3)(a)) and accessorial (Article 25(3)(b) to (d)) liability, with principals bearing more blameworthiness 'generally speaking and all other things being equal'.[75]

When all the elements of different variations under Article 25(3)(a) are proven, the ICC must elect which mode of responsibility best reflects the full scope of the accused's individual criminal responsibility. The accused can be convicted of only one form of Article 25(3)(a) commission for each incident or discrete type of criminal conduct, because to conclude otherwise not only contributes little to the fair labelling of the responsibility of the accused but it also punishes them twice for the commission of the same crime.[76]

For its part, the ICTY has developed the doctrine of 'joint criminal enterprise' to facilitate its prosecution of crimes committed by a large number of groups of people in different geographical locations. When a plurality of persons acts in unison to put into effect a 'joint criminal enterprise', all the participants in a joint criminal enterprise are equally guilty of the committed crime irrespective of the part played by each in its commission.[77] A person participates in a joint criminal enterprise by personally committing the agreed crime as a principal offender, or by assisting the principal offender in committing the agreed crime as a co-perpetrator (by undertaking acts that facilitate the commission of the offence by the principal offender), or by acting in furtherance of a particular system in which the crime is committed by reason of the accused's position of authority or function, and with knowledge of the nature of that system and intent to further that system.[78] The ICTY considers that a joint criminal enterprise, as a form of commission of a crime, has been established in customary international law since at least 1992.[79] Although the ICTR and hybrid tribunals have followed

74 *Prosecutor v Thomas Lubanga Dyilo*, Case ICC-01/04-01/06 A 5, ICC Appeals Chamber, Judgment, 1 Dec 2014 paras 445–7, 458, 463, 469, 472–3. Cf. *Ntaganda*, ICC Appeals Chamber, Judgment, 30 Mar 2021 paras 879–80,

75 *Lubanga Dyilo*, ICC Appeals Chamber, Judgment, 1 Dec 2014 para 462. See also *Ntaganda*, Case ICC-01/04-02/06, ICC Trial Chamber VI, Judgment, 8 July 2019 paras 772–80; *Ongwen*, ICC Trial Chamber IX, Judgment, 4 Feb 2021 paras 774–80.

76 *Al Mahdi*, ICC Trial Chamber VIII, Judgment and Sentence, 27 Sept 2016 para 60.

77 *Tadic*, ICTY Appeals Chamber, Judgment, 15 July 1999 para 227.

78 *Prosecutor v Mitar Vasiljevic*, Case IT-98-32-T, ICTY, Trial Chamber, 29 Nov 2002 para 67. For criticisms of this doctrine, see Jens D Ohlin, 'Three Conceptual Problems with the Doctrine of Joint Criminal Enterprise' (2007) 5 J Int'l Criminal Justice 69; id, 'Joint Intentions' in François Tanguay-Renaud and James Stribopoulos (eds.), *Rethinking Criminal Law Theory: New Canadian Perspectives in the Philosophy of Domestic, Transnational, and International Criminal Law* (Hart 2012) Chapter 14.

79 *Jadranko Prlić et al.*, ICTY Appeals Chamber, 29 Nov 2017 para 587. See also Mark Osiel, *Making Sense of Mass Atrocity* (Cambridge University Press 2009) 48–90; Daryl Robinson, *Justice*

this,[80] the ICC has not. In *Lubanga*, the ICC Appeals Chamber does not consider it is legally bound to follow the particular approach of the *ad hoc* tribunals. At issue in that case is the interpretation of the terms 'commits [...] jointly with another' under Article 25(3)(a) of the Rome Statute. The ICC Appeals Chamber recalls that Article 25(3) of this Statute has a different structure than the relevant provisions of the ICTY and ICTR Statutes, and that approaches to the interpretation and application of the latter two Statutes therefore cannot easily be transposed to the former. In circumstances where a plurality of persons was involved in the commission of crimes under the Rome Statute, the question of whether an accused 'committed' a crime – and therefore not only contributed to the crime committed by someone else – requires a normative assessment of the role of the accused in the specific circumstances of the case. The most appropriate tool for conducting such an assessment is an evaluation of whether the accused had 'control over the crime', by virtue of his or her essential contribution to it and the resulting power to frustrate its commission, even if that essential contribution was not made at the execution stage of the crime.[81]

As regards Article 25(3)(c) of the Rome Statute, the IIFMM's 110-page report entitled 'The economic interests of the Myanmar military' submitted to the UN Human Rights Council in August 2019 calls for dozens of Myanmar and foreign companies to be criminally investigated for *aiding and abetting* international crimes and crimes against humanity with financial contributions to the Myanmar military and Government. Specifically, at least 45 companies and organizations are said to have provided the Tatmadaw with US$6.15 million in financial donations solicited in September 2017 by senior Tatmadaw leadership in support of the 'clearance operations' that began in August 2017 against the Rohingya in northern Rakhine. The report also asserts that

> private companies with enduring links to the Tatmadaw are financing development projects in northern Rakhine in furtherance of the Tatmadaw's objective of re-engineering the region in a way that erases evidence of Rohingya belonging in Myanmar, and preventing their return to access their homeland and communities.

These projects, carried out under the Union Enterprise for Humanitarian Assistance, Resettlement and Development in Rakhine, are said to 'consolidate the consequences of war crimes, crimes against humanity and acts of genocide'. On the basis of these findings, the report has identified private companies with officials who may have made a substantial and direct contribution to

---

in Extreme Cases: Criminal Law Theory Meets International Criminal Law (Cambridge University Press 2020) Annex 2.

80 Gerhard Werle and Florian Jessberger, *Principles of International Criminal Law* (4th edn, Oxford University Press 2020) 241 (n 214).

81 *Lubanga Dyilo*, ICC Appeals Chamber's Judgment, 1 Dec 2014 paras 472–3.

the commission of crimes under international law, including the crime against humanity of 'other inhumane acts' and persecution, warranting their criminal investigation.[82]

Since the ICC has jurisdiction over natural persons, not corporations or companies, only natural persons who own, direct, manage or otherwise work for companies implicated in crimes within the ICC's jurisdiction may be prosecuted.

Case law of international criminal tribunals has clarified the elements of aiding and abetting as follows.

Aiding means giving assistance to someone, whereas abetting involves facilitating the commission of an act by being sympathetic thereto, including providing mere exhortation or encouragement.[83]

In the jurisprudence of the ICTY and the ICTR, liability for aiding and abetting is incurred by an act or omission of assisting, encouraging or lending moral support to the commission of a crime where this support has a substantial effect on the perpetration of the crime. Aiding and abetting by omission requires that the accused had the means to fulfil his or her duty to act. Aiding and abetting may occur before, during, or after the commission of the principal crime. The assessment of whether an act or omission had a substantial effect on the commission of a crime is a fact-based inquiry. When making this assessment, the Trial Chamber does not have to find that the acts carried out by the aider and abettor are specifically directed to assist, encourage or lend moral support to the perpetration of that crime. As regards the *mens rea* element, the aider and abettor must have knowledge that his or her acts or omissions assist in the commission of the crime of the principal perpetrator. The aider and abettor must also be aware of the principal perpetrator's criminal acts, although not their legal characterization, and his or her criminal state of mind. This includes the specific intent of the principal perpetrator, if the crime requires such intent, although the aider and abettor need share that specific intent. The aider and abettor does not need to know either the precise crime that was intended or the one that was actually committed; it is sufficient that he/she be aware that one of a number of crimes will probably be committed, if one of those crimes is in fact committed.[84] To put it another way, the aider and abettor must be aware of the 'essential elements' of the crime(s) ultimately committed by the principal offender, including his/her state of mind, and the requisite *mens rea* can be established if the aider and abettor is not certain which of a number of crimes will ultimately be committed as long as the aider and abettor is aware that one of a number of crimes will probably be committed, and one of those crimes is

82 A/HRC/42/CRP.3 (5 Aug 2019) para 180(c).

83 *Prosecutor v Jean-Paul Akayesu*, Case ICTR-96-4, ICTR Trial Chamber I, 2 Sept 1998 para 484; *Prosecutor v Furundzija*, Case IT-95-17/1-T, ICTY Trial Chamber, 10 Dec 1998 para 231.

84 *Prosecutor v Ratko Mladić*, Case IT-09-92-T, ICTY Trial Chamber I, 22 Nov 2017 para 3567 and the cases cited therein; *Prosecutor v Karadžić*, Case IT-95-5/18-T, ICTY Trial Chamber, 24 Mar 2016 para 577.

in fact committed.[85] The accused's conduct may in itself be perfectly lawful; it becomes criminal only when combined with the unlawful conduct of the principal offender.[86] Either aiding or abetting alone suffices to incur criminal liability of the aider or abettor.[87] Assistance given to the commission of a crime need not be tangible in the sense of providing material means or physical help, but may consist of omission that has a decisive effect on the commission of a crime provided that such omission is accompanied by the requisite intent of the aider or abettor to assist, encourage or lend moral support to the perpetration of the crime. Such omission is often in the form of voluntary and willing presence to give moral support or encouragement – silent approval – to the commission of a crime.[88] However, actual physical presence when the crime is committed is not necessary, provided that the aider or abettor is found to have knowingly participated in the commission of a crime and his participation substantially effected the commission of that crime through supporting the actual commission before, during or after the incident. The aider or abettor is also criminally responsible for all natural consequences of the commission of the act in question.[89] The aider or abettor is not exonerated by the mere fact that his or her assistance could easily have been obtained from another person.[90] The requirement that the assistance facilitates the commission of the crime means such assistance need not even constitute a precondition for the acts of the principal offender, as, for example, when the crime is also taking place the aider or abettor who is in a position to stop it allows it to go on and sustains or further facilitates its commission.[91] Aiding and abetting liability has attached to those who have provided assistance, encouragement or moral support to a variety of different crimes in a variety of contexts, including by providing financial support to an organization committing crimes, issuing directives and drafting laws, signing by senior officials of decrees, attending meetings and issuing reports.[92]

Whether a person is guilty as an aider or abettor is also a question of facts to be determined on a case-by-case basis. For instance, the physician who was in

85 *Prosecutor v Popović et al.*, Case IT-05-88-A, ICTY Appeals Chamber, 30 Jan 2015 paras 1751, 1794.

86 *Furundzija* para 243.

87 *Akayesu* para 484.

88 *Prosecutor Blaskic*, Case IT-95-14-T, ICTY Trial Chamber, 3 Mar 2000 para 284; *Prosecutor v Jean Kambanda*, Case ICTR-97-23-S, ICTR Trial Chamber, 4 Sept 1998 paras 39(v), (viii), (xi), 40(4); *Furundzija* paras 199–209.

89 *Prosecutor v. Dusko Tadic*, Case IT-94-1-T, ICTY Trial Chamber II, 7 May 1997 paras 691–2; *Prosecutor v Musema*, Case ICTR-96-13-A, ICTR Trial Chamber I, 27 Jan 2000 paras 125–6.

90 *Furundzija*, para 224; *Kambanda* paras 39(v), (viii), (xi), 40(4).

91 *Furundzija* para 209; *Akayesu* para 692.

92 *Prosecutor v Charles Ghankay Taylor*, Case SCSL-04-01-T, Special Court for Sierra Leone's Appeals Chamber, 26 Sept 2013 para 369, citing the case law of different international criminal tribunals.

charge of taking care of the guard personnel of a Nazi concentration camp and who confined himself to doing only that, would be not guilty of aiding and abetting murder of the camp's detainees. Neither would the doctor who treated prisoners in the camp and saved their lives, nor those who in their place put little obstacles in the way of this programme of murder, albeit in a subordinate position and without success.[93]

While the Prosecution must establish the acts of the principal perpetrators for which it seeks to hold the aider and abettor responsible, an accused may be convicted for having aided and abetted a crime – including a crime which requires specific intent – even where the principal perpetrators have not been tried or identified.[94]

Notwithstanding the above, the ICC Appeals Chamber in *Bemba* notes that the jurisprudence of the ICTY, ICTR and Special Court for Sierra Leone requires that the aider and abettor provide a 'substantial contribution'. Although this jurisprudence may inform the ICC's understanding of liability for aiding and abetting, it is not binding on the ICC. In accordance with Article 21 of the Rome Statute, the ICC shall apply in the first place its own Statute and Rules. Article 25(3)(c) of the Statute provides for individual criminal responsibility of a person who '[f]or the purpose of facilitating the commission of [...] a crime, aids, abets or otherwise assists in its commission or attempted commission'. The text of this provision therefore only requires that the assistance in the commission (or attempted commission) of the crime be provided for the purposes of facilitating such commission without indicating whether the conduct must have also had an effect on the commission of the offence. The Appeals Chamber considers the *actus reus* under Article 25(3)(c) is certainly fulfilled when the person's assistance in the commission of the crime facilitates or furthers the commission of the crime, as the showing of such an effect indicates that the person indeed assisted in its commission. Whether a certain conduct amounts to 'assistance in the commission of the crime' within the meaning of Article 25(3)(c) even without the showing of such an effect can only be determined in light of the facts of each case.[95]

In the Rohingya context, Myanmar and non-Myanmar nationals who aid or abet crimes against the Rohingya that are within the ICC's jurisdiction may be prosecuted before the ICC. It is a question of facts as to who fall within the category of aiders and abettor in this situation. The IIFFMM's aforesaid August

93 *Tadić*, ICTY Appeals Chamber's Judgment para 203 (n 254), citing the Judgment of a post-Second World War military tribunal in *Case against R. Mulka et al.* ('Auschwitz concentration camp case').

94 *Prosecutor v Brđanin*, Case IT-99-36-A, ICTY Appeals Chamber, 3 Apr 2007 para 355; *Prosecutor v Ngirabatware*, Case MICT-12-29-A, Mechanisms for International Criminal Tribunal's Appeals Chamber, 18 Dec 2014 para 149.

95 *Prosecutor v Jean-Pierre Bemba Gombo et al*, Case ICC-01/05-01/13 A A2 A3 A4 A5, ICC Appeals Chamber, Judgment, 8 Mar 2018 paras 1326–7.

2019 report stresses that criminal liability for aiding or abetting can arise when business officials engage in acts or omissions that assist, encourage or lend moral support to the perpetration of a crime, including by financial assistance and the provision of goods, information and services, including banking and communications services. Moreover, continues the report, if businesses rely on the services or resources of the State or encourage the State to provide it with services and resources, with the knowledge these services might result in crimes under international law, the relevant business officials risk criminal liability.[96] The IIFFMM also notes that several domestic legal systems have sought to punish corporate actors under their domestic criminal and civil law.[97]

As for liability for 'in any other way contribut[ing] to the commission or attempted commission of such a crime by a group of persons acting with a common purpose' pursuant to Article 25(3)(d) of the Rome Statute, The ICTY Appeals Chamber has distinguished between acting in pursuance of 'a common purpose' or design to commit a crime, on the one hand, and aiding and abetting, on the other hand, as follows.

(i) The aider and abettor is always an accessory to a crime perpetrated by another person, the principal.
(ii) In the case of aiding and abetting no proof is required of the existence of a common concerted plan, let alone of the pre-existence of such a plan. No plan or agreement is required: indeed, the principal may not even know about the accomplice's contribution.
(iii) The aider and abettor carries out acts specifically directed to assist, encourage or lend moral support to the perpetration of a certain specific crime (murder, extermination, rape, torture, wanton destruction of civilian property, etc.), ... By contrast, in the case of acting in pursuance of a common purpose or design, it is sufficient for the participant to perform acts that in some way are directed to the furthering of the common plan or purpose.
(iv) In the case of aiding and abetting, the requisite mental element is knowledge that the acts performed by the aider and abettor assist the commission of a specific crime by the principal. By contrast, in the case of common purpose or design more is required (i.e., either intent to perpetrate the crime or intent to pursue the common criminal design plus foresight that those crimes outside the criminal common purpose were likely to be committed), as stated above.[98]

96 A/HRC/42/CRP.3 (5 Aug 2019) paras 43–4, citing judgments of the ICTY, ICTR, Special Court of Sierra Leone, and Special Tribunal for Lebanon.
97 Ibid para 45.
98 *Prosecutor v Duško Tadić*, Case IT-94-1-A, ICTY Appeals Chamber, 15 July 1999 para 229.

In this connection, the IIFFMM's report of 12 August 2018 touches upon the role of civilian government officials in relation to the plight of the Rohingya as follows:

> The constitutional powers of the civilian authorities afford little scope for controlling the actions of the Tatmadaw, nor is there any indication that they participated directly in planning or implementing security operations or were part of the command structure. Nevertheless, nothing indicates that the civilian authorities used their limited powers to influence the situation in Rakhine state where crimes were being perpetrated. The State Counsellor, Daw Aung San Suu Kyi, has not used her *de facto* position as Head of Government, nor her moral authority, to stem or prevent the unfolding events, or seek alternative avenues to meet a responsibility to protect the civilian population. On the contrary, the civilian authorities have spread false narratives, denied the wrongdoing of the Tatmadaw, blocked independent investigations (including that of the fact-finding mission), and overseen the destruction of evidence. Through their acts and omissions, the civilian authorities have *contributed to the commission* of atrocity crimes.[99]

With respect to *indirect individual criminal responsibility* arising from the position of a commander and or superior, it is covered under Article 28 of the Rome Statute. A military commander or person effectively acting as a military commander shall be criminally responsible for crimes within the ICC's jurisdiction committed by forces under his/her effective command and control, or effective authority and control as the case may be, as a result of his/her failure to exercise control properly over such forces when the following two preconditions are met. First, that military commander or person either *knew* or, owing to the circumstances at the time, *should have known* the forces were committing or about to commit such crimes. Second, that military commander or person failed to take all necessary and reasonable measures within his/her power to prevent or repress their commission or to submit the matter to the competent authorities for investigation and prosecution. With respect to other, non-military, superior and subordinate relationships, a superior shall be criminally responsible for crimes within the ICC's jurisdiction committed by subordinates under his/her effective authority and control, as a result of his/her failure to exercise control properly over such subordinates when the following three preconditions are fulfilled. First, the superior either *knew, or consciously disregarded* information which clearly indicated, that the subordinates were committing or about to commit such crimes. Second, the crimes concerned activities that were within the effective responsibility and control of the superior. Third, the superior failed to take all necessary and reasonable

99 A/HRC/39/64 para 93 (emphasis added).

measures within his/her power to prevent or repress their commission or to submit the matter to the competent authorities for investigation and prosecution.[100]

The only case on command/superior responsibility decided by the ICC as of this writing concerns Jean-Pierre Bemba Gombo, a former Vice-President of the transitional government of DR Congo and president of the *Mouvement de libération du Congo* ('MLC'). The ICC Appeals Chamber in that case[101] acquits him of war crimes and crimes against humanity against civilians committed by troops under his control during an unsuccessful MLC operation that assisted the then President of the Central African Republic in resisting a *coup d'état* in 2002. The scope of the duty to take 'all necessary and reasonable measures' is held to be intrinsically connected to the extent of a commander's material ability to prevent or repress the commission of crimes or to submit the matter to the competent authorities for investigation and prosecution – a commander cannot be blamed for not having done something he or she had no power to do.[102] An assessment of whether a commander took all 'necessary and reasonable measures' must be based on considerations of what crimes the commander knew or should have known about and at what point in time.[103] A commander is not required to employ every single conceivable measure within his or her arsenal, irrespective of considerations of proportionality and feasibility. Article 28 only requires commanders to do what is necessary and reasonable under the circumstances.[104] Whilst a commander is required to act in good faith in adopting 'necessary and reasonable measures', the fact that a commander was *motivated* by a desire to preserve the reputation of his or her troops does not intrinsically render the measures he or she adopted any less necessary or reasonable.[105] A finding that the measures deployed by a commander were insufficient to prevent or repress an extended crime wave does not mean these measures were also insufficient to prevent or repress the limited number of specific crimes for which the commander

100 See further Kriangsak Kittichaisaree, *International Criminal Law* (Oxford University Press 2001) 251–7; Guénaël Mettraux, *The Law of Command Responsibility* (Oxford University Press 2009); Chantal Meloni, *Command Responsibility in International Criminal Law* (TMC Asser Press 2010); Maria L Nybondas, *Command Responsibility and Its Applicability to Civilian Superiors* (TMC Asser Press 2010); Roberta Arnold and Otto Triffterer, 'Responsibility of commanders and other superiors' in Kai Ambos and Otto Triffterer (eds.), *The Rome Statute of the International Criminal Court: A Commentary* (3rd edn, Nomos 2016) 1056; Miles Jackson, 'Command Responsibility' in Jérôme de Hemptinne, Robert Roth and Elies van Sliedregt (eds.), *Modes of Liability in International Criminal Law* (Cambridge University Press 2019) 409; Darryl Robinson, *Justice in Extreme Cases: Criminal Law Theory Meets International Criminal Law* (Cambridge University Press 2020) 194–223.

101 *Prosecutor v Jean-Pierre Bemba Gombo* (Judgment on the appeal of Mr Jean-Pierre Bemba Gombo against Trial Chamber III's 'Judgment pursuant to Article 74 of the Statute'), Case ICC-01/05-01/08 A, 8 June 2018.

102 Ibid para 5.

103 Ibid para 6.

104 Ibid para 8.

105 Ibid para 9.

is ultimately convicted.[106] As a matter of proper notice, the accused person must be informed of the factual allegations on the basis of which the ICC Prosecutor seeks to establish that he or she failed as a commander to take 'all necessary and reasonable measures' within his/her power to prevent or repress the commission of crimes or to submit the matter to the competent authorities for investigation and prosecution.[107] On the question of whether Bemba discharged his duty to take all 'necessary and reasonable measures' under Article 28 of the Rome Statute, the Appeals Chamber finds the Trial Chamber's error in considering Bemba's *motivation* had a material impact on the entirety of its findings on necessary and reasonable measures because it permeated the Trial Chamber's assessment of the measures Bemba had taken. Furthermore, the Trial Chamber's failure to fully appreciate the limitations Bemba would have faced in investigating and prosecuting crimes as a remote commander sending troops to a foreign country had an important impact on the overall assessment of the measures taken by Bemba. Indeed, in faulting the results of measures taken by Bemba, the Trial Chamber failed to appreciate that, as a remote commander, Bemba was not part of the investigations and was not responsible for the results generated. Had it done so, the Trial Chamber's assessment of the measures Bemba had taken would have been necessarily different, bearing in mind also that the MLC's military operation in question was conducted within the short space of a few months and in a foreign country with the attendant difficulties on Bemba's ability, as a remote commander, to take measures, which notwithstanding, Bemba took numerous measures in response to crimes committed by the troops under his command.[108]

The relevance of the geographical remoteness of the commander at the particular time is a factual consideration to be considered on a case-by-case basis. As rightly pointed out in the Separate Opinion of Judges Van den Wyngaert and Morrison, what is required of a commander, both in terms of how closely they should monitor the troops and in terms of what measures they are expected to take to prevent criminal behaviour, depends on how proximate they are to the physical perpetrators in the chain of command. The primary obligation to prevent/repress/refer criminal behaviour rests upon the immediate commander of the physical perpetrator (that is, the platoon or section commander). This follows from the fact that Article 28 of the Statute requires the commander to have effective control, and it is simply impossible for senior commanders to control

106 Ibid para 10.
107 Ibid paras 11, 188.
108 Ibid paras 189–93. In ruling that the Trial Chamber inappropriately took Bemba's motives into consideration when determining whether the measures he had taken were necessary and reasonable, the Appeals Chamber rejects Bemba's submission that the motives of an accused commander are always irrelevant to the assessment of 'necessary and reasonable measures' because a commander is required to act in good faith in adopting such measures and must show that he 'genuinely' tried to prevent or repress the crimes in question or submit the matter to the competent authorities. Nonetheless, the Appeals Chamber finds that the Trial Chamber erred by taking an unreasonably strict approach (ibid para 176).

hundreds or thousands of individual troops effectively since this is the role of those who work closely with them in the field. Command responsibility is not strict liability for all the crimes committed by subordinates. Commanders can only be held accountable for the crimes of those they are commanding directly and whose conduct they can actually monitor. Importantly, unit commanders are not only responsible under international humanitarian law to ensure that their troops do not commit crimes and to ensure that they are sanctioned if they do, they are also responsible *vis-à-vis* their own superiors who delegate their authority to lower-level commanders to keep their troops in check and to deal with deviant behaviour. The main responsibility of the higher-level commander is to make sure the unit commanders are up to the task of controlling their troops, but it is not the task of the higher-level commander to micro-manage all lower-level commanders or to do their jobs for them. The duty of higher-level commanders is to ensure that those immediately under them comply with their obligations. If it turns out that one of them is unable/unwilling to control his/her troops, it is the responsibility of the higher-level commander to replace the failing lower-level commander or to strengthen his/her authority. Strictly speaking, therefore, if a senior commander is held responsible for a crime committed by a soldier at the bottom of the chain of command, he/she is not blamed for not having supervised the individual soldier properly, but for not having monitored the superior(s) of the soldier adequately. Of course, it is the shared responsibility of every commander at every level of the chain of command to do what they can, within their own specific sphere of competence and authority, to avoid crimes being committed. In short, what the law expects from commanders depends on where they find themselves on the hierarchical ladder. In applying the test under Article 28 of the Rome Statute ((i) effective control, (ii) knowledge or should have known and (iii) necessary and reasonable measures), the ICC should abide by the principle that command responsibility is not strict liability and the military commander is not to do the impossible, regardless of how proximate the superior-subordinate relationship actually was.[109]

Article 33 of the Rome Statute delineates the parameter of the defence of superior orders. The fact that a crime within the ICC's jurisdiction has been committed by a person pursuant to an order of a government or of a superior, whether military or civilian, shall not relieve that person of criminal responsibility unless: the person was under a legal obligation to obey orders of the government or the superior in question; the person did not know that the order was unlawful; and the order was not manifestly unlawful. However, orders to commit genocide or crimes against humanity are deemed to be manifestly unlawful.[110]

109 Joint Separate Opinion of Judges Van den Wyngaert and Morrison paras 33–6.

110 See also Paola Gaeta, 'The Defence of Superior Orders: The Statute of the International Criminal Court *versus* Customary International Law' (1999) 10 EJIL 172; Stefanie Bock and Otto Triffterer, 'Superior orders and prescription of law ' in Ambos and Otto Triffterer (eds.), *The Rome Statute of the International Criminal Court: A Commentary* 1183.

Investigation, trial, appeal and punishment

At any time after the initiation of an investigation, an assigned Pre-Trial Chamber of the ICC shall, on the application of the ICC Prosecutor, issue a warrant of arrest of a person if, having examined the application and the evidence or other information submitted by the Prosecutor, it is satisfied that there are *reasonable grounds to believe that the person has committed a crime* within the ICC's jurisdiction; *and* the arrest of the person appears necessary: (i) to ensure the person's appearance at trial; (ii) to ensure that the person does not obstruct or endanger the investigation or the court proceedings; or (iii) where applicable, to prevent the person from continuing with the commission of that crime or a related crime which is within the ICC's jurisdiction and which arises out of the same circumstances.[111]

A State Party to the Rome Statute which has received a request for provisional arrest or for arrest and surrender shall immediately take steps to arrest the person in question in accordance with its laws and the provisions of Part 9 of the Statute regulating international cooperation and judicial assistance with the ICC in the ICC's investigation and prosecution of crimes within the ICC's jurisdiction.[112]

Upon the surrender of the person to the ICC, or the person's appearance before the ICC voluntarily or pursuant to a summons, the Pre-Trial Chamber assigned by the ICC Presidency shall satisfy itself that the person has been informed of the crimes which he/she is alleged to have committed, and of his/her rights under the Rome Statute, including the right to apply for interim release pending trial. A person subject to a warrant of arrest may also apply for interim release pending trial. If the Pre-Trial Chamber is satisfied that the conditions set forth for his or her arrest are met, the person shall continue to be detained. If it is not so satisfied, the Pre-Trial Chamber shall release the person, with or without conditions.[113]

Within a reasonable time after the person's surrender or voluntary appearance before the ICC, the Pre-Trial Chamber shall hold a *hearing to confirm the charges* on which the ICC Prosecutor intends to seek trial. The hearing *shall be held in the presence of the Prosecutor and the person charged, as well as his or her counsel.* The Pre-Trial Chamber may, upon request of the Prosecutor or on its own motion, hold a hearing in the absence of the person charged to confirm the charges on which the Prosecutor intends to seek trial when the person has: (a) waived his or her right to be present; or (b) fled or cannot be found and all reasonable steps have been taken to secure his or her appearance before the ICC and to inform the person of the charges and that a hearing to confirm those charges will be held. In that case, the person shall be represented by counsel where the Pre-Trial Chamber determines that it is in the interests of justice. At the hearing, the Prosecutor shall support each charge with sufficient evidence to establish substantial grounds to believe that the person committed the crime charged. The Prosecutor may rely

111 Rome Statute Art 58.
112 Ibid Art 59.
113 Ibid Art 60(1) and (2).

on documentary or summary evidence and need not call the witnesses expected to testify at the trial. At the hearing, the person may: (a) object to the charges; (b) challenge the evidence presented by the Prosecutor; and (c) present evidence. The Pre-Trial Chamber shall, on the basis of the hearing, determine whether there is sufficient evidence to establish *substantial grounds to believe* that the person committed each of the crimes charged. Based on its determination, the Pre-Trial Chamber shall: (a) confirm those charges in relation to which it has determined there is sufficient evidence, and commit the person to a Trial Chamber for trial on the charges as confirmed; (b) decline to confirm those charges in relation to which it has determined there is insufficient evidence; (c) adjourn the hearing and request the Prosecutor to consider: (i) providing further evidence or conducting further investigation with respect to a particular charge; or (ii) amending a charge because the evidence submitted appears to establish a different crime within the ICC's jurisdiction. Where the Pre-Trial Chamber declines to confirm a charge, the Prosecutor shall not be precluded from subsequently requesting its confirmation if the request is supported by additional evidence. After the charges are confirmed and before the trial has begun, the Prosecutor may, with the permission of the Pre-Trial Chamber and after notice to the accused, amend the charges. If the Prosecutor seeks to add additional charges or to substitute more serious charges, a hearing to confirm those charges must be held. After commencement of the trial, the Prosecutor may, with the permission of the Trial Chamber, withdraw the charges. Any warrant previously issued shall cease to have effect with respect to any charges which have not been confirmed by the Pre-Trial Chamber or which have been withdrawn by the Prosecutor. Once the charges have been confirmed, the ICC Presidency shall constitute a Trial Chamber which shall be responsible for the conduct of subsequent proceedings and may exercise any function of the Pre-Trial Chamber that is relevant and capable of application in those proceedings.[114]

Unless otherwise decided, the trial shall take place at the seat of the ICC in The Hague, Netherlands.[115] *Article 63 of the Statute requires the accused to be present during the trial.* However, if the accused, being present before the ICC, continues to disrupt the trial, the Trial Chamber may remove the accused and shall make provision for him or her to observe the trial and instruct counsel from outside the courtroom, through the use of communications technology, if required. Such measures shall be taken only in exceptional circumstances after other reasonable alternatives have proved inadequate, and only for such duration as is strictly required.

Presumption of innocence of the accused until proven guilty beyond reasonable doubt by the Prosecutor before the ICC and the rights of the accused are stipulated in Articles 66 and 67 of the Statute, respectively.

Article 68 of the Statute requires the ICC to take appropriate measures to protect the safety, physical and psychological well-being, dignity and privacy of

114 Ibid Art 61.
115 Ibid Arts 3(1) and 62.

victims and witnesses. In so doing, the ICC shall have regard to all relevant factors, including age, gender and health, and the nature of the crime, in particular, but not limited to, where the crime involves sexual or gender violence or violence against children. The ICC Prosecutor shall take such measures particularly during the investigation and prosecution of such crimes. These measures shall not be prejudicial to or inconsistent with the rights of the accused and a fair and impartial trial. In order to protect victims and witnesses or an accused, the Chambers of the ICC may conduct any part of the proceedings in private (*in camera*) or allow the presentation of evidence by electronic or other special means. In particular, such measures shall be implemented in the case of a victim of sexual violence or a child who is a victim or a witness, unless otherwise ordered by the ICC, having regard to all the circumstances, particularly the views of the victim or witness. Where the personal interests of the victims are affected, the ICC shall permit their views and concerns to be presented and considered at stages of the proceedings determined to be appropriate by the ICC and in a manner not prejudicial to or inconsistent with the rights of the accused and a fair and impartial trial. Such views and concerns may be presented by the legal representatives of the victims where the ICC considers it appropriate. The ICC's Victims and Witnesses Unit may advise the ICC Prosecutor and the ICC on appropriate protective measures, security arrangements, counselling and assistance. Where the disclosure of evidence or information pursuant to the Statute may lead to the grave endangerment of the security of a witness or his or her family, the ICC Prosecutor may, for the purposes of any proceedings conducted prior to the commencement of the trial, withhold such evidence or information and instead submit a summary thereof. Such measures shall be exercised in a manner which is not prejudicial to or inconsistent with the rights of the accused and a fair and impartial trial. In any event, a State may make an application for necessary measures to be taken in respect of the protection of its servants or agents and the protection of confidential or sensitive information.

The ICC may impose one of the following penalties on a person convicted of a crime within its jurisdiction: (a) imprisonment for a specified number of years, which may not exceed a maximum of 30 years; or (b) a term of life imprisonment when justified by the extreme gravity of the crime and the individual circumstances of the convicted person. In addition to imprisonment, the ICC may order: (a) a fine; (b) a forfeiture of proceeds, property and assets derived directly or indirectly from that crime, without prejudice to the rights of *bona fide* third parties.[116] When the person has served two-thirds of the sentence, or 25 years in the case of life imprisonment, the ICC shall review the sentence to determine whether it should be reduced. In its review, the ICC may reduce the sentence if one or more of the following factors are present: (a) the early and continuing willingness of the person to cooperate with the ICC in its investigations and

116 Ibid Art 77.

prosecutions; (b) the voluntary assistance of the person in enabling the enforcement of the ICC's judgments and orders in other cases, and in particular providing assistance in locating assets subject to orders of fine, forfeiture or reparation which may be used for the benefit of victims; or (c) other factors establishing a clear and significant change of circumstances sufficient to justify the reduction of sentence, as provided in the ICC's Rules of Procedure and Evidence.[117]

As regards reparations to victims, Article 75 of the Statute authorizes the ICC to make an order directly against a convicted person specifying appropriate reparations to, or in respect of, victims, including restitution, compensation and rehabilitation. Where appropriate, the ICC may order the award for reparations to be made through the Trust Fund set up under Article 79 of the Statute by decision of the Assembly of States Parties for the benefit of victims of crimes within the ICC's jurisdiction, and of the families of such victims. The ICC may order money and other property collected through fines or forfeiture to be transferred, by order of the ICC, to the Trust Fund, to be managed according to the criteria determined by the Assembly of States Parties.[118]

For example, the ICC has awarded reparations to victims of Thomas Lubanga Dyilo, convicted on 14 March 2012 by the ICC Trial Chamber I of the war crimes of conscripting and enlisting children under the age of 15 years into the paramilitary groups called the Union of Congolese Patriots and the Patriotic Forces for the Liberation of Congo and using them to participate actively in hostilities between 1 September 2002 and 13 August 2003. On 21 December 2017, the ICC Trial Chamber II, after finding that 425 of the 473 potentially eligible victims have shown on a balance of probabilities they are direct or indirect victims of the crimes of which Lubanga was convicted, decides to award the 425 victims collective reparations. Since those 425 victims are only a sample of the potentially eligible victims whereas hundreds and possibly thousands more victims suffered harm as a consequence of the crimes of which Lubanga was convicted, the Trial Chamber sets the reparations award for which Lubanga is liable at a total of US$10 million which consists of his liability in respect of the 425 victims in the sample, amounting to US$3.4 million and his liability in respect of any other victims who may be identified, amounting to US$6.6 million. Because Lubanga is indigent for the purposes of reparations at the time of this decision, the Board of Directors of the Trust Fund was ordered by the Chamber to inform it, by 15 February 2018, whether it was in a position to earmark additional funds for the implementation of collective reparations in the case or to continue its efforts to raise additional funds. The Chamber also directs the ICC Presidency to monitor, with the assistance of the ICC Registrar, Lubanga's financial situation

117 Ibid Art 110(3) and (4).
118 Ibid Art 79(2) and (3).

on an ongoing basis.[119] On 4 March 2021, the ICC Trial Chamber II issued a public redacted version of its decision dated 14 December 2020 approving the implementation of collective service-based reparations to victims in this case. The Trial Chamber approves the programme proposed by the partner of the Trust Fund for Victims, selected by the latter to implement collective reparations in the form of the provision of services encompass, among others, projects aimed at mental and physical health care, and projects aimed at improving the socio-economic situation, including school, university and professional training, language courses and remedial schooling, income-generating activities as well as subsistence allowances and pensions. Although the implementation of collective reparations will have to take place in a complex security and health context, this makes it possible to achieve most of the objectives set by the Appeals Chamber, namely to relieve the suffering caused by the crimes committed by Lubanga, to afford justice to the victims by alleviating the consequences of the wrongful acts and to contribute to the effective reintegration of former child soldiers as well as facilitate the reintegration of direct victims into society, taking into account the different repercussions of these crimes depending on whether the victim is a boy or a girl, and provide victims with educational and vocational training opportunities, and sustainable employment opportunities enabling them to play a meaningful role in society. The proposed programme will meet the varied and evolving needs of direct and indirect victims according to their specific circumstances, in a flexible manner. The Trial Chamber also ordered the Trust Fund for Victims to include in its next quarterly reports all relevant information regarding the progress made in the implementation of collective reparations. The legal representatives of victims and the Office of Public Counsel for Victims will have the right to submit observations in response to the Fund's forthcoming quarterly reports. The number of victims entitled to collective reparations in this case stands at 1,025 as of 4 March 2021.[120]

On 8 March 2021, the ICC Trial Chamber VI orders collective reparations with individualized components to be awarded to direct and indirect victims of the crimes for which Bosco Ntaganda was convicted (5 counts of crimes against humanity and 13 counts of war crimes, namely: murder and attempted murder, rape, sexual slavery, persecution, forcible transfer of population, intentionally directing attacks against civilians, pillage, ordering the displacement of the civilian population, conscripting and enlisting children under the age of 15 years into an armed group and using them to participate actively in hostilities, intentionally

119 *Prosecutor v Thomas Lubanga Dyilo*, Case ICC-01/04-01/06 (21 Dec 2017). This decision is upheld by the ICC Appeals Chamber on 18 July 2019 (Case ICC-01/04-01/06 A7 A8) although the Appeals Chamber reversed Trial Chamber II's rejection of 48 victim applicants for reparations, who will now be entitled to re-apply for collective reparations benefits before the Trust Fund for Victims.

120 *Prosecutor v Thomas Lubanga Dyilo*, Case ICC-01/04-01/06, ICC Trial Chamber II, Reparations Order (as corrected on 5 Mar 2021).

directing attacks against protected objects and destroying the adversary's property). The multiple, diverse and multi-faceted nature of the harms suffered by the victims in this case makes it difficult to reinstate the victims to the situation they were in before the commission of the crimes. In order to address the various harms suffered by the victims in the best manner possible, a combination of the different modalities of reparations available should be applied. These modalities are restitution (to the extent possible), compensation, rehabilitation, satisfaction measures aimed at acknowledging the violations and safeguard the dignity and reputation of the victims and symbolic reparations. Ntaganda's liability for these reparations is set at US$30 million. The Trust Fund for Victims is to design an implementation plan on the basis of all the modalities of reparations identified by the Chamber, in consultation with the victims, with priority given to victims who are in a particularly vulnerable situation or require urgent assistance, particularly individuals who require immediate physical and/or psychological medical care, victims with disabilities and the elderly, victims of sexual or gender-based violence, victims who are homeless or experiencing financial hardship, as well as children born out of rape and sexual slavery and former child soldiers. The Trust Fund for Victims was ordered to submit its general draft implementation plan to the Chamber by 8 September 2021, and an urgent plan for the priority victims by 8 June 2021. After finding Ntaganda indigent for the purposes of reparations at the time of the Order, the Trial Chamber requests the ICC Presidency's assistance, with the support of the Registry, to continue exploring whether Ntaganda possesses any undiscovered assets and to monitor Ntaganda's financial situation on an ongoing basis.[121]

The ICC's decisions may be appealed as follows. The ICC Prosecutor may make an appeal on any of the following grounds: procedural error, error of fact or error of law.[122]

The convicted person, or the ICC Prosecutor on that person's behalf, may make an appeal on any of the following grounds: procedural error, error of fact, error of law or any other ground that affects the fairness or reliability of the proceedings or decision.[123] A sentence may be appealed by the ICC Prosecutor or by the convicted person on the ground of disproportion between the crime and the sentence.[124]

The ICC's sentence of imprisonment shall be served in a State designated by the ICC from a list of States which have indicated to the ICC their willingness to

121 *Prosecutor v Bosco Ntaganda*, Case ICC-01/04-02/06, ICC Trial Chamber VI, Reparations Order, 8 Mar 2021.

122 See the explanation of the standard of review at the appellate stage in *Prosecutor v Jean-Pierre Bemba et al.*, Case ICC-01/05-01/13 A A2 A3 A4 A5, ICC Appeals Chamber, Judgment, 8 Mar 2018 paras 89–111; *Prosecutor v Jean-Pierre Bemba Gombo* (Judgment on the appeal of Mr Jean-Pierre Bemba Gombo against Trial Chamber III's 'Judgment pursuant to Article 74 of the Statute'), Case ICC-01/05-01/08 A, 8 June 2018 paras 35–70; *Ntaganda*, ICC Appeals Chamber, Judgment, 30 Mar 2021 paras 35–46.

123 See *Prosecutor v. Laurent Gbagbo and Charles Blé Goudé*, Case 02/11-01/15 A, ICC Appeals Chamber, 31 Mar 2021 paras 60–74.

124 Rome Statute Art 81.

accept sentenced persons.[125] The ICC's sentence of imprisonment shall be binding on the States Parties to the Rome Statute, which shall in no case modify it, and the ICC alone has the right to decide any application for appeal and revision by a sentenced person.[126] The enforcement of a sentence of imprisonment shall be subject to the ICC's supervision and shall be consistent with widely accepted international treaty standards governing treatment of prisoners.[127] The conditions of imprisonment shall be governed by the law of the State of enforcement and shall be consistent with widely accepted international treaty standards governing treatment of prisoners; in no case shall such conditions be more or less favourable than those available to prisoners convicted of similar offences in the State of enforcement.[128]

Following completion of the sentence, a person who is not a national of the State of enforcement may, in accordance with the law of the State of enforcement, be transferred to a State which is obliged to receive him or her, or to another State which agrees to receive him or her, taking into account any wishes of the person to be transferred to that State, unless the State of enforcement authorizes the person to remain in its territory. If no State bears the costs arising out of transferring the person to another State, such costs shall be borne by the ICC. The State of enforcement may also, in accordance with its national law, extradite or otherwise surrender the person to a State which has requested the extradition or surrender of the person for purposes of trial or enforcement of a sentence.[129] However, a sentenced person in the custody of the State of enforcement shall not be subject to prosecution or punishment or to extradition to a third State for any conduct engaged in prior to that person's delivery to the State of enforcement, unless such prosecution, punishment or extradition has been approved by the ICC at the request of the State of enforcement after hearing the views of the sentenced person. This requirement of the ICC's approval ceases to apply if the sentenced person remains voluntarily for more than 30 days in the territory of the State of enforcement after having served the full sentence imposed by the ICC, or returns to the territory of that State after having left it.[130]

Prosecution of high-ranking civilians in international criminal tribunals

Myanmar military and security officers appear to be the primary targets for prosecution before the ICC for crimes against the Rohingya, either on the basis of direct individual criminal responsibility or as commanders of those with direct

125 Ibid Art 103(1).
126 Ibid Art 105.
127 Ibid Art 106(1).
128 Ibid Art 106(2).
129 Ibid Art 107.
130 Ibid Art 108.

individual criminal responsibility. However, Myanmar civilians, including those in the leadership, can expect to face punishment by the ICC as well.

Indeed, civilians holding high-ranking government positions have come before international criminal tribunals on several occasions.

Jean Kambanda, Prime Minister of Rwanda from 8 April 1994 until he left Rwanda on or about 17 July 1994, was convicted and sentenced by the ICTR to life imprisonment after pleading guilty to the six counts contained in the indictment against him, namely genocide, conspiracy to commit genocide, direct and public incitement to commit genocide, complicity in genocide and crimes against humanity (murder and extermination).[131] Former Minister of Family and Women's Development Pauline Nyiramasuhuko was convicted by the ICTR of conspiracy to commit genocide by entering into an agreement with members of Rwanda's Interim Government to kill Tutsis within Butare Prefecture; genocide, extermination as a crime against humanity and war crimes of violence to life, health and physical or mental well-being of persons for ordering the killing of Tutsis who had sought refuge at the Butare Prefecture Office; and rape as a crime against humanity and outrages upon personal dignity as a war crime on the basis of responsibility as a superior for failing to prevent and punish rapes perpetrated by her subordinates at the Butare Prefecture Office. She was sentenced to 47 years' imprisonment.[132]

On 24 May 1999, the ICTY indicted Slobodan Milošević, then President of the Federal Republic of Yugoslavia, for crimes in Kosovo. He resigned from the Presidency in October 2000 and was subsequently surrendered to the ICTY. His trial began on 12 February 2002 and formally terminated on 14 March 2006, following his death in the ICTY's Detention Unit on 11 March 2006.

Radovan Karadžić, 'President of the Republic of Srpska' which was an entity of the then disintegrating Socialist Federal Republic of Yugoslavia, was convicted and sentenced by the ICTY to 40 years' imprisonment for genocide, crimes against humanity (persecution, murder, extermination, deportation, and forcible transfer) and violations of the laws or customs of war (murder, acts of violence the primary purpose of which was to spread terror among the civilian population, unlawful attacks on civilians and the taking of hostages). During the war in the former Yugoslavia, he was at the apex of political, governmental and military structures, including by supporting the military takeover of territory and the forcible movement of the non-Serb population.[133]

Another interesting case at the ICTY concerns Biljana Plavšić. Plavšić acted as a Serbian Representative to the Presidency of the Socialist Republic of Bosnia

131 *Jean Kambanda v Prosecutor*, Case ICTR-97-23-A, ICTR Appeals Chamber, 19 Oct 2000.

132 *Prosecutor v Pauline Nyiramasuhuko et al*, Case ICTR-98-42-A, ICTR Appeals Chamber, 14 Dec 2015.

133 *Prosecutor v Karadžić*, Case IT-95-5/18-T, ICTY Trial Chamber, 24 Mar 2016.

and Herzegovina on 11 November 1990 until December 1992. She was also active in the Presidency of the Serbian Republic of Bosnia and Herzegovina, and then became a member of the collective and expanded Presidencies of Republika Srpska. Numerous individuals participated in devising and executing the *persecutions* of the Bosnian Muslim, Bosnian Croat and other non-Serb populations of 37 municipalities in Bosnia and Herzegovina. There were differences both as to their knowledge of the details and their participation in the execution of the objective. For her part, Plavšić embraced and supported the objective and contributed to achieving it, but she did not participate in its conception and planning and had a lesser role in its execution than others. She supported the objective in various different ways, by: serving as co-President, thereby supporting and maintaining the government and military at local and national levels through which the objective was implemented; encouraging participation by making public pronouncements that force was justified because certain territories within Bosnia and Herzegovina were Serbian by right and Serbs should fear genocide being committed against them by Bosnian Muslims and Bosnian Croats; and inviting and encouraging paramilitaries from Serbia to assist Bosnian Serb forces in effecting *ethnic separation by force*. The Bosnian Serb forces, collaborating with the Yugoslav People's Army, the Ministry of Interior of Serbia and paramilitary units to implement the objective of ethnic separation by force, committed the *persecutions* in a campaign that included: killings during attacks on towns and villages; *cruel and inhumane treatment* during and after the attacks; *forced transfer and deportation*; *unlawful detention and killing*, forced labour and use of human shields; cruel and inhumane treatment and inhumane conditions in detention facilities; destruction of cultural and sacred objects; and plunder and wanton destruction. The Bosnian Serb leadership, including Plavšić, *ignored the allegations of crimes committed by their forces*: Plavšić *disregarded reports of widespread ethnic cleansing and publicly rationalized and justified it*. She was aware that the key leaders of the Serbian Republic of Bosnia and Herzegovina ignored these crimes despite the power to prevent and punish them. Plavšić pleaded guilty before the ICTY to the charge that, between 1 July 1991 and 30 December 1992, she, acting individually and in concert with others in a joint criminal enterprise, planned, instigated, ordered and aided and abetted *persecutions* of the Bosnian Muslim, Bosnian Croat and other non-Serb populations of 37 municipalities in Bosnia and Herzegovina. Sentencing Plavšić, then aged 72, to 11 years' imprisonment, the ICTY Trial Chamber explained that despite her guilty plea, no sentence could fully reflect the horror of what occurred or the terrible impact on thousands of victims – she participated in 'a crime of the utmost gravity, involving a campaign of ethnic separation which resulted in the death of thousands and the expulsion of thousands more in circumstances of great brutality'. However, the Trial Chamber accepted that her guilty plea (together with remorse and reconciliation), voluntary surrender, post-conflict conduct and age were substantial mitigating circumstances. In particular, her guilty plea and her acknowledgment of responsibility 'should promote reconciliation in Bosnia and Herzegovina and the region as a whole'.[134]

Milan Milutinović, President of the Republic of Serbia from 1997 to 2002, surrendered himself to the ICTY after the expiry of his term as President, to stand trial for deportation, murder as a crime against humanity, murder as violation of laws or customs of war, and other inhumane acts during the War in Kosovo and was found not guilty of all charges on 26 February 2009. Milutinović was found by the Trial Chamber not to have had command over the Federal Republic of Yugoslavia's army, even though he was a member of the collective Supreme Defence Council of the Federal Republic. In practice, it was Federal Republic's President Milosevic who exercised actual command authority over the army. Although, as President of Serbia, Milutinović had the potential power to exercise oversight over Serbian governmental institutions, the evidence shows he had little *de facto* control. It was Nikola Šainović, then Deputy Prime Minister of Serbia and head of the joint command which coordinated the actions of the army and Serbian police, who, in his capacity as Milosevic's right-hand man on Kosovo, had a great deal of influence on the events in Kosovo. Milutinović was not found to have significantly contributed to the joint criminal enterprise due to his lack of authority over the armed forces.[135] By contrast, Šainović was sentenced to 18 years' imprisonment after being found guilty, through his participation in a joint criminal enterprise, of deportation, other inhumane acts (forcible transfer), murder, and persecution as crimes against humanity and of murder as a violation of the laws or customs of war committed against ethnic Albanian civilians in 1999 during the war in Kosovo.[136]

Uhuru Kenyatta and William Ruto, both of whom were holders of high-level political offices in Kenya at the time of their indictments by the ICC, have appeared before the ICC but proceedings against them have not been able to proceed further, as will be explained in the next chapter.

Lauren Gbagbo, former President of Côte d'Ivoire at the time of the ICC's arrest warrant of 23 November 2011, was charged with four counts of crimes against humanity: murder, rape, other inhumane acts or – in the alternative – attempted murder, and persecution, allegedly committed during the 2010–2011 post-election violence in Côte d'Ivoire. On 15 January 2019, following a no case to answer motion, the ICC Trial Chamber I acquitted him of all charges for lack of evidence. In particular, having thoroughly analysed the evidence, the Chamber concluded by majority that the ICC Prosecutor has failed to demonstrate several core constitutive elements of the crimes as charged, including the existence of a 'common plan' to keep Gbagbo in power, which included the

134 *Prosecutor v Biljana Plavšić*, Case IT-00-39&40/1-S, ICTY Trial Chamber, Sentencing Judgment of 27 Feb 2003. See also Jasenka Ferizović, 'The Case of Female Perpetrators of International Crimes: Exploratory Insights and New Research Directions' (2020) 31 EJIL 455.

135 *Prosecutor v Milan Milutinović et al.*, Case IT-05-87-T, ICTY Trial Chamber, 26 Feb 2009.

136 *Prosecutor v Nicola Šainović et al.*, Case IT-05-87-A, ICTY Appeals Chamber, 23 Jan 2014.

commission of crimes against civilians 'pursuant to or in furtherance of a State or organizational policy'; and the existence of patterns of violence from which it could be inferred that there was a 'policy to attack a civilian population'. The Prosecutor also failed to demonstrate that Gbagbo's public speeches constituted ordering, soliciting or inducing the alleged crimes.[137] On 31 March 2021, the ICC Appeals Chamber upheld the Trial Chamber's decision in this case.[138]

137 *Prosecutor v Laurent Gbagbo and Charles Blé Goudé*, Case 02/11-01/15, ICC Trial Chamber I, 15 Jan 2019 as elucidated by the Trial Chamber's written reasons on 16 July 2019.
138 *Gbagbo and Blé Goudé*, Case 02/11-01/15 A, ICC Appeals Chamber, 31 Mar 2021.

6

PRACTICAL DIFFICULTIES FACED BY THE ICC

As of this writing, the ICC has had 30 cases, with some cases having more than one suspect.

ICC judges have issued 35 arrest warrants. Thanks to cooperation from States, 17 individuals have been detained in the ICC detention centre and have appeared before the ICC. Thirteen individuals subject to the ICC's arrest warrants remain at large. Charges have been dropped against four individuals due to their deaths (including former President Muammar Gaddafi of Libya). The ICC has issued nine summonses to appear and rendered judgments convicting nine and acquitting four accused persons.

The ones in the dock

The following are common features for those brought to stand trial before the ICC.

First, only Africans have been brought before the ICC so far. The ICC has been accused of being Western/Eurocentric and biased against Africans while turning a blind eye to perpetrators in other regions. Such criticisms should bear in mind that 33, or over one-fourth, of the 123 States Parties to the Rome Statute of the ICC[1] are from Africa, and that several African States themselves have referred the situations in their respective territories to the ICC for prosecution. Besides, on-going civil wars and large-scale unrests in several parts of Africa have often made it not feasible to prosecute perpetrators of crimes under the Statute in domestic courts.[2]

1 218 UNTS 90, in force 1 July 2002.

2 See also Errol P Mendes, *Peace and Justice at the International Criminal Court: A Court of Last Resort* (2nd edn, Edward Elgar Publishing 2020) Chapter 2.

DOI: 10.4324/9781003224211-6

Second, former high-ranking government office holders, such as Laurent Gbagbo, former President of Côte d'Ivoire, and Jean-Pierre Bemba Gombo, a Vice President of DR Congo from 2003 to 2006, were arrested and surrendered to the ICC after a regime change in their respective countries where the new regimes were happy to get rid of them. Charles Blé Goudé, Gbagbo's former Minister for Sports and Youth, was arrested on 17 January 2013 in Ghana which extradited him to Côte d'Ivoire which, in turn, surrendered him to the ICC on 22 March 2014 to stand trial for crimes against humanity. Likewise, Patrice-Edouard Ngaïssona, former Minister for Sports of the Central African Republic ('CAR') from 2003 to 2013, was forced into exile after a regime change. He was arrested by the French authorities on 12 December 2018 and surrendered to the ICC on 23 January 2019, upon completion of necessary national proceedings in France, to stand trial before the ICC for crimes against humanity and war crimes, including murder, torture and the recruitment of child soldiers. Ngaïssona was allegedly one of the most senior leaders of Christian-dominated militias that carried out widespread attacks on CAR's Muslim population between December 2013 and December 2014.

Most of the other defendants who have appeared before the ICC are 'rebels' – war lords or notorious members of paramilitary groups in civil wars whom their countries want punished by the ICC or who have lost protection from the powers that be in their countries. On 17 March 2006, Thomas Lubanga Dyilo became the first person ever arrested under an ICC arrest warrant, when the DR Congolese authorities arrested him and surrendered him into ICC custody. Lubanga, a leader of an armed group fighting in a civil war in DR Congo, was convicted by the ICC of the war crimes of enlisting and conscripting children under the age of 15 and using them to participate actively in hostilities. Germain Katanga, former leader of an armed group in Ituri Province, DR Congo, was surrendered by the DR Congolese authorities to the ICC in October 2007. He was convicted and sentenced to 12 years' imprisonment by the ICC in March 2014 for being an accessory of one count of crime against humanity (murder) and four counts of war crimes (murder, attacking a civilian population, destruction of property and pillaging) committed on 24 February 2003 during the attack on the village of Bogoro, in the Ituri district of DR Congo. Mathieu Ngudjolo Chui, a senior member of several rebel groups fighting the civil war in Ituri Province, DR Congo, was arrested in February 2008 by the DR Congolese authorities and surrendered to the ICC to stand trial on seven counts of war crimes and three counts of crimes against humanity, of which he was eventually acquitted. Bosco Ntaganda, a Rwandan national who became chief of staff of an armed militia group fighting a civil war in DR Congo, surrendered himself to the US Embassy in Kigali, Rwanda, in March 2013 and requested to be transferred to the ICC, reportedly after being pressured by the Rwandan Government to do so or to escape the fallout from the in-fighting among leaders of the armed militia group in DR Congo to which he belonged. On 8 July 2019, Trial Chamber VI of the ICC convicted Ntaganda of crimes against humanity (murder and attempted murder, rape, sexual slavery, persecution, forcible transfer and deportation) and war crimes (murder and attempted murder, intentionally directing attacks against civilians, rape, sexual slavery, ordering the displacement of the civilian population, conscripting and enlisting children under the age of 15 years into an armed group and using them to participate actively in hostilities, intentionally directing attacks against protected objects, and destroying the adversary's property). In October 2010 Callixte Mbarushiman, another Rwandan, was arrested in France and surrendered to the ICC in January 2011 to stand trial for crimes against humanity and war crimes allegedly committed in DR Congo in 2009. In December 2011, he was released after the ICC found there was insufficient evidence for prosecuting him.

Al Hassan Ag Abdoul Aziz Ag Mohamed Ag Mahmoud, a Malian national, was surrendered by Mali to the ICC in March 2018 on charges of crimes against humanity and war crimes committed in Timbuktu, Mali. He headed the Ansar Dine/al-Qaeda in the Islamic Maghreb Islamic Police in Timbuktu during the Malian civil war from January 2012 to April 2015. Ahmad Al Mahdi, another Malian, was surrendered to the ICC by the Government of Niger in September 2015. He pleaded guilty to the charges of intentionally directing attacks against historic monuments and/or buildings dedicated to religion, including nine mausoleums and one mosque in Timbuktu, Mali, between about 30 June 2012 and 10 July 2012.

Bahr Idriss Abu Garda, a Sudanese, was the first accused to appear voluntarily before the ICC after being summoned to appear. He was the leader of the United Resistance Front, a rebel group fighting the Sudanese Government in Darfur, and a commander of the Justice Equality Movement. In 2010, the ICC declined to confirm the charges against him due to insufficient evidence to establish substantial grounds to believe that he could be held criminally responsible either as a direct or as an indirect co-perpetrator for the commission of the crimes with which he was charged by the ICC Prosecution; namely, the war crimes of violence to life; intentionally directing attacks against personnel, installations, material, units and vehicles involved in a peacekeeping mission; and pillaging during an attack carried out on 29 September 2007, against the African Union peace-keeping mission stationed in North Darfur.

Dominic Ongwen, a Ugandan who was Brigade Commander of the Sinia Brigade of the Lord's Resistance Army ('LRA') at the time of the ICC's arrest warrant in 2005, was captured in CAR by the American Special Forces operating in the area at the end of 2014 after his escape from detention by the LRA's leader Joseph Kony for having disobeyed Kony's orders and having refused to answer Kony's radio messages. He was transferred to the Uganda forces and, subsequently, to CAR forces before being surrendered to the ICC. In February 2021, Ongwen was convicted of 61 counts of the 70 counts crimes against humanity and war crimes in northern Uganda he was charged with and was sentenced three months later to 25 years' imprisonment.

Alfred Yekatom, a commander in the Christian-dominated militias in CAR, a.k.a. 'Rambo', was arrested by CAR authorities in late October 2018 and surrendered to the ICC on 17 November 2018 to stand trial for war crimes and crimes against humanity committed against CAR's Muslim population in various locations in CAR between 5 December 2013 and August 2014.

In June 2020, after 13 years on the run and as a result of the regime change in Sudan that ousted Sudanese President Al-Bashir, Ali Muhammad Ali Abd-Al-Rahman (a.k.a. Ali Kushayb, alleged leader of the Janjaweed militia, accused of 53 counts of crimes against humanity and war crimes in Darfur) surrendered himself to CAR authorities and was taken into the ICC's custody.

On 24 January 2021, Mahamat Said Abdel Kani, an alleged rebel commander from CAR, was surrendered to the ICC by CAR authorities on charges of crimes against humanity and war crimes in Bangui, CAR's capital, in 2013, on the warrant issued by the ICC under seal on 7 January 2019.

The ICC have also convicted certain nationals of DR Congo of various offences against the administration of justice related to the false testimonies of defence witnesses before the ICC in the *Jean-Pierre Bemba* case.

The ones not (yet) in the dock

Domestic law enforcement authorities in every nation State face the perennial problem of not being able to apprehend all those under arrest warrants issued by the authorities. In the case of the ICC, it does not even have its own police force and must rely entirely on cooperation from States to arrest and surrender the wanted individuals. Worse still, crimes under the Rome Statute are crimes of inherently political dimensions, making the ICC a hostage to the political will of the States where the persons sought by the arrest warrants are present to arrest and surrender the persons to the ICC.[3]

As of this writing, the following 12 accused subject to the ICC's arrest warrants are still at large or not in the ICC's custody: former Sudanese President Omar Al-Bashir; Abdallah Banda Abakaer Nourain (Commander-in-Chief of Justice and Equality Movement Collective-Leadership, accused of war crimes in Darfur); Walter Basara and Philip Bett (accused of committing offences against the administration of justice consisting in corruptly influencing or attempting to corruptly influence three ICC witnesses regarding cases from the situation in Kenya); Saif Al-Islam Gaddafi (son of the late Libyan President Gaddafi and acting *de facto* Prime Minister of Libya at the time of the ICC's arrest warrant of 27 June 2011, accused of crimes against humanity of murder and persecution in Libya); Simone Gbagbo (wife of former President Laurent Gbagbo of Côte d'Ivoire, accused of crimes against humanity allegedly committed during

3 See Robert Cryer, *Prosecuting International Crimes: Selectivity and the International Criminal Law Regime* (Cambridge University Press 2005) 124–88.

the 2010–2011 post-election violence in Côte d'Ivoire); Ahmad Muhammad Harun (Sudan's Minister of Interior in 2007, accused of crimes against humanity and war crimes in Darfur); Abdel Raheem Muhammad Hussein (Minister of National Defence at the time of the ICC's arrest warrant in March 2012, accused of crimes against humanity and war crimes in Darfur); Al-Tuhamy Mohamed Khaled (alleged former Lieutenant General of the Libyan army and former head of the Libyan Internal Security Agency, accused of crimes against humanity and war crimes in Libya); Joseph Kony (alleged commander of the LRA, accused of crimes against humanity and war crimes in northern Uganda); Sylvestre Mudacumura (alleged Supreme Commander of the *Forces Démocratiques pour la Libération du Rwanda* at the time of the ICC's arrest warrant in July 2012, accused of war crimes in DR Congo); and Vincent Otti (second in command to Joseph Kony, accused of crimes against humanity and war crimes in northern Uganda).

In addition, the ICC has continued to monitor Libya's domestic prosecution of Colonel Abdullah Al Senussi, former head of Libya's Military Intelligence accused by the ICC Prosecutor of two counts of crimes against humanity allegedly committed in 2011 in Libya, as explained in Chapter 5.

The following accused subject to the ICC's arrest warrants have died: Muammar Gaddafi, President of Libya until his death in October 2011; Saleh Mohammed Jerbo Jamus, accused of war crimes in Darfur; and Raska Lukwiya and Okot Odhiambo, co-defendants in the case against Kony and Otti. Mahmoud Mustafa Busayf Al-Werfalli, Commander in the Al-Saiqa Brigade, who was subject to the ICC's arrest warrant for war crimes in Libya during 2016–2018, was shot dead by unidentified attackers in Benghazi, Libya, on 24 March 2021.

What is of special interest in the context of the Rohingya are the incumbent high-ranking government officials who have escaped the ICC's reach.

Article 27 of the Rome Statute stipulates in paragraph 1 that this Statute shall apply equally to all persons without any distinction based on official capacity. In particular, official capacity as a Head of State or Government, a member of a Government or parliament, an elected representative or a government official shall in no case exempt a person from criminal responsibility under this Statute, nor shall it, in and of itself, constitute a ground for reduction of sentence. By virtue of paragraph 2 of this Article, immunities or special procedural rules which may attach to the official capacity of a person, whether under national or international law, shall not bar the ICC from exercising its jurisdiction over such a person.

However, Article 98 of the Statute, under the heading 'Cooperation with respect to waiver of immunity and consent to surrender' provides in paragraph 1 that the ICC may not proceed with a request for surrender or assistance which would require the requested State to act inconsistently with its obligations under international law with respect to the State or diplomatic immunity of a person or property of a third State, unless the ICC can first obtain the cooperation of that third State for the waiver of the immunity. Paragraph 2 of the Article adds that the ICC may not proceed with a request for surrender which would require the requested State to act inconsistently with its obligations under international agreements pursuant to which the consent of a sending State is required to surrender a person of that State to the ICC, unless the ICC can first obtain the cooperation of the sending State for the giving of consent for the surrender.

The International Court of Justice has ruled in *Arrest Warrant of 11 April 2000 (DR Congo v Belgium)* that

> in international law it is firmly established that, as also diplomatic and consular agents, certain holders of high-ranking office in a State, such as the Head of State, Head of Government and Minister for Foreign Affairs, enjoy immunities from jurisdiction in other States, both civil and criminal.[4]

The case concerns the warrant issued by Belgium for the arrest of the incumbent Minister for Foreign Affairs of DR Congo.

The ICJ reasons that, in customary international law, the immunities accorded to Ministers for Foreign Affairs are not granted for their personal benefit, but to ensure the effective performance of their functions on behalf of their respective States. The nature of the functions exercised by a Minister for Foreign Affairs are such that, *throughout the duration of his/her office*, a Minister for Foreign Affairs when abroad enjoys full immunity from criminal jurisdiction and inviolability which protects the Minister against any act of authority of another State which would hinder him/her in the performance of his/her duties. In this respect, no distinction can be drawn between acts performed by a Minister for Foreign Affairs in an 'official' capacity and those claimed to have been performed in a 'private capacity', or, for that matter, between acts performed before the person concerned assumed office as Minister for Foreign Affairs and acts committed during the period of office. Even the mere risk that, by travelling to or transiting another State, a Minister for Foreign Affairs might be exposing himself/herself to legal proceedings could deter the Minister from travelling internationally when required to do so for the purposes of the performance of his/her official functions. The ICJ has been unable to deduct from State practice any exception under customary international law to the rule according immunity from criminal jurisdiction and inviolability to incumbent Ministers for Foreign Affairs, even where they are suspected of having committed war crimes or crimes against humanity. After also examining the rules concerning the immunity or criminal responsibility of persons having an official capacity contained in the legal instruments creating international criminal tribunals, *including Article 27 of the Rome Statute*, the ICJ in that case finds these rules likewise do not enable it to conclude that any such exception exists in customary international law *in regard to national*

4 *Arrest Warrant of 11 April 2000 (DR Congo v Belgium)* [2002] ICJ Rep 3, 20–1 [51]. Affirmed by the ICJ in *Certain Questions of Mutual Assistance in Criminal Matters (Djibouti v France)*, Judgment [2008] ICJ Rep 177, 236–7 [170].

courts. Thus, although various international conventions on the prevention and punishment of certain serious crimes impose on States obligations of prosecution or extradition, thereby requiring them to extend their criminal jurisdiction, such extension of jurisdiction in no way affects immunities under customary international law, including those of Ministers for Foreign Affairs. However, the *immunity* from jurisdiction enjoyed by incumbent Ministers for Foreign Affairs does not mean that they enjoy *impunity* in respect of any crimes they might have committed, irrespective of their gravity: jurisdictional immunity may bar prosecution for a certain period or for certain offences; it cannot exonerate the person to whom it applies from all criminal responsibility. Accordingly, there are circumstances where there can be criminal prosecution of the persons enjoying immunity arising from their status (immunity *ratione personae*). These circumstances are where such persons are tried in their own countries, where the State which they represent or have represented decides to waive that immunity, where such persons no longer enjoy all of the immunities accorded by international law in other States after ceasing to hold the office, and where such persons are subject to criminal proceedings before certain international criminal courts, where they have jurisdiction.[5]

By ruling that those entitled to personal immunity include 'certain holders of high-ranking office in a State, such as ...', the ICJ in *Arrest Warrant* seems to indicate the list is not closed to the 'troika' of Head of State, Head of Government and Minister for Foreign Affairs. However, the ICJ in *Djibouti v France* has denied immunity *ratione personae* to Djibouti's *procureur de la République* and Head of National Security.[6] Thus, being a high-ranking official within a State does not automatically entitle the official to immunity arising from their status before foreign criminal jurisdiction. There is uncertainty as to who besides the 'troika' may be entitled to this immunity. For example, China's position before the Sixth (Legal) Committee of the UN General Assembly is that immunity *ratione personae* should not be limited to the troika only, but should also be accorded to high-level State officials engaged in international political, economic, trade and cultural exchanges, bearing in mind each State's specific situation and political system.[7] The Swiss Federal Criminal Court in *Khaled Nezzar* recognizes that the accused, who was Algeria's Minister of Defence at the time of his alleged acts of war crimes, enjoyed immunity *ratione personae* during his official term of office.[8] By contrast, the Netherlands' position in the Sixth Committee is that immunity *ratione personae*, which it considers to be 'absolute', is limited to the troika only, due to the changing balance between immunity and the growing desire

5 [2001] ICJ Rep 3, 21–30 [53]–[71]. See also Ellen L Lutz and Caitlin Reiger (eds.), *Prosecuting Heads of State* (Cambridge University Press 2009).
6 [2008] ICJ Rep 177, 243–4.
7 A/C.6/66/SR.27 (8 Dec 2011) para 9.
8 *A v Ministère Public de la Confédération, B and C*, Case BB.2011.140, Decision of 25 July 2012.

to prevent impunity for international crimes.[9] Belgium[10] and Austria[11] consider State officials beyond the troika enjoy immunity only where relevant treaties, such as the Vienna Convention on Diplomatic Relations of 1961,[12] accord that immunity.

Regarding those individuals holding *de facto* positions of the 'troika', the French Court of Cassation (Criminal Division) recognized that Libya's *de facto* Head of State Colonel Muammar Gaddafi had immunity *ratione personae* despite his claim to have no official position in the Libyan Government. The Court found that Gaddafi, being the president of the Command Council of the Revolution, was the highest authority in Libya under the constitutional proclamation, and that he also participated in that capacity in international conferences such as meetings of Arab or African Heads of State and received the representatives of foreign States and the letters of accreditation of their ambassadors. The Court held that under international law as it currently stands, the acts of terrorism allegedly committed by Gaddafi, irrespective of its gravity, does not come within the exceptions to the principle of immunity from jurisdiction for incumbent foreign Heads of State.[13]

In practice, a State official on an official visit overseas is usually granted immunity from the criminal jurisdiction of the host State issuing an appropriate visa and/or permission to stay for the duration of his/her visit. This was the case of, for instance, Major Tomas Ricardo Anderson Kohatsu, a former official of Peru's Army Intelligence Service, sent by the Peruvian Government to appear before a hearing of the Inter-American Commission on Human Rights in Washington, DC in March 2000. Despite his being accused by US authorities of having committed horrendous crimes in Peru in 1997, he was entitled to diplomatic immunity by virtue of his G-2 visa issued to accredited members of the Peruvian Mission to the Organization of American States.[14] The G-2 diplomatic visa is a non-immigrant visa which allows accredited representatives of any rank of foreign governments recognized by the United States to enter into the United States to work for an international organization and not for personal business or pleasure. In the UK's practice, the UK accords immunity *ratione personae* to visiting ministers for whom international travel is intrinsic to their functions, such as incumbent ministers of defence and incumbent ministers of international trade. Germany cited personal immunity of Rose Kabuye, Chief of Protocol to the Rwandan President, in its decision not to arrest her during

9 A/C.6/66/SR.26 (7 Dec 2011) paras 58–9.
10 Ibid para 66.
11 Ibid para 78.
12 500 UNTS 95, in force 24 Apr 1964.
13 Court of Cassation, *Affaire Kadhafi*, Judgment 1414 (13 Mar 2001), (2001) 125 ILR 490, 495, 508–10.
14 Cf Aaron Solomon, 'The Politics of Prosecution under the Convention against Torture' (2001) 1 Chicago JIL 309, 311–3.

her official visit to Germany in April 2008. It seems that the UK, Germany and several other States have followed this practice despite not being party to the 1969 Convention on Special Missions,[15] which has 39 parties as of this writing.[16] Under that Convention, a 'special mission' is a temporary mission, representing the State, which is sent by one State to another State with the consent of the latter for the purpose of dealing with it on specific questions or of performing in relation to it a specific task. A 'representative of the sending State in the special mission' is any person on whom the sending State has conferred that capacity. The representatives of the sending State in the special mission and the members of its diplomatic staff enjoy immunity from the criminal jurisdiction of the receiving State. If a representative of the sending State in the special mission or a member of its diplomatic staff passes through or is in the territory of a third State while proceeding to take up his functions or returning to the sending State, the third State shall accord him inviolability and such other immunities as may be required to ensure his transit or return. Every member of the special mission enjoy the privileges and immunities to which he is entitled from the moment he enters the territory of the receiving State for the purpose of performing his functions in the special mission or, if he is already in its territory, from the moment when his appointment is notified to the Ministry of Foreign Affairs or such other organ of the receiving State as may be agreed. When the functions of a member of the special mission have come to an end, his privileges and immunities normally cease at the moment when he leaves the territory of the receiving State, or on the expiry of a reasonable period in which to do so, but shall subsist until that time, even in case of armed conflict. However, in respect of acts performed by such a member in the exercise of his functions, immunity shall continue to subsist.

Those enjoying immunity *ratione personae* will continue to enjoy functional immunity (immunity *ratione materiae*) after they leave office, for *official acts* performed while in office. Immunity *ratione materiae* is enjoyed by State officials in general, irrespective of their position in the hierarchy of the State.[17] Immunity *ratione materiae* derives from functional necessity required by all State agents in performing their official duties. As the ICTY Appeals Chamber explains in *Blaskić*, State officials acting in their official capacity are 'mere instruments of a State and their official action can only be attributed to the State'. As such, they are immune from sanctions or penalties for conduct that is not private but undertaken on behalf of a State and 'not attributable to them personally but to

15 1400 UNTS 231, in force 21 June 1985.

16 Argentina, Austria, Belarus, Bosnia and Herzegovina, Bulgaria, Chile, Colombia, Croatia, Cuba, Cyprus, Czech Republic, North Korea, Estonia, Fiji, Georgia, Guatemala, Indonesia, Iran, Liberia, Liechtenstein, Lithuania, Mexico, Montenegro, North Macedonia, Paraguay, Philippines, Poland, Rwanda, Serbia, Seychelles, Slovakia, Slovenia, Spain, State of Palestine, Switzerland, Tonga, Tunisia, Ukraine and Uruguay.

17 *The 'Enrica Lexi' Incident (Italy v India)*, PCA Case 2015-28, Award of 21 May 2020 para 848, and see also ibid paras 856, 859.

the State on whose behalf they act'. Functional immunity is said to be 'a well-established rule of customary international law going back to the eighteenth and nineteenth centuries, restated many times since'.[18] However, where the act proscribed by a treaty can only be committed on behalf of the State, there can be no immunity *ratione materiae*. This is the case of torture as defined by Article 1(1) of the 1984 Convention against Torture and Other Cruel, Inhuman or Degrading Treatment or Punishment[19] as an act 'inflicted by or at the instigation of or with the consent or acquiescence of a public official or other person acting in an official capacity'. This is why the UK House of Lords rules in *Pinochet (No 3)* that former Chilean President Augusto Pinochet enjoys no immunity for torture committed after the UK has become party to the Torture Convention and torture is a crime under UK law.[20] The same reasoning applies to offences under the 2006 International Convention for the Protection of All Persons from Enforced Disappearance,[21] Article 2 of which defines 'enforced disappearance' as 'the arrest, detention, abduction or any other form of deprivation of liberty by agents of the State or by persons or groups of persons acting with the authorization, support or acquiescence of the State'.

In 2017, the UN International Law Commission provisionally adopted Article 7 of the draft Articles on Immunity of State Officials from Foreign Criminal Jurisdiction.[22] According to Article 7 of the draft Articles, immunity *ratione materiae* from the exercise of foreign criminal jurisdiction shall *not* apply 'in respect of the following crimes under international law: crime of genocide; crimes against humanity; war crimes; crime of apartheid; torture; and enforced disappearance'. Whereas the prevailing view and practice among States support the position that there is no exception to immunity *ratione personae*, there are exceptions to immunity *ratione materiae* under treaties and 'emerging State practice' where the impugned acts are among the crimes enumerated in Article 7 of the draft Articles.[23] Indeed, many States (such as the Nordic countries, Belgium,

18 *Prosecutor v Blaskić* (Judgment on the Request of the Republic of Croatia for Review of a Decision of Trial Chamber II of 18 July 1997), Case IT-95-14-AR108*bis*, ICTY Appeals Chamber, 29 Oct 1997 para 38.

19 1465 UNTS 85, in force 26 June 1987.

20 *R v Bow Street Metropolitan Stipendiary Magistrate and others* ex parte *Pinochet Urgarte (Amnesty International and others intervening) (No 3)* [1999] 2 All England Law Reports 97. See also *R v Reeves Taylor* [2019] UKSC 51, where the 4:1 majority of the UK Supreme Court construes 'a person acting in an official capacity' for the purpose of committing torture under the Convention against Torture as being 'a person who acts or purports to act, otherwise than in a private and individual capacity, for or on behalf of an organization or body which exercises, in the territory controlled by that organization or body and in which the relevant conduct occurs, functions normally exercised by governments over their civilian populations [...] whether acting in peace time or in a situation of armed conflict'.

21 2716 UNTS 3, in force 23 Dec 2010.

22 A/CN.4/L.893 (10 July 2017).

23 Statement of the Chairperson of the Drafting Committee on the topic 'Immunity of State Officials from Foreign Jurisdiction', 20 July 2017; International Law Commission, ' Report on

Greece and Mexico) consider developments since the end of the Second World War up to the advent of the 1998 Rome Statute of the ICC deny immunity *ratione materiae* to perpetrators of such crimes. By virtue of Section 16 of the Netherlands' International Crimes Act of 2003, 'foreign Heads of State, Heads of Government, and Ministers of Foreign Affairs, as long as they are in office' enjoy personal or full immunity from the exercise of criminal jurisdiction by the Netherlands. In addition, they enjoy functional immunity under Dutch law after their term of office for acts performed during their term of office, but this functional immunity does not extend to international crimes, including genocide, crimes against humanity and war crimes.[24] As another example, on 25 July 2012 the Swiss Federal Criminal Court, while recognizing the immunity *rationae personae* of Khaled Nezzar as Algeria's Minister of Defence at the time of his alleged commission of war crimes in Algeria, ruled this immunity did not subsist after his tenure in that position came to an end. Recognizing a clear trend in international law to restrict the immunity of persons as regards serious crimes of international law, the Swiss Court held that former State officials are not entitled to immunity *ratione materiae* for their conducts contrary to fundamental values of the international legal order.[25]

The immunity issue comes into play for the ICC in the light of Articles 27 and 98 of the Rome Statute. Unlike the ICC, which is created by the Rome Statute binding on its States Parties, the obligation to surrender offenders to *ad hoc* international criminal tribunals established by the UN Security Council pursuant to Chapter VII of the UN Charter overrides the obligation to respect such immunity.[26] The same applies to *ad hoc* or hybrid courts not set up by the UN Security Council; they do not recognize immunity since they are established specifically to punish all persons who have committed crimes within their jurisdiction, including persons in, or used to be in, official positions.[27]

---

the work of its 69th Session (1 May–2 June and 3 July–4 August 2017' (A/72/10) 164–5, 177–91; Kriangsak Kittichaisaree, *The Obligation to Extradite or Prosecute* (Oxford University Press 2018) 257–61.

24 'Immunity of Foreign State Officials: Advisory Report by the Netherlands Government Advisory Committee on Issues of Public International Law' (2011) 58 Netherlands Int'l Law Rev 461–2.

25 Case BB. 2011.140. See also the German Federal Court of Justice's Judgment of 28 January 2021 (BGH, 28.01.2021 – 3 StR 564/19), ruling that the claim of Ahmad Zaheer D., a former Afghan officer, to immunity is no longer valid due to his alleged mistreatment and torture of prisoners – which constitutes a war crime, and cf. Claus Kress, 'On Functional Immunity of Foreign Officials and Crimes under International Law', *Just Security* (31 Mar 2021).

26 *Prosecutor v Radovan Karadžić* (Decision on Accused's Second Motion for Inspection and Disclosure: Immunity Issue), Case IT-95-5/18-PT, ICTY Trial Chamber, 17 Dec 2008 paras 17–8.

27 See, e.g., *Prosecutor v Charles Taylor* (Decision on Immunity from Jurisdiction), Case SCSL-2003-01-I, Special Court for Sierra Leone Appeals Chamber, 31 May 2004 paras 44–53. See also Charles C Jalloh, *The Legal Legacy of the Special Court for Sierra Leone* (Cambridge University Press 2020) 214–76.

In respect of the obligation to surrender to an international criminal tribunal set up by a treaty, such as the ICC, matters are much more complicated.

In prosecuting nationals of States Parties to the Rome Statute, there is no conflict between Article 27 and Article 98 of the Statute. By becoming party to this Statute, a State is deemed by virtue of Article 27 to have agreed to waive any immunity of its nationals under international law in proceedings before the ICC, including when the State is the 'third State' referred to in Article 98(1). Even so, as the ICC's attempted prosecution of certain high-ranking government officials of Kenya, a State Party to the Statute, has shown, there may be potentially insurmountable hurdles confronting the ICC Prosecutor.

In 2007–2008, approximately 1,300 Kenyans were killed and 350,000 displaced by deadly clashes following the disputed 2007 general elections in Kenya. In December 2014, the then ICC Prosecutor Luis Moreno Ocampo requested that charges be brought against six prominent Kenyans (the 'Ocampo Six') who had allegedly incited or facilitated the post-election violence; namely, Kenya's suspended Education Minister William Ruto, Finance Minister Uhuru Kenyatta, Industrialization Minister Henry Kosgey, secretary to the cabinet Francis Kirimi Muthaura, former police chief Mohammed Hussein Ali, and radio executive Joshua Arap Sang. On 23 January 2012, the ICC Pre-Trial Chamber II dismissed the charges against Kosgey and Ali, while confirming the charges against the other four.

Kenyatta was accused of five counts of crimes against humanity. When the ICC issued the summons to appear against him on 8 March 2011, he was Deputy Prime Minister and Minister of Finance. He and Ruto cooperated with the ICC proceedings at the beginning. They appeared voluntarily before the ICC, after being issued with summonses to appear in March 2011, to attend preliminary hearings in The Hague in April 2011 and confirmation of charges hearings in September of that year. Kenyatta became Kenya's President and Ruta became his Deputy President on 9 April 2013.

In addition to the 'Ocampo Six' prosecution before the ICC, on 2 October 2013 the ICC Prosecutor issued a statement explaining that the evidence collected so far indicated there was a network of people trying to sabotage the case against Ruto *et al.* by interfering with ICC Prosecution witnesses. Kenyan journalist Walter Barasa, against whom compelling evidence had been collected, was part of this network, and his actions fit into this wider scheme that the Office of the ICC Prosecutor ('OTP') continued to investigate. Under Article 70 of the Rome Statute, using bribes or threats to influence witnesses to change or recant their testimony is a crime punishable by the ICC. If found guilty, Barasa would face up to five years' imprisonment, a fine, or both. The OTP has continued to press Kenyan authorities to arrest Barasa and surrender him over to the ICC. Although the Kenyan High Court validated the ICC's arrest warrant dated 2 August 2013, Barasa has appealed the decision and the matter is currently before the Kenyan Court of Appeal. In a related development, on 2 November 2020 Kenyan lawyer Paul Gicheru, who was subject to the ICC's arrest warrant issued in 2015 on charges of attempting to bribe six ICC Prosecution witnesses at the trial of Ruto and Sang at the ICC, voluntarily turned himself in to Dutch authorities which, on the following day, transferred him to the ICC. Ruto has denied Gicheru was his lawyer and the Kenyan High Court has issued a ruling, dated 16 November 2017, to 'lift' the ICC's arrest warrants against Gicheru and his co-accused Philip Bett, who is still at large as of this writing, on allegations of witness tampering. The Kenyan High Court reasons that pursuant to the principle of complementarity under the Rome Statute, to which Kenya is a State Party, Kenya has the primary mandate to investigate, prosecute and try offences against the administration of justice allegedly committed in Kenya unless Kenya's inability or procrastination is established, and that, at least for the time being, the constitutional rights and freedoms of these Kenyan citizens to enjoy their liberty without restriction shall be protected unless the due process of the law is followed.[28]

Thanks to Kenya's initiative, the extraordinary session of the Assembly of the African Union ('AU') on 12 October 2013 reached the following outcome on Africa's relationship with the ICC. It reaffirmed the AU's 'strong conviction that the search for justice should be pursued in a way that does not impede or jeopardize efforts aimed at promoting lasting peace', while also reiterating its 'concern on the politicization and misuse of indictments against African leaders' especially when a sitting Head of State and his deputy were being tried in an international court at the same time 'which could undermine the sovereignty, stability and peace in that country and in other [AU] Member States as well as reconciliation and reconstruction and the normal functioning of constitutional institutions' including national and regional security affairs. Kenya was said to be a frontline State in the fight against terrorism at regional, continental and international levels. Following the 2007 post-election violence, the mediation process in Kenya was initiated by the AU which led to the enactment of the National Accord and Reconciliation Act 2008[29] and the agreement establishing the coalition Government, the implementation of which was under threat by the ICC's prosecution of the Kenyan leaders. The AU 'reaffirm[ed] the principles deriving from national laws and international customary law by which sitting Heads of State and other senior State officials [were] granted immunities during their tenure of office'. Hence, no charges were to be commenced or continued before any international court or tribunal against any serving AU Head of State or Government or anybody acting or entitled to act in such capacity during their term of office, and the trials of incumbent President Kenyatta and Deputy President Ruto were to be suspended until they completed their terms of office. The AU also set up a Contact Group to consult the UN Security Council

28 *Republic of Kenya v Paul Gicheru and Philip Kipkoech Bett*, Miscellaneous Criminal Application 193 of 2015, High Ct of Kenya, Order of 16 Nov 2017.

29 Act No 4 of 2008.

on all of the AU's concerns as regards the Security Council's relationship with the ICC, including the deferral by the Security Council under Article 16 of the Rome Statute of the Kenyan cases. The AU also decided that the Kenyan President would not appear before the ICC until such time as the concerns raised by the AU and its Member States had been adequately addressed by the Security Council and the ICC. According to Article 16, no investigation or prosecution may be commenced or proceeded with under the Rome Statute for a period of 12 months after the UN Security Council, in a resolution adopted under Chapter VII of the UN Charter, has requested the ICC to that effect; that request may be renewed by the Council under the same conditions.[30] Pursuant to Article 27 of the UN Charter, decisions of the Security Council on all substantive matters shall be made by an affirmative vote of nine members including the concurring votes of the five permanent members. This stringent condition prevented the Security Council from adopting a resolution to defer the Kenyan cases.

As a compromise, in November 2013 the Assembly of States Parties to the Rome Statute adopted Rule 134*quater* as an amendment to the ICC's Rules of Procedure and Evidence, to the effect that the ICC Trial Chamber may excuse the accused from continuous presence at his or her trial when the accused has to perform 'extraordinary public duties at the highest national level'. Thereafter, in February 2014 Ruto succeeded in having the Trial Chamber relieve him from having to attend all trial hearings for as long as he was Kenya's Deputy President, subject to the following nine conditions. The accused would have to be present at hearings before the Trial Chamber during the entirety of the closing statements of all parties and participants in the case; when victims presented their views and concerns in person; during the entirety of the delivery of the Judgment in the case; during the entirety of the sentencing hearing, if applicable; during the entirety of the sentencing, if applicable; during the entirety of the victim impact hearings, if applicable; during the entirety of the reparation hearings, if applicable; during the first five days of hearing starting after a judicial recess; and at any other attendance directed by the Chamber either on its own initiative or on a request of a party or participant as decided by the Chamber.[31]

The charges against Muthaura and Kenyatta were withdrawn by the OTP in March 2013 and March 2015, respectively, due to lack of sufficient evidence after the OTP had repeatedly asked for more time to build its case. On 5 April 2016, the charges against Ruto and Sang, the remaining two individuals of the 'Ocampo Six', were withdrawn. Nonetheless, it would be open to the ICC Prosecution to bring new charges against the accused at a later date, based on

30 See also Kamari Maxine Clarke, *Affective Justice: The International Criminal Court and the Pan-Africanist Pushback* (Duke University Press 2019) Chapter 6 (Retributions: The Refusal to Arrest and Surrender African Heads of State).

31 *Prosecutor v Willian Samoei Ruto and Joshua Arap Sang* (Reasons for the Decision on Excusal from Presence at Trial under Rule 134*quater*), Case ICC-01/09-01/11, ICC Trial Chamber V(A), 18 Feb 2014.

the same or similar factual circumstances, should it obtain sufficient evidence to support such a course of action.

On 26 November 2019, the ICC Prosecutor reports the outcome of the OTP's internal Kenya situation review exercise following the receipt of a report in February 2018 by a panel of independent external experts commissioned to assist the OTP with the review. External factors, including lack of sufficient cooperation, witness tampering and interference, were found to have played their role in the final outcome in the Kenya cases. The prosecutorial process was hampered by deadlines set by the first ICC Prosecutor – who was in office from 16 June 2003 to 15 June 2012 – that were based on considerations other than what they considered to be sound prosecutorial practice. The effectiveness of the investigations and prosecutions was significantly undermined by a 'decision over assessment' tactic respecting cases and a target-based – as opposed to evidence-based – approach to investigation and charging. This, coupled with other problems, meant prosecutions were burdened with weak cases, relying on one or only a small number of insider witnesses – whose evidence could not be independently verified by the OTP – to establish essential elements of the case. Additionally, the continued cooperation of these insiders was constantly threatened by a pervasive witness interference campaign, exacerbated by the difficulties encountered with the witness protection programme at that time. Witness issues, relating to both credibility and vulnerability to witness interference, were a problem from the beginning. The OTP was dilatory in responding robustly to the potential for witness interference and the interference itself, delaying comprehensive Rome Statute Article 70 investigations of alleged offences against the administration of justice until late in the process. The experts' report also draws attention to: the difficulty the ICC Registry's Victims and Witnesses Unit had at the time in dealing with pervasive witness protection issues; the inability of the OTP to secure adequate cooperation from States Parties, notably Kenya; the failure of the judges to be proactive with respect to effective witness protective measures, which might, in the experts' view, have been partly due to the OTP's failure compellingly to address these issues before the judges; and the first ICC Prosecutor's susceptibility to influence from domestic and international NGOs in his decision-making. The experts were also concerned that too many staff positions were filled by individuals who did not have the requisite experience and skill sets to deal with complex investigations and prosecutions against high level suspects. While these individuals worked to the best of their abilities, these abilities were not sufficient to cope with the complexities of the Kenya cases.[32]

Several impediments identified in the internal Kenya situation review exercise are prevalent when criminal investigation or prosecution is being pursued either internationally or domestically against national leaders or politically influential persons of countries where the rule of law is relatively weak. To be fair to the

32 www.icc-cpi.int/itemsDocuments/261119-otp-statement-kenya-eng.pdf.

OTP, in trying to gather evidence against incumbent high-ranking government officials in a State the OTP needs cooperation and assistance from that State to, ironically, prosecute some members of its political leadership.

It may be recalled that pursuant to Article 98(1) of the Rome Statute, a State in whose territory or jurisdiction a person subject to the ICC's arrest warrant is present may not be requested by the ICC to surrender, or provide assistance regarding, the person if such request 'would require the requested State to act inconsistently with its obligations under international law with respect to the State or diplomatic immunity of a person or property of a third State, unless the ICC can first obtain the cooperation of that third State for the waiver of the immunity'. What would happen if the third State is *not* party to the Rome Statute? This question has arisen in at least two cases before the ICC.

One case related to the arrest warrant issued by the ICC on 27 June 2011 for President Muammar Gaddafi of Libya, a State not party to the Rome Statute but the situation in whose State had been referred to the ICC Prosecutor by the UN Security Council under Article 13(b) of the Statute. The case was terminated on 22 November 2011 after his death and any debate on the actual application of Article 27 and Article 98(1) of the Statute to this case is otiose.

The other case concerns the ICC's arrest warrant for the then President Al-Bashir of Sudan, another State not party to the Rome Statute, after the UN Security Council has referred the situation in Darfur, Sudan, to the ICC Prosecutor pursuant to Article 13(b) of the Rome Statute in March 2005. In March 2009, a Pre-Trial Chamber of the ICC authorized the issuance of an arrest warrant against Al-Bashir for alleged war crimes and crimes against humanity in Darfur. A second arrest warrant was issued in July 2010 to include charges of genocide.

Where the UN Security Council refers the situation to the ICC pursuant to Article 13(b) of the Rome Statute, this entails the implementation of the Rome Statute as a whole, including Articles 27 and 98(1) thereof. Nonetheless, States Parties to the Statute have not cooperated with the ICC by arresting and surrendering Al-Bashir to the ICC, and Pre-Trial Chambers of the ICC have dealt on several occasions with non-compliance by these States Parties, including Chad,[33] Malawi[34] and South Africa.

The Judgment of the Supreme Court of Appeal of South Africa on 15 March 2016 in *Minister of Justice and Constitutional Development v Southern African Litigation Centre*[35] analyses the relationship between Article 27 and Article 98 of the Rome

33 *Decision on the Non-compliance of the Republic of Chad with the Cooperation Requests Issued by the Court Regarding the Arrest and Surrender of Omar Hassan Ahmad Al-Bashir*, Case ICC-02/05-01/09, ICC Pre-Trial Chamber II, 26 Mar 2013.

34 *Decision Pursuant to Article 87(7) of the Rome Statute on the Failure by the Republic of Malawi to Comply with the Cooperation Requests Issued by the Court with Respect to the Arrest and Surrender of Omar Hassan Ahmad Al Bashir*, Case ICC-02/05-01/09, ICC Pre-Trial Chamber I, 12 Dec 2011.

35 [2016] 2 All SA 365 (SCA).

Statute in relation to the immunity of visiting Sudanese President Al-Bashir. It finds 'a measure of consensus' that Article 98 of the Statute deals with requests for surrender or assistance in relation to nationals, including Heads of State, of non-States Parties to the Statute such as Sudan. The Supreme Court alludes to the ICC's decision in the *DR Congo* case concerning President Al-Bashir[36] to the effect that, while the ICC itself recognizes the customary international rule as propounded by the ICJ in *Arrest Warrant* of the immunity *ratione personae* of sitting Heads of State like President Al-Bashir, the ICC concludes that President Al-Bashir's immunity has been removed by the UN Security Council's Resolution 1593 (2005)[37] deciding that the Sudanese Government 'shall cooperate fully with and provide necessary assistance to the [ICC] and the Prosecutor pursuant to this resolution', thereby eliminating any impediment to the proceedings before the ICC, as this is also an implicit waiver by the UN Security Council of Al-Bashir's immunities. The ICC reiterates this justification in relation to President Al-Bashir's visit to South Africa.[38] The Supreme Court concludes, nevertheless, that customary international law recognizes the personal immunity of Heads of State and other officials entitled to such personal immunity from arrest and prosecution or any inviolability while visiting a foreign State, and that customary international law as it currently stands does not recognize any exception to this immunity. Section 4(1) of South Africa's Diplomatic Immunities and Privileges Act, 2001[39] embodies this rule and would apply to accord immunity from arrest to visiting President Al-Bashir of Sudan, a 'third State' referred to in Article 98(1) of the Rome Statute. That Act is, however, subject to the Implementation of the Rome Statute of the International Criminal Court Act, 2002[40] enacted to implement South Africa's obligations under the Rome Statute and remove a bar, including immunity, to the prosecution of international crimes in South Africa or to South Africa cooperating with the ICC by way of the arrest and surrender of persons charged with such crimes before the ICC, where an arrest warrant has been issued and a request for cooperation made. The Supreme Court, therefore, holds the conduct of the Government of South Africa in failing to take steps to arrest and detain Sudan's President Al-Bashir for surrender to the ICC after his arrival in South Africa on 13 June 2015 to attend the 25th Assembly of the African Union to be inconsistent with South Africa's obligations under the Rome Statute and Section 10 of the Implementation Act, and unlawful.

36 *Decision on the Cooperation of the Democratic Republic of the Congo Regarding Omar Al-Bashir's Arrest and Surrender to the Court*, Case ICC-02/05-01/09, ICC Pre-Trial Chamber II, 9 Apr 2014 paras 25, 29.

37 S/RES/1593 (2005).

38 *Decision following the Prosecutor's request for an order further clarifying that the Republic of South Africa is under the obligation to immediately arrest and surrender Omar Al-Bashir*, Case ICC-02/05-01/09, ICC Pre-Trial Chamber II, 13 June 2015 para 9.

39 Act 37 of 2001, Government Gazette, vol 437 (29 Nov 2001) No 22876.

40 Act 27 of 2002, Government Gazette, vol 445 (18 July 2002) No 23642.

On 6 July 2017, Pre-Trial Chamber II of the ICC issued its Decision under Article 87(7) of the Rome Statute on the non-compliance by South Africa with respect to the ICC's request for the arrest and surrender of Sudanese President Al-Bashir.[41] The first substantive question for the Pre-Trial Chamber was whether South Africa was entitled not to comply with the request for arrest and surrender contrary to the provisions of the Rome Statute.

The Pre-Trial Chamber finds, by majority, that because the rights and obligations as provided for in the Rome Statute, including Article 27(2), are applicable to Sudan (by imposition of the UN Security Council acting under Chapter VII of the UN Charter), the immunities of Al-Bashir as Head of State do not bar States Parties to the Rome Statute from executing the ICC's request of his arrest and surrender for crimes under the ICC's jurisdiction allegedly committed in Darfur within the parameters of the Security Council's referral. Article 98(1) of the Statute is held inapplicable to Al-Bashir's situation, and States Parties to the Rome Statute are under the duty to execute the warrants of arrest issued by the ICC, and to implement the ICC's request for the arrest of Al-Bashir and his surrender to the ICC. Besides, irrespective of whether South Africa considers itself obliged to respect his Head of State immunity under customary international law, it nevertheless has the duty under the Rome Statute to arrest him and surrender him to the ICC, as Article 98 of the Statute – even if applicable to the present situation – does not foresee the possibility for a requested State Party to unilaterally refuse compliance with a request by the ICC for arrest and surrender.

In passing, the ICC Pre-Trial Chamber also touches on the relevance of the 1948 Genocide Convention[42] to which both South Africa and Sudan are party. The majority cannot answer in the affirmative the question whether that Convention renders inapplicable, between South Africa and Sudan and with respect to implementation of the warrant for arrest for the alleged crime of genocide, Al-Bashir's Head of State immunity. According to the majority, the Genocide Convention, unlike the Rome Statute in Article 27(2), does not mention immunities based on official capacity, and there is no convincing basis for a constructive interpretation of the provisions in the Convention such that would give rise to an implicit exclusion of immunities. Article IV of the Convention speaks of individual criminal responsibility of 'persons committing genocide' – which, as the ICJ has explained in *Arrest Warrant*, must not be confused with immunity from criminal jurisdiction – and can be effective even without reading into it an implicit exclusion of immunities based on official capacity. Article VI of the Convention is concerned with the allocation of competence among the

41 *Decision under Article 87(7) of the Rome Statute on the non-compliance by South Africa with the request by the Court for the arrest and surrender of Omar Al-Bashir*, Case ICC-02/05-01/09, ICC Pre-Trial Chamber II, 6 July 2017.

42 78 UNTS 277, in force 12 Jan 1951.

national and international jurisdictions in trying 'persons charged with genocide' and does not bear upon immunities.

On 6 May 2019, in the appeal brought by Jordan, the ICC Appeals Chamber decides unanimously to confirm the decision of ICC Pre-Trial Chamber II that Jordan, a State Party to the Rome Statute since 2002, has failed to comply with its obligations by not arresting Al-Bashir, who was at all material times President of Sudan, and surrendering him to the ICC while he was on Jordanian territory attending the League of Arab States' Summit on 29 March 2017. The issue on this appeal is

> whether Head of State immunity finds application in a situation where the ICC requests a State Party of the Rome Statute to arrest and surrender the Head of State of another State (in this instance, Sudan), which, while not being party to the Rome Statute, is the subject of a referral to the ICC by the UN Security Council and, in terms of Resolution 1593, obliged to fully cooperate with the ICC.

The Appeals Chamber rules that Article 27(2) of the Rome Statute, stipulating that immunities are not a bar to the exercise of jurisdiction, reflects the status of customary international law. It concludes there is no Head of State immunity under customary international law *vis-à-vis* an international court. Thus, in the present circumstances, where Jordan (a State Party) is requested by the ICC to arrest and surrender Al-Bashir, when Sudan is under an obligation to cooperate fully with the ICC in accordance with the Rome Statute due to UN Security Council Resolution 1593, Head of State immunity is equally inapplicable.[43]

There was a movement among certain AU Member States which are also party to the Rome Statute to challenge the ICC's decisions on the lack of immunity of Al-Bashir. In their opinion, this immunity issue was one of customary international law that the ICJ, and not the ICC, would be the judicial body to authoritatively delineate its parameters. A possibility of having the UN General Assembly requesting the ICJ to render an advisory opinion on this issue has been broached but has not materialized as of this writing because Al-Bashir has ceased to be President of Sudan since 11 April 2019. The issue is now moot unless and until a similar situation arises in the future.[44]

43 *Judgment in the Jordan Referral re Al-Bashir Appeal, Situation in Darfur, Sudan in the case of the Prosecutor v Omar Hassan Ahmad Al-Bashir,* Case ICC-02/05-01/09 OA2, ICC Appeals Chamber, 6 May 2019. The Appeals Chamber further finds, by majority, that the Pre-Trial Chamber erroneously exercised its discretion in referring Jordan's non-compliance to the Assembly of States Parties to the Rome Statute and the UN Security Council based on an incorrect conclusion that Jordan had not sought consultations with the ICC.

44 During the 18th Session of the Assembly of States Parties to the Rome Statute of the ICC in December 2019, the AU and Kenya maintained their positions that incumbent Heads of State had immunity *ratione personae* from international criminal proceedings.

On 11 February 2020, the transitional government in Sudan agreed in principle with rebel groups from the Darfur region of Sudan that the ICC would be among the four mechanisms for transitional justice in Darfur, which would include a special criminal court and truth and reconciliation in Sudan. According to this agreement 'in principle', Al-Bashir and the other Sudanese nationals subject to the ICC's arrest warrants for their alleged crimes in Darfur would be surrendered to the ICC. However, the head of Sudan's Sovereign Council, the collective Head of State for Sudan for 39 months from 20 August 2019, gave a television interview on 15 April 2021 revealing an agreement between Sudan's judicial authorities and the ICC to try Al-Bashir and other Sudanese fugitives wanted by the ICC in Sudan or any other place to be agreed upon, adding that the ICC did not request that they be surrendered to the ICC but rather that they be tried to achieve justice. In any event, the above lesson about the ICC's futile efforts to put an incumbent Head of State in its dock is still valid.[45]

Any draft resolution for the UN Security Council to refer the Situation in Bangladesh/Myanmar to the ICC pursuant to Article 13(b) of the Rome Statute will most likely be vetoed by one or more permanent member of the Council. Therefore, a possibility of the ICC denying the immunity of any person whose crime is covered by a UN Security Council's referral to the ICC under Article 13(b) – on the grounds that the immunity is implicitly waived by the Security Council – is not realistic in the Situation in Bangladesh/Myanmar. The ICC Prosecutor will have to be content with seeking cooperation from States Parties to surrender Myanmar individuals accused of crimes against humanity under the ICC's jurisdiction which are allegedly committed by with transboundary effects in Bangladesh, a State Party to the Rome Statute.

Let's assume the ICC does approves the ICC Prosecutor's request for the issuance of arrest warrants against high-ranking Myanmar government officials such as ASSK. Several States Parties to the Rome Statute may argue that ASSK whom they still recognize as *de facto* Head of State even after the *coup d'état* of 1 February 2021 has immunity *ratione personae*. Some States Parties may even assert that the Command-in-Chief of the Tatmadaw is also entitled to immunity *ratione personae*. Some may even go further by recognizing his immunity *ratione personae* in his capacity as the head of the State Administrative Council (hence, *de facto* Head of State) set up after the *coup*. In any event, *former* Myanmar government officials

45 According to news reports subsequent to the agreement between the transitional government in Sudan and rebel groups from Sudan's Darfur region, the transitional government is reluctant to surrender the persons sought by the ICC because some members of the Sudanese military and militia elements, which once belonged to Al-Bashir's state apparatus, who are in Sudan's current leadership, may also stand accused of involvement in crimes in Darfur. However, in June 2021 after a visit to Sudan by the ICC Prosecutor who specifically requested the Sudanese Government to surrender to the ICC the remaining 4 Sudanese persons subject to the ICC's arrest warrants, the Sudanese Cabinet reportedly pledged, in a unanimous decision, to comply with this request.

who used to have immunity *ratione personae* will no longer have such immunity after they leave office. Nor will they enjoy immunity *ratione materiae* for official acts that amount to acts of genocide, crimes against humanity or war crimes, either. This rule governing immunity has caused a dilemma – human rights abusers holding high-ranking government positions would have every incentive to stay in office as long as possible, even to fight to the death, lest they be brought to justice either before the ICC, foreign domestic criminal courts exercising jurisdiction over the crimes, as the next chapter will discuss, or even in their own domestic courts.

Will the Office of the ICC Prosecutor be capable of discharging its mandate in relation to the Situation in Bangladesh/Myanmar?

The OTP is responsible for determining whether a situation meets the legal criteria established by the Rome Statute to warrant *investigation* by the OTP. For this purpose, the OTP conducts a *preliminary examination* of all communications and situations that come to its attention based on the criteria established under the Rome Statute and the information available. Article 53(1)(a)–(c) of the Rome Statute requires that, in order to determine whether there is a reasonable basis to proceed with an investigation into the situation, the Prosecutor shall consider: jurisdiction; admissibility (complementarity and gravity); and the interests of justice.

There is a high-profile communication about alleged events in Asia that has not been pursued further. On 6 July 2020, the OTP received a communication alleging that genocide and crimes against humanity (murder, deportation, imprisonment or other severe deprivation of liberty, torture, enforced sterilization, persecution, enforced disappearance and other inhumane acts) were committed by Chinese officials against Uyghurs and members of other Turkic minorities in the context of their detention in mass internment camps in China. Relying on the ICC Pre-Trial Chamber I's Decision of 6 September 2018 on the ICC's jurisdiction in the Rohingya case, the communication alleged that the aforesaid crimes occurred in part on the territories of Cambodia and Tajikistan, both of which are States Parties to the Rome Statute, as some of the victims were arrested (or 'abducted') there and deported to China as part of concerted and widespread persecution and destruction of the Uyghur community. Subsequently, the OTP announced it would take no further action on this communication because the precondition for the exercise of the ICC's territorial jurisdiction did not appear to have been met with respect to the majority of the crimes alleged in the communication. In the OTP's opinion, the conduct constituting each of these alleged crimes appeared to have been committed solely by nationals of China within the territory of China, a State not a party to the Rome Statute. The OTP separately assessed the alleged crimes for which the part of the conduct appeared to have taken place in Cambodia and Tajikistan, in particular alleged acts of deportation. The OTP observed that while the transfers of persons from Cambodia and Tajikistan to China appeared to raise concerns with respect to their conformity with national and international law, including international human rights law and international refugee law, it did not appear that such conduct would amount to the crime against humanity of deportation under Article 7(1)(d) of the Rome Statute within the ICC's jurisdiction. Not all conduct which involves the forcible removal of persons from a location necessarily constitutes the crime of forcible transfer or deportation, absent violation of the legal interest commonly protected by these crimes; namely, the right of individuals to live in their area of residence or in the State in which they are lawfully present. While the conduct of such officials might have served as a precursor to the subsequent alleged commission of crimes on China's territory, over which the ICC lacks jurisdiction, the conduct occurring on the territory of Cambodia and Tajikistan did not appear, on the information available, to fulfil material elements of the crime of deportation under Article 7(1)(d) of the Statute. Accordingly, the OTP found no basis to proceed at this time.[46]

In 2006, the ICC Prosecutor opened a preliminary examination into war crimes and crimes against humanity committed in Afghanistan, another Asian State, since May 2003. In November 2017, the ICC Prosecutor submitted a request to a ICC Pre-Trial Chamber to authorize the commencement of an investigation in relation to: crimes against humanity and war crimes allegedly committed by the Taliban and affiliated armed groups; war crimes allegedly committed by Afghan government forces and other members; war crimes allegedly committed by the US armed forces and members of the Central Intelligence Agency in Afghanistan and the territory of other States Parties to the Rome Statute since 1 July 2002. The US Government has threatened to block any potential ICC investigation that might include US nationals or nationals of US allies. On 12 April 2019, Pre-Trial Chamber II of the ICC rejected the ICC Prosecutor's request. It reasoned that notwithstanding the fact all the relevant requirements under the Rome Statute were met as regards both jurisdiction and admissibility, the current circumstances of the situation in Afghanistan were such as to make the prospects for a successful investigation and prosecution extremely limited. Subsequent changes within the relevant political landscape both in Afghanistan and in key States (both parties and non-parties to the Rome Statute), coupled with the complexity and volatility of the political climate still surrounding the Afghan scenario, made it extremely difficult to gauge the prospects of securing meaningful cooperation from relevant authorities for the future, whether in respect of investigations or of surrender of suspects. In the Pre-Trial Chamber's opinion, suffice it to say that nothing in the present conjuncture gave any reason to believe such cooperation could be taken for granted. Indeed, the Prosecution acknowledged the difficulties in securing albeit minimal cooperation from the

46 OTP, *Report on Preliminary Examination Activities 2020*, issued on 14 Dec 2020 paras 70–6.

relevant authorities as one of the reasons explaining the unusual duration of the preliminary examination. Even neutral, low-impact activities proved unfeasible. Accordingly, the Pre-Trial Chamber found it reasonable to assume these difficulties would prove even trickier in the context of an investigation proper, making it unlikely that pursuing an investigation would result in meeting the objectives listed by the victims favouring the investigation, or otherwise positively contributing to it. The Pre-Trial Chamber, therefore, decided an investigation into the situation in Afghanistan at this stage would not serve the interests of justice and, accordingly, rejected the request.[47] This Decision has since been overturned by the ICC Appeals Chamber's Judgment of 5 March 2020.[48] According to the Appeals Chamber, pursuant to Article 15 of the Rome Statute the ICC Prosecutor may initiate an investigation *propio motu* (on her own motion) as in the case at hand, without having received a referral from a State Party to the Statute or the UN Security Council, provided that the investigation must be authorized by a Pre-Trial Chamber. The Appeals Chamber finds that the Pre-Trial Chamber erred in deciding that 'an investigation into the situation in Afghanistan at this stage would not serve the interests of justice'. The Pre-Trial Chamber's decision at this stage should have addressed only whether there is a reasonable factual basis for the Prosecutor to proceed with an investigation, in the sense of whether crimes have been committed, and whether the potential case(s) arising from such investigation would appear to fall within the ICC's jurisdiction. The Appeals Chamber, therefore, amends the impugned Decision and authorizes the ICC Prosecutor to commence an investigation

> in relation to alleged crimes committed on the territory of Afghanistan in the period since 1 May 2003, as well as other alleged crimes that have a nexus to the armed conflict in Afghanistan and are sufficiently linked to the situation and were committed on the territory of other States Parties in the period since 1 July 2002.

Notwithstanding the Appeals Chamber's Judgment, the difficulties and impediments faced by the Prosecutor as described by the Pre-Trial Chamber in its impugned Decision remain to be overcome.

Between 6 December 2019 and 11 December 2020, the OTP completed four *preliminary examinations* – with respect to the situations in Palestine (for alleged crimes committed in the occupied Palestinian territory, including East Jerusalem, since 13 June 2014), Iraq/UK, Ukraine and Nigeria. The OTP also commenced two new preliminary examinations following Rome Statute State

47 *Decision Pursuant to Article 15 of the Rome Statute on the Authorisation of an Investigation into the Situation in the Islamic Republic of Afghanistan*, Pre-Trial Chamber II, 12 Apr 2019.

48 *Judgment on the appeal against the decision on the authorisation of an investigation into the situation in the Islamic Republic of Afghanistan*, Appeals Chamber, 5 Mar 2020.

Party referrals received from the Government of Venezuela on 13 February 2020 and from the former Government of Bolivia on 4 September 2020 regarding the situation in the respective territories. The former Government of Bolivia alleges that crimes against humanity were committed in August 2020, when members of political party *Movimiento al Socialismo* and associated organizations engaged in a course of conduct pursuant to an organizational policy to attack the Bolivian population by coordinating hundreds of blockades at various points throughout the country that connected different cities to prevent the passage of convoys, transport and communications in order to, among other things, prevent the civilian population in those cities from accessing public health supplies and services during the COVID-19 pandemic. In its referral, the Government of Venezuela alleges crimes against humanity have been committed on Venezuela's territory as a result of the application of unlawful coercive measures adopted unilaterally by the US Government against Venezuela, at least since 2014.

The ICC Prosecutor has continued with preliminary examinations of other possible cases in Colombia (for crimes against humanity and war crimes allegedly committed there by different actors since 1 November 2002 and 1 November 2009, respectively), Venezuela (the 'Venezuela I' situation, prior to the Venezuelan Government's self-referral to the ICC Prosecutor on 13 February 2020, for alleged crimes committed since at least April 2017, in the context of demonstrations and related political unrest); extrajudicial killing in the war on drugs in the Philippines between 1 July 2016 and 16 March 2019 when the Philippines withdrew from the Rome Statute; and Guinea (for crimes against humanity allegedly committed against the opposition gathering which was violently suppressed by the security forces in the national stadium in Conakry on 28 September 2009 and in the immediate aftermath).

Most of the situations currently under *investigation* by the ICC Prosecutor are in Africa: DR Congo, Uganda, Darfur/Sudan, CAR, Kenya, Libya, Côte d'Ivoire, Mali, Central African Republic Part II and Burundi. Apart from the Situation in Bangladesh/Myanmar regarding the Rohingya, the only other two non-African situation for which the ICC Prosecutor is authorized by the ICC to investigate is the Situation in Georgia and the Situation in Palestine. The former covers the period from 1 July 2008 to 10 October 2008, for all crimes within the ICC's jurisdiction related to the conflict in and around South Ossetia between 1 July and 10 October 2008.[49] On 3 January 2020, the ICC Prosecutor considered there was a reasonable basis to proceed with an investigation into the situation in Palestine, referred to her by the State of Palestine, which became party to the Rome Statute in 2015, since war crimes had been or were being committed in the West Bank, including East Jerusalem, and the Gaza Strip. Before proceeding

49 *Decision on the Prosecutor's Request for Authorization of an Investigation (Situation in Georgia)*, Case ICC-01/15, Pre-Trial Chamber I, 27 Jan 2016.

further, she asked an ICC Pre-Trial Chamber to rule on the territory over which the ICC has jurisdiction because of the unique and highly contested legal and factual issues attaching to this situation. On 5 February 2021, the ICC Pre-Trial Chamber I decided, by a majority of 2 to 1, that the ICC's territorial jurisdiction in the Situation in Palestine, a State party to the Rome Statute, extends to the territories occupied by Israel since 1967, namely Gaza and the West Bank, including East Jerusalem.[50] On 3 March 2021, the OTP officially launched an investigation in respect of the Situation in Palestine, covering crimes within the ICC's jurisdiction that are alleged to have been committed in the Situation since 13 June 2014.

Unlike *ad hoc* or hybrid criminal tribunals, the ICC's mandate is not confined to specific geographical areas or time frames. In order to maximize available financial and human resources, the OTP has to be pragmatic against all odds.

The ICC Prosecutor's Prosecution Strategic Plan dated 17 July 2019 for the years 2019–2021 recognizes that despite a number of successes in the ICC's prosecution during 2016–2019 (e.g., the *Al Mahdi* case and the *Ntaganda* case), there have also been significant setbacks (e.g., the Situation in Kenya, the *Bemba* case and the *Gbagbo & Blé Goudé* case). Different factors have caused these unsatisfactory outcomes, including cooperation and security challenges. The OTP has set six strategic goals for the period 2019–2021. One of them aims to achieve a high rate of success in court by strengthening its existing strategy of conducting open-ended and in-depth investigations so as to be trial-ready as early as possible in the judicial proceedings as well as further developing its ability to investigate in complex operating environments. The OTP also aims to increase the speed, efficiency and effectiveness of preliminary examinations, investigations and prosecutions by focusing on optimizing preliminary examinations, further prioritizing among investigations and prosecutions, developing a clear completion strategy for situations under investigation, developing narrower cases as appropriate where the evidence requires it, preparing and advocating for more expeditious court proceedings, improving its business processes and optimizing cooperation with partners.

In addition, an Independent Expert Review was commissioned by the Assembly of State Parties to the Rome Statute to make concrete, achievable and actionable recommendations aimed at enhancing the performance, efficiency and effectiveness of the ICC and the Rome Statute system as a whole in three clusters: governance; judiciary and judicial process; and preliminary examinations, investigations and prosecutions. The last mentioned cluster, which is of direct relevance to the Rohingya context, involves reviewing the OTP's structure, organization, management, staffing and working methods, with special attention to, among other things, prosecutorial strategies, including on case selection and prioritization; investigations and case-preparations (including

50 *Decision on the 'Prosecution request pursuant to article 19(3) for a ruling on the Court's territorial jurisdiction in Palestine'*, Case ICC-01/18-143, Pre-Trial Chamber I, 5 Feb 2021.

investigative techniques, strategies and tools and financial investigations); and completion strategies (focusing on the mechanism for closure). The final report dated 30 September 2020 makes the following recommendations on this cluster. The OTP should focus on a narrower range of situations, and limit their interventions to the extent possible, focusing on situations of the highest gravity and on those most responsible for the crimes, which may well include mid-level perpetrators. The ICC Prosecutor should adopt a higher threshold for the gravity of the crimes alleged to have been perpetrated. The OTP should consider adopting an overall strategy plan for each preliminary examination, with benchmarks and provisional timelines for all its phases and activities, including its closure, and, if relevant, re-opening. Upon authorization of an investigation, this plan should provide the foundation on which to build the OTP's targets and strategies for the investigation. In parallel, the OTP's Investigations Division should develop long-term situation-specific investigative strategies that cover all stages of the situations, from the opening of a preliminary examination/investigation, to possible de-prioritization, hibernation and closure of an investigation. These plans should have flexible benchmarks to enable appropriate responses and monitoring of their implementation. Preliminary examinations should last no longer than two years. Extensions could be granted by the ICC Prosecutor, but only in exceptional and justified circumstances. The OTP should *not* have regard to prospective national proceedings and focus solely on whether national proceedings are or were ongoing and whether tangible steps are or have been taken at the national level in this regard. The OTP and the Assembly of States Parties should consider the development of a uniform cooperation framework, including collection of evidence, for all States Parties, or for regional groups of States Parties. Agreements with international and intergovernmental agencies with which the OTP engages frequently, such as the UNHCR and International Organization for Migration, could also be revisited.

On 12 February 2021, Karim A.A. Khan, QC, a UK national, was elected by States Parties to the Rome Statute to succeed Fatou Bensouda as ICC Prosecutor for a nine-year non-renewable term starting from 16 June 2021. At the time of his election, Khan was an Assistant UN Secretary-General and Special Adviser and Head of the UN Investigative Team for the Promotion of Accountability for Crimes Committed by Da'esh/ISIL in Iraq, set up by the UN Security Council[51] to support domestic efforts to hold Da'esh/ISIL accountable for acts that may amount to genocide, crimes against humanity and war crimes in Iraq. In his career spanning over 27 years, Khan worked for almost every international criminal tribunal in prosecution and defence roles, as well as counsel for victims. He has promised to reform the OTP to make it more efficient.

The Myanmar leadership, led by ASSK, has appeared before the ICJ to defend Myanmar against The Gambia's Application invoking Myanmar's State

51 A/RES/S/2376 (21 Sept 2017).

responsibility for violation of the Genocide Convention. After the *coup* of 1 February 2021, will Myanmar's military and civilian leaders, past and present, voluntarily appear before the ICC to defend themselves against charges of crimes against humanity under the Rome Statute at the risk of being convicted and sentenced to imprisonment as well as fined and ordered to pay reparation to the victims? Indeed, there is no guarantee the ICC Trial Chamber will apply Rule 134*quater* of the ICC's Rules of Procedure and Evidence to excuse the Myanmar accused from continuous presence at his/her trial when the accused has to perform 'extraordinary public duties at the highest national level', as in the case of Kenya's Deputy President Ruto a while ago. Above all, it is extremely rare for someone to voluntarily appear before the ICC to defend oneself, unless they are certain the ICC Prosecution will not succeed, as in the cases of Bahr Idriss Abu Garda, Kenyatta and Ruto.

The OTP can prosecute the Myanmar individuals accused of committing crimes under the ICC's jurisdiction only if, against all odds, States, especially States Parties to the Rome Statute, cooperate in arresting and surrendering these individuals to the ICC. Maybe a regime change in Myanmar after 1 February 2021 or not long thereafter will make this happen?

PART IV

Justice in foreign domestic courts

7

EXERCISE OF UNIVERSAL CRIMINAL JURISDICTION BY ARGENTINA AND OTHER NATION STATES

On 13 November 2019, the Burmese Rohingya Organization UK and two Argentine human rights groups – Grandmothers of the Plaza de Mayo (*Abuelas de Plaza de Mayo*) and the Foundation for Peace and Justice (*Fundacion Servicio Paz y Justicia*) – submitted a complaint to a federal court in Buenos Aires, Argentina, seeking the criminal prosecution of Myanmar's top military and political leaders, including Commander-in-Chief Senior General Min Aung Hlaing and Aung San Suu Kyi for their acts amounting to 'existential threat', or genocide, against the Rohingya Muslim minority.[1] The complaint was collaborated by Tomás Ojea Quintana, an Argentine who was the UN Human Rights Council's Special Rapporteur on the situation of human rights in Myanmar between 2008 and 2014 and who has seen first-hand the alleged sufferings of the Rohingya.

On 9 December 2019, an Argentine court dismissed the lawsuit on the grounds that it would duplicate the investigation launched by the ICC Prosecutor. That decision was overturned by Argentina's Federal Criminal Chamber No 1 in Buenos Aires on 29 May 2020. In accepting the complaint, the latter court requested more information from the ICC so as to ensure the case in Argentina would not duplicate other efforts to bring justice to the Rohingya.[2]

Why Argentina? One explanation could be the involvement and support of Tomás Ojea Quintana. Another, and more important reason, is that Argentine law recognizes the exercise of 'universal jurisdiction'.

1 www.brouk.org.uk/argentinean-courts-urged-to-prosecute-senior-myanmar-military-and-government-officials-for-the-rohingya-genocide/.

2 www.aa.com.tr/en/americas/argentinian-court-decision-brings-hope-for-rohingya/1861967.

DOI: 10.4324/9781003224211-7

Criminal jurisdiction

Jurisdiction is the authority of a nation State to regulate conduct of natural persons or legal entities by its own domestic law. Jurisdiction to prescribe is the State's authority to legislate or prescribe law and regulations. Jurisdiction to enforce is the State's authority to enforce the law and regulations legislated or prescribed by it. There is also an adjudicatory jurisdiction of national courts of the State to interpret its law and regulations. Jurisdiction is primarily territorial. A State may exercise jurisdiction over an incident in its territory or an incident originating in a State's territory but consummated elsewhere. It may also exercise territorial jurisdiction over individuals where an incident has effects on the State's territory although the act was initiated elsewhere. This territorial jurisdiction extends to the airspace superjacent to the land territory and territorial waters under the State's sovereignty as well as to the crime committed on board a ship or aircraft registered in that State. In addition, it has become acceptable for a State to exercise jurisdiction based on passive personality, active personality and protective principles. Under the active personality principle of jurisdiction, a State may exercise jurisdiction over the offender on the basis that the offender is a national of that State. Several States have also asserted jurisdiction over the offender on the basis that the offender's victim is a national of that State – this is based on the passive personality principle of jurisdiction. A State may, based on the protective principle, exercise jurisdiction over the offender whose conduct abroad threatens that State's security or interferes with the operation of its government functions.[3]

The most controversial base of jurisdiction is universal jurisdiction, whereby a State asserts jurisdiction over a crime which has no connection (*nexus*) with that State at all. In other words, the crime is committed outside its territory, does not have any effect therein and neither the perpetrator nor the victim is its national. It has long been accepted that every State may exercise universal jurisdiction over perpetrators of piracy. Apart from that, it is still controversial whether a State may exercise universal jurisdiction absent treaty obligations binding on the States concerned – as in the case of the obligation to prosecute or extradite commonly found in many multilateral conventions on suppression of serious crimes of international concern like international terrorism.[4]

With regard to the jurisdiction to enforce, a State may not enforce its criminal law, that is, investigate crimes or arrest suspects, in the territory of another State without that other State's consent.[5]

3 Malcolm Shaw, *International Law* (8th edn, Cambridge University Press 2017) 488–500; James Crawford, *Brownlie's Principles of Public International Law* (9th edn, Oxford University Press 2019) Chapter 21.

4 See the discussion in the Separate Opinion of President Guillaume in *Arrest Warrant of 11 April 2000 (DR Congo v Belgium)* [2002] ICJ Rep 3, 36–45 and in the Joint Separate Opinion of Judges Higgins, Kooijmans and Buergenthal ibid 76–83.

5 Shaw, *International Law* 509–10; Jacques Semmelman, 'Criminal Jurisdiction–extradition treaties – U.S. government-sponsored abduction of Mexican citizen: *United States v*

A frequently cited rationale for universal jurisdiction is that because of the atrocious nature of the crime in question, each State has a vested interest in its suppression and punishment despite the absence of a *nexus* with the forum State, otherwise its perpetrator may escape punishment. As the ICTY Appeals Chamber puts it in *Tadić*, 'Universal jurisdiction [is] nowadays acknowledged in the case of international crimes'.[6] In the view of the ICTY Trial Chamber in *Furundžija*, as international crimes are universally condemned wherever they occur, every State is entitled to prosecute and punish the perpetrators of such crimes.[7]

The legality or illegality of universal jurisdiction has yet to be decided by the International Court of Justice. In the *Arrest Warrant* case between DR Congo and Belgium before the ICJ, the dispute involved the arrest warrant issued by a Belgian investigating judge in exercise of his purported universal jurisdiction for the arrest of DR Congo's incumbent Minister of Foreign Affairs. DR Congo originally challenged the legality of the arrest warrant before the ICJ on two separate grounds: Belgium's claim to exercise universal jurisdiction and the alleged violation of the immunities of the Minister for Foreign Affairs then in office. However, in the submissions in its Memorial, and in its final submissions at the close of the oral proceedings, DR Congo invoked only the second ground. The ICJ, therefore, only addressed the question whether, assuming Belgium had jurisdiction under international law to issue and circulate the arrest warrant, Belgium in so doing violated the immunities of the then Minister for Foreign Affairs of DR Congo. Having found Belgium in violation of the personal immunity (or immunity *ratione personae*) of the Minister, the ICJ abstained from deciding on the issue of universal jurisdiction originally raised by DR Congo.[8]

In Europe, the European Court of Human Rights' decision of 12 July 2007 in *Jorgic v Germany* upheld the jurisdiction of German courts under the German Criminal Code[9] to try persons charged with genocide committed abroad, regardless of the accused and the victims' nationalities, and despite the wording of Article VI of the 1948 Convention on the Prevention and Punishment of the

Alvarez-Machain' (1992) 86 AJIL 811; Candace R Somers, '*United States v Alvarez-Machain*: Extradition and the Right to Abduct' (1992) 18 North Carolina JIL 213; Abraham Mohit, 'The Customary International Law of International Abductions: Limits and Boundaries' (2006) 11 Asian YBIL 123.

6 *Prosecutor v Tadić, Decision on the defence motion of interlocutory appeal on jurisdiction*, Case IT-94-1, ICTY Appeals Chamber, 2 Oct 1995 para 62.

7 *Prosecutor v Furundžija*, Case IT9517/1T, ICTY Trial Chamber, Judgment, 10 Dec 1998 para 156, quoting the Supreme Court of Israel in *Eichmann* which is also endorsed by a US court in *Demjanjuk*, that 'it is the universal character of the crimes in question ... which vests in every State the authority to try and punish those who participated in their commission' (*Attorney-General of the Government of Israel v Adolf Eichmann* (1968) 36 ILR 277, 298; *In the Matter of the Extradition of John Demjanjuk*, 612 F.Supp 544, 558 (N.D. Ohio 1985)).

8 [2002] ICJ Rep 3, 19 [45]–[46]; ibid 35 [1] (Separate Opinion of President Guillaume); ibid 59–62 (Separate Opinion of Judge Koroma).

9 Strafgesetzbuch – StGB, Federal Law Gazette I, 945 at 3322.

Crime of Genocide,[10] to which Germany is a State Party, that persons charged with genocide or any of the other acts enumerated in the Convention

> shall be tried by a competent tribunal of the State in the territory of which the act was committed, or by such international penal tribunal as may have jurisdiction with respect to those Contracting Parties which shall have accepted its jurisdiction.

According to the European Court of Human Rights,

> the Contracting Parties to the Genocide Convention, despite proposals in earlier drafts to that effect, had not agreed to codify the principle of universal jurisdiction over genocide for the domestic courts of all Contracting States in [Article VI] … However, pursuant to Article I of the Genocide Convention, the Contracting Parties were under an *erga omnes* obligation to prevent and punish genocide, the prohibition of which forms part of the *jus cogens*. In view of this, the [German] national courts' reasoning that the purpose of the Genocide Convention, as expressed notably in that Article, did not exclude jurisdiction for the punishment of genocide by States whose laws establish extraterritoriality in this respect must be considered as reasonable (and indeed convincing). Having thus reached a reasonable and unequivocal interpretation of Article VI of the Genocide Convention in accordance with the aim of that Convention, there was no need, in interpreting the said Convention, to have recourse to the preparatory documents, which play only a subsidiary role in the interpretation of public international law (see Articles 31(1) and 32 of the Vienna Convention on the Law of Treaties of 23 May 1969).[11]

The European Court of Human Rights also noted that this interpretation of Article VI of the Genocide Convention in the light of Article I of that Convention and the establishment of universal jurisdiction to try the applicant on charges of genocide was widely confirmed by the statutory provisions and case-law of numerous other Contracting States to the 1950 European Convention for the Protection of Human Rights and Fundamental Freedoms[12] and by the Statute and case-law of the ICTY. Furthermore, Article 9(1) of the ICTY Statute[13] was

10 78 UNTS 277, in force 12 Jan 1951.

11 *Jorgić v Germany*, Case 74613/01 para 68, ECHR 2007III. *Erga omnes* means 'towards all' or 'towards everyone', whereas '*jus cogens*' means 'peremptory norms of general international law' accepted and recognized by the international community of States as a whole as norms from which no derogation is permitted and which can be modified only by subsequent norms of general international law having the same character.

12 ETS 5, in force 3 Sept 1953.

13 S/25704 at 36, annex (1993) and S/25704/Add.1 (1993).

held to have confirmed the German courts' view, providing for concurrent jurisdiction for genocide of the ICTY and national courts, without any restriction to domestic courts of particular States.[14] The European Court of Human Rights cited the relevant law of the following States authorizing the exercise of universal jurisdiction over the crime of genocide: Spain, France, Belgium (at least until 2003), Finland, Italy, Latvia, Luxembourg, Netherlands (since 2003), Russia, Slovakia, Czech Republic, Hungary, Austria, Denmark, Estonia, Poland, Portugal, Romania, Sweden and Switzerland (since 2000).[15]

There have been unsuccessful attempts to request courts in several western European States to exercise universal jurisdiction. For example, attempts were made to resort to Belgium's 1993 universal jurisdiction law against former US President George Bush, Vice President Dick Cheney and Secretary of State Colin Powell for war crimes allegedly committed during the Iraq War in 1991, and Israeli Prime Minister Ariel Sharon for war crimes allegedly committed by him in the West Bank. In August 2003, Belgium, after intense international pressure, amended its universal jurisdiction law of 1993. The 2003 Belgian Code of Criminal Procedure recognizes the personal immunity based on a person's official position. Moreover, for Belgian courts to exercise jurisdiction over a serious crime committed outside Belgium, the accused must be a Belgian national or has his primary residence in Belgium; or the victim is a Belgian national or has had his/her actual place of normal and legal residence in Belgium for at least three years at the time of its commission; or where Belgium is bound by treaty to exercise jurisdiction over the case. Unless the accused is a Belgian national or has his/her primary residence in Belgium, only the Belgian federal prosecutor may pursue such case, and his/her decision is not subject to appeal. Consequently, in September 2003 the Brussels Court of Appeal dismissed all cases against Bush and Sharon and others for lack of jurisdiction.[16]

In October 2010, pro-Moluccan human rights activists requested a Dutch court to order the arrest of the then Indonesian President Susilo Bambang Yudhoyono, who was about to travel on a State visit to the Netherlands, for his alleged human rights violations in Indonesia. The court rejected the request on the grounds that the President had immunity *ratione personae*. However, the President had to cancel his planned visit as a precaution. Not until April 2016 did Indonesian President Joko Widodo become the first Indonesian President to pay an official visit to the Netherlands after Indonesia's independence from the latter (but only for one day and as part of his European tour).

14 *Jorgić v Germany* para 69.

15 Ibid paras 53–4.

16 On 19 December 2019, the Brussels Criminal Court found Fabien Neretsé, a Rwandan residing in France at the time of his extradition to Belgium, guilty of genocide and war crimes and sentenced him to 25 years' imprisonment for the murder of *a Belgian national*, her Tutsi husband and their daughter on 9 April 1994 in Kigali, Rwanda. His sentence was upheld by the Belgian Supreme Court on 27 May 2020.

On 15 September 2011, the UK amended its Police Reform and Social Responsibility Act[17] by requiring the consent of the Director of Public Prosecutions before an arrest warrant can be issued in cases brought by private individuals against alleged perpetrators of crimes committed outside and with no connection to the UK. This puts an end to private individuals' right to initiate criminal prosecutions in such cases by applying to a magistrate for an arrest warrant. In the past, arrest warrants sought by private individuals were often seen by their opponents as being 'politically-motivated', and the threats of arrest deterred high-profile foreign politicians such as former US Secretary of State Henry Kissinger, senior Chinese Communist Party official and Minister of Commerce Bo Xilai and former Israeli Foreign Minister Tzipi Livni from visiting the UK.

Spain's Judicial Power Organization Act of 1985[18] allowed Spanish courts to exercise jurisdiction over crimes committed by Spaniards or foreign citizens outside Spain when such crimes can be described according to Spanish criminal law as genocide, terrorism or some other international crimes, as well as any other crime that, according to international treaties or conventions, must be prosecuted in Spain. Spain has amended this law in 2009 and 2014 to limit the scope of the exercise of universal jurisdiction. Spain's Organic Act no 1/2009 of 3 November 2009 provides, among other things, that, without prejudice to treaty provisions binding on Spain, for Spanish courts to have universal jurisdiction over the offences enumerated under the Act, the accused must be present in Spain, there are victims of Spanish nationality or there is some special link with Spain and, in any event, there is no other State or competent international court which has initiated proceedings, including an effective investigation and, where appropriate, prosecution of such crimes. Proceedings already initiated in Spain shall be temporarily stayed if proceedings connected with the same offence and against the same accused are initiated by a court in another State or an international court. Organic Act no 1/2014 of 13 March 2014 expands the list offences subject to universal jurisdiction to encompass, among others, torture, enforced disappearance and corruption of public officials. It also provides that only the victim and the Public Prosecution Service have the legal standing to initiate proceedings in such cases. Article 23(4)(a) of the original Organic Act no 6/1985, as amended in 2014, stipulates that Spanish courts shall have universal jurisdiction over genocide, crimes against humanity or war crimes against protected persons or property where proceedings are brought against a Spanish national, a foreign national who is a habitual resident in Spain or a foreign national present in Spain whose extradition has been denied by Spanish authorities. Paragraph 5 of the Article excludes the universal jurisdiction of Spanish courts over the offences listed in paragraph 4 in two situations, based on the principle of complementarity and that of subsidiarity, respectively. First, an international court

17 UK Public General Acts 2011 c. 13.
18 Organic Act no 6/1985 of 1 July 1985.

set up by a treaty or agreement to which Spain is party has initiated proceedings. Second, the State where the offence is committed or the State of nationality of the accused has initiated proceedings and either the accused is not present in Spanish territory or proceedings have been initiated to extradite the accused from Spain to either of the aforesaid States or to surrender the accused to a competent international court, unless the extradition is not granted by Spain. The second exception is inapplicable where the State having jurisdiction over the case is unwilling or unable genuinely to undertake the investigation. As of this writing, the case against Argentine military officer Adolfo Scilingo was the first and only one based on universal jurisdiction to have resulted in convictions from both the National High Court and the Supreme Court of Spain.[19] Criminal proceedings in many universal jurisdiction cases in Spain did not progress much due to a combination of three main factors. Some of the accused enjoyed immunity from the jurisdiction of Spanish courts by virtue of their status as incumbent or former Heads of State, Heads of Government or Ministers of Foreign Affairs. In other cases, Spain extradited the accused to another State to face on-going prosecution. In the rest of the cases, a third State denied extradition of the accused to Spain, as when the UK declined Spain's request to have former Chilean President Pinochet extradited from the UK to Spain.

As a means to bridge differences in the understanding of the scope and application of universal jurisdiction, the African Union, or AU, and the European Union set up the AU-EU Technical *ad hoc* Expert Group on the Principle of Universal Jurisdiction in November 2008[20] in response to the AU's concerns over 'abusive applications of the principle of universal jurisdiction'. The *ad hoc* Expert Group was entrusted with clarifying the respective understanding of the African and the European Union Member States on the principle of universal jurisdiction. The *ad hoc* Expert Group, having met in January and March 2009, issued its report on 15 April 2009. The *ad hoc* Expert Group states categorically:

> International law, both customary and conventional, regulates States' assertion of universal criminal jurisdiction. States by and large accept that customary international law permits the exercise of universal jurisdiction over the international crimes of genocide, crimes against humanity, war crimes and torture, as well as over piracy. In addition, numerous treaties

19 *Scilingo Manzorro (Adolfo Francisco) v Spain*, Appeal judgment, Case 798, ILDC 1430 (ES 2007), 1 Oct 2007, Spain's Supreme Court. On 11 September 2020, the Spanish National Court convicted Inocente Orlando Montano Morales, a Salvadoran citizen who was a military officer and El Salvador's Vice Minister of Public Security from 1989 to 1992, and sentenced him to 133 years of prison for the murder in November 1989 of five *Spanish* Jesuit priests, but acquitted him of the murder of Salvadoran victims because Spain lacked jurisdiction over these cases.

20 The independent experts appointed by the EU were the first President of the ICTY Antonio Cassese (Italy), Pierre Klein (Belgium) and Roger O'Keefe (Australia). The independent experts appointed by the AU were: former President of the ICJ Mohammed Bedjaoui (Algeria), Chaloka Beyani (Zambia) and Chris Maina Peter (Tanzania).

> oblige States Parties to empower their criminal justice systems to exercise universal jurisdiction over the crimes defined in those treaties, although this obligation extends only to the exercise of such jurisdiction when a suspect is subsequently present in the territory of the forum State.[21]

In exercising universal jurisdiction, the *ad hoc* Expert Group recommends that a priority be given to a State having a significant link with the crime in question, especially the territorial State where the crime is committed. When exercising universal jurisdiction, States have to bear in mind the need to avoid impairing friendly international relations. National criminal justice authorities considering exercising universal jurisdiction 'should consider refraining from taking steps that might publicly and unduly expose the suspects, thereby discrediting and stigmatizing them, curtailing their right to be presumed innocent until found guilty by a court of law and hampering the discharge of their official functions'. National criminal justice authorities considering exercising universal jurisdiction 'are legally bound to take into account all the immunities to which foreign State officials may be entitled under international law'. Where either the territorial State or the State of nationality of the victim/accused seems 'manifestly unwilling or unable to prosecute the suspect, and the suspect is a foreign State official exercising a representative function on behalf of his or her State', the national criminal justice authorities considering exercising universal jurisdiction should seek and issue a summons to appear or an equivalent measure, rather than an arrest warrant, for the suspect to appear before the court and to produce, with the assistance of counsel, any exculpatory evidence. States should specify an appropriate level of court for prosecuting such serious crimes.

Since October 2011, the Working Group on the Scope and Application of the Principle of Universal Jurisdiction has been set up under Sixth (Legal) Committee of the UN General Assembly 'to undertake a thorough discussion of the scope and application of universal jurisdiction', open to all UN Member States and members of the specialized agencies and of the International Atomic Energy Agency.[22] There is no substantive progress in the Working Group's work as of this writing.[23]

As a general rule, it seems that insofar as the State in whose territory a crime is committed is unable or unwilling to exercise its territorial jurisdiction to punish the offender, another State may exercise universal jurisdiction over the crime, provided that the latter State acts in good faith, without ulterior political agenda and avoids the criticisms against its potential 'abuse' and arbitrariness as much as

21 Report of the AU-EU Technical *ad hoc* Expert Group on the Principle of Universal Jurisdiction dated 15 April 2009, Annexed to the Council of the European Union Doc 8672/1/09 (16 Apr 2009) para 9 (footnotes omitted).

22 A/RES/65/33 (6 Dec 2010).

23 See a detailed summary in Kriangsak Kittichaisaree, *The Obligation to Extradite or Prosecute* (Oxford University Press 2018) 213–8.

possible. In addition, the latter State may do so unless the person accused of the crime is extradited to another State willing and able to exercise jurisdiction over the crime or that person is surrendered to the ICC. The list of crimes subject to universal jurisdiction under customary international law are 'core crimes' such as genocide, war crimes, crimes against humanity and torture. Otherwise, a State may exercise jurisdiction in the absence of any jurisdictional link between the State and the crime in question only where that State is obligated to do so under a treaty binding upon it.

A proper exercise of universal jurisdiction over the perpetrator of any such core crime is most likely to meet the least opposition or resistance from the international community of nations. A case in point is the *Zimbabwe Torture Docket Case* decided by the Constitutional Court of South Africa, holding that the South African Police Service ('SAPS') has a duty to investigate crimes against humanity committed in Zimbabwe by Zimbabweans against Zimbabweans.[24] While South Africa is a State Party to both the 1984 Convention against Torture and Other Cruel, Inhuman or Degrading Treatment or Punishment[25] and the 1998 Rome Statute of the International Criminal Court,[26] Zimbabwe is party to neither. It was alleged that six Cabinet Ministers and Directors General and the ruling party in Zimbabwe itself were implicated as suspects in the commission of these crimes. The Constitutional Court of South Africa explains:

> We have found that our applicable legislative scheme, understood in the light of international customary law and other international obligations, places an obligation on our country through the SAPS to investigate crimes against humanity, including torture, committed outside our territory. However, the universal jurisdiction to investigate international crimes is not absolute. It is subject to at least two limitations. The first limitation arises from the principle of subsidiarity. It requires that ordinarily there must be a substantial and true connection between the subject-matter and the source of the jurisdiction. And once jurisdiction is properly founded, the principle of non-intervention in the affairs of another country must be observed; investigating international crimes committed abroad is permissible only if the country with jurisdiction is unwilling or unable to prosecute and only if the investigation is confined to the territory of the investigating State. Simply put, we may not investigate or prosecute international crimes in breach of considerations of complementarity and subsidiarity.[27]

24 *National Commissioner of the South African Police Service v Southern African Human Rights Litigation Centre and Another* (CCT02/14) [2014] ZACC 30.

25 1465 UNTS 85, in force 26 June 1987.

26 2187 UNTS 90, in force 1 July 2002.

27 *National Commissioner of the South African Police Service* para 61.

The second limitation is that of practicality, whereby 'it must be considered whether embarking on an investigation into an international crime committed elsewhere is reasonable and practicable in the circumstances of each particular case ... in light of all the relevant circumstances', particularly 'whether the investigation is likely to lead to a prosecution and accordingly whether the alleged perpetrators are likely to be present in South Africa on their own or through an extradition request'.[28]

On the facts of that case, the Constitutional Court of South Africa concludes that, due to 'the international and heinous nature of the crime', South Africa has 'a substantial connection to it'. The Court considers as 'the cornerstone of the universality principle, in general, and the Rome Statute, in particular', the obligation 'to hold torturers, genocidaires, pirates and their ilk, the so-called *hostis humani generis*, the enemy of all humankind, accountable for their crimes, wherever they may have committed them or wherever they may be domiciled'. The alleged acts of torture were perpetrated in Zimbabwe, by and against Zimbabwean nationals, and none of the perpetrators was present in South Africa. However, 'the duty to combat torture travels beyond the borders of Zimbabwe'. Torture forms part of the category of crimes in which all States have an interest under customary international law. Therefore, South Africa can, through universal jurisdiction, assert prescriptive and, to some degree, adjudicative jurisdiction by investigating the allegations of torture as a precursor to taking a possible next step against the alleged perpetrators such as a prosecution or an extradition request. There is no evidence that Zimbabwe has launched any investigation or indicated its willingness to do so, given the period of time since the alleged commission of the crimes. While political inter-State tensions are, in most instances, virtually unavoidable in implementing universal jurisdiction, the exercise of universal jurisdiction for purposes of the investigation of an international crime committed outside the territory of South Africa may occur in the absence of a suspect without offending international law. As South Africa is not exercising enforcement jurisdiction against the Zimbabwean suspects within the South African territory, this will not offend against the principle of non-intervention. Furthermore, there is a reasonable possibility that the SAPS will gather evidence that may satisfy the elements of the crime of torture allegedly committed in neighbouring Zimbabwe, and the possible presence of the suspects in South Africa in the future cannot be discounted.[29]

Decline or rise in the exercise of universal jurisdiction?

The article 'The Quiet Expansion of Universal Jurisdiction' written by Professor Máximo Langer of the University of California Los Angeles and Mackenzie

28 Ibid paras 63–4.
29 Ibid paras 47, 49, 74–9.

Eason, a PhD student at that University, published in 2019,[30] is a result of their extensive and original worldwide survey of all universal jurisdiction complaints filed between 1961 and 2017 over the alleged commission of one or more of the four core international crimes: crimes against humanity, genocide, war crimes and torture. Their finding shows universal jurisdiction practice has been quietly expanding as there has been a significant growth in the number of universal jurisdiction trials, in the frequency with which these trials take place year by year and in the geographical scope of universal jurisdiction litigation. However, as Langer and Eason are at pains to point out, the expansion of universal jurisdiction has been quiet because most tried defendants have been low-level, and universal jurisdiction States have not made an effort to publicize these trials. Most universal jurisdiction investigations and trials have focused on 'low-cost' defendants and defendants who were already residing in the prosecuting State. Low-cost defendants are those defendants whose prosecutions do not impose substantial diplomatic and other costs to the political branches of the prosecuting State, whether because – among other possible factors – the defendant's home State is relatively weak in its ability to exert pressure, or does not protest or does not otherwise impose substantial costs, on the prosecuting State – hence, in practice, universal jurisdiction has not been global vigilante justice. Out of the total number of universal jurisdiction trials, 45.9% have been against African defendants (from Chad, DR Congo, Mauritania, Rwanda and Tunisia), 26.2% against European defendants (former Nazis and Yugoslavs), 18% against Middle Eastern defendants, 8.2% against Asian defendants (from Afghanistan and Nepal) and 1.6% against Central and South American defendants (Argentines). In the last decade of 2008–2017, the percentage of African trial defendants has gone up to 52.9%, compared with the 32.4% of concluded trials against Middle Eastern defendants (Iraqis and Syrians) and 11.8% of concluded trials against European defendants. Langer and Easton have found the amendments to Belgium's universal jurisdiction statute in 2003 and the amendments to the statute governing universal jurisdiction in Spain in 2009 and 2014 did have a noticeable effect, causing the number of complaints and investigations initiated in Belgium and Spain to drop sharply after 2003 and 2009, respectively. However, France and Germany have continued to be active universal jurisdiction States, maintaining or increasing the number of cases they hear over the ensuing decades, and there is a steady growth of universal jurisdiction litigation in new venues – including, notably, *Argentina* and several Scandinavian States including Denmark, Finland, Iceland, Norway and Sweden as well as in States that have adopted national law to implement their obligations under the Rome Statute of the ICC.[31]

30 Maximo Langer and Mackenzie Eason, 'The Quiet Expansion of Universal Jurisdiction' (2019) 30 EJIL 779.

31 See also TRIAL International, *Universal Jurisdiction: Annual Review 2021: A year like no other? – The impact of COVID-19 on universal jurisdiction.*

France is where a number of Rwandans suspected of playing some roles in the 1994 Rwandan genocide have fled to. The ICTR has referred some cases to France for prosecution by the latter. One concerned Laurent Bucyiabaruta, who was arrested and released in 2000 by the French authorities, and rearrested in 2007 under an international arrest warrant issued by the ICTR. In October 2015, the charges against him were dismissed by a French court. Another case referred by the ICTR concerned Wenceslas Munyeshyaka, a priest accused of genocide and crimes against humanity, whose case was dismissed on 2 October 2015 by a French court for lack of sufficient evidence. In February 2014, Pascal Simbikangwa, a former Rwandan intelligence chief, was brought to trial by France's newly created War Crimes Unit.

On 14 March 2014, a court in Paris found Simbikangwa guilty of genocide and complicity in crimes against humanity and sentenced him to 25 years' imprisonment.[32] On 16 October 2019, the French Supreme Court upheld the life sentences of Octavien Ngenzi and Tito Barahira, two former mayors in Rwanda, for genocide and crimes against humanity by overseeing the systematic practice of summary executions of ethnic Tutsis in Rwanda in 1994.[33] When France denies Rwanda's requests for extradition of Rwandan suspects, France takes upon itself to prosecute them, as in the case of Marcel Hitayezu, whose extradition to Rwanda was rejected by France's Cour de Cassation in 2016, as it did similar requests by the Rwandan Government for others suspected of having taken part in the 1994 Rwandan genocide. Hitayezu, a Rwandan priest at the time of the genocide, was charged by the French authorities on 14 April 2021 with genocide and being an accomplice to crimes against humanity by providing, among other things, food to militiamen who massacred Tutsis in his church during the genocide.

In November 2009, Ignace Murwanashyaka and Straton Musoni, two leaders of the Democratic Forces for the Liberation of Rwanda, were arrested in Germany on charges of belonging to a terrorist organization and having command responsibility for war crimes and crimes against humanity committed in DR Congo. In September 2015, they were found guilty by the Higher Regional Court in Stuttgart of committing grave breaches of international law in eastern DR Congo in 2008–2009, and were sentenced to 13 and 8 years' imprisonment, respectively.[34] On 29 December 2015, the Higher Regional Court of Frankfurt convicted former mayor Onesphore Rwabukombe and sentenced him to life imprisonment for committing genocide in Rwanda.[35]

32 Helen L Trouille, 'France, Universal Jurisdiction and Rwandan *génocidaires*: The *Simbikangwa* Trial' (2016) 14 J Int'l Criminal Justice 195.

33 https://trialinternational.org/latest-post/octavien-ngenzi/.

34 Oberlandersgericht Stuttgart Urteil vom 28.9.2015, 5-3 StE 6/10.

35 Oberlandesgericht Frankfurt am Main Urt. v. 29.12.2015, Az.: 4-3 StE 4/10-4-1/15.

In the case of Sweden, Chapter 2, section 2 of the Swedish Penal Code[36] provides that crimes committed abroad can be adjudged by a Swedish Court under Swedish law if committed by an alien not habitually resident in Sweden who, after the offence, has become a Swedish citizen or become habitually resident in Sweden, or who is a Danish, Finnish, Icelandic or Norwegian citizen and is in Sweden; or by any other alien who is in Sweden and the offence can, under Swedish law, result in imprisonment for more than six months. In addition, Chapter 22, section 6 of the Code proscribes 'a serious violation of a treaty or agreement with a foreign power or an infraction of a generally recognized principle or tenet relating to international humanitarian law concerning armed conflicts' as 'crimes under international law' punishable up to four years' imprisonment. If the offence is grave, the penalty is imprisonment for a term not exceeding 18 years, or for life. In determining whether the offence is serious, particular account shall be taken of whether it has been committed in a large number of separate acts or whether many people have been killed, injured or suffered significant loss of property as a result of the commission of the offence. Regarding war crimes committed in the former Yugoslavia, the Stockholm District Court convicted Ahmet Makitan of war crimes for his role during the conflict in Bosnia and Herzegovina when he was a member of the Croatian Defence Forces and prison guard for Serbian detainees.[37] As for the 1994 Rwandan genocide, Theodore Tabaro, a native Rwanda who became a Swedish citizen in 2006, was sentenced by the Stockholm District Court on 27 June 2018 to life imprisonment for genocide through murder, attempted murder and abduction of members of the Tutsi ethnic minority in Rwanda in 1994. Tabaro was ordered to compensate 16 victims, with each awarded approximately US$2,800 to 11,600.[38] In April 2019, his verdict and sentence were upheld by the Appeal Chamber,[39] which became final. Of interest is the fact that the War Crimes Commission of the Swedish police and the Appeals Chamber travelled to Rwanda to examine the crime scenes and hear testimonies. In another case, Stanislas Mbanenande, a Swedish citizen of Rwandan origin, was convicted and sentenced on 20 June 2013 to life imprisonment (maximum of 18 years) by the Stockholm District Court for his involvement in the 1994 Rwandan genocide. The Svea Court of Appeal in Stockholm upheld his conviction of complicity of genocide and serious violations of common Article 3 to the 1949 Geneva Conventions.[40]

36 Brottsbalken, SFS 1962:700; SFS 2009: 396; SFS 2014:381.

37 *Prosecutor v Ahmet Makitan*, Stockholm District Court, Case B 382-10, Judgment of 4 Aug 2011.

38 *Prosecutor v Theodore Tabaro*, Stockholm District Court, Case B 13688-16, Judgment of 27 June 2018.

39 *Prosecutor v Theodore Tabaro*, Svea Court of Appeal, Case B 6814-18, Judgement of 29 Apr 2019.

40 *Prosecutor v Stanislas Mbanenande*, Stockholm District Court, Case B 18271-11, Judgment of 20 June 2013; Svea Court of Appeal, Case B 6659-13, Judgment of 19 June 2014. See also *Prosecutor*

Raed Abdulkareem, an Iraqi national and a member of the Iraqi armed forces fighting Islamic State fighters in 2015, posed for pictures with the dead bodies of enemy fighters which he subsequently posted on Facebook in July 2015 showing him standing in military uniform among several decapitated bodies and a severed head on a plate. On 6 December 2016, Abdulkareem was found guilty of war crimes and sentenced to 6 months' imprisonment by Sweden's Blekinge District Court.[41] His sentence was affirmed on appeal.[42] In a similar incident, Kurda Bahaalddin H Saeed has been convicted in Sweden of four counts of the war crime of subjecting protected persons to humiliating or degrading treatment by posting pictures and videos of dead Islamic State fighters on Facebook with intent to commit outrages upon personal dignity. A soldier in the Iraqi army who fought the Islamic State in Kirkuk, northern Iraq, in 2015, Saeed took several photographs and videos of himself posing with the bodies of enemy fighters, some of whom had been mutilated. He was sentenced to one year's imprisonment.[43]

Several warlords who committed atrocities during the First Liberian Civil War (1989–1996) or the Second Liberian Civil War (1999–2003) have been put on trial in the West. Alieu Kosiah, a former commander of the United Liberation Movement of Liberia for Democracy ('ULIMO'), a rebel group fighting another rebel group called the National Patriotic Front of Liberia ('NPFL'), who became a permanent resident in Switzerland, was arrested by Swiss authorities in November 2014 after Civitas Maxima, an NGO working on independent legal representation of victims or war crimes and crimes against humanity, presented the Swiss Attorney General with evidence of his involvement in war crimes in northern Liberia during the First Liberian Civil War. His case was Switzerland's first war crimes trial in a civilian court exercising universal jurisdiction, and Kosiah became the first Liberian ever convicted for crimes committed during the Liberian Civil Wars. On 18 June 2021, the Swiss court in Bellinzona found him guilty of 21 out of the 25 charges against him, including ordering the killing of 13 civilians and two unarmed soldiers, murdering four civilians, raping a civilian, repeated orders to loot, an act of cannibalism and using a child soldier in armed hostilities. He was sentenced to 20 years' imprisonment, ordered deported from Switzerland for a period of 15 years, and ordered to pay compensation to seven plaintiffs. On 23 February 2021, the criminal trial of Gibril Massaquoi commenced in a criminal court in Finland, which subsequently held hearings in Liberia and Sierra Leone. The defendant, a resident of Finland, was arrested in

---

v Claver Berinkindi, Stockholm District Court, Case B 12882-14, Judgment of 16 May 2016; Svea Court of Appeal, Case B 4951-16, Judgment of 15 Feb 2017.

41 *Prosecutor v Raed Abdulkareem*, Blekinge District Court, Case B 569-16, Judgment of 6 Dec 2016.

42 *Prosecutor v Raed Abdulkareem*, Scania and Blekinge Court of Appeal, Case B 3187-16, Judgement of 11 April 2017.

43 *Prosecutor v Kurda Bahaalddin H Saeed*, Swedish Supreme Court, Case B 5595-19, Judgment of 5 May 2021.

2020 on the charges of killing civilians, rape and recruiting child soldiers during the civil war in Liberia. Massaquoi, a Sierra Leonean, had given evidence to the UN-backed Special Court for Sierra Leone set up to investigate war crimes committed in the armed conflict in Sierra Leone. He was relocated to Finland in 2008 as part of a witness protection programme, which provided immunity for crimes committed in Sierra Leone, but not in Liberia.[44] On 5 April 2021 the investigating chamber of the Paris Court of Appeals confirmed the referral to trial in France of Kunti K, former Liberian commander of ULIMO, for crimes against humanity, torture and other acts of barbarism allegedly committed during the First Liberian Civil War. He was arrested in September 2018 after a complaint filed by Civitas Maxima, the NGO working on independent legal representation of victims or war crimes and crimes against humanity, and several Liberian plaintiffs it represents. In the United States, immigration law has been used to put ex-Liberian warlords in prison. Mohammed Jabateh was sentenced by a US court in April 2018 to 30 years' imprisonment after being convicted of two counts of fraud in immigration documents and two counts of perjury stemming from statements he made in connection with his applications for asylum and for legal permanent residence in the United States, both of which were granted to him in December 1999. The prosecution was able to prove that during the First Liberian Civil War Jabateh either committed himself or ordered his troops to commit crimes such as the murder of civilians, sexual enslavement of women, public rapes, conscription of child soldiers and maiming and torture of non-combatants. His conviction and sentence were subsequently affirmed on appeal.[45] In another case, Thomas Woewiyu, Defence Minister and a co-founder of the NPFL, widely believed to have perpetrated serious war crimes in Liberia, was convicted by a US court of immigration fraud in July 2018 on two counts of fraudulently attempting to obtain citizenship, two counts of fraud in immigration documents, two counts of false statements in relation to naturalization and five counts of perjury. Among other things, when asked if he has ever been a member of or associated with any organization, association, fund, foundation, party, club, society or similar group in the United States or any other place, he did not disclose his NPFL membership. When asked if he ever advocated (directly or indirectly) to overthrow any government by force or violence, he answered no and did not disclose his advocacy to overthrow the government of former

44 For the exercise of universal jurisdiction by Finland, see Mikaela Heikkilä 'The Criminalisation and Prosecution of International Core Crimes in Finland' (2020) 66 Scandinavian Studies in Law 457.

In *Prosecutor v Ahmed Jabbar Hasan* (Case R 18/6593, Judgment, District Court of Helsinki, 10 Jan 2019), a Finnish Court sentenced Ahmed Jabbar Hasan, Iraqi national and former corporal in the Iraqi army, to a suspended sentence of 18-month imprisonment for war crimes of desecrating and violating the dignity of a dead body. The accused did not appeal and the judgment is now final.

45 *United States v Jabateh*, 974 F.3d 281.

Liberian President Samuel Doe. When asked if he ever persecuted (directly or indirectly) any person because of race, religion, national origin, membership in a particular social group, or political opinion, he answered no and did not disclose his NPFL membership and persecution of others based on political opinions and race. In April 2020, Woewiyu died of COVID-19 before his sentencing. Once those convicted of violation of the US immigration law have served their sentence in US prisons, they can be expected to be deported to their country of origin or surrendered to a competent international criminal tribunal to face other criminal charges against them.[46]

The influx of Syrian immigrants/asylum seekers into Germany, Finland, Switzerland, Norway, Sweden, France, Netherlands and other European States has led to an increase in cases involving the exercise of universal jurisdiction, since some of these Syrians might have committed serious crimes in Syria. The following cases are just some examples.

In February 2015, Mohannad Droubi, a member of the Free Syrian Army fighting the forces loyal to Syrian President Bashar al-Assad who was granted asylum in Sweden in December 2013, was convicted by the Södertörn District Court in Sweden of crimes against international law (war crimes) as defined by Section 6 of Chapter 22 of the Swedish Penal Code and gross assault as provided by Section 6 of Chapter 3 of the Code. He was sentenced to five years' imprisonment. In a final judgment on 5 August 2016, the Svea Court of Appeal sentenced him to eight years' imprisonment.[47] On 16 February 2017, the District Court of Stockholm convicted and sentenced Haisam Omar Sakhanh, a former member of a Syrian armed group fighting the Syrian Government, to life imprisonment for his participation in the summary execution 'under particularly cruel circumstances' of seven injured Syrian soldiers in Syria in 2012, one year before he was granted a refugee status in Sweden.[48] On 31 May 2017, the Court of Appeals confirmed his life sentence and on 20 July 2017 his leave to appeal was denied by the Swedish Supreme Court.[49] In September 2017, Mohamad Abdullah, a Syrian soldier who posed with dead and severely injured bodies and posted photographs

46 As in the case of Beatrice Munyenyezi who was deported from the United States in mid-April 2021 back to Rwanda and charged for crimes ranging from murder to complicity in rape during the Rwandan genocide in 1994. She had been stripped of her naturalized US citizenship and imprisoned for ten years in 2013 after being found guilty by a court of misrepresenting material facts when she secured the naturalization.

47 *Prosecutor v Mohannad Droubi*, Södertörn District Court, Case B 13656-14, Judgment of 6 Feb 2015; Svea Court of Appeal, Case B 4770-16, Judgment of 5 Aug 2016.

48 *Prosecutor v Haisam Omar Sakhanh*, District Court of Stockholm, Case B 3787-16, Judgment of 16 Feb 2017.

49 *Prosecutor v Haisam Omar Sakhanh*, Svea Court of Appeal, Case B 3787-16, Judgment of 31 May 2017; *Prosecutor v Haisam Omar Sakhanh*, Swedish Supreme Court, Case B 3157-17, Decision of 20 July 2017.

thereof on social media, was convicted of war crimes by Sweden's Södertörn District Court.[50]

On 24 February 2021, the High Regional Court in Koblenz, Germany, sentenced Eyad al-Gharib, a former sergeant major in Syria's General Intelligence Directorate ('GID'), to four-and-a-half years' imprisonment for aiding and abetting crimes against humanity under Section 7(1) No 5 (torture) and No 9 (serious deprivation of physical liberty in violation of a general rule of international law) of Germany's Code of Crimes against International Law of 26 June 2002[51] by accompanying the transportation of 30 detained demonstrators to the notorious Al-Khatib prison in Damascus in 2011 despite his knowing about the systematic torture in that prison. The case was the first-ever such trial and conviction anywhere in the world over alleged atrocities committed by Syrian President Bashar al-Assad's regime. Al-Gharib was given a relatively lenient sentence due to his low rank in the command hierarchy and for providing information that ultimately led to the indictment against Anwar Raslan, a former Syrian brigadier general.[52] Raslan is charged with 58 counts of murder as well as rape and sexual assault when he was in charge of the GID's Al-Khatib prison. Both al-Gharib and Raslan fled Syria's civil war and got asylum in Germany before their arrest in Berlin in February 2019 and were put on trial in April 2020 based on universal jurisdiction over crimes in international law pursuant to Section 1 of the aforesaid Code. In Germany and elsewhere, the prosecution's evidence against Syrians who used to work for the al-Assad's regime is supported by the 53,000 images smuggled out of Syria by a military police photographer known as 'Caesar' who defected in 2013 showing 6,786 people who starved or were tortured to death inside Syrian government detention centres. Also in Germany, Taha Al-J., an Iraqi national, is being tried since April 2020 in the Higher Regional Court of Frankfurt for, *inter alia*, genocide, war crimes, and crimes against humanity committed against members of the Yazidi religious minority in Iraq when he was a member of the Islamic State.

On 2 March 2021, three NGOs – the Paris-based Syrian Centre for Media and Freedom of Expression together with the Open Society Foundation's Justice Initiative and Syrian Archive – filed a criminal complaint in France against certain Syrian officials on behalf of a group of survivors of the coordinated sarin gas attacks in Douma and the Eastern Ghouta region just southeast of Damascas, Syria, in August 2013 that killed more than 1,400 victims, making the attacks the world's deadliest use of chemical weapons in the twenty-first century. The complaint requests an independent investigation that can ultimately issue arrest warrants against Syrian President al-Assad, his brother, Maher, and senior advisers

50 *Prosecutor v Mohamad Abdullah*, Södertörn District Court, Case B 11191-17, Judgment of 25 Sept 2017.

51 www.gesetze-im-internet.de/englisch_vstgb/englisch_vstgb.html#p0016.

52 https://syriaaccountability.org/updates/2021/03/04/reflections-on-the-eyad-al-gharib-judgement/.

and military officials forming the chain of command who are suspected of having committed these crimes against civilians. Officials in the al-Assad regime are not the only Syrians subject to the reach of universal jurisdiction in France. In February 2020, Majdi Mustafa Ne'ma (a.k.a. Islam Alloush), the spokesperson and a senior official of Jaysh al-Islam (or 'Army of Islam') with more than 20,000 fighters who carried out a reign of terror in the rebel areas in Syria it controlled until April 2018, was arrested and indicted by the War Crimes Unit of the Paris Tribunal for war crimes, torture, enforced disappearance and complicity in these crimes.

On 21 April 2021, the District Court of The Hague convicted Ahmed al-Y., a Syrian who had applied for asylum in the Netherlands, of membership in a terrorist organization and the war crime of outrage upon personal dignity. He was sentenced to six years' imprisonment.[53]

F. Hassan, a Syrian who had been a commander of a small Islamic State unit in Syria entrusted with terrorizing and executing civilians and religious leaders who refused to side with the group and who was subsequently granted a refugee status in Greece, was arrested at Budapest airport in December 2018 after presenting forged travel documents for himself and a female travel partner. In December 2020, a Hungarian court sentenced him to life imprisonment for terrorism and crimes against humanity including by personally taking part in the beheading of an imam in the town of al-Sukhnah and in the murder of another civilian in the area in May 2015. Authorities in Malta, Greece and Belgium as well as in Hungary participated in the investigation coordinated by Eurojust, the Hague-based EU agency dealing with judicial cooperation in criminal matters among agencies of the EU Member States, and witnesses in Belgium, Malta and Hungary came to give testimony against him.[54]

With respect to Argentina, where a case against Myanmar leaders has been brought for their alleged crimes against the Rohingya, Amnesty International's *Universal Jurisdiction: A Preliminary Survey of Legislation Around the World – 2012 Update*[55] lists Argentina's laws permitting the exercise of universal jurisdiction. They comprise the 1853 National Constitution, as amended in 1994; Penal Code of 1922, as amended; and Law on the implementation of the Rome Statute of the ICC, 2007, covering genocide (Article 8), crimes against humanity (Article 9) and war crimes (Article 10). Article 118 of the 1994 Constitution allows the exercise of jurisdiction over violations of international norms outside the national borders. Pursuant to Article 3(d) of the Law on the implementation of the Rome Statute, Argentine courts shall exercise jurisdiction over foreigners who commit crimes abroad as long as so provided for in treaties and

53 Cases 09/748011-19(dagv.I) and 09/748004-21(dagv.II), ECLI:NL:RBDHA:2021:3998.

54 www.barrons.com/news/hungary-jails-syrian-is-commander-over-imam-beheading-01607010606.

55 www.amnesty.org/download/Documents/24000/ior530192012en.pdf at 25–6.

international conventions to which Argentina is a party. With respect to war crimes, Argentina is party to the four Geneva Conventions of 1949 and their Protocols I and II of 1977 and the Second Protocol to the Hague Convention of 1954 for the Protection of Cultural Property in the Event of Armed Conflict of 1999. By virtue of Article 4 of the Law on the implementation of the Rome Statute, *when an alleged perpetrator* of genocide, a crime against humanity or a war crime *is found in any territory subject to Argentina's jurisdiction* an investigation shall be open before national courts, unless that person is extradited to another State or surrendered to the ICC. Article 114*ter* of the Penal Code permits the exercise of universal jurisdiction over torture, either committed by State officials and non-State agents. In addition, the 1984 Convention against Torture has constitutional hierarchy under Argentine Law and all its provisions are considered as part of the National Constitution.

The National Office of the Prosecutor of Argentina has established a Working Group on Universal Criminal Jurisdiction within the Crimes against Humanity Prosecution Unit to support the work of prosecutors on the interpretation and application of universal jurisdiction.

The Rohingya case is not the first high-profile case brought before Argentine courts on the basis of universal jurisdiction. On 17 December 2009, after four years of investigation Federal Judge Octavio de Lamadrid requested Interpol to issue an arrest warrant against China's former President Jiang Zemin and former security chief Luo Gan for 'crimes against humanity committed in China' including genocide and torture of certain members of the Falun Gong religious sect. Jiang was China's President from 1993 to 2003. To date, neither of them has been arrested and brought before Argentine courts.[56]

Legal proceedings on the basis of universal jurisdiction have also been brought in Argentina against lower-ranking government officials than the two aforementioned Chinese. In April 2010, some 250 Spaniards presented a complaint to a federal court in Buenos Aires asking the court to render justice for genocide and crimes against humanity (including torture, forced disappearances and kidnapping of children) committed during the Spanish Civil War and the dictatorship of General Francisco Franco in Spain between 17 July 1936 and 15 June 1977. After protracted legal proceedings, arrest warrants were issued against several Spaniards, but Spanish courts rejected the extradition requests regarding these individuals on the grounds that the statute of limitations applied to these cases under Spanish law.

Universal jurisdiction complaints have also been filed before Argentine courts for crimes allegedly committed in Gaza against Palestinians and in Paraguay

56 A similar complaint was filed by Falun Gong practitioners in South Korea in 2003 against Jiang Zemin and Luo Gan; and in Poland and in Russia against Bo Xilai, then China's Minister of Commerce during his visit to Poland and Russia in 2004, for his alleged crimes against humanity and torture of Falun Gong members. These complaints did not even lead to the opening of formal proceedings by the prosecutors in the respective countries.

against indigenous people and other victims of the Stroessner regime from 1954 to 1989.

In November 2018, Human Rights Watch, a human rights NGO, filed a complaint before an Argentine federal court to seek prosecution of Saudi Arabia's Crown Prince Mohammed bin Salman who was scheduled to come to Buenos Aires to attend a two-day G20 summit. He was accused of war crimes of causing mass civilian casualties as a result of the Saudi-led coalition's military campaign in Yemen since March 2015 and the torture of Saudi citizens, including the *Washington Post* columnist Jamal Khashoggi, who was murdered in the Saudi consulate in Istanbul on 2 October 2018. The Argentine Government's position was that the Crown Prince would be protected by diplomatic immunity, that he was also travelling in his official status as representative of a foreign Head of State, and that cases involving diplomatic immunity could only be decided by the Argentine Supreme Court and his visit would be too brief for the complaint to reach the Supreme Court. Indeed, although the federal court had accepted Human Rights Watch's complaint, and a prosecutor had asked a judge to determine if either Saudi Arabia or Yemen was investigating the Crown Prince for the alleged crimes before an Argentine court might exercise universal jurisdiction, the Saudi Crown Prince left Argentina after the G20 summit before the proceedings could reach the Argentine Supreme Court for a ruling whether he was covered by diplomatic immunity.

A similar situation occurred in Australia regarding ASSK. In March 2018, the Rohingya community in Australia sought leave from the Australian Attorney-General to prosecute Myanmar's then State Counsellor and Foreign Minister ASSK, who was attending the ASEAN-Australia summit in Sydney, for crimes against humanity of deportation and forced transfer of the Rohingya from Myanmar. They invoked as the basis of Australian courts' universal jurisdiction over the crimes and ASSK the provisions in Australia's Commonwealth Criminal Code that implement Australia's obligations under the Rome Statute of the ICC. They also lodged an application with the Magistrates' Court of Victoria to bring a private prosecution against ASSK. They accused ASSK of failing to use her position of authority and power, and, as such, permitting the Myanmar security forces to deport and forcibly remove Rohingyas from their homes. In response, Australia's Attorney-General affirmed that incumbent Heads of Government and Ministers of Foreign Affairs had immunity from prosecution.

The tussle between the executive and the judicial branches of government in a nation State with regard to the exercise of universal jurisdiction is not uncommon. For the executive branch, it generally prefers smooth bilateral relations with as many foreign States as possible, and arresting and prosecuting foreign State officials, especially those with high ranks, strain such relations. For the judiciary, including judges and prosecutors, the letter of the law must be upheld – *fiat justitia, ne pereat mundus* (Let justice be done lest the world perish).

The story of the prosecution in Switzerland of former Algerian Minister of Defence Khaled Nezzar, accused of war crimes and crimes against humanity committed in Algeria, is a case in point.[57]

Nezzar was the Minister of Defence in Algeria and a member of the High Council of State. In addition, he was considered the most influential person within the junta between 1990 and 1994, during which period he is suspected of having authorized and incited the army and public officials to commit countless crimes within the context of the 'dirty war', which resulted in approximately 200,000 dead and 20,000 disappeared persons in Algeria. Algeria's law prevents the prosecution of State agents involved in the fight against terrorism. In October 2011, during a visit to Switzerland, Nezzar was arrested in Geneva as a result of a report filed by TRIAL International, a human rights NGO, and complaints by two victims of torture. After being interviewed by the Swiss Federal Prosecutor, he was released on the condition that he would attend the subsequent proceedings. In the early months of 2012, Nezzar filed an appeal against the prosecution of his case, arguing that his position as Minister of Defence at the time of the events protected him from criminal prosecution in Switzerland.

On 25 July 2012, the Swiss Federal Criminal Court rejects an appeal for reasons of immunity by the defendant, on the grounds that immunity cannot be invoked in case of war crimes, crimes against humanity or genocide. With regard to the requirement of the presence of the accused in Switzerland for the exercise of criminal jurisdiction by Swiss authorities, the Court rules the accused must be present in Switzerland when a criminal investigation is opened, but the fact that the accused in specific cases subsequently leaves Switzerland does not automatically extinguish the competence of Swiss authorities to proceed to prosecute the said accused. The prosecutor may suspend, close or continue the investigation. The Court takes note of the fact that Nezzar is not being prosecuted in Algeria where Article 45 of the amnesty law of 27 February 2006 bars, without any exception, prosecution of members of Algeria's defence and security forces for actions taken to protect persons and property, safeguard the nation and preserve the institutions of Algeria. Algeria is also not party to the Rome Statute of the ICC. Therefore, due to the principle of 'extradite or prosecute' (*aut dedere aut judicare*), reasons the Swiss Court, since the Swiss authorities cannot extradite the accused to stand trial in Algeria or surrender him to the ICC, Swiss authorities are competent to prosecute him.

As regards Nezzar's claim to immunity from the jurisdiction of Swiss courts, the Court disagrees with the opinion dated 21 November 2011 of the Directorate of Public International Law of the Federal Department of Foreign Affairs of Switzerland that the accused in his capacity as *former* Minister of Defence of Algeria continues to enjoy immunity *ratione materiae* from the jurisdiction of

57 See https://trialinternational.org/latest-post/khaled-nezzar/; https://trialinternational.org/latest-post/nezzar-case-swiss-court-orders-resumption-or-war-crimes-investigation/.

Swiss authorities for all the acts committed in the exercise of his official functions, but not for those committed in a private capacity during his term of office or for the acts committed prior or after such period. The Court rules that since the accused is no longer Minister of Defence, he has no immunity *ratione personae* and he cannot assert immunity *ratione materiae* either because the conducts he is accused of constitute international crimes and gross violations of human rights norms.

On 4 January 2017, the Office of the Attorney General of Switzerland decided to drop the charges against Khaled Nezzar and to end the case after more than five years, on the grounds that the precondition of an armed conflict for the purpose of war crimes committed in Algeria was not met at the time he was charged. The Swiss Federal Criminal Court disagrees, finding the confrontations between the Algerian regime and the Islamist opposition during that particular period to be an 'armed conflict' in the light of detailed data on the organizational structure of the conflict parties and on the intensity of the conflict. Besides, Switzerland is responsible for the prosecution of the alleged offences because, at the time of the relevant incidents, both Switzerland and Algeria were party to the 1984 Convention against Torture and the alleged torture is not time-barred. On 30 May 2018, the Swiss Federal Criminal Court approved the complaints of three alleged victims of torture and arbitrary arrests in the *Nezzar* case, thereby requiring the Office of the Attorney General to re-investigate the case. Hearings for the case resumed in September 2019.[58]

In a twist of fate, in August 2019 while Nezzar was in Spain, the Algerian military justice issued an international arrest warrant against him after the investigation against Said Bouteflika, the brother of deposed Algerian President Abdelaziz Bouteflika. Said Bouteflika and Nezzar are accused of 'conspiracy against the State and breach of public order', punishable by death penalty under Algeria's Penal Code. On 25 September 2019, after a three-day trial, Said Bouteflika was sentenced to 15 years' imprisonment, while Nezzar and the other defendants were sentenced *in absentia* to 20 years' imprisonment. In December 2020, Nezzar returned to Algeria apparently after obtaining guarantees for a retrial and suspension of the international arrest warrant issued against him. On 2 January 2021, an Algerian military appeals court overturned the convictions and 15-year-imprisonment sentences of Said Bouteflika and two former Presidential security chiefs for plotting the army and the State, but Said Bouteflika remained in custody awaiting a separate trial over alleged corruption during his brother's rule. Indeed, Khaled Nezzar is an example of a former high-ranking official punished by a

58 Another case in Switzerland against a former high-ranking foreign official is that of Ousman Sonko, former Gambian Minister of Interior, arrested in Bern in January 2017 when he was applying for asylum. He has been charged with crimes against humanity and torture committed in The Gambia (https://trialinternational.org/latest-post/ousman-sonko/).

regime change in his own country as well as being a fugitive from criminal justice in foreign domestic criminal courts.

On the whole, in the Rohingya context, Argentina and any other nation State wanting to exercise universal jurisdiction over the individuals accused of committing serious crimes against the Rohingya must bear in mind the various practical considerations mentioned above. The Myanmar Government's diplomatic clout and bilateral relations with the States concerned are also of importance, since the executive branch of these States may prefer not to cooperate with efforts to bring Myanmar officials to account before their respective domestic courts. In any event, high-ranking Myanmar government officials, especially the President, Head of Government and Foreign Minister, who are still in office should feel comfortable that they will be immune from the exercise of universal jurisdiction by foreign domestic criminal courts. Former officials are in a riskier position. Nonetheless, the *coup d'état* in Myanmar on 1 February 2021 has led to uncertainties as to who are still in office as incumbent President, Head of Government, Foreign Minister and so forth, as will be seen in Chapter 9. One should also bear in mind that Rohingya refugees have been admitted to reside permanently in more and more States around the globe. These Rohingya individuals may thus avail themselves of the right to bring cases against Myanmar nationals in States whose law permits the exercise of jurisdiction over crimes committed abroad by foreign nationals provided that certain conditions are met, such as the victims or their relatives are permanent residents or nationals of the forum State.

8

SANCTIONS AND REDRESS UNDER DOMESTIC LAW FOR VICTIMS OF SERIOUS HUMAN RIGHTS VIOLATIONS ABROAD

Some States impose sanctions against serious human rights violations overseas and domestic law of certain States allow redress for victims of such violations.

Unilateral sanctions

The IIFFMM's report of September 2018 considers targeted individual sanctions, including travel bans and asset freezes, could support a reduction in violations of international law in Myanmar, particularly acts amounting to gross human rights violations and serious crimes under international law. The IIFFMM encourages the UN Security Council to adopt such sanctions as well as impose an arms embargo on Myanmar. Regardless of the imposition of a global arms embargo, States should not authorize the transfer of arms to Myanmar.[1]

The IIFFMM's 110-page report entitled 'The economic interests of the Myanmar military' submitted to the UN Human Rights Council in August 2019[2] identifies Myanmar Economic Holdings Limited ('MEHL') and Myanmar Economic Corporation ('MEC') as being owned and influenced by senior military leaders, including Senior General Min Aung Hlaing and Deputy Commander-in-Chief Vice Senior General Soe Win, both of whom the IIFFMM has identified for the purpose of their investigation and prosecution for genocide, crimes against humanity and war crimes. MEHL and MEC own at least 120 businesses in construction, pharmaceuticals, manufacturing, insurance, tourism and banking, among others. Both companies, along with at least 26 of their subsidiaries,

1 A/HRC/39/64 (12 Sept 2018) paras 105, 114.
2 A/HRC/42/CRP.3 (5 Aug 2019).

DOI: 10.4324/9781003224211-8

hold licences for jade and ruby mining in Kachin and Shan states.[3] The IIFFMM asks businesses and consumers to conduct heightened due diligence to ensure they are not purchasing, selling, trading or otherwise using gems produced or sold by enterprises owned or influenced by the Tatmadaw. The IIFFMM also finds no fewer than 15 foreign firms have joint ventures with the Tatmadaw, while 44 others have some form of commercial ties with Tatmadaw businesses, thereby risking contributing to, or being linked to, violations of international human rights and humanitarian law, including forced labour and sexual violence. These companies, argues the IIFFMM, are bound by international law to divest from Myanmar's military. The IIFFMM recommends that these alternative sources of revenue and economic interests of the Tatmadaw be eliminated, with the Myanmar Government placing the Tatmadaw fully under civilian control and oversight through the adoption of necessary laws and policies, including through the amendment of the Constitution. Until then, the UN Security Council, UN Member States, relevant regional and international intergovernmental organizations should impose targeted financial sanctions against all Tatmadaw-owned companies, especially MEHL, MEC and their subsidiaries, and do so in a manner that respects human rights and gives due consideration to any negative socio-economic impact of such sanctions on the civilian population. This should be accompanied by a comprehensive arms embargo on Myanmar, with a monitoring and enforcement mechanism. In addition, the report reiterates the IIFFMM's recommendation from its aforesaid September 2018 report for targeted individual sanctions. The IIFFMM's full and final report submitted to the Human Rights Council on 17 September 2019 clarifies that the IIFFMM does not support general economic sanctions on Myanmar because such sanctions in the past may have contributed to the impoverishment of the Myanmar people generally while having little impact on those most responsible for serious human rights violations. The IIFFMM supports continuing efforts to reduce the poverty in which most people in Myanmar live, through increased economic engagement and development assistance, provided that the engagement and assistance is carefully targeted to avoid any benefit to the Tatmadaw generally or to its leaders individually or to others responsible for serious human rights violations.[4]

Since October 2018, Australia has imposed targeted financial sanctions and travel bans on members of the Tatmadaw in response to the release of the IIFFMM's 2018 report. Australia also continues to maintain an arms embargo and restrictions on the export or provision of services to Myanmar, due to ongoing concerns about armed conflict, weapons proliferation and human rights. Australian sanction laws apply to activities in Australia

3 According to Global Witness, a UK-based NGO, Myanmar's jade industry was worth up to US$31 billion in 2014 alone, or 48 per cent of Myanmar's official GDP (Global Witness, *Jade: Myanmar's 'Big State Secret'* (Oct 2015)). See also Amnesty International, *Myanmar: Leaked documents reveal global business ties to military crimes* (10 Sept 2020).

4 A/HRC/39/CRP.2 (17 Sept 2019) paras 1166–8.

and activities undertaken overseas by Australian citizens and Australian-registered bodies corporate. It is a serious criminal offence to contravene a sanction measure (or a condition of a sanctions permit) and is punishable by up to ten years' imprisonment and substantial fines.

Canada, since 13 December 2007, has imposed trade embargo on arms and related material, as well as on related technical and financial assistance, with Myanmar, as well as imposed sanctions against certain listed Myanmar individuals and entities. In October 2017, Canada's Prime Minister appointed a Special Envoy to Myanmar, who submitted his final report in April 2018, outlining 17 recommendations for Canadian action. In May 2018, the Canadian Government released Canada's Strategy to respond to the Rohingya Crisis, informed by the Special Envoy's report, recognizing the need for Canada to enhance the effectiveness of targeted sanctions against those who have committed gross human rights violations in the course of the crisis faced by the Rohingya. Canada will continue to work to identify senior military officials in Myanmar with the aim of imposing sanctions for their role in the security operations against the Rohingya. On 25 June 2018, seven additional Myanmar individuals were added to the list of persons subject to sanctions. The seven were senior Tatmadaw officials who occupied positions of authority during the military operations against the Rohingya in Rakhine, which led to the humanitarian and security crisis in Myanmar and Bangladesh. Canada continues to review the need for further sanctions as appropriate.

The UK Treasury has imposed sanctions against 14 top-ranking Tatmadaw officers over alleged human rights violations during military operations in northern Rakhine since 2017, freezing any UK assets held by them and criminalizing financial transactions with them for anyone in the UK. They are also barred from entering the UK. The Global Human Rights Sanctions Regulations of 2020[5] put in place the aforesaid sanctions measures to deter, and provide accountability for, activities which, if carried out by or on behalf of a State within the territory of that State, would amount to a serious violation by that State of an individual's right to life; right not to be subjected to torture or cruel, inhuman or degrading treatment or punishment; or right to be free from slavery, not to be held in servitude or required to perform forced or compulsory labour. Since 6 July 2020, two Myanmar nationals have been specifically sanctioned under the 2020 Regulations. The first one is Senior General Min Aung Hlaing, Commander-in-Chief of the Tatmadaw, for his responsibility for military operations in Rakhine state in 2017 and in 2019 when atrocities and serious human rights violations were committed by the Tatmadaw against the Rohingya population by, *inter alia*, unlawful killings – including through systematic burning of Rohingya houses and buildings – massacre, torture, forced labour, systematic rape and other forms of targeted sexual violence, and enforced labour. The

5 UK Statutory Instruments 2020 No 680.

other one is Vice Senior General Soe Win, Deputy Commander-in-Chief of the Tatmadaw and Commander-in-Chief of the Myanmar Army, with responsibility for the Tatmadaw troops which carried out the aforesaid serious human rights violations against the Rohingya population. Soe Win was also involved in the financing of the Tatmadaw military operations in Rakhine state during which these violations took place, knowing this financing would contribute to the commission of these violations. After the February 2021 *coup*, on 25 March 2021 the UK imposed sanctions on MEHL for its involvement in serious human rights violations against the Rohingya and its association with senior Myanmar military figures. The UK sanction is in response to evidence that MEHL contributed funds to support the Tatmadaw 'in their campaign on ethnic cleansing against the Rohingya in 2017, having reasonable cause to suspect that the funds would or may contribute to the serious human rights violations committed, and that MEHL is associated with the Commander-in-Chief and Deputy Commander-in-Chief'.[6]

The European Union has imposed an arms embargo on Myanmar in various forms since the 1990s. In general, the embargo covers arms, munitions and military equipment and suspension of non-humanitarian aid or development programmes, with possible exceptions for projects and programmes in support of human rights and democracy as well as those concentrating on poverty alleviation and, in particular, the provision of basic needs for the poorest sections of the population, in the context of decentralized cooperation through local civilian authorities and NGOs. In response to the political developments in Myanmar in April 2013, the EU lifted all sanctions against Myanmar, except for the arms embargo, which has been extended annually since 2013. In February 2018, the EU Council, after condemning widespread, systematic grave human rights violations committed by the Myanmar military and security forces, confirmed the relevance of the existing embargo and on 26 April 2018 it expanded the restrictive measures on Myanmar to include an embargo on arms and equipment that can be used for internal repression, an export ban of dual-use goods for use by the military and border guard police and export restrictions of equipment for monitoring communications that might be used for internal repression. It also prohibits the provision of military training to and military cooperation with the Tatmadaw. The sanction also covers targeted restrictive measures on 14 individuals for serious human rights violations, or association with such violations, committed against the Rohingya population, ethnic minority villagers or civilians in Rakhine, Kachin and Shan states. These individuals are high-ranking officials from the Tatmadaw and the border guard police.

On 7 December 2020, the foreign ministers of EU Member States agreed to establish a regime that will allow EU Member States to sanction individuals

6 www.gov.uk/government/news/uk-sanctions-major-military-business-interests-in-further-measures-against-myanmar-military-regime.

and entities – both State and non-State actors – responsible for, involved in, or associated with human rights violations or abuses worldwide. The sanction imposes travel bans on the targeted individuals and the freezing of funds for targeted individuals and entities. Persons and entities in the EU will be also forbidden from making funds available to those listed, either directly or indirectly. The human rights violations or abuses subject to the EU sanction regime are atrocious acts such as genocide, crimes against humanity, torture, slavery, extrajudicial killings and arbitrary arrests or detentions. Other human rights violations or abuses can also fall under the scope of the EU sanctions regime where those violations or abuses are widespread, systematic or are otherwise of serious concern as regards the objectives of the EU's common foreign and security policy. It is for the European Council, consisting of all EU Member States, to decide by unanimity to act upon a proposal from an EU Member State or from the High Representative of the EU for Foreign Affairs and Security Policy, to establish, review and amend the sanctions list. On 19 April 2021, the European Council imposed sanctions on ten individuals, MEHL and MEC in response to the *coup d'état* in Myanmar on 1 February 2021 and the ensuing military and police repression against peaceful demonstrators.[7]

On 10 December 2019, the United States imposed sanctions on four Myanmar military leaders for their alleged human rights abuses against the Rohingya and other minorities in Myanmar. The sanctions target Senior General Min Aung Hlaing, his deputy Soe Win and two subordinates. The sanction was imposed on the same day as the start of the ICJ's hearing on The Gambia's request for provisional measures in its case brought against Myanmar. The US sanctions were implemented under the Global Magnitsky Human Rights Accountability Act,[8] enacted by US Congress in 2016 to authorize the US Executive Branch to impose visa bans and target sanctions on individuals anywhere in the world who are responsible for committing human rights violations or acts of significant corruption. The sanctions imposed on 10 December 2019 freeze any US assets held by those targeted and prohibit Americans from doing business with them. The US Treasury Department has described the sanctions as measures supporting a transition towards democracy in Myanmar. The US action has fallen short of re-imposing economic sanctions on Myanmar as a nation State which has been lifted after the Myanmar military began loosening its grip on power. It also does not target Myanmar's military-owned companies that dominate some sectors of Myanmar's economy and which are still doing business with US firms.

With its global political and economic dominance, the United States seems to have a much freerrein than other nation States in imposing unilateral sanctions

7 Council Implementing Regulation (EU) 2021/638 of 19 April 2021 implementing Regulation (EU) No 401/2013 concerning restrictive measures in view of the situation in Myanmar/Burma, OJ L 132I, 19.4.2021 at 1–11.

8 Pub. L. 114-328; 22 USC §2656.

against human rights abusers virtually anywhere in the world. In November 2019, for example, the United States passed the Hong Kong Human Rights and Democracy Act.[9] Among other things, the Act requires the US President to report to US Congress a list of individuals responsible for committing acts that violate internationally recognized human rights in Hong Kong, including the extrajudicial rendition or torture of any person in Hong Kong. Such individuals shall be barred from entering the United States and be subject to sanctions.

There is always a geopolitical consideration in imposing unilateral sanctions. Imposing such sanctions naturally pushes the targeted State to depend more and more on those States which are friendly to it. In the case of Myanmar, such sanctions may serve to deepen the isolation of a country well-versed in digging in its heels in the face of international pressure. To survive, Myanmar is reported to have been trying to circumvent the sanctions by various means, such as by using front companies to purchase embargoed goods or equipment from countries imposing sanctions on Myanmar or by trading with countries not imposing sanctions on Myanmar.[10] Also a crucial question is whether such unilateral sanction is legal under international law.

Article 2(1) of the UN Charter[11] – coming under Chapter I: Purposes and Principles of the United Nations – affirms that the UN is based on the principle of the sovereign equality of all its Members. Article 2(7) stipulates that nothing in the Charter shall authorize the UN 'to intervene in matters which are essentially within the domestic jurisdiction of any State or shall require the Members to submit such matters to settlement under the present Charter', except where the UN Security Council applies enforcement measures under Chapter VII of the Charter against threats to the peace, breaches of the peace and acts of aggression.

The applicability of Article 2(7) of the UN Charter has been increasingly curtailed in practice, especially in relation to human rights. For example, starting from 1962 until the end of apartheid in South Africa in 1993, UN organs adopted a series of resolutions to allow intervention to end the apartheid policy, law and practice in South Africa. Since the adoption by the African Union in 2002 of the Protocol Relating to the Establishment of the AU's Peace and Security Council ('PSC')[12], the PSC as the AU's standing organ may recommend to the AU's Assembly of Heads of State and Government to intervene in an AU Member State in respect of grave circumstances, namely war crimes, genocide and crimes against humanity, which are the most serious violations of human rights. As of this writing, the Protocol is binding on 52 AU Member States. The three AU Member States not party to the Protocol are Cabo Verde, DR Congo and South

9 Pub. L. 116-76; 22 USC §5721.

10 Jarred Ferrie and Timothy McLaughlin, *From Jordanian Planes to German Software: Myanmar's 'Genocidal' Military Stocks Up* (Organized Crimes and Corruption Reporting Project, 8 Dec 2020).

11 1 UNTS XVI, in force 24 Oct 1945.

12 www.peaceau.org/uploads/psc-protocol-en.pdf.

Sudan. ASEAN, of which Myanmar is a Member State, does not allow any of its Member States to do what the PSC of the AU may do. Nonetheless, the UN General Assembly and Human Rights Council, among other international organizations, have intervened in the human rights situations in Myanmar, as narrated in Chapter 2.

Indeed, no State may now legitimately maintain that an abuse of human rights of individuals within its territory, jurisdiction or effective control is a matter essentially within its domestic jurisdiction and is not subject to international law, especially the applicable rules of international human rights law. The world's leaders, meeting at the UN Headquarters in New York from 14 to 16 September 2005, came up with the 2005 World Summit Outcome, which was subsequently endorsed by the UN General Assembly on 16 September 2005. The World Summit Outcome contains a section on 'Responsibility to protect populations from genocide, war crimes, ethnic cleansing and crimes against humanity', which is owed by each State. This responsibility entails the prevention of such crimes, including their incitement, through appropriate and necessary means. The international community should, as appropriate, encourage and help States to exercise this responsibility and support the UN in establishing an early warning capability. The international community, through the UN, also has the *responsibility* to use appropriate diplomatic, humanitarian and other peaceful means, in accordance with Chapters VI and VIII of the Charter, to help *to protect* populations from genocide, war crimes, ethnic cleansing and crimes against humanity.[13]

By recognizing human rights might be connected to international peace and security, the UN makes human rights a formal part of international relations and international politics. In discharging its mandate under the UN Charter, the UN Security Council is implicated wherever human rights violations may lead to threats to, or breaches of, international peace and security; commission of international crimes, especially crimes proscribed under peremptory norms of international law (*jus cogens*); massive refugee outflows or internal displacements; or potential humanitarian disasters and other comparable catastrophes. The Council has discharged this mandate in relation to the Balkan wars, by setting up the ICTY, and the Rwandan genocide, by setting up the ICTR. Unfortunately, owing to political considerations and the veto power of its five permanent members, the Security Council does not always effectively discharge this mandate. With the Council's shortcomings, can a State unilaterally impose sanctions against another State or foreigners?

As pointed out in Chapter 2, the treaty bodies monitoring the implementation of the 1989 Convention on the Rights of the Child[14] and the 1979 Convention

13 A/RES/60/1 (24 Oct 2005).
14 1577 UNTS 3, in force 2 Sept 1990.

on the Elimination of All Forms of Discrimination against Women,[15] to which Myanmar is party, have expressed several serious concerns regarding the Myanmar Government's treatment of Rohingya children and women, respectively. In addition, Myanmar might also fall short of its obligations regarding the Rohingya under the 1966 International Covenant on Economic, Social and Cultural Rights,[16] to which it has become party as of January 2018. However, unlike the 1948 Genocide Convention[17] binding upon Myanmar, the three aforesaid human rights treaties do not have any dispute settlement provision pursuant to which a State Party may ask the ICJ to compel Myanmar to implement its obligations thereunder. By virtue of Article 26 of the 1969 Vienna Convention on the Law of Treaties,[18] to which Myanmar is party since 1998, every treaty in force is binding upon its parties and must be performed by them in good faith. Article 27 of the 1969 Convention makes it clear a party to a treaty may not invoke the provisions of its internal law as justification for its failure to perform the treaty. Other States Parties to the relevant treaties that consider Myanmar in breach of their provisions are thus entitled to ask Myanmar to abide by its treaty obligations. However, a question may be asked whether these States may impose sanctions on Myanmar to compel it to respect its treaty obligations and/or other obligations under customary international law outside treaties which these States consider Myanmar to have violated.

Some Governments do argue that external pressure exerted on them to improve human rights of persons within their respective territories, jurisdiction or effective control amounts to intervention or interference in their internal affairs. The ICJ's Judgment in *Military and Paramilitary Activities in and against Nicaragua (Nicaragua v the United States of America)* explains that the principle of non-intervention, which represents customary international law, 'involves the right of every sovereign State to conduct its affairs without outside interference' because, between independent States, respect for territorial sovereignty is an essential foundation of international relations and international law requires political integrity also to be respected.[19] This principle of non-intervention forbids all States or groups of States from intervening directly or indirectly in internal or external affairs of other States. A prohibited intervention must accordingly be one bearing on matters in which each State is permitted, by the principle of State sovereignty, to decide freely, such as the choice of a political, economic, social and cultural system and the formulation of foreign policy. Intervention is 'wrongful when it uses methods of coercion in regard to such choices, which must remain free ones'.[20] The ICJ substantiates its aforesaid conclusion by refer-

15 1249 UNTS 13, in force 3 Sept 1981.
16 993 UNTS 3, in force 3 Jan 1976.
17 78 UNTS 277, in force 12 Jan 1951.
18 1155 UNTS 331, in force 27 Jan 1980.
19 [1986] ICJ Rep 14, 106 [202].
20 Ibid 107–8 [205].

ring to the Declaration on Principles of International Law concerning Friendly Relations and Cooperation among States in accordance with the Charter of the United Nations,[21] adopted by the UN General Assembly without a vote in October 1970.

The Declaration proclaims, among others, the principle concerning the duty not to intervene in matters within the domestic jurisdiction of any State, in accordance with the UN Charter and elucidates this principle as prohibiting any State or group of States from intervening, directly or indirectly, for any reason whatever, in the internal or external affairs of any other State as well as prohibits any State from using or encouraging the use of economic political or any other type of measures 'to coerce another State in order to obtain from it the subordination of the exercise of its sovereign rights and to secure from it advantages of any kind'. However, the Declaration also stipulates the duty of States to cooperate with one another in accordance with the UN Charter that includes 'the promotion of universal respect for, and observance of, human rights and fundamental freedoms for all and in the elimination of all forms of racial discrimination and all forms of religious intolerance'. The principle of sovereign equality of States means equal rights and duties and equal membership of the international community, including the duty to comply fully and in good faith with its international obligations and to live in peace with other States.

Therefore, asking or even putting pressure on a foreign government to improve its human rights records is not prohibited by international law insofar as there is no coercion exerted upon the government 'in order to obtain from it the subordination of the exercise of its sovereign rights and to secure from it advantages of any kind'. Since every sovereign State is equally bound to comply in good faith with its international human rights obligations, prompting it to do so does not violate the principle of non-interference, especially if the method(s) and manner of persuasion is not 'coercive'.[22] Of course, in the subjective view of the State targeted by a unilateral sanction by another State, the sanction is 'coercive' and, as such, unlawful – in which case the targeted State may have recourse to the ICJ, where the ICJ has jurisdiction to end the sanction. Alternatively, it may resort to a countermeasure against the foreign State imposing a unilateral sanction against it. The ICJ has held in *Gabčikovo-Nagymaros Project (Hungary/ Slovakia)* that, in order to be justifiable, a countermeasure must meet certain conditions. First, it must be taken in response to a previous international wrongful act of another State and must be directed against that State. Secondly, the injured State must have called upon the State committing the wrongful act to discontinue its wrongful conduct or to make reparation for it. Thirdly, the effects of a

21 A/RES/25/2625 (24 Oct 1970).

22 See also Mohamed S Helal, 'On Coercion in International Law' (2019) 52 NYU JIL & Politics 1, 4, 49–54, 58–89, 94–5, 98, 101–7; Surya P Subedi, *Unilateral Sanctions in International Law* (Hart 2021).

countermeasure must be commensurate with the injury suffered, taking account of the rights in question. Fourthly, the countermeasure's purpose must be to induce the wrong-doing State to comply with its obligations under international law, and the measure must therefore be reversible.[23]

The UN International Law Commission has dealt with the issue of countermeasures in its Articles on Responsibility of States for Internationally Wrongful Acts,[24] finalized and submitted to the UN General Assembly in 2001. Article 50(b) of the Articles stipulates that countermeasures shall not affect obligations for the protection of fundamental human rights. In this connection, the International Law Commission cites the award in the '*Naulilaa*' arbitration, where the tribunal stated that a lawful countermeasure must be 'limited by the requirements of humanity and the rules of good faith applicable in relations between States';[25] the *Institut de droit international* in its 1934 resolution stating that in taking countermeasures a State must 'abstain from any harsh measure which would be contrary to the laws of humanity or the demands of the public conscience'; and the development since 1945 of the international human rights law that prohibits derogation of important human rights norms even in time of war or other public emergency. Interestingly, the International Law Commission also alludes to General Comment No 8 (1997) of the Committee on Economic, Social and Cultural Rights, which monitors the implementation of the International Covenant on Economic, Social and Cultural Rights, emphasizing the need to distinguish between the basic objective of applying political and economic pressure upon the governing elite of a country to persuade them to conform to international law, on the one hand, and the collateral infliction of suffering upon the most vulnerable groups within the targeted country, on the other hand – with the latter to be avoided as much as possible, as in, for example, the sanctions regimes established by the UN Security Council that include humanitarian exemptions designed to permit the flow of essential goods and services destined for humanitarian purposes.[26]

On the whole, if the Myanmar Government fails to abide by the ICJ's Order indicating provisional measures and subsequent Judgment on the merits against Myanmar, several States may find it justifiable under the rules of international law mentioned above to impose targeted sanctions against Myanmar and the Myanmar nationals concerned. The same can be said if the ICC issues international arrest warrants against Myanmar individuals accused of crimes within the ICC's jurisdiction. Unless and until the ICJ and the ICC eventually exonerate Myanmar and the Myanmar accused, respectively, may the sanctions imposed by States become unjustifiable under international law.

23 [1997] ICJ Rep 7, 55–6 [83]–[85], [87].

24 A/RES/56/83 (12 Dec 2001) Annex and A/56/49(Vol. I)/Corr.4.

25 *Portuguese Colonies case (Naulilaa incident)*, (1928) Reports of International Arbitral Awards, vol II (1949) 1011, 1026.

26 E/C.12/1997/8 (12 Dec 1997).

Should the Myanmar Government wish to take countermeasures against the foreign States imposing unilateral sanctions against Myanmar and/or Myanmar nationals, it must calculate all the related costs and effectiveness of its countermeasures taken against such States.

Damages and other forms of reparation under the domestic law of foreign States

In addition to the possibility of having recourse to foreign domestic criminal courts to exercise universal jurisdiction over alleged crimes against the Rohingya in Myanmar, there may also be room for seeking damages and other forms of reparation for the Rohingya in foreign domestic courts if certain conditions are met.

Domestic law of several States authorizes their courts to award compensation to victims of crime,[27] as in the case of Theodore Tabaro who was convicted by the Stockholm District Court to life imprisonment for genocide and ordered to compensate 16 victims, with each awarded approximately US$2,800 to 11,600.[28]

Civil actions may entail higher amounts of compensation. In the United States, the Torture Victim Protection Act of 1991[29] allows the filing of civil suits for damages in the United States against *individuals* – meaning 'natural persons', not organizations, corporations or foreign States – who, acting in an official capacity for any foreign nation, committed torture and/or extrajudicial killing, provided that a plaintiff, who may be a US or *non-US citizen*, has exhausted adequate and available local remedies in the State where the crime is committed. Any action under this Act must be commenced within ten years after the cause of action arose.[30] *Mamani et al. v Sánchez de Lozada and Sánchez Berzaín* is the first case in US history that a former Head of State was tried before his accusers in a human rights trial before a US court. On 26 November 2007, nine Bolivian residents and citizens initiated a civil law suit under the 1991 Act against former Bolivian President Gonzalo Sánchez de Lozada and former Minister of Defence

27 See also the Declaration of Basic Principles of Justice for Victims of Crime and Abuse of Power, adopted by UN General Assembly Resolution 40/34 of 29 November 1985 (A/RES/40/34) paras 8–13; Theo van Boven, 'Victims' Rights to a Remedy and Reparation: The New United Nations Principles and Guidelines' in Carla Fertsman, Mariana Goetz and Alan Stephens (eds.), *Reparation for Victims of Genocide, War Crimes and Crimes against Humanity* (Martinus Nijhoff 2009) 19.

28 *Prosecutor v Theodore Tabaro*, Stockholm District Court, Case B 13688-16, Judgment of 27 June 2018.

29 106 Stat. 73.

30 In *United States v Samantar* (560 US 305 (2010)), the US Supreme Court held that the Foreign Sovereign Immunities Act of 1976 (28 USC §§1330, 1602 *et seq.*) does not provide a former First Vice President and Prime Minister of Somalia with immunity from a suit brought under the 1991 Act based on actions taken in his official capacity, and that his claim to immunity is governed by the common law because it is not a claim against a foreign State as defined by the 1976 Act.

José Carlos Sánchez Berzaín who have been living in exile in the United States since 2003, seeking damages against the defendants for their involvement in the extrajudicial killings of 67 Bolivian civilians participating in street protests in Bolivia in September and October 2003 against a controversial economic policy of the Bolivian Government. The plaintiffs are relatives of eight Bolivian civilians killed. After years of the defendants challenging the jurisdiction of US courts, the trial eventually commenced in June 2013. In April 2018, after a three-week long jury trial, the federal jury found both defendants responsible for extrajudicial killings in 2003 and awarded the plaintiffs a total of US$10 million in compensatory damages, but declined to award any punitive damages. In May 2018, the US District Court Southern District of Florida overturned the unanimous jury's decision, citing insufficient evidence to support the verdict.[31] On 3 August 2020 the Court of Appeals for the Eleventh Circuit overturned the District Court's Judgment by affirming that the eight killings at the heart of the trial were each potentially covered by the 1991 Act. However, the Court of Appeal left it to the District Court to evaluate whether each of the deaths were 'military reaction[s] to just provocation, which is lawful under international law' or indiscriminate and/or deliberate killings of civilians that are international crimes. On these matters, the Court of Appeals ordered the District Court to consider in the first instance whether, for each decedent, the plaintiffs produced sufficient evidence to demonstrate that each death was not lawful under international law and thus extrajudicial and, if so, whether the plaintiffs produced sufficient evidence to link the defendants to that wrongdoing via the command-responsibility doctrine.[32]

Another high-profile case brought under the Torture Victims Protection Act is *Ahimsa Wickrematunge v Nandasena Gotabaya Rajapaksa*. The plaintiff is the daughter of slain journalist, Lasantha Wickremetunge, one of Sri Lanka's most fiercely independent journalists, who accused then-Secretary of Defence Gotabaya Rajapaksa of embezzling over US$10 million in government funds in an arms deal. Rajapaksa sued him for defamation. On 8 January 2009, weeks before he could testify in court, he was assassinated by an armed group. Ahimsa Wickrematunge's lawsuit, filed in a US court in April 2019, sought to hold Rajapaksa responsible for his alleged involvement in the assassination of her father and in the widespread and systematic targeting of journalists critical of the Sri Lankan Government. On 27 February 2020, the Ninth Circuit Court of Appeals granted Ahimsa Wickrematunge's request to vacate the lower court's ruling that Rajapaksa is entitled to common law foreign official immunity for acts committed while he was Sri Lanka's Secretary of Defence. The Ninth Circuit Court of Appeals also granted the plaintiff's request to dismiss her case *without prejudice*, as Rajapaksa's accession to the Presidency of Sri Lanka in November 2019 gave

31 *Mamani v Berzaín*, Case 07-22459-CIV-COHN/SELTZER (S.D. Fla. 30 May 2018).
32 *Mamani v Berzaín* ('*Mamani* II'), 825 F.3d 1304 (11th Cir. 3 Aug 2020).

him immunity from suits in US courts for so long as he remains President.[33] The Ninth Circuit's decision clears the way for future litigation against Rajapaksa once he no longer enjoys immunity as Head of State.

With regard to claims against *a foreign State*, on 31 January 2019 the US District Court for the District of Columbia rendered its Judgment in *Cathleen Colvin et al v Syrian Arab Republic*.[34] An intense artillery assault on the Baba Amr Media Centre in Homs, Syria, killed Marie Colvin, an American war journalist for *The Sunday Times* who was there covering the war between the Syrian Government and rebel groups. The case was brought by plaintiffs who are Colvin's relatives, asserting that Colvin was the victim of the Syrian Government's policy to surveil, capture and even kill journalists to prevent reporting on the Syrian Government's suppression of the political opposition, and that her death constitutes an extrajudicial killing in violation of the US Foreign Sovereign Immunities Act of 1976. Under that Act, a foreign State is presumptively immune from the jurisdiction of US courts and, unless a specified exception applies, a US federal court lacks subject-matter jurisdiction over a claim against a foreign State. This case falls within the exception provided in the Act stipulating that a foreign State shall not be immune from the jurisdiction of US courts in which money damages are sought against the foreign State for personal injury or death caused by an act of torture, extrajudicial killing, aircraft sabotage, hostage taking or the provision of material support or resources for such an act if such act or provision of material support or resources is engaged in by an official, employee or agent of such foreign State while acting within the scope of his/her office, employment or agency. The Act lists the following additional conditions for a US federal district court to hear a claim: (i) the foreign State must be designated a State sponsor of terrorism[35] at the time of the act giving rise to the claim, (ii) the claimant or the victim must be a US national, a member of the armed forces or a government employee at the time of the act, and (iii) the claimant must have afforded the foreign State a reasonable opportunity to arbitrate the claim in accordance with the accepted international rules of arbitration. Because the plaintiffs in that case have demonstrated all of these elements, the Court finds Syria is not immune from suit. The Court grants the plaintiffs' motion for default judgment and enter judgment in the amount of US$302,511,836, comprising US$300 million in punitive damages, US$2.5 million in compensation to Colvin's sister and US$11,836 in funeral expenses. In awarding the punitive damage, the Court refers to Section 1605A(c) of the Act that authorizes punitive damages to be assessed against foreign State sponsors of terrorism in order to punish and deter defendants for their bad acts. In this respect, US courts shall calculate punitive damages by considering the

33 *Ahimsa Wickrematunge v Nandasena Gotabaya Rajapaksa*, Case CV 19-02577-R (RAOx), US District Ct Central District of California, 8 Apr 2020.

34 363 F.Supp.3d 141 (2019).

35 Pursuant to the Anti-terrorism and Effective Death Penalty Act of 1996 (Pub. L. No 104–132, 110 Stat. 1214).

following four factors: (1) the character of the defendants' act, (2) the nature and extent of harm to the plaintiffs that the defendants caused or intended to cause, (3) the need for deterrence, and (4) the wealth of the defendants. The Court remarks, in particular, that a targeted murder of an American citizen, whose courageous work was not only important, but vital, to our understanding of war zones and of wars generally, is outrageous and therefore warrants a punitive damages award that multiples the impact on the responsible State. The main hurdle thereafter for the plaintiffs is to enforce the award. This Judgment will form the grounds for a legal claim to seize Syria's overseas assets, if the assets can be proved to belong to Syria or the Syrian Government and not Syrian individuals or entities who are not holders of the assets as agents or on behalf of Syria or the Government. In any event, the plaintiffs may seek compensation from the fund set up under the Justice for United States Victims of State Sponsored Terrorism Act,[36] which compensates eligible US persons who hold a final judgment issued by a US district court awarding them compensatory damages arising from acts of international terrorism for which a foreign State sponsor of terrorism was found not immune from the jurisdiction of US courts under the US Foreign Sovereign Immunities Act.

After a regime change, the new Government in the State designated as a State sponsor of terrorism may agree to pay compensation in return for the termination of such designation which entails a series of US restrictions including a ban on defence exports and sales and restrictions on US foreign assistance. On 11 March 2021, Sudan's civilian-led transitional Government paid a US$335 million settlement to victims and families of more than 200 individuals killed and thousands injured by the 1998 bombings at the US Embassies in Tanzania and Kenya, the attack on the USS Cole in 2000 and the murder of a USAID employee in Khartoum in 2008. Under the US$335 million settlement, those who were US citizens at the time of the bombings would receive more than those who became citizens after the fact and foreign national embassy employees. The legislation signed into law as part of the omnibus included US$150 million in additional funds to allow for equitable compensation between birthright and naturalized citizens. The aforesaid settlement is in addition to US$72.5 million in an already paid private settlement with a number of the USS COLE victims. With the settlement, Sudan is no longer designated as a State sponsor of terrorism and its sovereign immunities are restored so as to shield it from litigation in US courts for further compensation claims.[37]

With respect to the Rohingya, between 2008 and 4 December 2018, more than 8,300 Rohingya refugees had been admitted to the United States.[38] This is a

36 34 USC §20144.

37 Jennifer Hansler, 'US receives $335M from Sudan for victims of terrorist attacks', *CNN* (31 Mar 2021), https://edition.cnn.com/2021/03/31/politics/sudan-settlement-received/index.html.

38 US Dept of State Bureau of Population, Refugees and Migration, www.wuwm.com/post/milwaukee-likely-has-largest-rohingya-refugee-community-us#stream/0.

sizeable Rohingya community in any country, and there is strong likelihood that most of them have been victims of the atrocities in Rakhine state (otherwise they would not have been granted a refugee status in the first place) as well as still have relatives in Rakhine and/or in refugee camps in Bangladesh and elsewhere who are victims of the aforesaid. Civil lawsuits in US courts seeking damages from the Myanmar Government and/or certain Myanmar individuals are thus likely.

However, the US Supreme Court has strictly limited the applicability of the Alien Tort Statute ('ATS'),[39] passed in 1789, stipulating '[t]he [US] district courts shall have original jurisdiction of any civil action by an alien for a tort only, committed in violation of the law of nations or a treaty of the United States'.

In *Kiobel v Royal Dutch Petroleum Co*,[40] decided in 2013, certain Nigerian nationals, having been granted asylum in the US, filed suit under the ATS, alleging that Dutch, British and Nigerian corporations aided and abetted the Nigerian Government in committing violations of the law of nations in Nigeria. The complaint alleges that in the 1990s Nigerian Government forces attacked villages, beating, raping, killing and arresting residents and destroying or looting property, and that the corporations provided food, transportation, compensation and a staging ground for these attacks. According to the petitioners, the respondents violated the law of nations by aiding and abetting the Nigerian Government in committing: (1) extrajudicial killings, (2) crimes against humanity, (3) torture and cruel treatment, (4) arbitrary arrest and detention, (5) violations of the rights to life, liberty, security and association, (6) forced exile and (7) property destruction. The question before the US Supreme Court is whether and under what circumstances US courts may recognize a cause of action under the ATS for violations of the law of nations occurring within the territory of a sovereign other than the United States. The US Supreme Court rules that nothing in the text of the ATS suggests the US Congress intended causes of action recognized under it to have extraterritorial reach. The ATS covers actions by aliens for violations of the law of nations, but that does not imply extraterritorial reach – such violations affecting aliens can occur either within or outside the United States. Nor does the fact that the text reads 'any civil action' suggest application to torts committed abroad; it is well established that generic terms like 'any' or 'every' do not rebut the presumption against extraterritoriality. Two notorious episodes involving violations of the law of nations occurred in the United States shortly before passage of the ATS. Each concerned the rights of ambassadors, and each involved conduct within US territory. The United States was embarrassed by its potential inability to provide judicial relief to foreign officials injured in the United States, hence, the enactment of the ATS. The third example of a violation of the law of nations familiar to the then US Congress that enacted the ATS was piracy.

39 28 USC §1350.

40 569 US 108 (2013). See also the US Supreme Court's Judgments of 17 June 2021 in *Nestlé USA, Inc v Doe I, et al* and *Cargill Inc v Doe I, et al*, 593 U. S. ____ (2021).

Piracy typically occurs on the high seas, beyond the territorial jurisdiction of the United States or any other country. The US Supreme Court has generally treated the high seas the same as foreign soil for purposes of the presumption against extraterritorial application. Applying US law to pirates, however, does not typically impose the sovereign will of the United States onto conduct occurring within the territorial jurisdiction of another sovereign, and therefore carries less direct foreign policy consequences. Pirates were fair game wherever found, by any nation, because they generally did not operate within any jurisdiction. Finally, there is no indication the ATS was passed to make the United States 'a uniquely hospitable forum for the enforcement of international norms' by providing a cause of action for conduct occurring in the territory of another sovereign State. Indeed, far from avoiding diplomatic strife, providing such a cause of action could have generated it. The presumption against extraterritoriality guards against US courts triggering such serious foreign policy consequences, and instead defers such decisions, quite appropriately, to the political branches.

According to Justice Souter delivering the opinion of the US Supreme Court in *Sosa v Alvarez-Machain et al.* in 2004, 'the judicial power should be exercised on the understanding that the door is still ajar subject to vigilant doorkeeping, and thus open to a narrow class of international norms today'.[41] The US Supreme Court in *Jesner v Arab Bank, PLC*, decided in 2018,[42] is more circumspect – any consideration of *Sosa*'s discretion must also account for proper limits on the judicial function in which US federal courts generally lack the institutional expertise and constitutional authority to oversee foreign policy and national security, and should be wary of straying where they do not belong. It is one thing for US courts to assume the task of creating new causes of action to ensure US citizens abide by the law of nations and *avoid* reprisals against the United States. It is altogether another thing for US courts to punish *foreign* parties for conduct that could not be attributed to the United States and thereby *risk* reprisals against the United States. If a foreign State or citizen violates an 'international norm' in a way that offends another foreign State or citizen, the US Constitution arms the US President and Congress with ample means to address it, as in the case of the enactment by Congress of the Torture Victim Protection Act of 1991 creating an express cause of action for victims of torture and extrajudicial killing in violation of international law. Or, if they think best, the political branches may choose to look the other way. But in all events, the decision to impose sanctions in disputes between foreigners over international norms is not for US courts to make. It is a decision that belongs to those answerable to the people and assigned by the US Constitution to defend the United States. If they wish help from US courts, they are free to enlist the courts, but US courts should not ever be in the business of elbowing their way in.

41 542 US 692, 729 (2004).
42 138 US 1386 (2018).

PART V

Stock taking

9

LESSONS LEARNT AND FUTURE POSSIBILITIES

The chapter sums up the challenges identified in the preceding chapters and assesses the likely scenarios and their legal implications, especially after the 1 February 2021 *coup d'état* in Myanmar.

Where are we now?

Bilateral and multilateral diplomatic forums have failed to alleviate the Rohingya's grievances. Multilaterally, the United Nations works within the confine of UN politics and the veto power of the five permanent members of the UN Security Council, whereas ASEAN's non-intervention in domestic affairs of an ASEAN Member State prevents it from being able to do more than what it has done so far. Myanmar is not a member of the OIC, and the OIC can only use indirect means, including by entrusting The Gambia with bringing the case against Myanmar before the ICJ, to compel Myanmar to abide by Myanmar's obligations under the 1948 Genocide Convention.[1]

In the ICJ, legal technicalities (especially proof of the specific genocidal intent based on evidence and reports of non-judicial bodies and attribution of responsibility to Myanmar from conducts of its officials) will be determinative. Proceedings before the ICJ usually take several years before the ICJ renders its final Judgments or dismisses the cases. The ICJ's decisions on the request for the indication of provisional measures take the least time to deliver because this is an urgent proceeding with priority over other proceedings. After that, the Respondent usually challenges the ICJ's jurisdiction on various grounds.

1 78 UNTS 277, in force 12 Jan 1951.

DOI: 10.4324/9781003224211-9

In the Bosnian genocide case, Bosnia and Herzegovina instituted proceedings against Yugoslavia on 20 March 1993 and requested the ICJ to indicate provisional measures pending the final Judgment, which was ordered by the ICJ on 8 April 1993. On 27 July 1993, Bosnia and Herzegovina submitted a new request for the indication of provisional measures. On 10 August 1993, Yugoslavia also submitted a request for the indication of provisional measures. By an Order dated 13 September 1993, the ICJ, after hearing the parties, reaffirmed the measures indicated in its Order of 8 April 1993 and declared those measures should be immediately and effectively implemented. Thereafter, Yugoslavia submitted its 'preliminary objections' to the ICJ's jurisdiction, contending that the ICJ had no jurisdiction to decide on the merits of the case. Not until 11 July 1996 did the ICJ give Judgment rejecting the preliminary objections raised by Yugoslavia as well as finding the Application filed by Bosnia and Herzegovina admissible. Subsequently, Yugoslavia filed counter-claims requesting the ICJ to adjudge and declare Bosnia and Herzegovina was responsible for acts of genocide committed against the Serbs in Bosnia and Herzegovina and for other violations of the Genocide Convention. In its Order of 17 December 1997, the ICJ ruled the counter-claims admissible as such and formed part of the proceedings in the case. During 1999 and 2000, various exchanges of letters took place concerning new procedural difficulties which had emerged in the case. In April 2001, Yugoslavia informed the ICJ of its wish to withdraw its counter-claims. On 4 May 2001, Yugoslavia submitted to the ICJ a document asserting the ICJ had no jurisdiction over Serbia and Montenegro, a new nation State which succeeded Yugoslavia, and requested the ICJ to suspend proceedings regarding the merits of the case until a decision on this jurisdictional issue had been rendered. On 1 July 2001, it also filed an Application for revision of the Judgment of 11 July 1996. These submissions were found to be inadmissible by the ICJ on 12 June 2003 and 3 February 2003, respectively. Following public hearings held between 27 February 2006 and 9 May 2006, the ICJ rendered its Judgment on the merits in that case on 26 February 2007.

In the Croatian genocide case, on 2 July 1999 Croatia filed an Application against Yugoslavia for violations of the Genocide Convention. On 11 September 2002, Yugoslavia filed preliminary objections to the ICJ's jurisdiction and to the admissibility of the claims made by Croatia. The ICJ delivered its Judgment on the preliminary objections on 18 November 2008, rejecting the preliminary objections and finding the Application filed by Croatia admissible. The ICJ then fixed 22 March 2010 as the time-limit for the filing of a Counter-Memorial by Serbia, which succeeded Yugoslavia as a new nation State. That pleading, containing counter-claims, was filed on 4 January 2010. By an Order of 4 February 2010, the ICJ directed the submission of a Reply by Croatia and a Rejoinder by Serbia. The ICJ fixed 20 December 2010 and 4 November 2011, respectively, as the time-limits for the filing of those written pleadings. By an Order of 23 January 2012, to ensure strict equality between the parties, the ICJ decided to authorize the submission by Croatia of an additional written pleading relating to the counter-claims of Serbia. Croatia filed the additional pleading within the time-limit of 30 August 2012 as fixed by that Order. The ICJ eventually delivered its Judgment on the merits of the case on 3 February 2015.

Each of the two genocide cases before the ICJ just mentioned took 14 to 16 years before the ICJ rendered its final Judgments on the merits. The two cases are exceptional in many ways. In particular, the jurisdictional issues revolving around the international status of the Respondent and its UN membership (and, consequently, as a party to the ICJ Statute) as well as founding the ICJ's jurisdiction on the basis of State succession to responsibility under Article IX of the Genocide Convention permeated all phases of the cases as a result of the State succession arising out of the disintegration of the Socialist Federal Republic of Yugoslavia in the early 1990s. Besides, the amount of factual evidence presented to the ICJ was enormous. The ICJ has also been criticized for yielding to the Respondent's delay tactics of submitting frivolous Applications that were not legally sound. In the amendment of the Rules of the ICJ that has entered into force as of 21 October 2019, Article 80(1) of the Rules stipulates that the ICJ may entertain a counter-claim only if it comes within the ICJ's jurisdiction and is directly connected with the subject-matter of the claim of the other party. This amendment should lay to rest any potential abuse by resorting to counter-claims to delay or impede proceedings before the ICJ. In any event, Myanmar should not be able to make any counter-claim that The Gambia was also responsible for acts of genocide and/or for violations of the Genocide Convention. Any counter-claim part can thus be omitted from *The Gambia v Myanmar*, making the proceedings much shorter in duration than those in the two genocide cases previously decided by the ICJ.

On 23 January 2020, the ICJ issued an Order fixing the following time-limits for the filing of the written pleadings: 23 July 2020 for the Memorial of The Gambia and 25 January 2021 for the Counter-Memorial of Myanmar. In fixing the above time-limits instead of the period of nine months from 23 January 2020 as requested by The Gambia and another nine months for Myanmar to submit its Counter-Memorial subsequent to The Gambia's submission of its Memorial, the ICJ took into account 'the exceptional circumstances of the case and its gravity'. On 24 April 2020, The Gambia requested the ICJ to grant at least a three-month extension for the filing of the Memorial, owing to the COVID-19 pandemic, adding that 'the principle of equality of arms would entitle Myanmar to a similar extension of time for filing its Counter-Memorial'. On 28 April 2020, Myanmar replied that, although the COVID-19 pandemic did not appear to constitute in and of itself a sufficient justification for The Gambia's request, Myanmar took no position on that request and left it to the ICJ 'to decide whether The Gambia ha[d] established a sufficient justification for an extension of time'. By an Order dated 18 May 2020, the ICJ extended from 23 July 2020 to 23 October 2020 and from 25 January 2021 to 23 July 2021 the respective time-limits for the filing of The Gambia's Memorial and Myanmar's Counter-Memorial.

Article 45(2) of the ICJ Rules allows it to authorize or direct that there shall be a Reply by the Applicant and a Rejoinder by the Respondent if the parties are so agreed, or if the ICJ decides, at its own initiative or at the request of one of the parties, that these pleadings are necessary.

On 20 January 2021, Myanmar filed preliminary objections to the ICJ's jurisdiction and admissibility in this case, thereby suspending the ICJ's proceedings on the merits until the preliminary objections are adjudicated by the ICJ.[2] The ICJ fixed 20 May 2021 as the time-limit within which The Gambia might present a written statement of its observations and submissions on Myanmar's preliminary objections. The ICJ may consider it necessary to resolve first of all the question of its jurisdiction and that of the admissibility of The Gambia's Application before any proceedings on the merits.[3] If the ICJ decides it has no jurisdiction and/or that the Application is inadmissible, the case will end in approximately three years' time from November 2019. If the ICJ rejects Myanmar's preliminary objections but the merits phase is not combined with the phase of preliminary objections, an additional two or three years might be expected before the ICJ renders its final Judgment on the merits. In any event, as evident from its Order of 23 January 2020 fixing the time-limits, the ICJ is anxious to expedite proceedings in this case as much as possible.

Regarding the prosecution in the ICC, the OTP always faces a daunting challenge in gathering sufficient evidence to secure the accused's conviction, if the accused is ever brought before the ICC. After the initial appearance and confirmation of charges of each accused person, a trial can proceed during which evidence will be presented and witnesses (including alleged victims) summoned to testify and cross-examined. The entire duration of the trial depends on the amount of the evidence and the number of witnesses. After the Judgment of the Trial Chamber, the accused may appeal to the ICC Appeals Chamber, which will take at least a year to deliver its appeal judgment.

2 Under Rule 79(1) of the ICJ Rules, following the submission of the Application and after the ICJ President has met and consulted with the parties, the ICJ may decide, if the circumstances so warrant, that questions concerning its jurisdiction or the admissibility of the Application shall be determined separately.

Article 79*bis* provides that when the ICJ has not taken any decision under Article 79, an objection by the Respondent to the ICJ's jurisdiction or to the admissibility of the Application, or other objection the decision upon which is requested before any further proceedings on the merits, shall be made in writing as soon as possible, and not later than three months after the delivery of the Memorial by the Applicant. Upon receipt by the ICJ Registry of a preliminary objection, the proceedings on the merits shall be suspended. Nonetheless, the ICJ shall give effect to *any agreement between the parties* to have a preliminary objection heard and determined within the framework of the merits.

3 As the ICJ did in, e.g., *Relocation of the United States Embassy to Jerusalem (Palestine v United States of America)* Order of 15 November 2018 [2018] ICJ Rep 708, 710.

Proceedings in Argentina may be the easiest challenge for the Myanmar accused insofar as the record of Argentine courts prosecuting high-ranking foreign government officials, even former ones, is not promising.

When courts outside Myanmar – be they the ICJ, ICC or foreign domestic criminal courts – are taking their time to dispense justice sought by the Rohingya, situations inside Myanmar have kept on evolving *vis-à-vis* the Rohingya. Again, a crucial question is whether in a foreseeable future there can be justice for the Rohingya under the Myanmar domestic system that is meted out according to international standards.

As of this writing, there are two most likely scenarios as regards seeking justice for the Rohingya *beyond* Myanmar's domestic criminal justice system.

In the first scenario, the ICJ rules it has jurisdiction to proceed to consider the merits of The Gambia's Application and the Application is admissible, but The Gambia fails to discharge its burden of proving genocide of the Rohingya. Meanwhile, the ICC issues international arrest warrants against certain Myanmar individuals accused of crimes against humanity against the Rohingya in Bangladesh, a State Party to the Rome Statute of the ICC.[4] Some States may also seek prosecution of such Myanmar individuals on the basis of universal jurisdiction and/or other jurisdictional bases, such as the nationality of the Rohingya victims who have become naturalized citizens of these countries. The crimes for which these States may seek to punish can include war crimes, as conceded by Myanmar before the ICJ and by the ICOE to have been committed against the Rohingya, and crimes against humanity. In this first scenario, the issue of absolute immunity *ratione personae* of Myanmar's Head of State, Head of Government, Foreign of Minister of Myanmar and some other high-ranking government officials will come into play as explained in Chapters 6 and 7. Those States claiming no genocide has been committed against the Rohingya will be vindicated, but it is uncertain how they would react to the international arrest warrants issued by the ICC and the criminal proceedings in States exercising jurisdiction over other alleged crimes against the Rohingya.

The second scenario is the same as the first with the sole exception that the ICJ rules The Gambia has proved genocide against the Rohingya thereby placing the genocide deniers in a difficult position, with the scope of their credible and justifiable response options or excuses severely limited.

These two scenarios must be considered in the context of what is taking place inside Myanmar itself. First, there may be a regime change in Myanmar, with those accused of crimes of genocide, crimes against humanity and/or war crimes ousted from power, in which case the accused individuals will cease to have of immunity *ratione personae*, if they did have it while still in office, and will not have immunity *ratione materiae* for their conducts amounting to such crimes. They will become 'fair game' to be arrested and prosecuted in Myanmar, or surrendered to

4 2187 UNTS 90, in force 1 July 2002.

the ICC or extradited to States able and willing to prosecute them. Second, the *coup d'état* of 1 February 2021 may end up as a complete fiasco for the Tatmadaw, with civilians gaining full control over the governance of Myanmar, bringing full and true democracy to Myanmar free from the Tatmadaw's influence. Unfortunately, having denied the Tatmadaw's wrongs against the Rohingya, the civilian powers that be may find it difficult to put Tatmadaw members in the dock without also implicating some in the civilian leadership for these wrongs. In this latter scenario, certain kinds of national reconciliation or an acceptable soft landing for the Tatmadaw are likely, such as granting amnesty to selected Tatmadaw members while setting up a truth commission to deal with what has happened to the Rohingya.

Alternatives to prosecution

Instead of prosecution of wrongdoers, some societies have resorted to restorative (or reparative) justice, whereby the perpetrators acknowledge and take responsibility for their conducts by giving reparation to their victims after having dialogue with them.[5]

Restorative justice through the mechanism of truth commissions has been used as a crucial part of a political process of transition when the previous oppressive regime transfers its government power to a new regime that better protects human rights of those under its jurisdiction or control. Truth commissions are normally entrusted with investigating and documenting atrocities, identifying the perpetrators of atrocities and involving them in a process of public assumption of their individual responsibilities, providing redress to victims of mass atrocities and making recommendations for reform, and establishing a mechanism to ensure accountability for future atrocities. After the end of the apartheid regime in South Africa, the mechanism of a Truth and Reconciliation Commission was resorted to instead of prosecuting hundreds of thousands of individuals involved in implementing the racially oppressive regime, which would be costly, time-consuming and disrupting national reconciliation and harmony. The work of

5 Restorative justice may form part of the process known as 'transitional justice' resorted to by societies emerging from civil wars and systematic or widespread human rights abuses. In the UN system, 'transitional justice is the full range of processes and mechanisms associated with a society's attempt to come to terms with a legacy of large-scale past abuses, in order to ensure accountability, serve justice and achieve reconciliation'. It consists of both judicial and non-judicial processes and mechanisms, including prosecution initiatives, truth-seeking, reparations programmes, institutional reform or an appropriate combination thereof, in conformity with international legal standards and obligations. Transitional justice should further seek to take account of the root causes of conflicts and the related violations of all rights so as to contribute to achieving the broader objectives of prevention of further conflict, peacebuilding and reconciliation (United Nations, *Guidance Note of the Secretary General: United Nations Approach to Transitional Justice* (Mar 2010) 3). See also Cheryl Lawther and Luke Moffett (eds.), *Research Handbook on Transitional Justice* (Edward Elgar Publishing 2019).

some truth commissions – like the ones in Argentina, Chile and Peru – facilitated subsequent national prosecution of perpetrators of crimes covered under their respective mandates. In the case of Sierra Leone, a special tribunal has been set up to prosecute crimes alongside a truth and reconciliation commission set up to promote national healing and reconciliation.[6] These national mechanisms cannot supersede the international criminal tribunals or foreign domestic criminal courts having jurisdiction over the crimes in question.

Amnesty and pardon

Not infrequently, governments grant amnesty to or pardon those accused of committing serious human rights abuses. Amnesty is given to a group of individuals who have not faced a trial and been convicted or before the final judgment of the court trying them, whereas a pardon is granted individually to convicted persons although their criminal records are not erased after the pardon. Pursuant to Article 204(b) of the 2008 Constitution of Myanmar,[7] Myanmar's President has the power to grant amnesty in accordance with the recommendation of the National Defence and Security Council.

There are conflicting views as to the permissibility of amnesties and pardons under international law. *Ad hoc* international or 'hybrid' criminal courts as well as the Inter-American Court of Human Rights and the African Commission on Human and Peoples' Rights do not recognize amnesties or pardons granted by States. For example, in 2011 the Inter-American Court of Human Rights refused to recognize, and even condemned, Uruguay's amnesty law which had been confirmed in a plebiscite. According to the Court, the fact that a law has been approved in a democratic regime and ratified or supported by the public does not automatically or by itself grant legitimacy under international law. The Court reasons that the democratic legitimacy of specific facts in a society is limited by the norms of protection of human rights recognized in international treaties, such as the 1969 American Convention on Human Rights,[8] in such a form that the existence of one true democratic regime is determined by both its formal and substantial characteristics and therefore, particularly in cases of serious violations of non-revocable norms of international law, the protection of human rights constitutes 'an impassable limit to the rule of the majority'.[9]

In June 2018 the Inter-American Court of Human Rights ruled in *Barrios Altos and La Cantuta v Peru* that Peruvian courts had to review whether the 'pardon on humanitarian [health] reasons' granted by Peru's President on 24 December 2017 to former Peruvian President Alberto Fujimori, then aged 79, constituted

6 See Charles C Jalloh, *The Legal Legacy of the Special Court for Sierra Leone* (Cambridge University Press 2020) 306–37.

7 www.constituteproject.org/constitution/Myanmar_2008.pdf?lang=en.

8 1144 UNTS 123, in force 18 July 1978.

9 *Gelman v Uruguay*, Merits and Reparations, 24 Feb 2011, Series C, No 110 paras 238–9.

an unnecessary and disproportionate impact on the right of access to justice of the victims of serious human rights violations which constituted crimes against humanity, as determined and confirmed by Peru's own highest courts. The Inter-American Court of Human Rights reasons that a measure designed to protect the physical integrity or life of the person convicted of these crimes should only be applied in very extreme cases and should not necessarily result in his release, much less extinguish his criminal liability. On 3 October 2018, the Peruvian Supreme Court complied with Inter-American Court of Human Rights' decision in that case and, after examining the merits of the presidential pardon through a special procedure set up to assess the pardon's conformity with international human rights law, annulled the Presidential pardon. Fujimori, therefore, had to serve his sentence of 25 years' imprisonment, passed in 2009, for ordering, when he was President, the killings of 25 people by a government-backed death squad.

State practice outside Latin America is far from universal, however. No international treaty explicitly prohibits amnesties or pardons. Article 6(5) of the 1977 Additional Protocol II to the four Geneva Conventions of 1949,[10] applicable to internal armed conflicts, even stipulates:

> At the end of hostilities, the authorities in power shall endeavour to grant the broadest possible amnesty to persons who have participated in the armed conflict, or those deprived of their liberty for reasons related to the armed conflict, whether they are interned or detained.

A possibility of including a provision on amnesty was too controversial for the negotiations for both the 1998 Rome Statute of the ICC and the 2006 International Convention for the Protection of All Persons from Enforced Disappearance[11] that the final Statute and Convention omit any such provision. The European Court of Human Rights cautions, in passing, that while there is the 'growing tendency in international law' against amnesties to grave breaches of fundamental human rights as they are incompatible with the unanimously recognized obligation of States to prosecute and punish such crimes, amnesties may be possible in particular circumstances, such as a reconciliation process and/or as a form of compensation to victims.[12]

From the United Nations' perspective,[13] the removal of statutory limitations, amnesties or immunities that prevent prosecution of State officials and other indi-

10 1225 UNTS 609, in force 7 Dec 1978.

11 2716 UNTS 3, in force 23 Dec 2010.

12 *Marguš v Croatia* [GC], no 4455/10 para 139, 27 May 2014. See also Mark Osiel, *Making Sense of Mass Atrocity* (Cambridge University Press 2009) 218–40; Jalloh, *The Legal Legacy of the Special Court for Sierra Leone* 277–305.

13 Report of the UN Secretary-General on Implementing the Responsibility to Protect: Accountability for Prevention, A/71/1016 –S/2017/556 (10 Aug 2017).

viduals responsible for atrocities can help strengthen national legal frameworks for accountability. In addition, addressing past violations is a helpful measure to restore the dignity of victims, facilitate redress of violations and enable national reconciliation. Therefore, States must ensure that those responsible for atrocities such as genocide, war crimes or crimes against humanity in their territory are prosecuted, and if they fail to do so, the international community should consider all legal options available to secure justice for victims and to prevent recurrence.

As a rule of thumb, blanket amnesties issued by those suspected or accused of mass atrocities are self-serving efforts to evade the rule of law and should not be recognized. The broader amnesty offered by South Africa's Truth and Reconciliation Commission was not unilaterally issued by those who themselves were alleged to have committed mass atrocities, but as an essential part of joint efforts by all stakeholders for the sake of national peace and unity. In any case, the granting of an amnesty or a pardon by one State has no direct effect on prosecutions in another State with concurrent jurisdiction over the crime(s) in question. For instance, in *Public Prosecutor v Guus Kouwenhoven*, the Dutch Supreme Court rejected the defence's appeal that the blanket amnesty for acts and crimes committed during the Liberian civil war, approved by the then Liberian President Charles Taylor on 7 August 2003 shortly before his resignation, prevented prosecution of the defendant, a Dutch national, in the Netherlands for grave international crimes.[14]

Moreover, an amnesty or a pardon cannot override treaty obligations binding on the granting State to the contrary or the obligations owed by that State to victims of the crime.

The case of former Guatemalan President General Efrain Ríos Montt is illustrative. In 1982, Ríos Montt staged a *coup d'état* to overthrow the then Guatemalan Government, but he was toppled by another *coup d'état* led by another army general in 1983. In 1986, the latter general granted an amnesty to Ríos Montt and his aides for their acts while in office. Ríos Montt also enjoyed immunity from prosecution while he served as a Guatemalan congressman for 15 years until he lost his re-election bid late in 2011 and was put under house arrest. On 1 March 2012, a Guatemalan court ruled that the 1986 amnesty decree was invalidated by the 1948 Genocide Convention to which Guatemala had become a State Party in 1950 and which was implemented in Guatemala's domestic law in 1973. Therefore, Ríos Montt has no amnesty or immunity from prosecution for the charges, brought in January 2012, of ordering 1,771 murders, 1,400

14 HR 18 December 2018, Case 17/02109, *NJB* 2019, 25 at para 5. The Dutch Supreme Court cites the European Court of Human Rights' *dicta* in *Marguš v Croatia* that in exceptional circumstances it may be permissible to grant an amnesty for war crimes. Yet, the amnesty approved by Taylor was not mentioned in the peace agreement concluded one week after Taylor's resignation and the transitional government set up under the agreement evidently decided not to introduce a general amnesty.

human rights violations, including rapes and torture, and displacement of 29,000 indigenous Guatemalans in a 'scorched earth' campaign aimed at eliminating the support for a left-wing guerrilla movement during his regime in 1982–1983. On 10 May 2013 he was found guilty of genocide for the slaughter of 1,771 members of the Mayan Ixil indigenous group and was sentenced to 80 years' imprisonment. This was the first time that a former Head of State had been convicted of genocide within his/her own country. However, ten days later, Guatemala's Constitutional Court overturned his conviction on a technicality. A three-judge panel in 2015 ordered a retrial, which commenced in 2017, this time for the genocide by the killing of some 200 persons during a massacre in 1982. On 1 April 2018, he died of a heart attack at the age of 91. Since Myanmar, like Guatemala, is a State Party to the Genocide Convention, the decisions of the Guatemalan courts invalidating Ríos Montt's amnesty on the grounds of Guatemala's obligations under the Genocide Convention are very pertinent. Article IV of the Convention stipulates that persons committing genocide or any of the other acts enumerated in Article III 'shall be punished, whether they are constitutionally responsible rulers, public officials or private individuals'. Pursuant to Article V, the Contracting Parties to the Convention undertake to enact, in accordance with their respective Constitutions, the necessary legislation to give effect to the provisions of this Convention, and, in particular, 'to provide effective penalties' for persons guilty of genocide or any of the other acts enumerated in Article III. According to Article VI of the Convention, persons charged with genocide or any of the other acts enumerated in Article III 'shall be tried by a competent tribunal of the State in the territory of which the act was committed', or by such international penal tribunal as may have jurisdiction with respect to those Contracting Parties which shall have accepted its jurisdiction. These provisions negate the possibility of an amnesty or a pardon for genocidaires.

The case of Simone Gbagbo, former First Lady of Côte d'Ivoire, who has been subject to the ICC's arrest warrant on charges of four counts of crimes against humanity allegedly committed during the 2010–2011 post-election violence in Côte d'Ivoire, is of relevance. The Government of Côte d'Ivoire has refused to surrender her to the ICC. Instead she was tried by Côte d'Ivoire's Assize Court which, on 10 March 2015, convicted her and other pro-Gbagbo supporters for political crimes in relation to the post-election violence, including disturbing the peace, forming and organizing armed gangs and undermining State security. The ICC Appeals Chamber ruled in May 2015 that the domestic proceedings in Côte d'Ivoire did not cover the same crimes as those charged by the ICC, and that Côte d'Ivoire remains obliged to surrender her to the ICC.[15]

15 *Prosecutor v Simone Gbagbo*, Case ICC-02/11-01/12 OA, ICC Appeals Chamber, Judgment on the appeal of Côte d'Ivoire against the decision of Pre-Trial Chamber I of 11 December 2014 entitled 'Decision on Côte d'Ivoire's challenge to the admissibility of the case against Simone Gbagbo', 27 May 2015.

Simone Gbagbo was retried at an Ivorian court, this times on charges of crimes against humanity similar to those on which her ICC arrest warrant was based. In March 2017, she was acquitted due to lack of evidence. On 7 August 2018, after serving three of her 20 years' sentence imposed by Côte d'Ivoire's Assize Court in March 2015, she was pardoned by Côte d'Ivoire's President. Nevertheless, the ICC has not withdrawn its arrest warrant against her and has continued to press the Government to surrender her to the ICC. Until Simone Gbagbo is surrendered to the ICC, the case will remain in the ICC's Pre-Trial stage. This episode shows how a pardon granted to an individual so as to circumvent justice from being served may not be recognized by international criminal tribunals or foreign domestic criminal courts with concurrent jurisdiction over the crime(s) in question.

The 2016 peace accord between the Colombian Government and the insurgent or 'rebel' group called the Revolutionary Armed Forces of Colombia is interesting. It aims at ending the conflict ravaging Colombia since 1964, with more than 220,000 persons estimated to have been killed. There is *no amnesty or pardon* for

> crimes against humanity, genocide, serious war crimes (that is, any violation of international humanitarian law committed as part of a systematic attack), hostage taking or other serious deprivations of freedom, torture, extrajudicial executions, forced disappearances, rape and other forms of sexual violence, child abduction, forced displacement and the recruitment of minors, in every case as established in the Rome Statute.

Amnesties or pardons may be granted for 'the crime of rebellion and other politically motivated crimes' as narrowly defined by the accord, but without prejudice to the victims' right for any damages caused by those crimes. The accord refers to Article 6(5) of the 1977 Additional Protocol II to the Geneva Conventions of 1949, to which Colombia is a State Party, as a basis for amnesties and pardons.[16]

Statute of limitations

The 1968 Convention on the Non-Applicability of Statutory Limitations to War Crimes and Crimes Against Humanity[17] has 55 parties, including Lao DPR, Philippines and Vietnam, but not Myanmar, from among the ASEAN Member States. Article 29 of the Rome Statute of the ICC excludes the crimes within the ICC's jurisdiction from being subject to a statute of limitations, or time-barred. In addition, according to Rule 160 of the International Committee of the Red

16 Final Agreement to End the Armed Conflict and Build Stable and Lasting Peace, 24 Nov 2016, Chapter 5, www.peaceagreements.org/viewmasterdocument/1845.

17 754 UNTS 73, in force 11 Nov 1970.

Cross's authoritative *Customary International Law*, updated in December 2019, the principle that statutes of limitations do not apply to war crime committed in both international and non-international armed conflicts is a norm of customary international law binding on all States.

International cooperation to extradite or prosecute perpetrators of serious crimes of international concern

There is currently no global or regional treaty devoted exclusively to extradition of alleged perpetrators of crimes against humanity, war crimes committed in an internal armed, and Article VII of the Genocide Convention is rudimentary in nature, stipulating that the Contracting Parties to the Genocide Convention 'pledge themselves in [the cases of genocide and related acts proscribed by the Genocide Convention] to grant extradition in accordance with their laws and treaties in force'. Even in relation to war crimes in international armed conflict, Article 88(2) of the 1977 Additional Protocol I to the four Geneva Convention of 1949[18] merely requires that 'when circumstances permit, the High Contracting Parties shall cooperate in the matter of extradition', giving 'due consideration to the request of the State in whose territory the alleged offence has occurred'.

The establishment of international networks of cooperation with active judicial and prosecutorial assistance will be especially important to the effective exercise of universal jurisdiction as well as to the surrender to the ICC of persons subject to its arrest warrants.

Argentina, Belgium, Mongolia, Netherlands, Senegal and Slovenia have launched an initiative for the adoption of the Convention on International Cooperation in the Investigation and Prosecution of the Crime of Genocide, Crimes against Humanity and War Crimes. The goal of this initiative is to set up a modern procedural multilateral treaty on mutual legal assistance and extradition, replacing incomplete and outdated ones, so as to facilitate better practical cooperation between States investigating and prosecuting genocide, crimes against humanity and war crimes.

The Draft Convention is based on existing procedural provisions found in relatively recent treaties on mutual legal assistance dealing with international or transnational crimes, such as the 2000 UN Convention against Transnational Organized Crime[19] and the 2003 UN Convention against Corruption,[20] which are adapted for cooperation in the investigation and prosecution of crimes of genocide, crimes against humanity and war crimes. It also draws upon the UN General Assembly's Principles of International Cooperation in the Detection, Arrest, Extradition and Punishment of Persons Guilty of War Crimes and

18 1125 UNTS 3, in force 7 Dec 1978.
19 2225 UNTS 209, in force 29 Sept 2003.
20 2349 UNTS 41, in force 14 Dec 2005.

Crimes against Humanity,[21] which stipulates, among other things, that 'States shall cooperate with each other on a bilateral and multilateral basis with a view to halting and preventing war crimes and crimes against humanity, and shall take the domestic and international measures necessary for that purpose'. The Draft Convention will complement the Rome Statute mechanism and fill gaps in existing treaty regimes for the prosecution of core crimes under international law as well as enable States to prosecute crimes under the Rome Statute in the first instance according to the principle of complementarity, failing which the ICC may exercise jurisdiction over such crimes pursuant to the Rome Statute where applicable. Its procedural provisions will include freezing of assets, seizure and confiscation; protection of witnesses; transfer of criminal proceedings; disposal of confiscated proceeds of crime or property; taking of evidence or statements from persons; service of judicial documents; searches and seizures; identification or tracing of proceeds of crime, property, instrumentalities or other things of evidentiary purposes; facilitation of the voluntary appearance of persons in the requesting State Party; video-conference; assistance to and protection of victims; and training and technical assistance.

As of this writing, the Draft Convention has deleted a previous draft provision permitting States to grant amnesty and pardon for genocide, crimes against humanity and war crimes. It has included a provision allowing States to surrender a person suspected of criminal responsibility to an international criminal court as well as included torture and forced disappearance as crimes covered by the Draft Convention.

As of 19 March 2021, the initiative received support from 76 States. Sixty-nine of them are party to the Rome Statute; namely, Albania, Andorra, *Argentina*, Austria, Belgium, Benin, Bolivia, Bosnia and Herzegovina, Botswana, Bulgaria, Burkina Faso, Canada, Chile, Costa Rica, Côte d'Ivoire, Croatia, Cyprus, Czech Republic, Denmark, Ecuador, El Salvador, Estonia, Finland, France, Gambia, Georgia, Germany, Greece, Guinea, Hungary, Ireland, Italy, Latvia, Liechtenstein, Lithuania, Luxembourg, Madagascar, Malawi, Mali, Malta, Mexico, Moldova, Mongolia, Montenegro, Netherlands, Nigeria, North Macedonia, Norway, Panama, Paraguay, Peru, Poland, Portugal, Romania, Saint Kitts and Nevis, Samoa, Senegal, Serbia, Seychelles, Slovakia, Slovenia, South Africa, Spain, Suriname, Sweden, Switzerland, Trinidad and Tobago, UK and Uruguay. The remaining seven are not party to the Statute; namely, Belarus, Kazakhstan, Rwanda, São Tomé and Principe, Togo, Ukraine and Vietnam. Several States cannot support the initiative because they are not party to the Rome Statute and their domestic law does not criminalize some or even all of

21 A/RES/26/3074 (3 Dec 1973).

the crimes covered by the initiative – thus being unable to prosecute or even extradite (due to the lack of double criminality)[22] persons accused of such crimes.

In parallel, from 2015 to 2019 the UN International Law Commission took up the topic 'Crimes against humanity', resulting in the submission of the Articles on the Prevention and Punishment of Crimes against Humanity[23] to the UN General Assembly to consider convening a diplomatic conference to conclude an international convention based on the Articles. Crimes against humanity are the only core crimes under international law not yet discretely regulated by any treaty.

Article 4 (Obligation of prevention) of the Articles requires each State to undertake to prevent crimes against humanity, in conformity with international law, through: (a) effective legislative, administrative, judicial or other appropriate preventive measures in any territory under its jurisdiction; and (b) cooperation with other States, relevant intergovernmental organizations, and, as appropriate, other organizations. Article 6 (Criminalization under national law) obligates each State to take the necessary measures to ensure that crimes against humanity constitute offences under its criminal law. Article 7 (Establishment of national jurisdiction) provides in paragraph 1 that each State shall take the necessary measures to establish its jurisdiction over the offences covered by the Articles in the following cases: (a) when the offence is committed in any territory under its jurisdiction or on board a ship or aircraft registered in that State; (b) when the alleged offender is a national of that State or, if that State considers it appropriate, a stateless person who is habitually resident in that State's territory; (c) when the victim is a national of that State if that State considers it appropriate. Paragraph 2 of Article 7 requires each State to also take the necessary measures to establish its jurisdiction over the offences covered by the Articles in cases where the alleged offender is present in any territory under its jurisdiction and it does not extradite or surrender the person in accordance with the Articles. However, Article 7(3) provides that the Articles do not exclude the exercise of any criminal jurisdiction established by a State in accordance with its national law.

Under Article 9 (Preliminary measures when an alleged offender is present), upon being satisfied, after an examination of information available to it, that the circumstances so warrant, any State in the territory under whose jurisdiction a person alleged to have committed any offence covered by the Articles is present

22 Double criminality, or dual criminality, is a requirement in extradition, according to which a suspect may be extradited from one State to stand trial in another State only if the offence in the latter State for which the suspect is sought for extradition is also an offence in the extraditing State. This requirement is met if the necessary character of the criminal acts of these State is the same and if the characterization of the criminal acts as an offence under their respective laws is substantially similar.

23 ILC, 'Report of the International Law Commission on the Work of the work of the seventy-first session (29 April–7 June and 8 July–9 August 2019', GAOR, 74th Session Suppl. No 10 (A/71/10) Chapter IV.

shall take the person into custody or take other legal measures to ensure his or her presence. The custody and other legal measures shall be as provided in the law of that State, but may be continued only for such time as is necessary to enable any criminal, extradition or surrender proceedings to be instituted. Such State shall immediately make a preliminary inquiry into the facts. When a State, pursuant to this Article, has taken a person into custody, it shall immediately notify the States referred to in Article 7(1) of the fact that such person is in custody and of the circumstances which warrant his or her detention. The State which makes the preliminary inquiry shall, as appropriate, promptly report its findings to the said States and shall indicate whether it intends to exercise jurisdiction.

Article 10 (*Aut dedere aut judicare*) requires the State in the territory under whose jurisdiction the alleged offender is present, if it does not extradite or surrender the person to another State or competent international criminal court or tribunal, to submit the case to its competent authorities for the purpose of prosecution. Those authorities shall take their decision in the same manner as in the case of any other offence of a grave nature under the law of that State.

On the whole, the international community is trying its best to close gaps that would give impunity to perpetrators of serious crimes of international concern. Victims should welcome and benefit from this kind of treaty-based international cooperation to either extradite or prosecute the perpetrators.

Business as usual with Myanmar, especially after the February 2021 military takeover?

There have been calls for all investments in and trade with Myanmar to be conducted in strict adherence with the Guiding Principles on Business and Human Rights: Implementing the United Nations 'Protect, Respect, and Remedies' Framework,[24] endorsed by the UN Human Rights Council in June 2011.

The Guiding Principles are based on the recognition of: (a) States' existing obligations to respect, protect and fulfil human rights and fundamental freedoms; (b) the role of business enterprises as specialized organs of society performing specialized functions required to comply with all applicable laws and to respect human rights; and (c) the need for rights and obligations to be matched to appropriate and effective remedies when breached. Although the Guiding Principles should be implemented in a non-discriminatory manner, particular attention should be given to the rights and needs of, as well as the challenges faced by, individuals from groups or populations that may be at heightened risk of becoming vulnerable or marginalized, and with due regard to the different risks that may be faced by women and men.

24 www.ohchr.org/documents/publications/guidingprinciplesbusinesshr_en.pdf.

In addition, the UN has endorsed the UN Global Compact initiative[25] since 26 July 2000 to support businesses to do business responsibly by aligning their strategies and operations with ten principles on human rights, labour, environment and anti-corruption; and take strategic actions to advance broader societal goals, such as the UN Sustainable Development Goals, with an emphasis on collaboration and innovation. Principle 1 encourages businesses to support and respect the protection of internationally proclaimed human rights, whereas Principle 2 encourages them to ensure they are not complicit in human rights abuses. The Global Compact acts as a forum for discussion and networking among businesses, national and local governments, labour organizations, the academia, NGOs and other interested stakeholders. Participating businesses are required to submit annual communication on progress publicly disclosing details of their work to embed the Initiative's principles into their strategies and operations, as well as efforts to support societal priorities. Any business failing to submit a communication on progress that meets all the requirements within a year of becoming non-communicating will be expelled from the Global Compact and the name of expelled participants will be made public on the Global Compact website. Non-business participants submit biennially communication on engagement regarding the principles as a public disclosure of specific activities they undertake to support the Global Compact and the result of their activities. As of this writing, 13,043 companies in 160 countries have joined the Global Compact.

For its part, the Organization for Economic Development and Cooperation ('OECD')[26] has adopted its Guidelines for Multinational Enterprises[27] comprising recommendations jointly addressed by governments to multinational enterprises to provide principles and standards of good practice consistent with applicable laws and internationally recognized standards. As a general policy, multinational enterprises should respect the internationally recognized human rights of those affected by their activities. More specifically, enterprises should, within the framework of internationally recognized human rights, the international human rights obligations of the States in which they operate as well as relevant domestic laws and regulations, avoid infringing on the human rights of others and should address adverse human rights impacts with which they are involved. Within the context of their own activities, they should avoid causing or contributing to adverse human rights impacts and address such impacts when they occur. Moreover, they should seek ways to prevent or mitigate adverse human rights

25 www.unglobalcompact.org/.

26 The OECD's members are Australia, Austria, Belgium, Canada, Chile, Czech Republic, Denmark, Estonia, Finland, France, Germany, Greece, Hungary, Iceland, Ireland, Israel, Italy, Japan, South Korea, Luxembourg, Mexico, Netherlands, New Zealand, Norway, Poland, Portugal, Slovakia, Slovenia, Spain, Sweden, Switzerland, Turkey, UK and United States. The EU participates in the work of the OECD.

27 *OCED Guidelines for Multinational Enterprises 2011 Edition*, www.oecd.org/daf/inv/mne/48004323.pdf.

impacts directly linked to their business operations, products, or services by a business relationship, even if they do not contribute to those impacts. Enterprises should have a policy commitment to respect human rights; carry out human rights due diligence as appropriate to their size, the nature and context of operations, and the severity of the risks of adverse human rights impacts; and provide for or cooperate through legitimate processes in the remediation of adverse human rights impacts where they identify that they have caused or contributed to these impacts.

The aforesaid initiatives are not legally binding. On 26 June 2014, the UN Human Rights Council established an open-ended intergovernmental working group on transnational corporations and other business enterprises with respect to human rights, whose mandate is to elaborate an international legally binding instrument to regulate, in international human rights law, the activities of transnational corporations and other business enterprises.[28] The latest revised draft instrument as of this writing requires State Parties to the instrument to regulate effectively by domestic legislation all persons conducting business activities, *including those of a transnational character*, in their territory or jurisdiction, for them to respect human rights and prevent human rights violations or abuses throughout their operations. The domestic law must provide for a comprehensive and adequate system of legal liability for human rights violations or abuses in the context of business activities and liability of legal persons shall be without prejudice to the liability of natural persons. Also, civil liability shall not be made contingent upon finding of criminal liability or its equivalent for the same acts. Moreover, States Parties shall adopt legal and other measures necessary to ensure that their domestic jurisdiction provides for effective, proportionate and dissuasive criminal and/or administrative sanctions and reparations to the benefit of the victims where business activities, including those of transnational character, have caused harm to victims. State Parties may require natural or legal persons engaged in business activities to establish and maintain financial security, such as insurance bonds or other financial guarantees to cover potential claims of compensation. States Parties shall ensure that their domestic legislation provide for the liability of natural or legal persons conducting business activities, including those of transnational character, for its failure to prevent *another* natural or legal person with whom it has a business relationship, from causing human rights abuses, when the former legally or factually controls or supervises such person or the relevant activity that caused or contributed to the human rights abuses, or *should have foreseen* risks of human rights abuses in the conduct of their business activities, including those of transnational character, or in their business relationships, but failed to put adequate measures to prevent the abuses. Human rights due diligence shall not automatically absolve a legal or natural person conducting business activities from liability for causing or contributing to human rights

28 A/HRC/RES/26/9.

abuses or failing to prevent such abuses by a natural or legal person. Subject to their legal principles, States Parties shall ensure that their domestic law provide for the criminal or functionally equivalent liability of legal persons for human rights abuses that amount to criminal offences under international human rights law binding on the State Party, customary international law or their domestic law. Regardless of the nature of the liability, States Parties shall ensure the applicable penalties are commensurate with the gravity of the offence. Acts or omissions constituting attempt, participation or complicity in a criminal offence are also to be criminalized. Jurisdiction with respect to claims brought by *victims, irrespective of their nationality or place of domicile*, arising from acts or omissions that result or may result in human rights abuses covered under this instrument shall vest in the courts of the State where: (a) the human rights abuse occurred; (b) an act or omission contributing to the human rights abuse occurred; or (c) the legal or natural persons alleged to have committed an act or omission causing or contributing to such human rights abuse in the context of business activities, including those of a transnational character, are domiciled.

For its part, the EU is moving towards making corporate due diligence and accountability in preventing human rights and environmental harm an enforceable legal obligation in all EU Member States, with proportionate sanctions which shall be effective, proportionate and dissuasive and shall take into account the severity of the infringements committed and whether or not the infringement has taken place repeatedly. The competent national authorities may in particular impose proportionate fines calculated on the basis of a corporation's turnover; temporarily or indefinitely exclude the corporation from public procurement, State aid, public support schemes and loans; and resort to the seizure of commodities and other appropriate administrative sanctions.[29]

A landmark development in this connection is the Canadian Supreme Court's Judgment in *Nevsun Resources Ltd v Araya*,[30] decided on 28 February 2020. Three Eritrean workers brought action on behalf of more than 1,000 individuals against Nevsun, a Canadian corporation in British Columbia, alleging they were forced to work at the gold, copper and zinc mine owned by Nevsun in Eritrea and were subjected to violent, cruel, inhuman and degrading treatment. They sought damages from Nevsun for, among others, breaches of customary international law prohibitions. The Supreme Court rules customary international law can give rise to a direct claim for damages in Canada with respect to allegations of forced labour; slavery; cruel, inhumane and degrading treatment; and crimes against humanity, and corporations may be liable for violations of customary international law since it is not plain and obvious that corporations today enjoy a blanket

29 P9_TA-PROV(2021)0073 Corporate due diligence and corporate accountability European Parliament resolution of 10 March 2021 with recommendations to the Commission on corporate due diligence and corporate accountability (2020/2129(INL).

30 *Nevsun Resources Ltd v Araya*, 28 Feb 2020, 2020 SCS 5 (CanLII), 443 DLR (4th) 183.

exclusion under customary international law from direct or indirect liability for violations of obligatory, definable and universal norms of international law.[31] The workers claim breaches not only of norms of customary international law, but of norms accepted to be of such fundamental importance as to be characterized as *jus cogens*. In Canada, customary international law is automatically adopted into domestic law without any need for legislative action and, consequently, a breach by a Canadian company can theoretically be directly remedied. Besides, the Canadian Government has adopted policies to ensure that Canadian companies operating abroad respect international human rights norms. With respect specifically to the allegations raised by the workers, like all State Parties to the 1966 International Covenant on Civil and Political Rights,[32] Canada has international obligations under Article 2 thereof to ensure an effective remedy to victims of violations of those rights. Appropriately remedying the violations of *jus cogens* and norms of customary international law requires different and stronger responses than typical tort claims, given the public nature and importance of the violated rights involved, the gravity of their breach, the impact on the domestic and global rights objectives and the need to deter subsequent breaches. Since the customary international law norms raised by the Eritrean workers form part of the Canadian common law, and since Nevsun is a company bound by Canadian law, the claims of the Eritrean workers for breaches of customary international law are allowed to proceed.[33]

Those businesses identified in the IIFFMM's report entitled 'The economic interests of the Myanmar military' submitted to the Human Rights Council in August 2019[34] may find it hard to withstand international pressure for them to heed the recommendations in the IIFFMM's report, otherwise their corporate image will severely suffer and they may also be subject to civil litigations in some States. Those natural persons responsible for providing financial support to atrocities against the Rohingya may also be criminally liable under the domestic law of certain States and/or under the Rome Statute of the ICC as explained in Chapter 5.

Indeed, there are cases in which corporations and natural persons who are senior members of the corporations have been convicted or are being investigated for their human rights violations abroad amounting to crimes of international concern. For instance, in April 2017 the Court of Appeal in 's-Hertogenbosch, Netherlands, sentenced Guus Kouwenhoven, a Dutch national who was the

31 Ibid para 113 and see also para 127.

32 999 UNTS 171, in force 23 Mar 1976.

33 See also the UK Supreme Court's Judgment in *Vedanta Resources PLC and another v Lungowe and others* [2019] UKSC 20, finding jurisdiction in UK courts over a tort lawsuit by Zambian farmers against Vedanta Resources, a UK parent company, and its majority-owned Zambian subsidiary, alleging that the farmers' health and livelihoods were harmed by water pollution caused by a copper plant owned and operated by the subsidiary in Zambia.

34 A/HRC/42/CRP.3.

owner and president of two logging companies in Liberia, to 19 years' imprisonment for his role in the second Liberian Civil War (1999–2003). The Court found him guilty of illegal trafficking of weapons and ammunitions and complicity in war crimes committed by the Liberian armed forces through making an active contribution to the war efforts by providing weapons, transportation, facilities and armed personnel while he must have been aware these weapons would be used in the armed conflict and thus exposed himself to a high probability that war crimes would be committed by third parties. In other words, the defendant had deliberately provided the means for the war crimes committed by the Liberian armed forces and had therefore deliberately been an accomplice to these war crimes.[35] His appeal was dismissed by the Dutch Supreme Court.[36] In France, a judicial investigation was opened on 26 August 2020 regarding the alleged complicity of BNP Paribas ('BNPP') in crimes committed by the Sudanese Government against its citizens between 2002 and 2008, with BNPP as a company and its senior staff as individuals being subject to these proceedings. Acts amounting to genocide and crimes against humanity were allegedly facilitated by BNPP through its provision of credit facilities, access to foreign financial markets and petrol exports to the Sudanese Government in defiance of the sanctions imposed on Sudan by the UN, the EU and individual States.[37] Also in France, as of this writing there are ongoing proceedings against Amesys, as a company, for allegedly aiding and abetting crimes of torture committed in Libya under Muammar Gaddafi's regime as a result of the company's sale of surveillance material to the regime.[38]

Epilogue

The military takeover of government in Myanmar on 1 February 2021 has had impact on the Rohingya's quest for justice.

Myanmar's general election held on 8 November 2020, the second since the end of a half-century of direct military rule, saw approximately 71% of eligible voters turn out to cast their votes. ASSK's National League for Democracy ('NLD') candidates won 920 (or 82%) of the total 1,117 elected seats to be filled, including seats in both houses of Myanmar's bicameral Parliament and the state/regional parliaments, as well as ethnic affairs minister posts, giving the NLD another landslide victory – with 61 more seats in all parliaments than it had won in the previous general election held in 2015. Myanmar's new legislatures whose term was scheduled to begin on 1 February 2021 included representatives

35 *Public Prosecutor v Guus Kouwenhoven*, Hof s-Hertogenbosch, Case 20/001906-10, 21 Apr 2017, *NJFS* 2017, 153.

36 *Public Prosecutor v Guus Kouwenhoven*, HR 18 December 2018, Case 17/02109, *NJB* 2019, 25.

37 TRIAL International, *Universal Jurisdiction: Annual Review 2021: A year like no other? – The impact of COVID-19 on universal jurisdiction* 35.

38 Ibid 36.

of 19 political parties and four independents. The main opposition party, the Union Solidarity and Development Party ('USDP') set up by the Tatmadaw, won 71 seats, or 6.4% of all elected seats (down from 117 in 2015), losing several of its seats to the NLD and the ethnic parties. In Rakhine state, where the election were cancelled on the grounds of security threats and violence in the entire nine townships and parts of four other townships, the Arakan National Party ('ANP') won a majority in the Rakhine state parliament. Although the NLD won 82% of elected seats, the 2008 Constitution of Myanmar reserves 25% of seats in every parliament for the military, thereby making the NLD's share of seats in the Union Parliament, where the key legislation is enacted or amended, stand at 62%, as the Union Parliament's 642 seats include the 166 seats held by the military.[39] The NLD's landslide was largely attributed to ASSK's immense popularity among Myanmar's Bamar Buddhist majority, especially after her personal defence of Myanmar against accusations of genocide at the ICJ in December 2019. Western commentators are concerned that the general election outcome would threaten to further divide rather than unify Myanmar since ethnic minority leaders perceive the landslide to serve to marginalize their voices while validating a cult of personality around ASSK as an icon only for the Bamar majority. In particular, some 1.4 million people in minority townships in Rakhine, Shan, Kachin and Kayin states were denied the right to vote, after election officials either fully or partially cancelled elections in those areas, citing security situations and violence. The decisions of the Union Election Commission ('UEC'), a partisan body appointed by the Government, were criticized for lack of transparency and consultation. Many of the areas cancelled were where the NLD was almost guaranteed to lose. Hundreds of thousands of Rohingya were also disenfranchised, as in the previous general election in 2015.

The Tatmadaw alleged there were widespread voter irregularities in the November 2020 election with evidence of more than ten million cases of voter irregularities and fraud in the polls, and asked the UEC to release the electoral roll for cross-checking and the start of the new parliament scheduled for 1 February 2021 be delayed until the issues around the election were resolved. Senior General Min Aung Hlaing himself asserted on 27 January 2021 that Myanmar's Constitution could be 'revoked' under certain circumstances. On 29 January 2021, Myanmar's Supreme Court heard applications of writs from the USDP and the Democratic Party of National Politics, two political parties aligned with the Tatmadaw, naming President U Win Myint, State Counsellor ASSK, the UEC chairman and 14 other election officials as defendants for election misconduct during the November general election which, according to the applicants, made the election unfair and marred by mass fraud.

39 'Official Results Show Another Election Landslide for Myanmar's Ruling NLD', *Irrawaddy* (16 Nov 2020).

Early in the morning of 1 February 2021, the day when the new 664-seat bicameral Parliament was to convene, ASSK, President Win Myint and other senior members of the NLD were detained by the military. So were politicians from states and regions, as well as prominent political activists. Subsequently, the military announced its takeover of the government and declared a one-year state of emergency, with Senior General Min Aung Hlaing, who was due to retire from the armed forces in July 2021 at the age of 65, taking over the government. He was so appointed by the Tatmadaw-nominated Vice President General Myint Swe who was acting President while the President was being detained. Sections 417 through 431 of the 2008 Constitution deal with the state of emergency. Section 417 reads:

> If there arises or if there is sufficient reason for a state of emergency to arise that may disintegrate the Union or disintegrate national solidarity or that may cause the loss of sovereignty, due to acts or attempts to take over the sovereignty of the Union by insurgency, violence and wrongful forcible means, the President may, after coordinating with the National Defence and Security Council, promulgate an ordinance and declare a state of emergency. In the said ordinance, it shall be stated that the area where the state of emergency in operation is the entire Nation and the specified duration is one year from the day of promulgation.

In citing Section 417 to justify the nationwide state of emergency, the Tatmadaw asserted as follows. The voter lists used during the multi-party general election in November 2020 were found to have huge discrepancies and the UEC failed to settle this matter. Although the sovereignty of the nation must derive from the people, there was terrible fraud in the voter list during the democratic general election which runs contrary to ensuring a stable democracy. A refusal to settle the issue of voter list fraud and a failure to take action and follow a request to postpone lower-house and upper-house parliament sessions were not in accordance with Section 417 that refers to 'acts or attempts to take over the sovereignty of the Union by wrongful forcible means' and could lead to a 'disintegration of national solidarity'. Due to such acts, there had been many protests going on in townships and cities in Myanmar to demonstrate their mistrust toward the UEC. Other parties and people had also been found conducting different kinds of provocations including displaying flags which were very damaging to national security. Unless this problem was resolved, it would obstruct the path to democracy and it, therefore, had to be resolved according to the law. In order to perform scrutiny of the voter lists and to take action, the authority of the nation's law making, governance and jurisdiction was handed over to the commander in chief in accordance with Sections 418 and 419 of the Constitution.

In invoking Section 417 of the Constitution, the Tatmadaw did not seem to have followed its procedural requirement as regards the 'coordination' with the National Defence and Security Council before declaring the state of emergency.

Several members of the Council (whose membership comprises the President of Myanmar, two Vice Presidents and the speakers of the two houses of the Assembly of the Union, the Foreign Minister, the army chief and his deputy and the three military-appointed ministers – Border Affairs, Defence and Home Affairs) had apparently not been consulted. Those attending the Council's meeting in the morning of 1 February 2021 to approve the state of emergency decree were the six military representatives, chaired by Vice President General Myint Swe in the President's absence. This is why this military takeover is widely considered a *coup d'état* by the Tatmadaw.

The Tatmadaw removed 24 ministers, including the President and ASSK, and deputies of the NLD-led government, replacing them with 11 ministers in the new administration under Acting President General Myint Swe. Yet, the *de facto* leader of Myanmar is Senior General Min Aung Hlaing. On 2 February 2021, the Tatmadaw announced the establishment of the State Administrative Council ('SAC'), with the Senior General as Chairman and Vice Senior General Soe Win as Vice Chairman. SAC appointed State and Regional Administrative Council chairmen for Myanmar's 12 states and regions, as well as Self-Administrative Council chairmen for Myanmar's six self-administered zones. Of special interest is the appointment as a member of the Rakhine State Administrative Council of U Than Tun, a nationalist allegedly opposed to the Rohingya in general and their repatriation from Bangladesh. Key government officials replaced by SAC included the Attorney-General, the Central Bank of Myanmar chairman and the Naypyitaw Council chairman. All the UEC members before the *coup* were replaced.

The Senior General, who was supposed to give up his position as Commander-in-Chief in 2016 when he was 60 and who extended his tenure and promised to finally retire in July 2021, is believed to have long aspired to be President of Myanmar. The outcome of the November 2020 general election made it impossible to achieve this ambition. The 2008 Constitution allocates 166 seats or 25% of seats in the Parliament, and the USDP would have needed to secure another 167 seats to appoint the Senior General as Myanmar's President but the USDP won only 33 of the 498 available seats, compared to the NLD's 396 seats. As the *coup* leader, the Senior General's tenure as Commander-in-Chief of the Tatmadaw is indefinitely extended. Although soon after the *coup* the Senior General pledged to hold new elections in 18 months, respect the ensuing election results and transfer power to the winner, in early April 2021 the Tatmadaw's spokesman told *CNN* that due to the ongoing 'riotous' protests against the Government the state of emergency could be extended for an additional 'six months or more' over 'two terms' and 'if the duties are not done yet', expecting to hold 'a free and fair election' within two years from 1 February 2021.[40]

40 Clarissa Ward *et al.*, 'Myanmar military denies responsibility for child deaths and says elections could be pushed back', *CNN* (8 Apr 2021), https://edition.cnn.com/2021/04/08/asia/myanmar-zaw-min-tun-interview-intl-hnk/index.html.

Starting from 3 February 2021, ASSK has been charged with various criminal offences punishable by years of imprisonment, including illegal import and use, without permission, of communications equipment; violation of the Natural Disaster Management Law[41] for apparently violating COVID-19 restrictions in the run-up to the general election; incitement by publication of information that may cause fear or alarm or disrupt public tranquillity proscribed under Section 505(b) of the Penal Code;[42] violation of the Telecommunications Act[43] because the communications equipment seized did not have licences; illegally accepting US$600,000 and 11 kilogrammes of gold from the chief minister of Yangon before the *coup*; and violation of official secrets law. The ousted President Win Myint was accused, under the National Disaster Management Law, of meeting supporters in a 220-vehicle motorcade during the election campaign in breach of COVID-19 restrictions. Ironically, thousands of people were reported to have gathered at People's Park in Yangon on the day after the Tatmadaw takeover to show support for the declaration of the state of emergency and its ramifications, although the Park was supposed to be closed as part of the measures to curtail the spread of COVID-19. These charges against ASSK and the ousted President could be thinly-veiled pretexts to keep them in custody at least beyond any future general election. Many other prominent politicians opposed have been arrested and charged with various offences.

On 26 February 2021, the chairman of the military-appointed UEC 'confirmed' the results of the 2020 November general election were no longer valid after SAC had taken control of the country.

Senior General Min Aung Hlaing has already been subject to sanctions in the United States and the UK, among others, for his alleged role in the plight of the Rohingya. It has become more and more difficult to get the Rohingya who have run away from their homes in Rakhine to be voluntarily repatriated during the government under the full control of the person accused of having perpetrated serious atrocities against them. This is despite the Tatmadaw's operation starting on 15 February 2021 to clear landmines in some areas of Rakhine state to allow internally displaced people to return. Shortly after the *coup* and apparently prompted by the need to deflect international criticisms against the *coup*, the Senior General gave a speech, saying that efforts to repatriate Rohingya refugees from Bangladesh would continue. Because of the *coup*, the long-awaited working committee meeting between Bangladesh and Myanmar on Rohingya repatriation, scheduled to be convened on 5 February 2021 was deferred. According to the UNHCR, about 2,400 Rohingya attempted to travel by sea in overcrowded rickety wooden boats to find countries of asylum in 2020, and 200 died as a result.

41 Pyidaungsu Hluttaw Law No 21/2013 .
42 Penal Code 1986 (1 May 1981).
43 Pyidaungsu Hluttaw Law No 31/2013.

Right after the *coup*, the ASEAN Chairman (Brunei) issued a statement on behalf of ASEAN, recalling 'the purposes and principles of the ASEAN Charter, including the adherence to the principles of democracy, the rule of law and good governance, respect for and protection of human rights and fundamental freedom'. The statement 'reiterates that the political stability in ASEAN Member States is essential to achieving a peaceful, stable and prosperous ASEAN Community', and encourages 'the pursuance of dialogue, reconciliation and the return to normalcy in accordance with the views and interests of the people of Myanmar'. ASEAN subsequently issued a modest collective position as regards the developments in Myanmar after the Informal ASEAN Ministerial Meeting convened on 2 March 2021 via video-conference, with the Foreign Minister of Myanmar also participating. The ASEAN Chair's Statement[44] has ten paragraphs, the last one of which 'underscored the importance of Myanmar's continued efforts in addressing the situation in the Rakhine state, including commencing the repatriation process, in voluntary, safe and dignified manner in accordance with its bilateral agreements with Bangladesh'. On 24 April 2021, a special ASEAN Summit was convened at the ASEAN Secretariat in Jakarta, chaired by Brunei, 'with the view to [advancing] ASEAN Community building, hasten recovery from the Coronavirus Disease 2019 (COVID19) pandemic, strengthen ASEAN's external relations and address pressing issues of common interest to all ASEAN Member States'.[45] The Chairman's Statement issued after the Summit has two paragraphs on the situation in Myanmar. The 'ASEAN Leaders' expressed their 'deep concern on the situation in the country, including reports of fatalities and escalation of violence' and 'acknowledged ASEAN's positive and constructive role in facilitating a peaceful solution in the interest of the people of Myanmar and their livelihoods, and therefore agreed to the "Five-Point Consensus" attached to this Chairman's Statement'. They also 'heard calls for the release of all political prisoners including foreigners'.[46] The Leaders 'also underscored the importance of Myanmar's continued efforts in addressing the situation in the Rakhine state, including commencing the repatriation process, in a voluntary, safe and dignified manner in accordance with its bilateral agreements with Bangladesh'. In this regard, they looked forward to the resumption of repatriation of verified displaced persons as soon as possible as well as underscored the importance of efforts to addressing the root causes of the situation in Rakhine state.[47]

44 https://asean.org/storage/FINAL-Chairmans-Statement-on-the-IAMM.pdf.

45 Para 1 of the Chairman's Statement on the ASEAN Leaders' Meeting, 24 Apr 2021.

46 Ibid para 8.

47 Ibid para 9. The 'Five-Point Consensus' attached to the Chairman's Statement reads: First, there shall be immediate cessation of violence in Myanmar and all parties shall exercise utmost restraint; second, constructive dialogue among all parties concerned shall commence to seek a peaceful solution in the interests of the people; third, a special envoy of the ASEAN Chair shall facilitate mediation of the dialogue process, with the assistance of the Secretary General

On 4 February 2021, the UN Security Council issued a press statement without condemning the *coup*. It merely expressed the Security Council members' 'deep concern' at the declaration of the state of emergency imposed in Myanmar by the military on 1 February and the arbitrary detention of members of the Government, including ASSK and President Win Myint and others. The Council called for the immediate release of all those detained as well as emphasized the need for the continued support of the democratic transition in Myanmar. It stressed the need to uphold democratic institutions and processes, refrain from violence and fully respect human rights, fundamental freedoms and the rule of law. The statement encouraged the pursuance of dialogue and reconciliation in accordance with the will and interests of the people of Myanmar. It also reiterated 'the need to address the root causes of the crisis in Rakhine state and to create conditions necessary for the safe, voluntary, sustainable and dignified return of displaced persons'. Subsequently, on 10 March 2021, the President of the Security Council issued a statement that, among other things, expressed concern that recent developments posed particular serious challenges for the voluntary, safe, dignified and sustainable return of Rohingya refugees and internally displaced persons. After the special ASEAN summit of 24 April 2021, the Council on 30 April 2021 issued a statement reiterating its demand for the restoration of democracy in Myanmar and the release of all detainees including ASSK, as well as expressing its support for ASEAN's Five-Point Consensus and demanding that the UN Secretary-General's Special Envoy on Myanmar be allowed to visit Myanmar as soon as possible.

On 12 February 2021, the UN Human Rights Council adopted a resolution on 'Human rights implications of the crisis in Myanmar',[48] proposed by the UK and the EU, without a vote. Of special interest is the resolution's stress on 'the need to address the root causes of the crisis in Rakhine state and to create the conditions necessary for the safe, voluntary, sustainable and dignified return of displaced persons, including of Rohingya Muslims and other minorities'. It further called for full cooperation with and the granting of full and unrestricted access to UN mandate holders and human rights mechanisms, including the Special Rapporteur on the situation of human rights in Myanmar and the Office of the UN High Commissioner for Human Rights.

Unilateral sanctions of different scales and dimensions have been imposed by several States in response to the *coup*, starting from that of New Zealand on 9 February 2021, the United States on 10 February 2021 and thereafter,

---

of ASEAN; fourth, ASEAN shall provide humanitarian assistance through the ASEAN Coordinating Centre for Humanitarian Assistance on Disaster Management; and fifth, the special envoy and delegation shall visit Myanmar to meet with all parties concerned. The Senior General reportedly informed the Summit the Five-Point Consensus would be positively considered if it would facilitate the implementation of SAS' own roadmap and serve Myanmar's interests.

48 A/HRC/RES/S-29/1 (15 Feb 2021).

the Canadian Government on 17 February 2021, the UK Government on 17 February 2021 and thereafter, and the EU on 22 February 2021 and thereafter. Of note is the US sanction on Myanmar Economic Corporation and Myanmar Economic Holdings Ltd imposed on 25 March 2021 freezing any assets they have in the Unites States and banning US individuals and businesses from trading with them – something the US Government did not do when imposing sanctions on 10 December 2019 on four Myanmar military leaders for their alleged human rights abuses against the Rohingya and other minorities in Myanmar.[49] How effective these sanctions will be depends on the leverage the sanctioning States and group of States have *vis-à-vis* Myanmar. In their telephone conversation on 4 February 2021, Vice Senior General Soe Win told UN Secretary-General's Special Envoy on Myanmar Christine Schraner Burgener: 'We are used to sanctions and we survived', and, as regard the prospect of international isolation: 'We have to learn to walk with only few friends'.[50]

The February 2021 *coup* was the third one after Myanmar's independence from British rule in 1948. The Tatmadaw set up a junta named the Revolutionary Council after the *coup* in 1962; the State Law and Order Restoration Council following the 1988 coup, which was changed to the State Peace and Development Council in 1997; and the State Administrative Council after the February 2021 *coup*. Unlike the two previous *coups*, the most recent one came at the time when Myanmar has experienced five years or more of freedom and the social media revolution not seen during the aftermath of the two previous *coups*. These have motivated and mobilized relentless mass protests and civil disobedience movement against the February 2021 *coup*. Hundreds of protesters against the *coup* have been reportedly killed by Myanmar government security forces. The confrontation between the Tatmadaw and the protesters who are supported by several ethnic armed groups might escalate into a civil war.[51]

49 On 21 April 2021, the US Government added to the sanction list the State-owned Myanma [*sic*] Timber Enterprise and Myanmar Pearl Enterprise, which are responsible for timber and pearl exports from Myanmar. The timber and pearl industries are among Myanmar's key economic resources.

50 www.reuters.com/article/us-myanmar-politics-un-idUSKCN2AV2CJ.

51 The ethnic armed groups that have pledged their support to civilian protesters against the coup and demanded the end to the violent suppression include the Restoration Council for Shan State, the Karen National Union, the Kachin Independence Organization, the Brotherhood Alliance, the Myanmar National Democratic Alliance Army and the Ta'ang National Liberation Army. The protesters were initially unarmed but some of them subsequently used home-made firearms, knives and firebombs to counter the junta's violent suppression. Although ethnic armed groups in Myanmar may not support ASSK or the NLD, this is probably the best time to attack the Tatmadaw to advance their strategic positions and agendas. Armed clashes in several areas controlled by ethnic armed groups escalated after the *coup*. On 13 April 2021, the UN High Commissioner for Human Rights warned 'there are clear echoes of Syria in 2011' when peaceful protests met with 'unnecessary and clearly disproportionate force', escalating into a full-blown conflict amidst the failure of the international community to respond with united resolve (Office of the High Commissioner for Human Rights, News Release, 13 Apr 2021).

Economically, the latest *coup* has had immediate serious repercussions for Myanmar. Several multinational corporations running business in Myanmar are concerned over *the safety of their employees and those employed by their suppliers, communications* network instability that impeded manufacturing and inspection processes, and difficulties in accessing information due to the volatile situation and political instability. The safety situation has deteriorated after 13 March 2021, when 32 Chinese factories were attacked and damaged by groups of people armed with iron bars, axes and petrol who opposed the *coup* and accused China of being supportive of the *coup*. A modern industrial hub project worth several hundred million US dollars backed by Thailand's largest industrial estate developer Amata Corporation suspended work due to possible sanctions by the West, particularly the United States and the EU. From 20 March 2021, Électricité de France suspended the Shweli-3 Project, a 671 megawatt hydropower project worth more than US$1.5 billion in Myanmar's Shan state, including the activities of its subcontractors. The company explained it adhered to fundamental human rights principles, the relevant conventions of the International Labor Organization and the UN Guiding Principles on Business and Human Rights in every project in which it participated. Kirin Holdings from Japan announced on 5 February 2021 the termination of its joint-venture partnership with MEHL. One month after the *coup*, Myanmar's Central Bank issued a directive ordering banks in Myanmar to limit cash withdrawals. The UN Development Programme, therefore, has warned that in the worst-case scenario, 48.2% of Myanmar's population will live in poverty (compared to the 24.8% in 2017), and that if the situation on the ground persists, the poverty rate could double by the beginning of 2022.[52]

Natural gas is Myanmar's second biggest export after manufactured goods, with Myanmar earning nearly US$1 billion a year from natural gas sales. Almost all of Myanmar's hydrocarbon revenues come from Yanada and three other giant gas projects operated by France's Total (with Chevron from the United States owning 28% of the project), South Korea's Posco, Malaysia's Petronas and Thailand's PTTEP, respectively. The revenues from natural gas are paid to Myanmar's Oil and Gas Enterprise, a State enterprise closely linked to the Tatmadaw, which does not open its accounts to public scrutiny. Insofar as international sanctions do not adversely affect this source of revenue, the Tatmadaw will continue to survive financially. In response to criticisms against Total, Total's chief executive has explained Total has to keep its offshore Yadana site operational to avoid cutting off electricity supplies to a large population in Yangon, adding to their suffering, and Total has been alerted by the Thai authorities not to interrupt

Two days after the special ASEAN Summit of 24 April 2021, the junta's spokesman said it would give careful consideration to suggestions made by ASEAN leaders when the situation returned to stability in the country since priorities at the moment were to maintain law and order and to restore community peace and tranquillity.

52 UN Development Programme, *COVID-19,* COUP D'ÉTAT *AND POVERTY: Compounding Negative Shocks and Their Impact on Human Development in Myanmar* (Apr 2021).

supply of this source of energy for power plants in Thailand. Total has considered whether it should place payments on taxes owed to the Myanmar Government in an escrow account, as suggested by some human rights NGOs, but this could make its local managers liable under the local law. Total has halted new projects and drilling in Myanmar in response to the repressive action taking place there, and would donate the equivalent of the taxes payable to the Myanmar authority to associations working towards human rights in Myanmar.[53]

For ASSK, her decision to defend the Tatmadaw for its alleged atrocities against the Rohingya, either for personal, political or patriotic reasons, helped her gain popularity and the NLD win the November 2020 general election by a landslide. The Tatmadaw, with one of the two Vice President posts, three cabinet portfolios in charge of internal and external security as well as border affairs, wields the real power and influence in Myanmar under the 2008 Constitution. Had ASSK dared to enrage the Tatmadaw by bringing those accused by the international community of serious crimes against the Rohingya to justice – domestically or elsewhere, the *coup* might have come much sooner. Alas, ASSK's stance towards the plight of the Rohingya, while placating the Tatmadaw, has not saved her from being ousted by the Tatmadaw or Myanmar from being returned to the days of military rule it emerged from not too long ago – from 1962 until 2011, when successive military regimes ruled Myanmar with ruthless suppression of dissent before the gradual transition to democracy that culminated in the general elections in 2015 and 2020. The international condemnation of ASSK over her failure to protect the rights of the Rohingya arguably made her an international pariah and a soft target at home for the Tatmadaw to prey on. After the *coup*, those implicated for alleged atrocities against the Rohingya would still be held accountable before the ICC and foreign criminal courts exercising universal jurisdiction over their respective conducts which were already consummated before the *coup*. If conducts amounting to crimes continue after the *coup*, those responsible therefor could be held criminally liable for such conducts. Those accused who have been forced into exile would be vulnerable to arrest and prosecution in the ICC and/or the foreign criminal courts. ASSK is in a very strange situation – she might be sought for prosecution before the ICC and certain foreign domestic criminal courts exercising universal jurisdiction, while, at the same time, she has once again become an icon of democracy in Myanmar in the eyes of the international community and the approximately 35 million Bamars, the majority ethnic group accounting for around 68% of Myanmar's total population as of 2018. Ironically, unlike the February 2021 *coup*, allegations of the Tatmadaw's atrocities against the Rohingya have been met with indifference both from the majority population and democracy activists

53 Patrick Pouyanné, 'Pourquoi Total reste en Birmanie', *Le Journal de Dimanche* (4 Apr 2021), www.lejdd.fr/International/exclusif-pourquoi-total-reste-en-birmanie-la-tribune-de-patrick-pouyanne-4035902.

in Myanmar. The EU and its Member States were the first to directly raise the fate of the Rohingya when addressing the February 2021 *coup* – even before ASEAN. During the UN General Assembly Informal Meeting of the Plenary on Myanmar, held on 26 February 2021, they reiterated their support for the mandate of the IIMM to collect evidence and build criminal case files wherever there are indications of serious international crimes or violations of international law and the ongoing discrimination against ethnic minorities, including the Rohingya. They also recalled that Myanmar had to address the root causes of conflict, especially in Rakhine state, and create conditions necessary for the safe, voluntary, sustainable and dignified return of refugees and displaced persons, and this encompassed ensuring adequate assistance including health services and education, and access to justice to survivors of sexual and gender-based violence. They called on Myanmar to fully implement the provisional measures following the ICJ's Order. They also took note of the ICC's authorization of the Prosecutor to investigate alleged crimes within the ICC's jurisdiction.[54]

One crucial issue arising from international opposition to the February 2021 *coup* is the existence or non-existence of the immunity of State officials in the Myanmar Government installed by the *coup* that is not recognized by foreign Governments in whose domestic criminal courts the officials' immunity is asserted or by those Governments requested to surrender the officials to the ICC for prosecution. During the second week of March 2021, Mahn Win Khaing Than, a Karen who was the speaker of the Upper House in the previous parliament, was appointed acting Vice President of Myanmar's parallel civilian Government by the Committee for Representing Pyidaungsu Hluttaw ('CRPH').[55] The CRPH, comprising mainly MPs elected at the November 2020 general election who managed to escape arrest after the *coup*, on 31 March 2021 released the 20-page Federal Democracy Charter as the basis of the forthcoming declaration of a Federal Democratic Union under a National Unity Government ('NUG') composed of a President, a State Counsellor, a Vice President, a Prime Minister, ministers and deputy ministers. The NUG aims at weakening the governance mechanisms of the military Government, supporting the civil disobedience movement, and making arrangements for national defence, among others. The Charter, said to have been drafted and approved by 'federal democratic forces' comprising both ethnic Bamars and ethnic minorities, outlines the political roadmap according to which legislative and judicial bodies will be created after the formation of the NUG, a national convention established to draft a new Constitution to be subject to approval by a national referendum and a National Unity Consultative Council instituted to coordinate

54 Statement by the Head of Delegation of the EU to the United Nations on behalf of the EU and its Member States. Turkey, North Macedonia, Montenegro, Serbia, Albania, Bosnia and Herzegovina, Ukraine, Moldova, Monaco and San Marino aligned themselves with this statement.

55 Pyidaungsu Hluttaw means 'national parliament'.

cooperation among the federal democracy forces. The Council will include representatives of the CRPH, political parties, ethnic armed groups, civil society organizations and civil disobedience movement groups. The new Constitution will have to guarantee equality and autonomy, end the root causes of conflict in Myanmar, ensure the inclusiveness of all ethnic groups, and build up a 'federal democratic union' which can guarantee equality and self-determination through a democratic system based on the freedom, equality and justice for all citizens. After making the Charter public, the CRPH announced the repeal of the 2008 Constitution. Some of Myanmar's largest ethnic armed organizations controlling vast swaths of territory across Myanmar have pledged their support to the CRPH. The military Government has declared the CRPH illegal and warned that anyone involved with it could be charged with treason, punishable by 20 years' imprisonment or death, whereas the CRPH itself has declared the military Government a 'terrorist organization'. On 16 April 2021, the CRPH eventually announced the NUG with U Win Myint as President, followed by ASSK as State Counsellor, Duwa Lashi La as Vice President, Mahn Win Khaing Than as Prime Minister and Zin Mar Aung as Foreign Minister in that hierarchical order. The NUG's Cabinet has 11 ministers and 12 deputy ministers. Thirteen members of the Cabinet belong to ethnic minorities, but none is a Rohingya. Besides trying to win international support and recognition, the NUG intends to form a federal army under its command and has been in talks with ethnic minority forces, but the Arakan Army has refused to join in since the AA wants outright independence from Myanmar and nothing less.

As an English court opined in 1921, a *de jure* Government is one which, in the opinion of the person using the phrase, ought to possess the powers of sovereignty, though at the time it may be deprived of them, whereas a *de facto* Government is 'one which is really in possession of them, although the possession may be wrongful or precarious.[56] The Secretariat of the UN International Law Commission has compiled practices of nation States as regards the immunity from foreign criminal jurisdiction of officials of the Government not recognized by the Government of the forum State where criminal proceedings are brought against the officials. In the judicial practice in some States (e.g., the United States and the UK), a formal statement by the executive branch that it recognizes or does not recognize an entity or person as a *de jure* and/or *de facto* State, ruler or Government is conclusive before the judiciary; therefore recognition plays a decisive role in the granting of immunity.[57] In other States, domestic

56 *Luther v Sagor* [1921] 3 KB 532, 543.

57 The present author: up to 1980, it was the UK Government's policy to formally announce a decision 'recognizing' the new Government formed after an unconstitutional change of regime. Since 1980, the UK Government no longer makes such a formal announcement, although it has to decide the nature of its dealings with the regime and in some exceptional circumstances it will make an express public statement, as on 4 February 2019 when the UK Foreign Secretary issued a statement that the UK 'now recognises Juan Guaidó as the constitutional

courts consider this determination to be a factual issue arising in the context of the judicial case, which they solve on the basis of an autonomous study of the relevant domestic rules, and national and international practice: in this context, the recognition of the State or the Government concerned (in particular by the Government of the State where the courts sits) is only one element (albeit carrying a certain authority) among others that are taken into consideration in making that determination.[58] State practice shows that Heads of State in exile are granted immunity *ratione personae* in the country where they have found refuge.[59] However, Heads of State or Government not recognized by the State where of the court sits are not entitled to immunity from criminal prosecution, as was the case against the ousted *de facto* ruler of Panama, General Manuel Noriega, in the United States where his claim to Head of State immunity was dismissed since the United States had never recognized Noriega as Panama's Head of State.[60]

When Senior General Min Aung Hlaing went to Jakarta, Indonesia, to attend the special ASEAN Summit, officially entitled 'ASEAN Leaders' Meeting', on 24 April 2021, the Indonesian hosts described him only as Myanmar's Armed Forces Commander-in-Chief and not the head of a legitimate government. The Malaysian Ministry of Foreign Affairs' press release prior to this Meeting states: 'The ASEAN Leaders' Meeting will be attended by ASEAN Leaders, as well as ASEAN Secretary General, and Senior General Min Aung Hlaing of Myanmar [during which t]he unfolding development in Myanmar is also high on the meeting's agenda'. The Chairman's Statement on the ASEAN Leaders' Meeting issued after the Meeting did not specifically identify who these 'ASEAN Leaders' were, merely stating in the opening paragraph that 'The ASEAN Leaders' Meeting was convened on 24 April 2021 at the ASEAN Secretariat in Jakarta, Republic

---

interim President of Venezuela, until credible presidential elections can be held', and that the 'oppression of the illegitimate, kleptocratic Maduro regime must end' and those who continue to violate the human rights of ordinary Venezuelans under 'an illegitimate regime' will be called to account. In March 2021, Myanmar's Ambassador to the UK Kyaw Zwar Minn, who had criticized the military coup and called for the release of ASSK, was dismissed and replaced by the junta. Although the British Foreign Secretary has condemned the 'bullying actions' by the junta against the Ambassador, the UK Government has no choice but to accept the change after the UK Foreign and Commonwealth Office received the notification by 'the sending State' of the termination of the Ambassador's appointment pursuant to Article 43(a) of the 1961 Vienna Convention on Diplomatic Relations (500 UNTS 95, in force 24 Apr 1964) to which both the UK and Myanmar are party.

58 Secretariat of the International Law Commission, *Immunity of State officials from foreign criminal jurisdiction*, A/CN.4/596 (31 Mar 2008) paras 109, 112–3, 174–7.

59 Ibid para 112; Stefan Talmon, *Recognition of Governments in International Law: With Particular Reference to Governments in Exile* (Oxford University Press 1998) 259–61.

60 *United States v Noriega*, District Court, Southern District of Florida, Omnibus order of 8 June 1990, 746 F.Supp. 1506, affirmed by the Court of Appeals for the Eleventh Circuit, *United States v Noriega*, 7 July 1997, 117 F 3d 1206 (1997). On the complexity of the modern-day recognition or non-recognition of government, see Federica Paddeu and Alonso Gurmendi Dunkelberg, 'Recognition of Governments: Legitimacy and Control Six Months after Guaidó', *Opinio Juris* (18 Aug 2019).

of Indonesia, and chaired by His Majesty [the Sultan of Brunei Darussalam]'. This was a departure from the standard formula adopted in the Statements of the ASEAN Chair stating: 'We, the Heads of State/Government of ASEAN Member States, gathered for the … ASEAN Summit on …' Also of importance is the fact that the open letter dated 23 April 2021 sent to the Meeting by NUG's Spokesperson was read out by the ASEAN Secretary General, with copies thereof distributed, at the Meeting.[61] It may, therefore, be argued that Senior General Min Aung Hlaing has not been recognized by the other ASEAN Member States as Myanmar's Head of State/Government, either *de jure* or *de facto*. He was, at best, the head of a special mission[62] from Myanmar attending the Summit to hear the concerns as well as demands expressed by the Leaders from nine ASEAN

61 It reads:

> 'On principle, the meetings that can contribute to a solution to the deepening crisis in Myanmar are welcome, meetings that exclude the people of Myanmar but include murderer in chief Min Aung Hlaing who is murdering the people of Myanmar are unlikely to be helpful.
>
> The legitimate representatives of the people and country of Myanmar, the National Unity Government (NUG) stands ready to engage and attend any ASEAN meeting on Myanmar, including the one scheduled for April the 24th that starts in less than 24 hours.
>
> We firmly believe that a meeting on Myanmar should not include illegal, illegitimate military junta unless the following serious conditions are met. The military junta must meet the following conditions and demonstrate that it is adhering to them. This is the only way to restore democracy, stability and prevent the great civil war that will end in genocide.
>
> 1. Stop murdering civilians. The junta has killed over 740 Myanmar civilians since the *coup* and the number of its victims increase daily;
> 2. Stop systematically attacking neighbourhoods and randomly discharging weapons into civilians' homes that have claimed the lives of many civilians, including children;
> 3. Stop bombing and shelling villages, which has caused significant casualties and has led to tens of thousands of civilians being displaced;
> 4. Stop preventing those who need medical care from receiving it, including agreeing to immediately stop: (i) occupying medical facilities, (ii) arresting and attacking medical personnel, and (iii) preventing emergency medical personnel from reaching victims;
> 5. Unconditionally release the over 3,300 political prisoners detained since the *coup* and stop arbitrarily detaining protesters, CDM members and others who are exercising their fundamental right to the freedom of expression.
> 6. End the *coup*, end all violence and return the power to elected Government of Myanmar – the National Unity Government – NUG.

We once again express our sincere appreciation to the Association of Southeast Asian Nations (ASEAN) willingness to help Myanmar address the crisis that has gripped our nation, and indeed our region, following the illegal *coup d'etat* on 1 February.

Dr. Sasa, Union Minister of International Cooperation and Spokesperson National Unity Government of Myanmar.'

62 For special missions, see Chapter 6.

Member States and, on the sidelines of the summit, the UN Secretary-General's Special Envoy on Myanmar.

With respect to the ICJ, on 4 June 2021, the NUG's Deputy Foreign Minister U Moe Zaw Oo said during an online press conference that the NUG would not participate in defending Myanmar in the Rohingya genocide case in the ICJ. The NUG has promised to work with the ICJ as well as to accept the ICJ's decision in the case. For its part, the Myanmar military regime has organized a new legal team led by its Foreign Minister, U Wunna Maung Lwin, to defend Myanmar at the ICJ.[63]

Even if Myanmar stops appearing or participating further in the on-going ICJ proceedings against Myanmar, its absence or failure to defend its case does not constitute a bar to the proceedings. Article 53 of the ICJ Statute[64] provides that whenever one of the parties does not appear before the ICJ, or fails to defend its case, the other party may call upon the ICJ to decide in favour of its claim. By virtue of Article 36(6) of the ICJ Statute, the ICJ has jurisdiction to determine any dispute as to its own jurisdiction, and its judgment on that matter is final and binding on the parties under Articles 59 and 60 of this Statute. A State which decides not to appear must accept the consequences of its decision – despite its non-participation the case will continue and the non-appearing party remains a party to the case and is bound by the eventual judgment. There is however no question of a judgment automatically in favour of the party appearing. When Article 53 of the Statute applies, the ICJ is bound to satisfy itself, not only that it has jurisdiction in accordance with Articles 36 and 37, but also that the claim of the party appearing is well founded in fact and law, implying that the ICJ must attain the same degree of certainty as in any other case that the claim of the party appearing is sound in law, and, so far as the nature of the case permits, that the facts on which it is based are supported by convincing evidence. The burden laid upon the ICJ is somewhat lightened where the currently non-appearing party participated in the earlier phases of the case, when it submitted certain arguments on the law which have a bearing also on the merits. Nevertheless, the ICJ cannot by its own enquiries entirely make up for the absence of one of the Parties; that absence, in a case involving extensive questions of fact, must necessarily limit the extent to which the ICJ is informed of the facts. The absent party also forfeits the opportunity to counter the factual allegations of its opponent. It is of course for the party appearing to prove the allegations it makes, yet although formally absent from the proceedings, the non-appearing party frequently submits to the ICJ letters and documents, in ways and by means not contemplated by the ICJ's Rules. The ICJ has thus to strike a balance. On the one hand, it is valuable for the ICJ to know the views of both parties in whatever form those views may have

63 www.irrawaddy.com/news/burma/myanmar-junta-reorganizes-legal-team-for-icj-rohingya-genocide-case.html.

64 (1945) 39 AJIL Supp 215, in force 24 Oct 1945.

been expressed. Furthermore, where one party is not appearing it is especially incumbent upon the ICJ to satisfy itself that the ICJ is in possession of all the available facts. On the other hand, due to the principle of equality of the parties to a dispute, in a case of non-appearance neither party should be placed at a disadvantage and the non-appearing party cannot be permitted to profit from its absence, since this would amount to placing the party appearing at a disadvantage. The vigilance which the ICJ can exercise when aided by the presence of both parties to the proceedings has a counterpart in the special care the ICJ has to devote to the proper administration of justice in a case in which only one party is present.[65]

On 30 May 2021, the NUG issued a press statement stating, *inter alia*, that the NUG 'is also actively considering accepting the exercise of jurisdiction by the International Criminal Court over the killings, torture and other crimes against civilians that have occurred since the attempted *coup* started on 1 February 2021'. It is debatable whether such *ad hoc* acceptance of the ICC's jurisdiction pursuant to Article 12(3) of the Rome Statute by the NUG which has not yet exercised effective control over Myanmar is valid, and the ICC itself is likely to be reluctant in getting involved in the politically controversial issue of recognition of government. In addition, it is questionable whether the acceptance can be narrowly confined to the suppression by the Myanmar security forces against those opposed to the *coup*. Paragraph 3 of Article 12, when read in conjunction with paragraphs 1 and 2 of the same Article, requires the State making such declaration to accept the exercise of jurisdiction by the ICC with respect to any one or more of 'the crimes referred to in Article 5': crimes against humanity, war crimes, genocide, and/or, where applicable, aggression, and over the entire territory, not at a specific location, of the accepting State although specific incidents may form part of the charges falling under one of such crimes within the ICC's jurisdiction. Therefore, such declaration would also entail the acceptance of the ICC's jurisdiction over crimes against humanity allegedly committed against the Rohingya in Myanmar's territory and/or by Myanmar nationals, including those implicated in the IIFFMM's reports, when such crimes are committed or continue as of 1 February 2021, the date indicated by the NUG.

The Rohingya's quest for justice will have to pursue several long and winding roads. According to an old legal maxim, 'Justice delayed is justice denied'. But *if* the Rohingya's claims are eventually upheld by the ICJ, the ICC and/or foreign domestic courts, a delayed justice is still better than no justice at all, isn't it?

65 *Military and Paramilitary Activities in and against Nicaragua (Nicaragua v United States of America)* (Merits) Judgment [1986] ICJ Rep 14, 23–26.

INDEX

For Product Safety Concerns and Information please contact our EU
representative GPSR@taylorandfrancis.com
Taylor & Francis Verlag GmbH, Kaufingerstraße 24, 80331 München, Germany

www.ingramcontent.com/pod-product-compliance
Ingram Content Group UK Ltd.
Pitfield, Milton Keynes, MK11 3LW, UK
UKHW020017200926
475702UK00014B/1940

* 9 7 8 1 0 3 2 1 2 3 4 1 7 *